W9-DES-992

# HOW TO BE
# ACE

## A MEMOIR OF GROWING UP ASEXUAL

# REBECCA BURGESS

**Jessica Kingsley Publishers**
London and Philadelphia

FIRST PUBLISHED IN GREAT BRITAIN IN 2021 BY JESSICA KINGSLEY PUBLISHERS
AN HACHETTE COMPANY

1



FRONT COVER IMAGE SOURCE: REBECCA BURGESS.



A CIP CATALOGUE RECORD FOR THIS TITLE IS AVAILABLE FROM THE BRITISH LIBRARY AND THE LIBRARY OF CONGRESS

ISBN 978 1 78775 215 3
EISBN 978 1 78775 216 0

PRINTED AND BOUND IN CHINA BY LEO PAPER PRODUCTS

JESSICA KINGSLEY PUBLISHERS' POLICY IS TO USE PAPERS THAT ARE NATURAL, RENEWABLE AND RECYCLABLE PRODUCTS AND MADE FROM WOOD GROWN IN SUSTAINABLE FORESTS. THE LOGGING AND MANUFACTURING PROCESSES ARE EXPECTED TO CONFORM TO THE ENVIRONMENTAL REGULATIONS OF THE COUNTRY OF ORIGIN.

JESSICA KINGSLEY PUBLISHERS
73 COLLIER STREET
LONDON N1 9BE, UK

WWW.JKP.COM

**TRIGGER WARNING: THIS BOOK MENTIONS BULLYING, ANXIETY, OCD, RAPE, SEX AND ALCOHOL.**

# CONTENTS

# CHAPTER ONE

## HOW TO PRETEND
## TO BE SOMETHING YOU'RE NOT

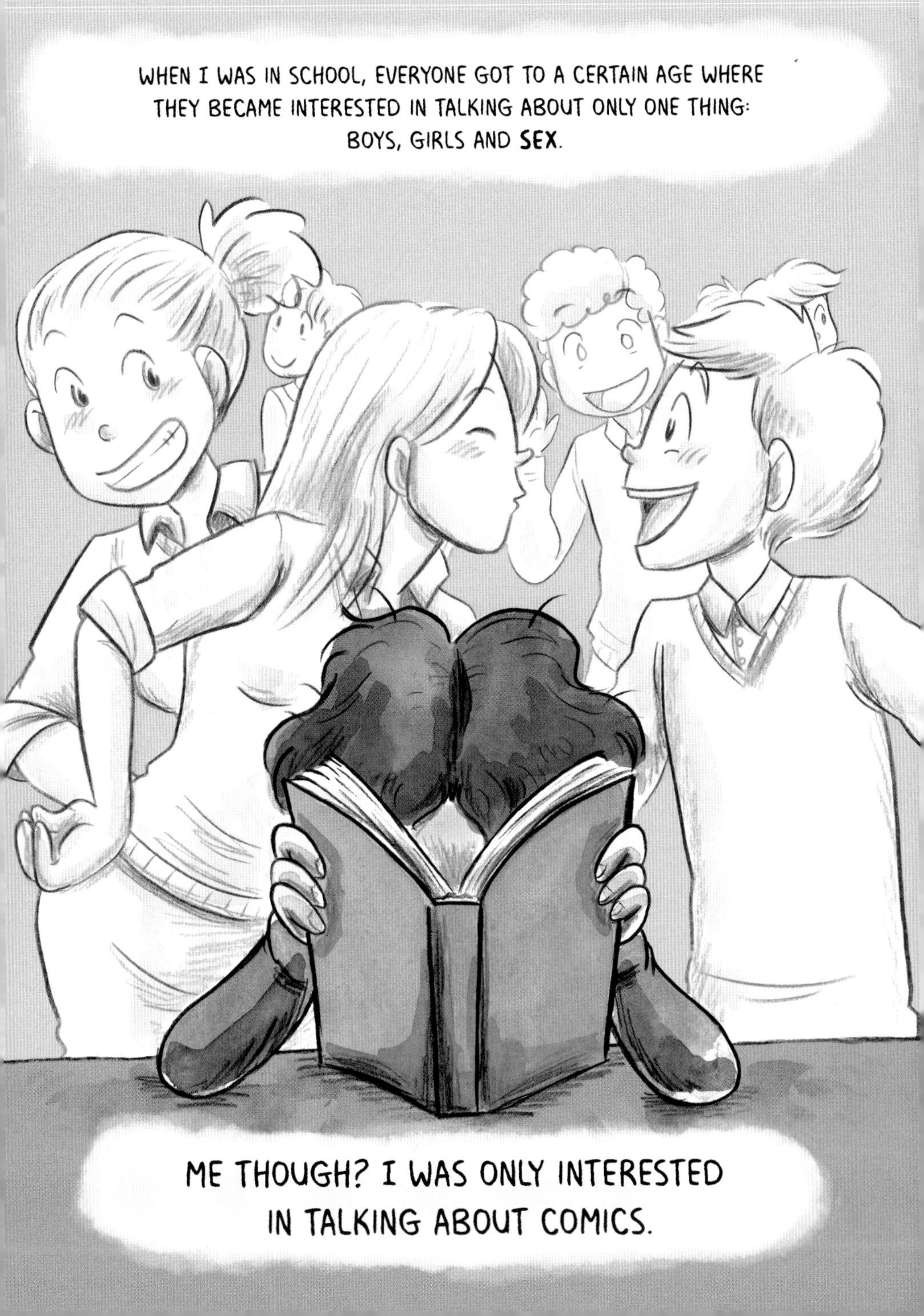
WHEN I WAS IN SCHOOL, EVERYONE GOT TO A CERTAIN AGE WHERE THEY BECAME INTERESTED IN TALKING ABOUT ONLY ONE THING: BOYS, GIRLS AND **SEX**.
ME THOUGH? I WAS ONLY INTERESTED IN TALKING ABOUT COMICS.

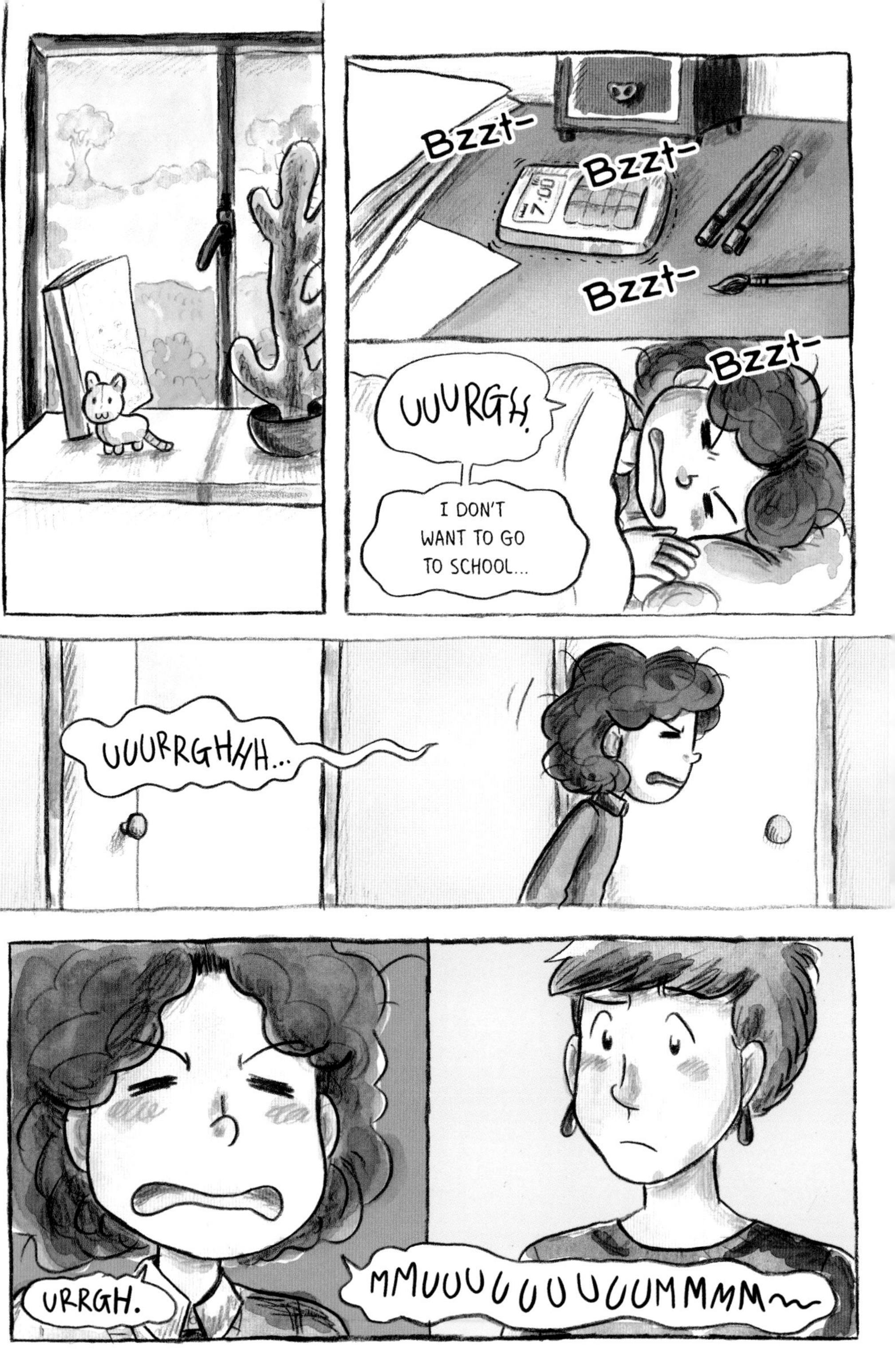
Bzzt-
Bzzt-
Bzzt-
Bzzt-
UUURGH!
I DON'T WANT TO GO TO SCHOOL...
UUURRGHHH...
URRGH.
MMUUUUUUUUUMMMM~

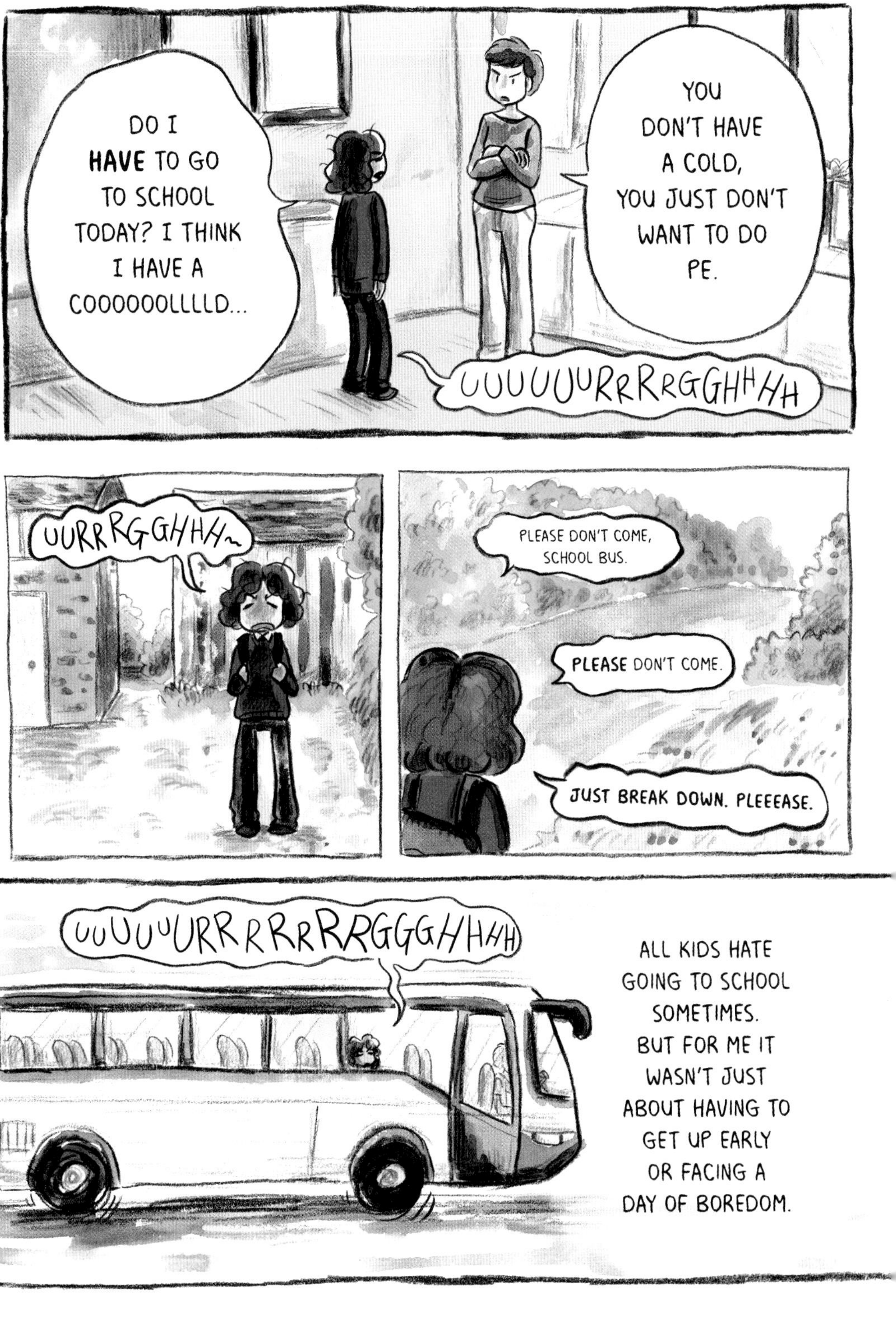
DO I **HAVE** TO GO TO SCHOOL TODAY? I THINK I HAVE A COOOOOOLLLLD...
YOU DON'T HAVE A COLD, YOU JUST DON'T WANT TO DO PE.
UUUUUURRRRGGHHHH
UURRRGGHHH
PLEASE DON'T COME, SCHOOL BUS.
**PLEASE** DON'T COME.
**JUST BREAK DOWN. PLEEEASE.**
UUUUUURRRRRRGGGHHHH
ALL KIDS HATE GOING TO SCHOOL SOMETIMES. BUT FOR ME IT WASN'T JUST ABOUT HAVING TO GET UP EARLY OR FACING A DAY OF BOREDOM.

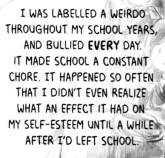

I WAS LABELLED A WEIRDO THROUGHOUT MY SCHOOL YEARS, AND BULLIED **EVERY** DAY. IT MADE SCHOOL A CONSTANT CHORE. IT HAPPENED SO OFTEN THAT I DIDN'T EVEN REALIZE WHAT AN EFFECT IT HAD ON MY SELF-ESTEEM UNTIL A WHILE AFTER I'D LEFT SCHOOL.

AT THE TIME, IT WAS JUST A PART OF DAILY LIFE FOR ME!

WHAT'S WRONG WITH YOUR HAIR? DON'T YOU EVER BRUSH IT?

WHY DON'T YOU EVER MAKE EYE CONTACT?? **FREAK!**

OH.

AW, YOU DON'T HAVE ANY FRIENDS, DO YOU?

THEY'RE IN OTHER CLASSES.

**HAHA!** WHAT'S THAT **DORKY** THING HANGING OFF YOU?

...I THOUGHT IT LOOKED COOL.

A Dragon Keychain... it _was_ dorky!

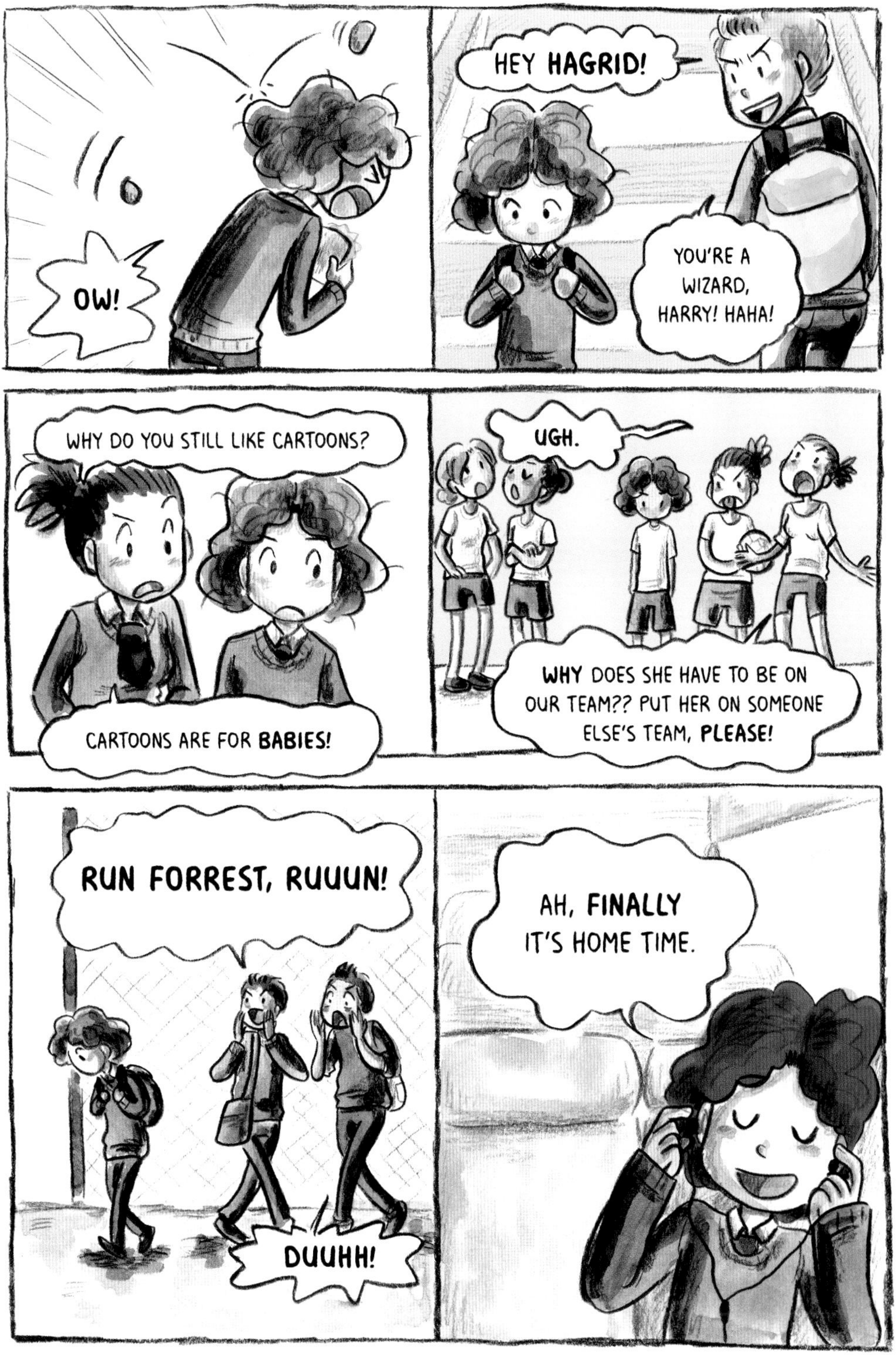
OW!
HEY HAGRID!
YOU'RE A WIZARD, HARRY! HAHA!
WHY DO YOU STILL LIKE CARTOONS?
CARTOONS ARE FOR BABIES!
UGH.
WHY DOES SHE HAVE TO BE ON OUR TEAM?? PUT HER ON SOMEONE ELSE'S TEAM, PLEASE!
RUN FORREST, RUUUN!
DUUHH!
AH, FINALLY IT'S HOME TIME.

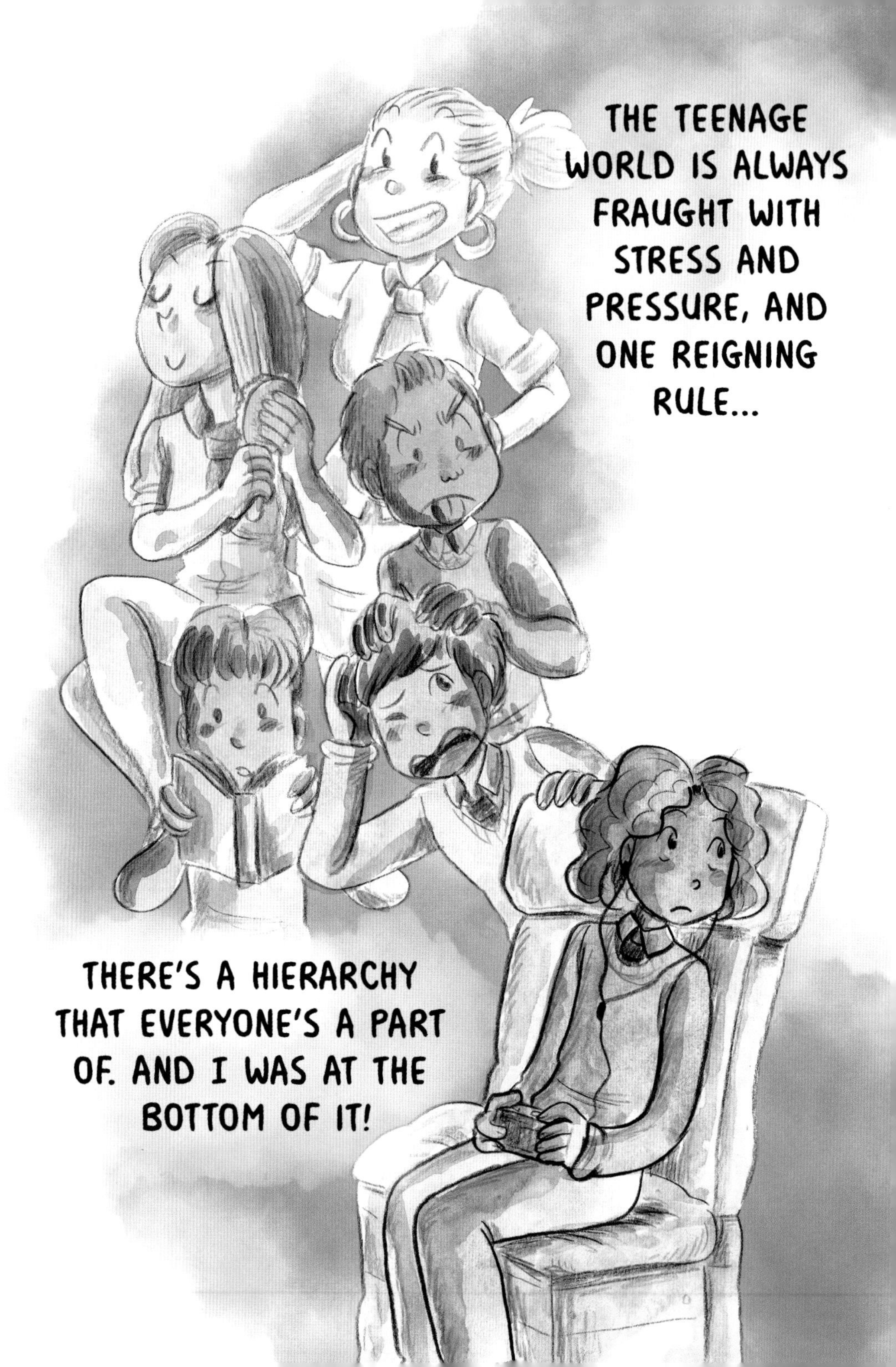
THE TEENAGE WORLD IS ALWAYS FRAUGHT WITH STRESS AND PRESSURE, AND ONE REIGNING RULE...
THERE'S A HIERARCHY THAT EVERYONE'S A PART OF. AND I WAS AT THE BOTTOM OF IT!

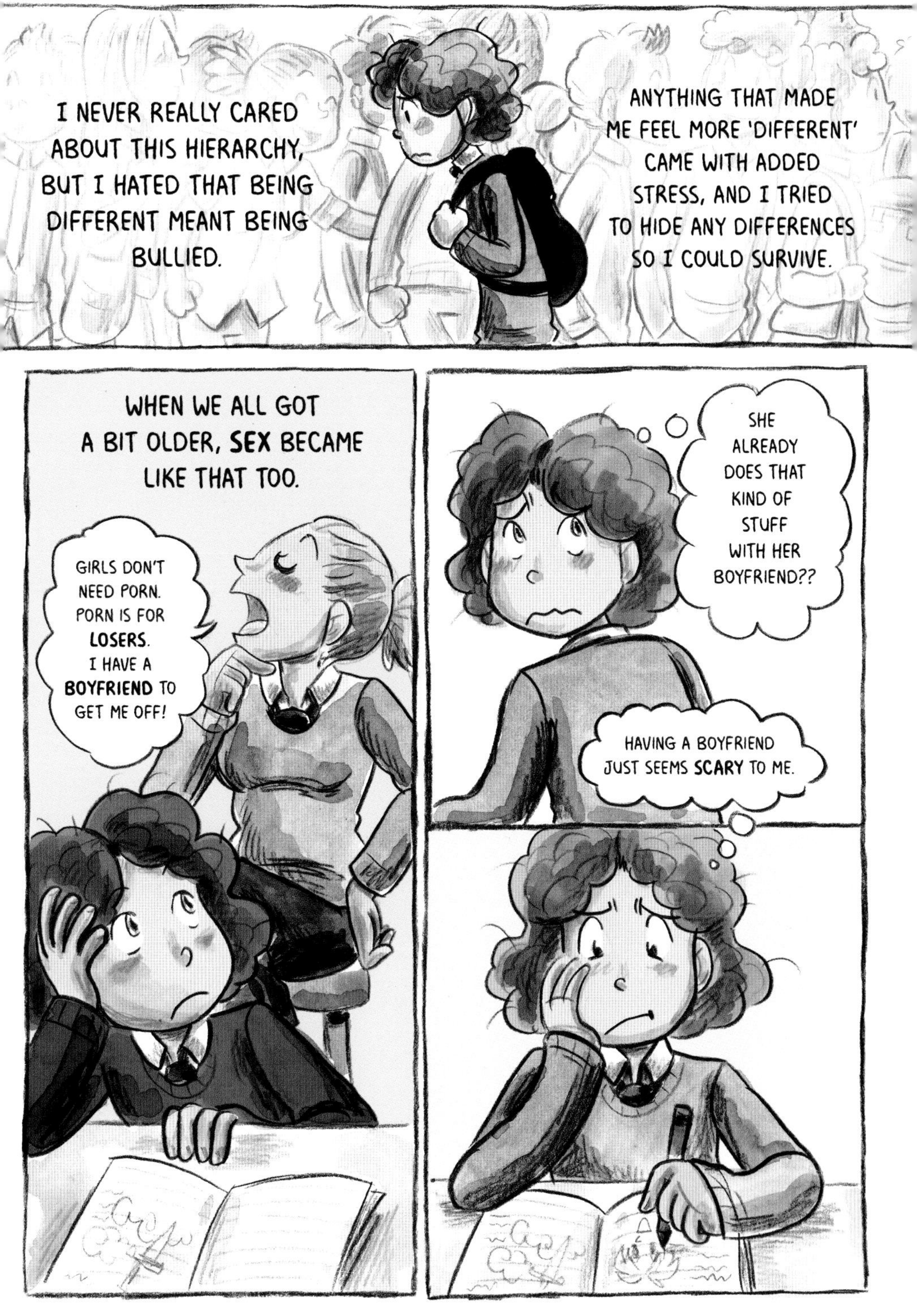
I NEVER REALLY CARED ABOUT THIS HIERARCHY, BUT I HATED THAT BEING DIFFERENT MEANT BEING BULLIED.
ANYTHING THAT MADE ME FEEL MORE 'DIFFERENT' CAME WITH ADDED STRESS, AND I TRIED TO HIDE ANY DIFFERENCES SO I COULD SURVIVE.
WHEN WE ALL GOT A BIT OLDER, **SEX** BECAME LIKE THAT TOO.
GIRLS DON'T NEED PORN. PORN IS FOR **LOSERS**. I HAVE A **BOYFRIEND** TO GET ME OFF!
SHE ALREADY DOES THAT KIND OF STUFF WITH HER BOYFRIEND??
HAVING A BOYFRIEND JUST SEEMS **SCARY** TO ME.

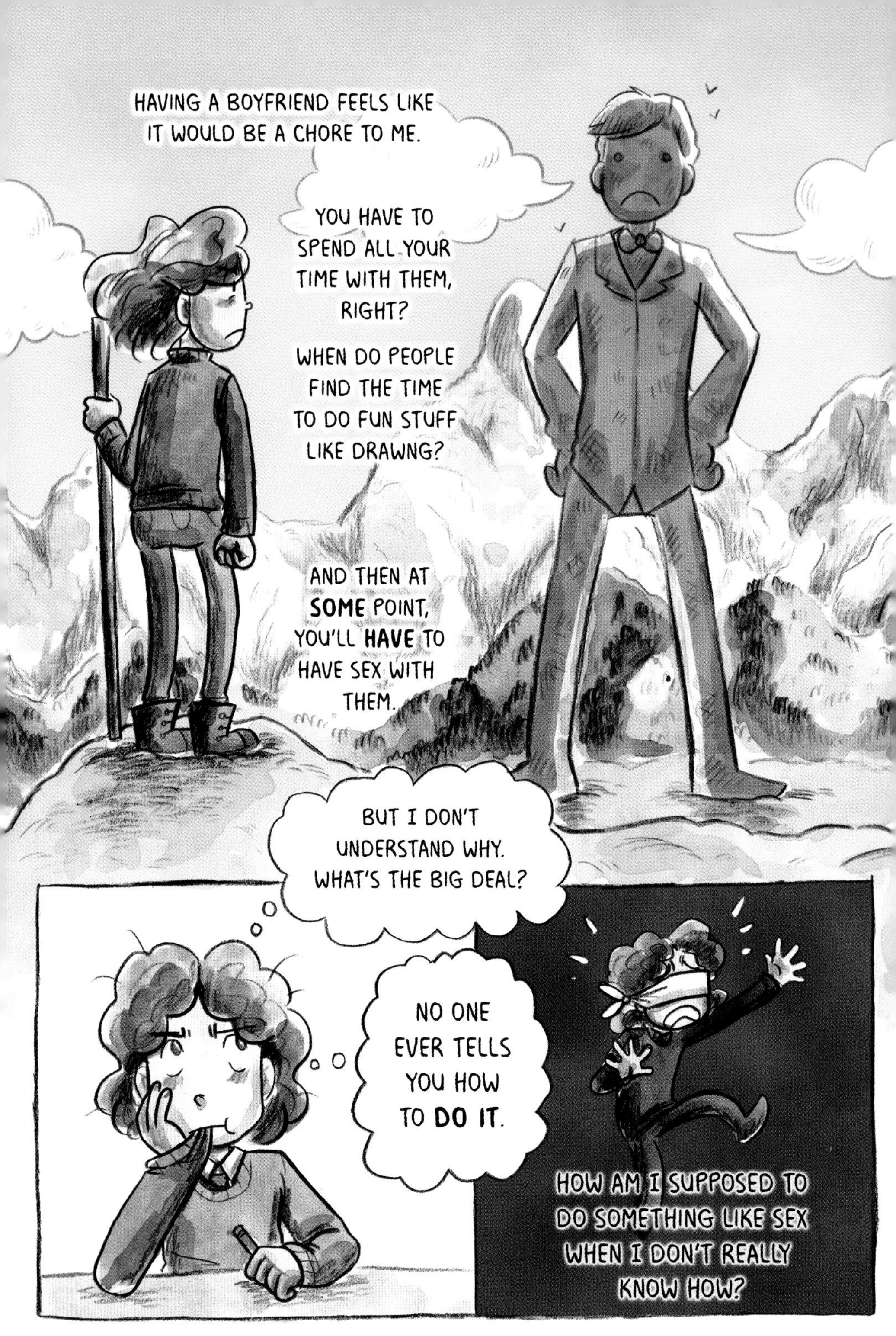
HAVING A BOYFRIEND FEELS LIKE IT WOULD BE A CHORE TO ME.
YOU HAVE TO SPEND ALL YOUR TIME WITH THEM, RIGHT?
WHEN DO PEOPLE FIND THE TIME TO DO FUN STUFF LIKE DRAWNG?
AND THEN AT **SOME** POINT, YOU'LL **HAVE** TO HAVE SEX WITH THEM.
BUT I DON'T UNDERSTAND WHY. WHAT'S THE BIG DEAL?
NO ONE EVER TELLS YOU HOW TO **DO IT**.
HOW AM I SUPPOSED TO DO SOMETHING LIKE SEX WHEN I DON'T REALLY KNOW HOW?

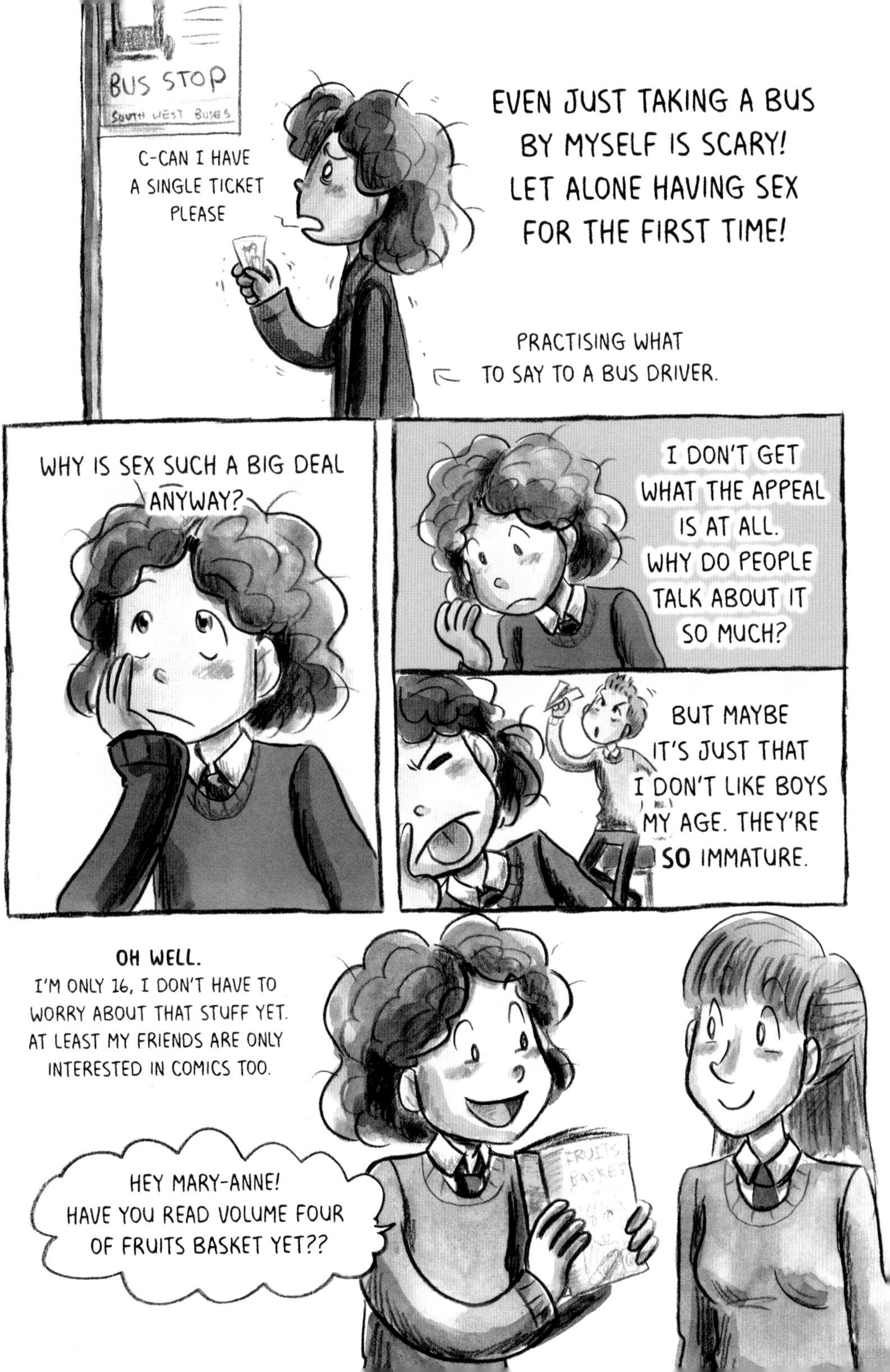
BUS STOP
SOUTH WEST BUSES
C-CAN I HAVE A SINGLE TICKET PLEASE
EVEN JUST TAKING A BUS BY MYSELF IS SCARY! LET ALONE HAVING SEX FOR THE FIRST TIME!
PRACTISING WHAT TO SAY TO A BUS DRIVER.
WHY IS SEX SUCH A BIG DEAL ANYWAY?
I DON'T GET WHAT THE APPEAL IS AT ALL. WHY DO PEOPLE TALK ABOUT IT SO MUCH?
BUT MAYBE IT'S JUST THAT I DON'T LIKE BOYS MY AGE. THEY'RE **SO** IMMATURE.
**OH WELL.**
I'M ONLY 16, I DON'T HAVE TO WORRY ABOUT THAT STUFF YET. AT LEAST MY FRIENDS ARE ONLY INTERESTED IN COMICS TOO.
HEY MARY-ANNE! HAVE YOU READ VOLUME FOUR OF FRUITS BASKET YET??
FRUITS BASKET

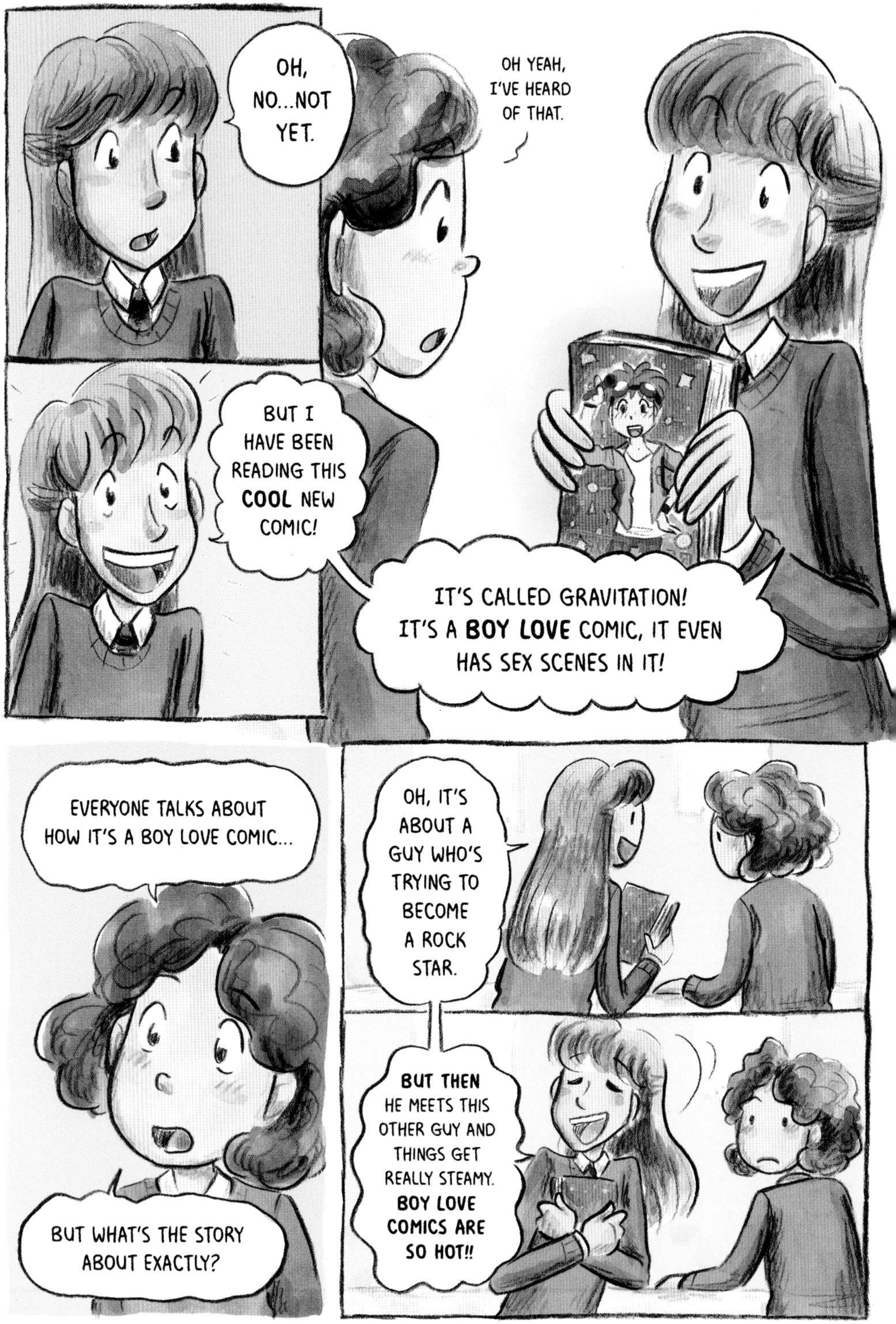
OH, NO...NOT YET.
OH YEAH, I'VE HEARD OF THAT.
BUT I HAVE BEEN READING THIS **COOL** NEW COMIC!
IT'S CALLED GRAVITATION! IT'S A **BOY LOVE** COMIC, IT EVEN HAS SEX SCENES IN IT!
EVERYONE TALKS ABOUT HOW IT'S A BOY LOVE COMIC...
BUT WHAT'S THE STORY ABOUT EXACTLY?
OH, IT'S ABOUT A GUY WHO'S TRYING TO BECOME A ROCK STAR.
**BUT THEN** HE MEETS THIS OTHER GUY AND THINGS GET REALLY STEAMY. **BOY LOVE COMICS ARE SO HOT!!**

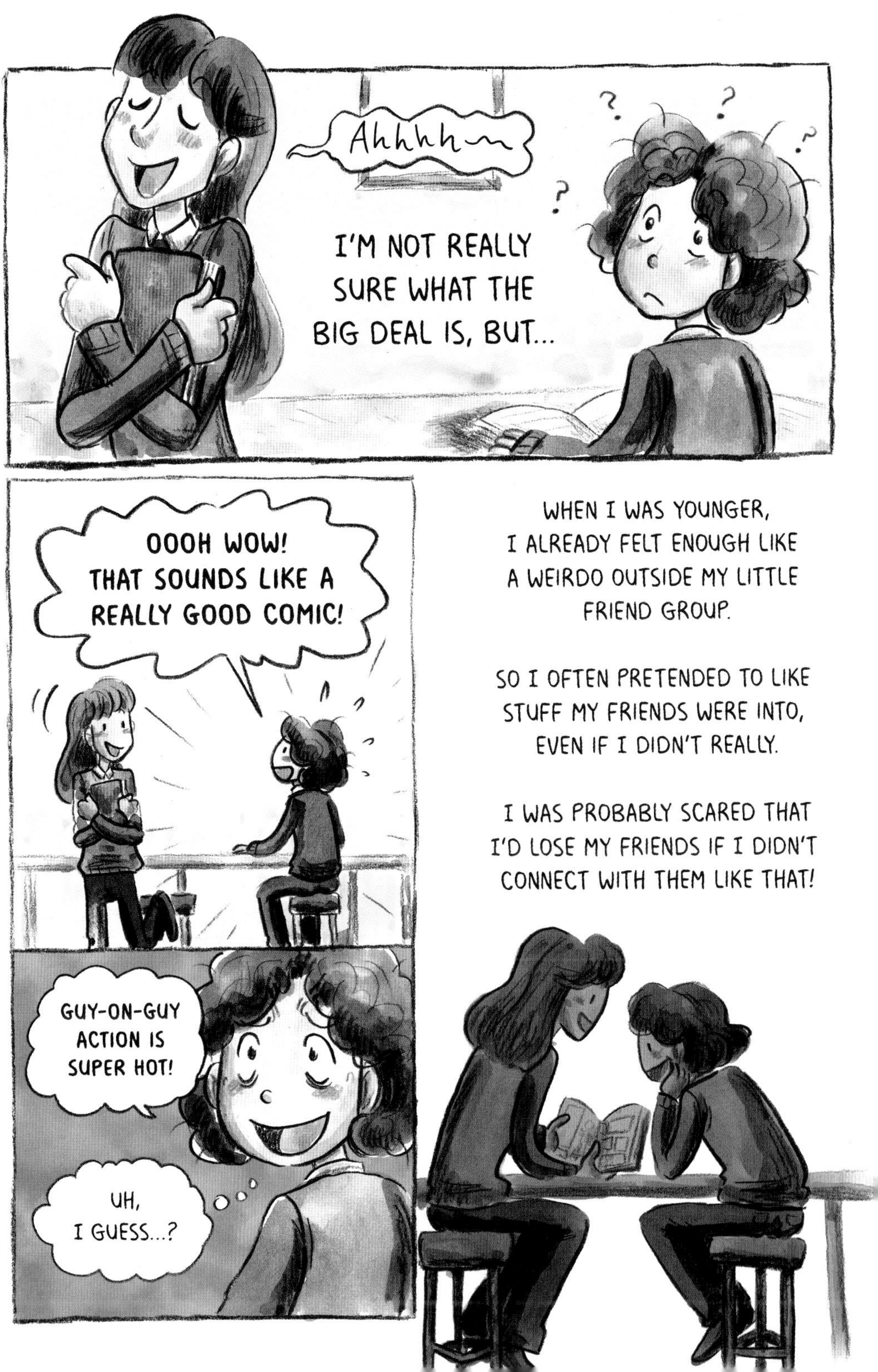
Ahhhh~
I'M NOT REALLY SURE WHAT THE BIG DEAL IS, BUT...
OOOH WOW! THAT SOUNDS LIKE A REALLY GOOD COMIC!
GUY-ON-GUY ACTION IS SUPER HOT!
UH, I GUESS...?
WHEN I WAS YOUNGER, I ALREADY FELT ENOUGH LIKE A WEIRDO OUTSIDE MY LITTLE FRIEND GROUP.
SO I OFTEN PRETENDED TO LIKE STUFF MY FRIENDS WERE INTO, EVEN IF I DIDN'T REALLY.
I WAS PROBABLY SCARED THAT I'D LOSE MY FRIENDS IF I DIDN'T CONNECT WITH THEM LIKE THAT!

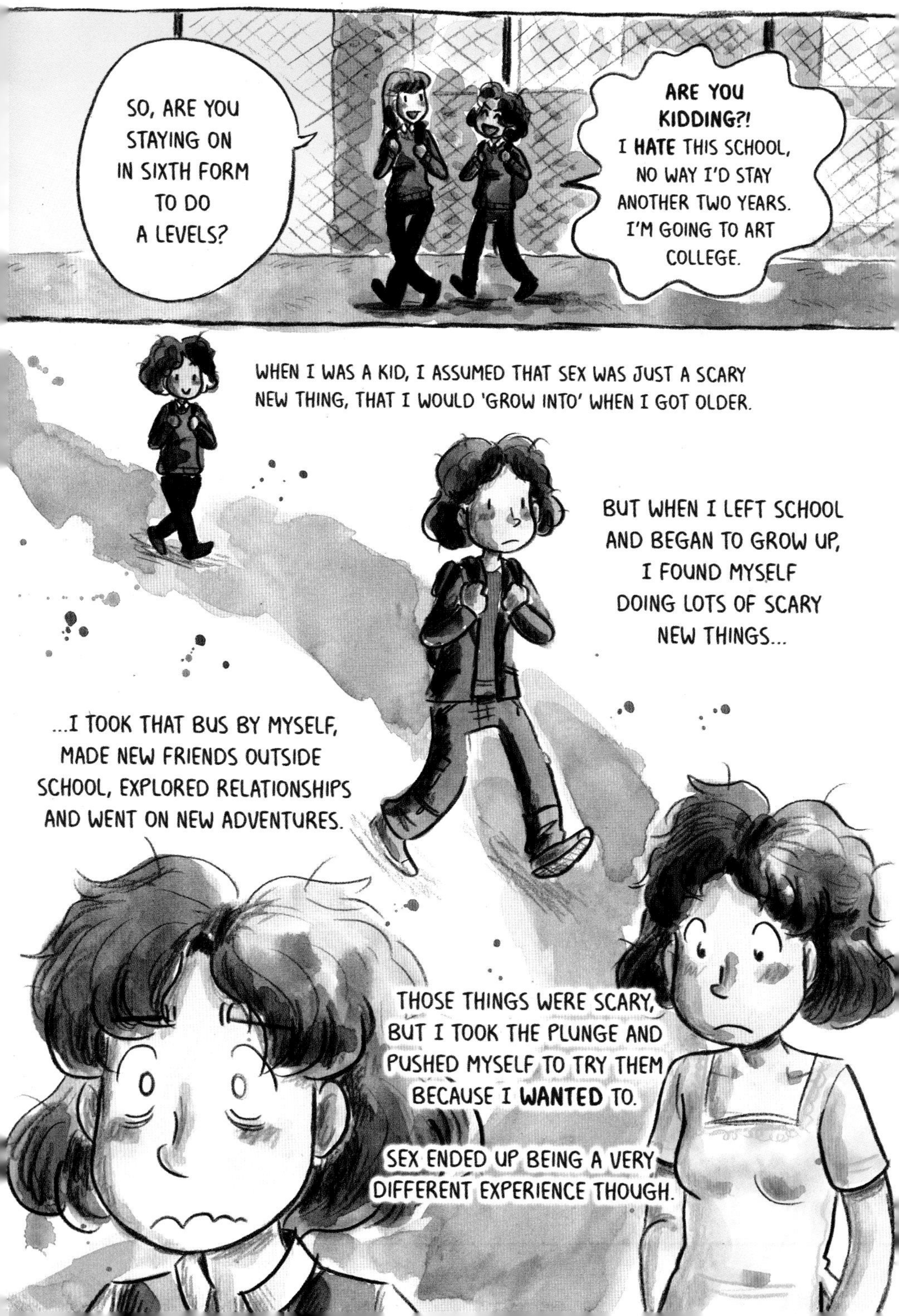
SO, ARE YOU STAYING ON IN SIXTH FORM TO DO A LEVELS?
ARE YOU KIDDING?! I HATE THIS SCHOOL, NO WAY I'D STAY ANOTHER TWO YEARS. I'M GOING TO ART COLLEGE.
WHEN I WAS A KID, I ASSUMED THAT SEX WAS JUST A SCARY NEW THING, THAT I WOULD 'GROW INTO' WHEN I GOT OLDER.
BUT WHEN I LEFT SCHOOL AND BEGAN TO GROW UP, I FOUND MYSELF DOING LOTS OF SCARY NEW THINGS...
...I TOOK THAT BUS BY MYSELF, MADE NEW FRIENDS OUTSIDE SCHOOL, EXPLORED RELATIONSHIPS AND WENT ON NEW ADVENTURES.
THOSE THINGS WERE SCARY, BUT I TOOK THE PLUNGE AND PUSHED MYSELF TO TRY THEM BECAUSE I WANTED TO.
SEX ENDED UP BEING A VERY DIFFERENT EXPERIENCE THOUGH.

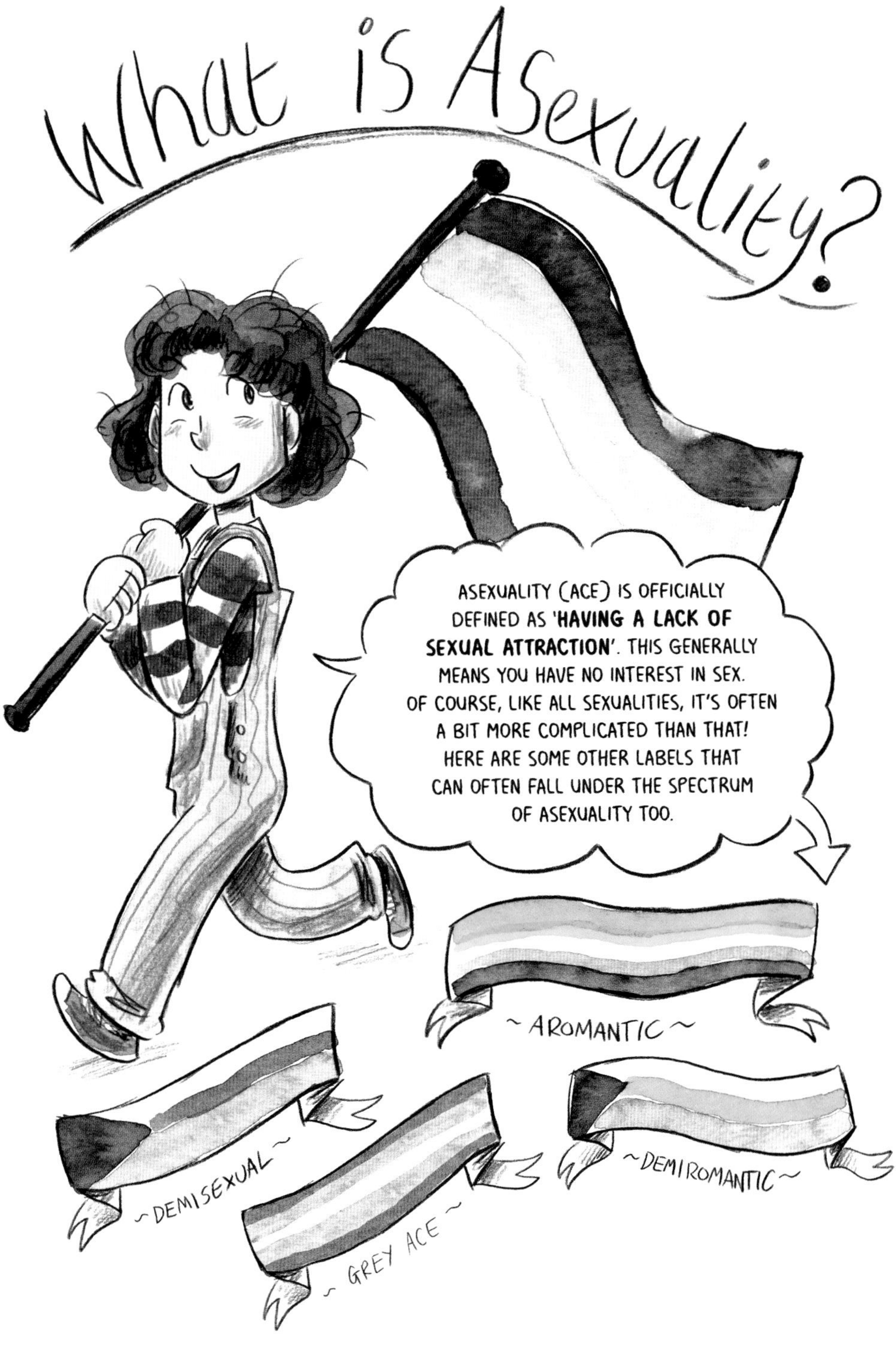
What is Asexuality?
ASEXUALITY (ACE) IS OFFICIALLY DEFINED AS 'HAVING A LACK OF SEXUAL ATTRACTION'. THIS GENERALLY MEANS YOU HAVE NO INTEREST IN SEX. OF COURSE, LIKE ALL SEXUALITIES, IT'S OFTEN A BIT MORE COMPLICATED THAN THAT! HERE ARE SOME OTHER LABELS THAT CAN OFTEN FALL UNDER THE SPECTRUM OF ASEXUALITY TOO.
~ AROMANTIC ~
~ DEMISEXUAL ~
~ GREY ACE ~
~ DEMIROMANTIC ~

# CHAPTER TWO

## HOW TO EXPERIMENT

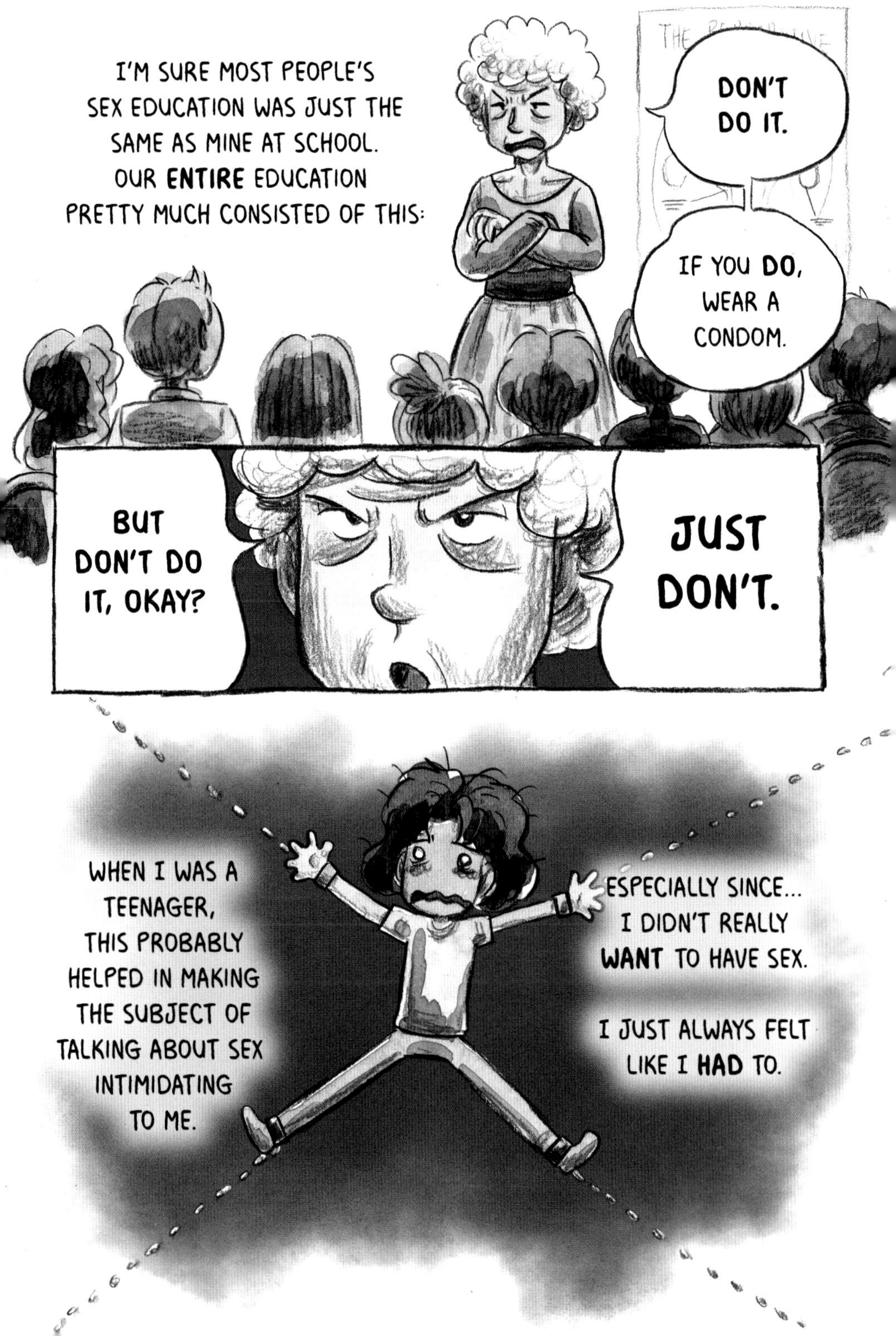
I'M SURE MOST PEOPLE'S SEX EDUCATION WAS JUST THE SAME AS MINE AT SCHOOL. OUR **ENTIRE** EDUCATION PRETTY MUCH CONSISTED OF THIS:
DON'T DO IT.
IF YOU **DO**, WEAR A CONDOM.
BUT DON'T DO IT, OKAY?
JUST DON'T.
WHEN I WAS A TEENAGER, THIS PROBABLY HELPED IN MAKING THE SUBJECT OF TALKING ABOUT SEX INTIMIDATING TO ME.
ESPECIALLY SINCE... I DIDN'T REALLY **WANT** TO HAVE SEX.
I JUST ALWAYS FELT LIKE I **HAD** TO.

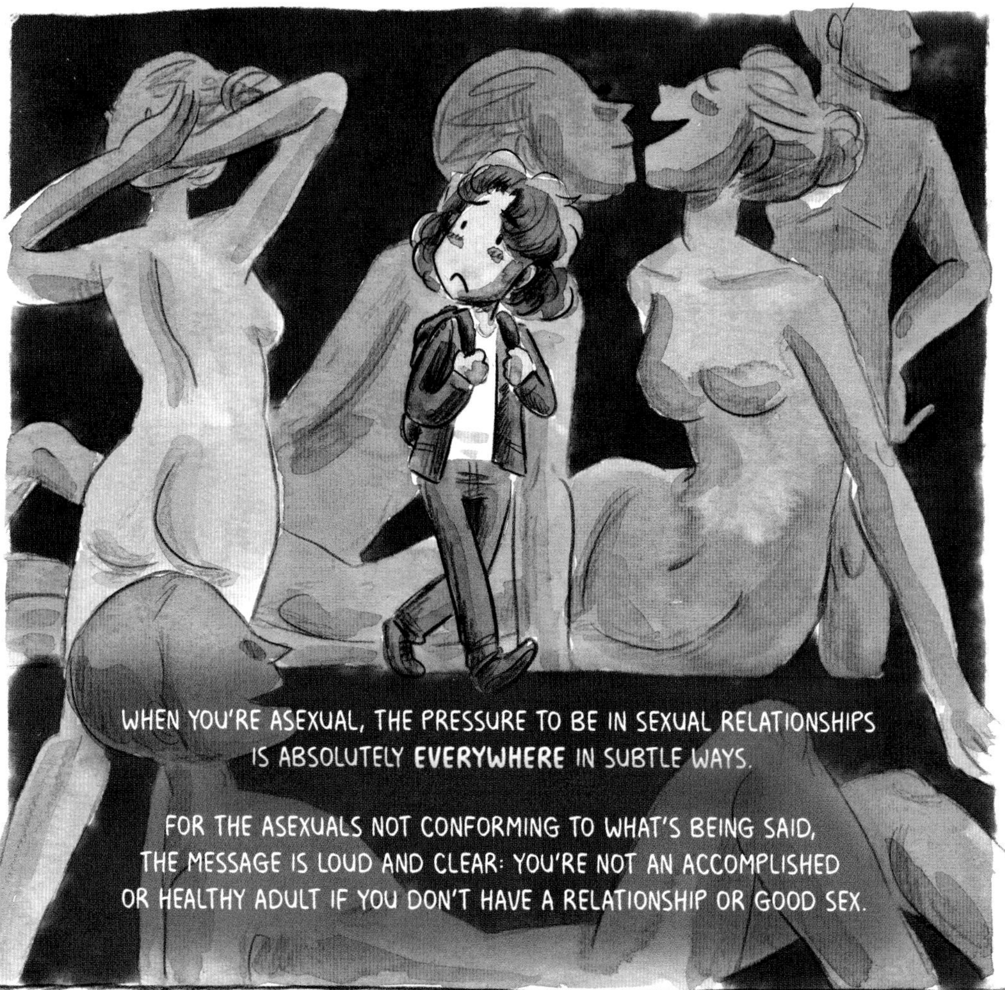
WHEN YOU'RE ASEXUAL, THE PRESSURE TO BE IN SEXUAL RELATIONSHIPS IS ABSOLUTELY **EVERYWHERE** IN SUBTLE WAYS.
FOR THE ASEXUALS NOT CONFORMING TO WHAT'S BEING SAID, THE MESSAGE IS LOUD AND CLEAR: YOU'RE NOT AN ACCOMPLISHED OR HEALTHY ADULT IF YOU DON'T HAVE A RELATIONSHIP OR GOOD SEX.

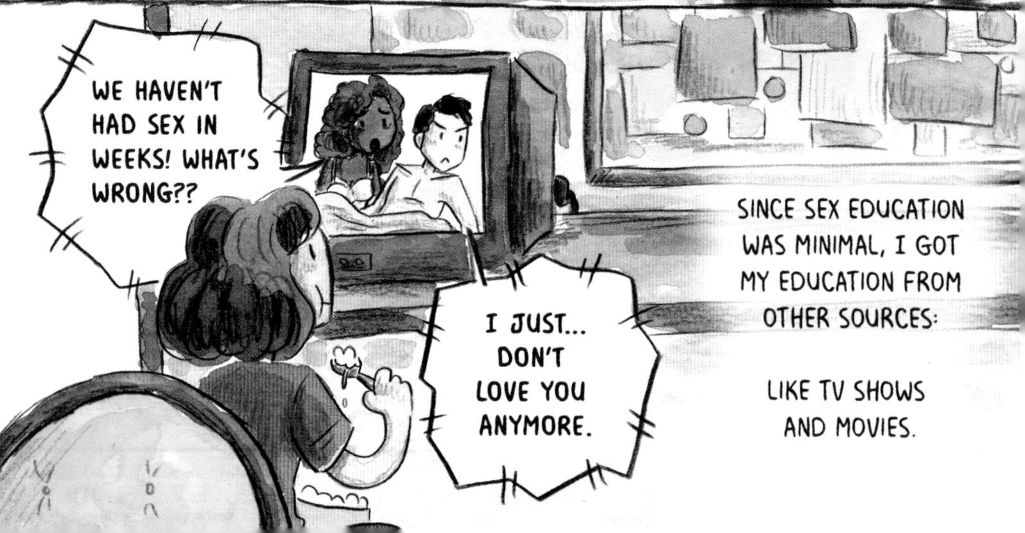
WE HAVEN'T HAD SEX IN WEEKS! WHAT'S WRONG??
I JUST... DON'T LOVE YOU ANYMORE.
SINCE SEX EDUCATION WAS MINIMAL, I GOT MY EDUCATION FROM OTHER SOURCES:
LIKE TV SHOWS AND MOVIES.

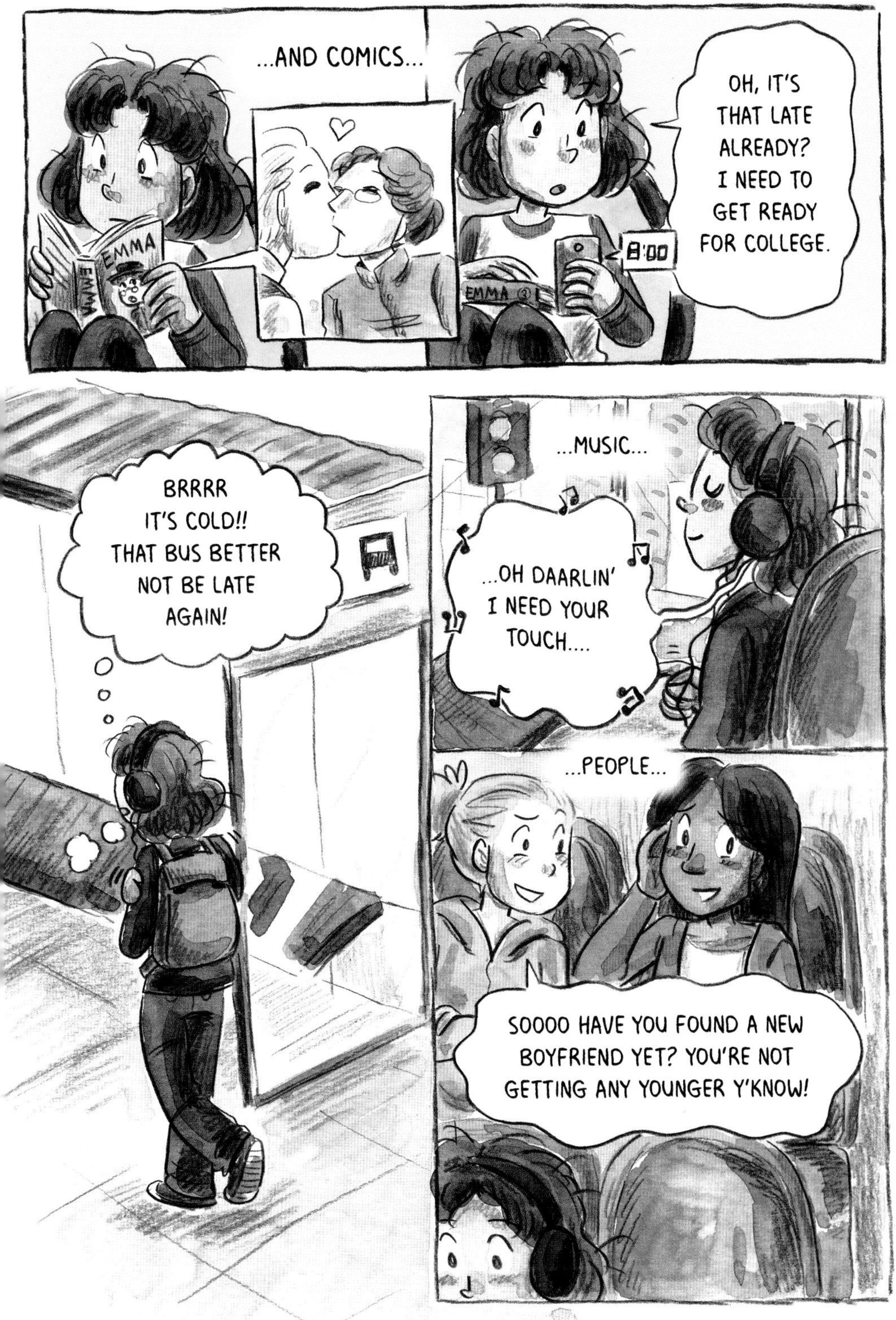
...AND COMICS...
EMMA
OH, IT'S THAT LATE ALREADY? I NEED TO GET READY FOR COLLEGE.
BRRRR IT'S COLD!! THAT BUS BETTER NOT BE LATE AGAIN!
...MUSIC...
...OH DAARLIN' I NEED YOUR TOUCH....
...PEOPLE...
SOOOO HAVE YOU FOUND A NEW BOYFRIEND YET? YOU'RE NOT GETTING ANY YOUNGER Y'KNOW!

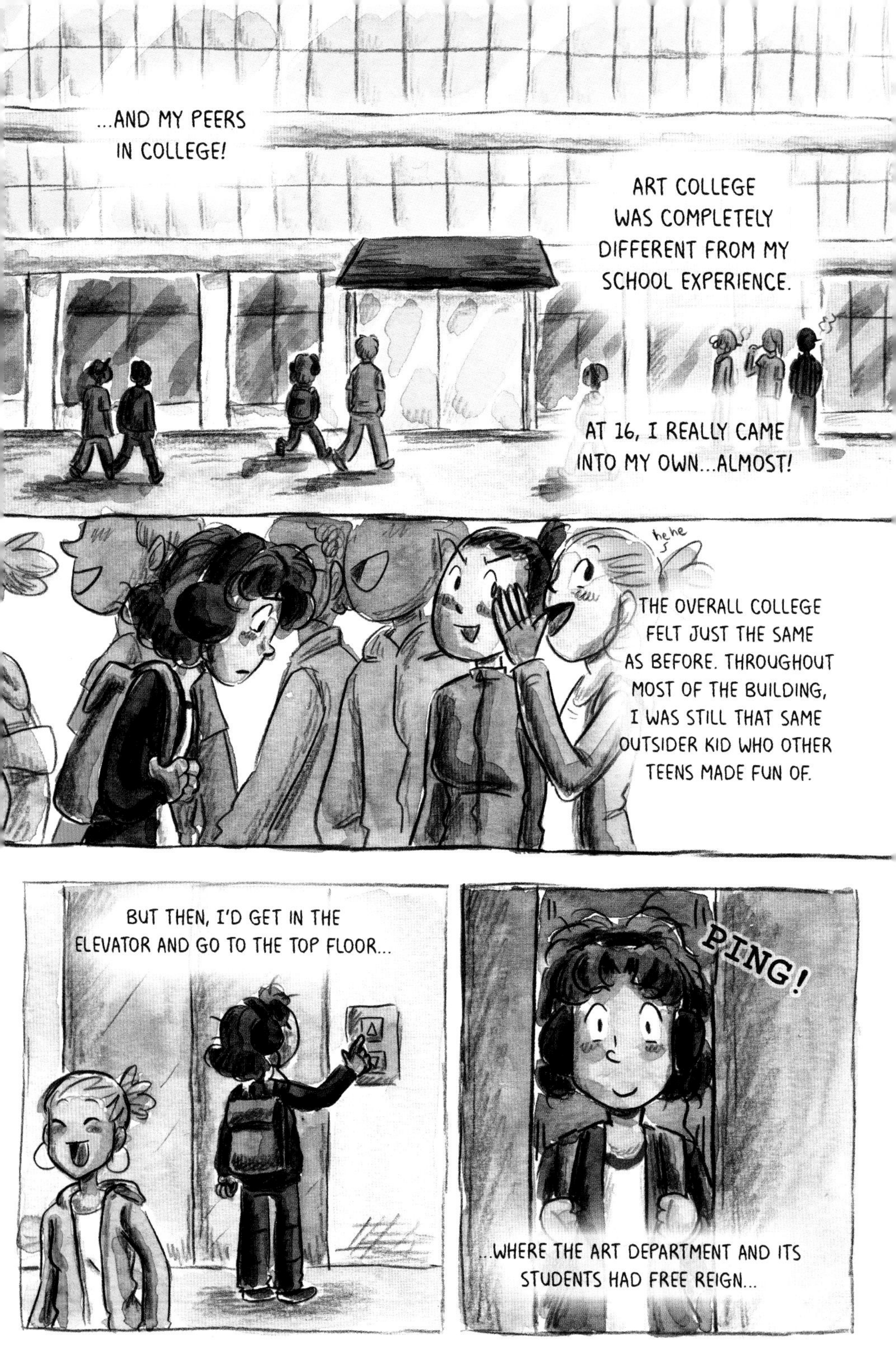
...AND MY PEERS IN COLLEGE!
ART COLLEGE WAS COMPLETELY DIFFERENT FROM MY SCHOOL EXPERIENCE.
AT 16, I REALLY CAME INTO MY OWN...ALMOST!
he he
THE OVERALL COLLEGE FELT JUST THE SAME AS BEFORE. THROUGHOUT MOST OF THE BUILDING, I WAS STILL THAT SAME OUTSIDER KID WHO OTHER TEENS MADE FUN OF.
BUT THEN, I'D GET IN THE ELEVATOR AND GO TO THE TOP FLOOR...
PING!
...WHERE THE ART DEPARTMENT AND ITS STUDENTS HAD FREE REIGN...

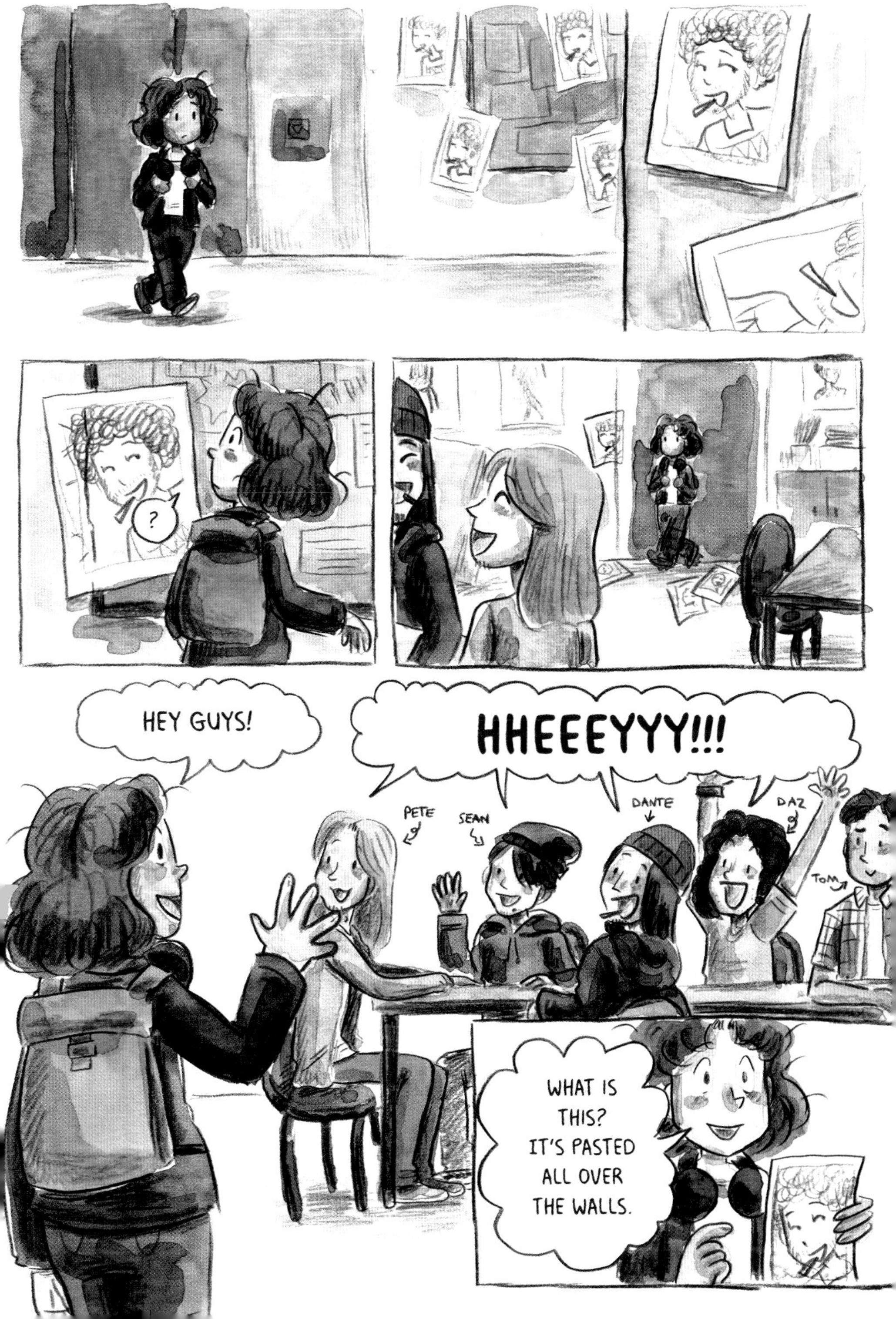
?
HEY GUYS!
HHEEEYYY!!!
PETE
SEAN
DANTE
DAZ
TOM
WHAT IS THIS? IT'S PASTED ALL OVER THE WALLS.

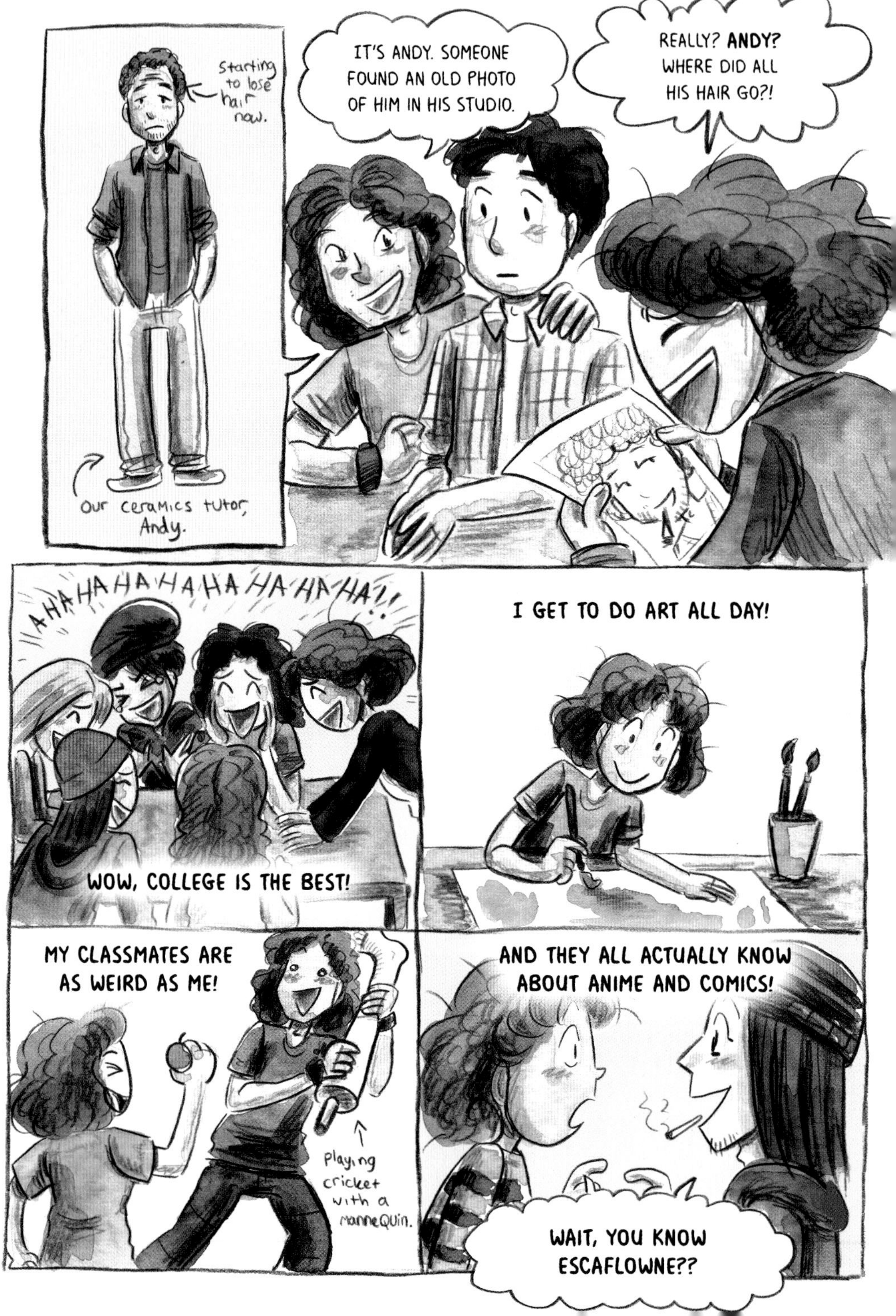
Starting to lose hair now.
Our ceramics tutor, Andy.
IT'S ANDY. SOMEONE FOUND AN OLD PHOTO OF HIM IN HIS STUDIO.
REALLY? ANDY? WHERE DID ALL HIS HAIR GO?!
AHAHAHAHAHAHAHAHAHA!!
WOW, COLLEGE IS THE BEST!
I GET TO DO ART ALL DAY!
MY CLASSMATES ARE AS WEIRD AS ME!
Playing cricket with a mannequin.
AND THEY ALL ACTUALLY KNOW ABOUT ANIME AND COMICS!
WAIT, YOU KNOW ESCAFLOWNE??

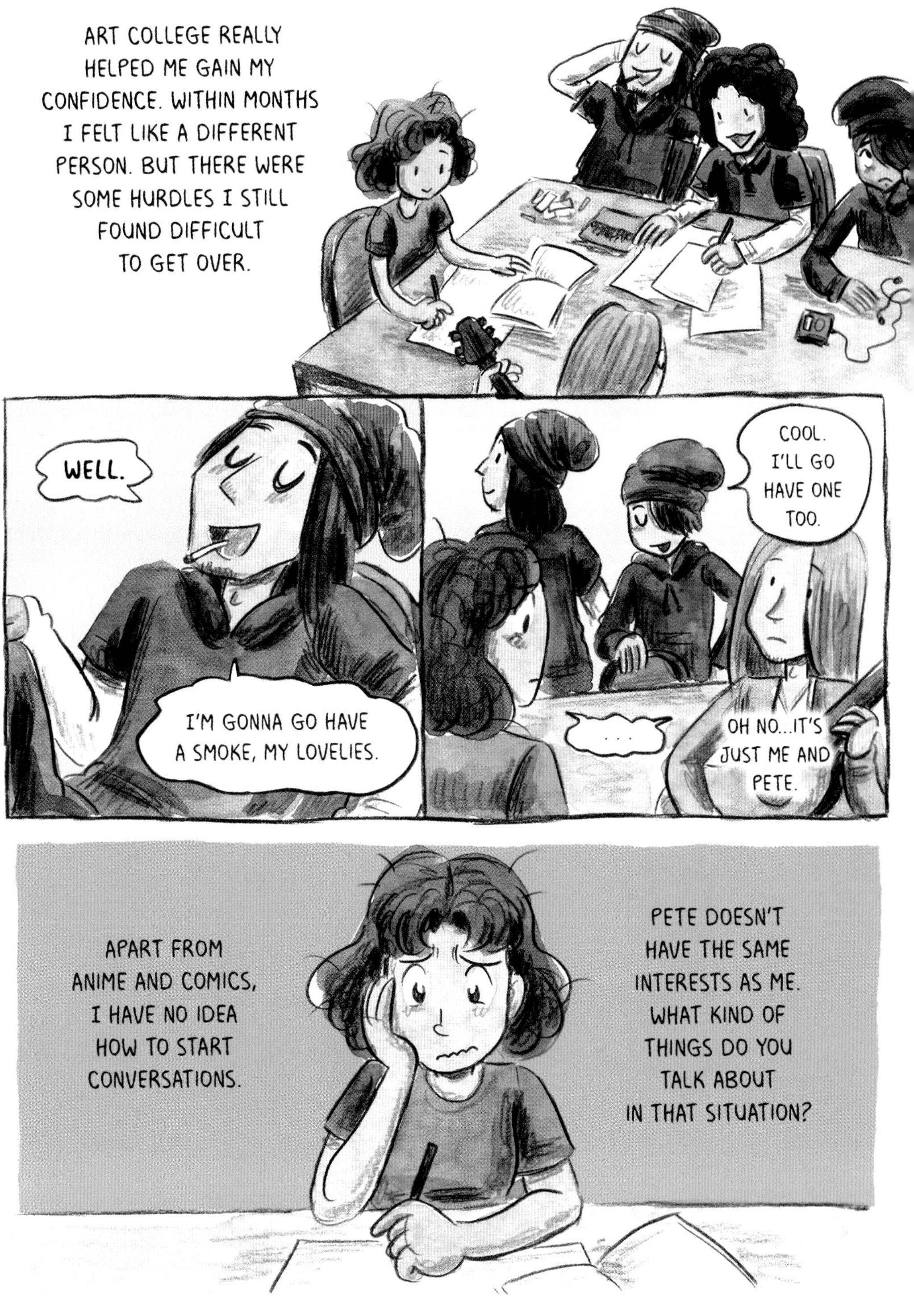
ART COLLEGE REALLY HELPED ME GAIN MY CONFIDENCE. WITHIN MONTHS I FELT LIKE A DIFFERENT PERSON. BUT THERE WERE SOME HURDLES I STILL FOUND DIFFICULT TO GET OVER.
WELL.
I'M GONNA GO HAVE A SMOKE, MY LOVELIES.
COOL. I'LL GO HAVE ONE TOO.
. . .
OH NO...IT'S JUST ME AND PETE.
APART FROM ANIME AND COMICS, I HAVE NO IDEA HOW TO START CONVERSATIONS.
PETE DOESN'T HAVE THE SAME INTERESTS AS ME. WHAT KIND OF THINGS DO YOU TALK ABOUT IN THAT SITUATION?

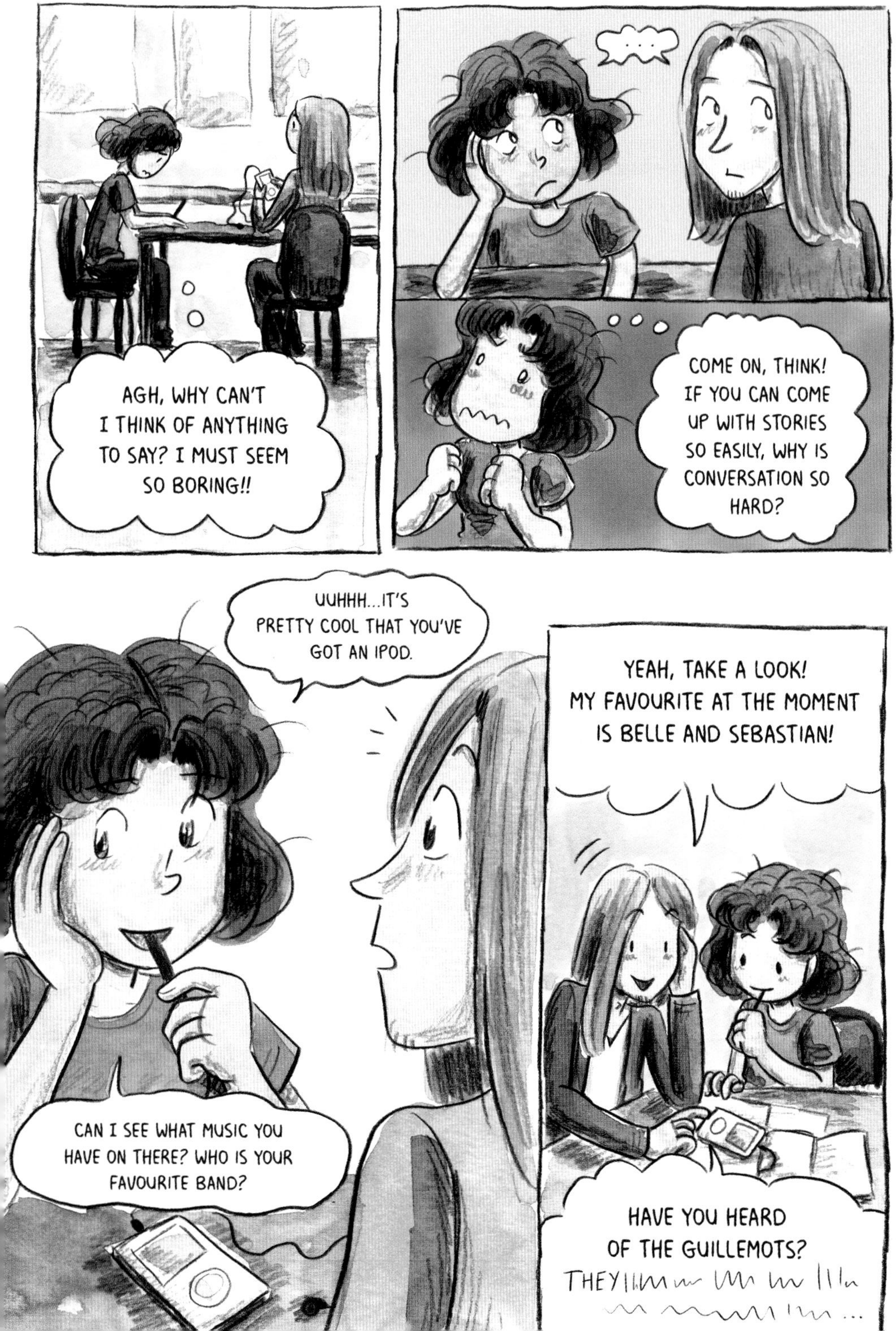
AGH, WHY CAN'T I THINK OF ANYTHING TO SAY? I MUST SEEM SO BORING!!
...
COME ON, THINK! IF YOU CAN COME UP WITH STORIES SO EASILY, WHY IS CONVERSATION SO HARD?
UUHHH...IT'S PRETTY COOL THAT YOU'VE GOT AN IPOD.
CAN I SEE WHAT MUSIC YOU HAVE ON THERE? WHO IS YOUR FAVOURITE BAND?
YEAH, TAKE A LOOK! MY FAVOURITE AT THE MOMENT IS BELLE AND SEBASTIAN!
HAVE YOU HEARD OF THE GUILLEMOTS?

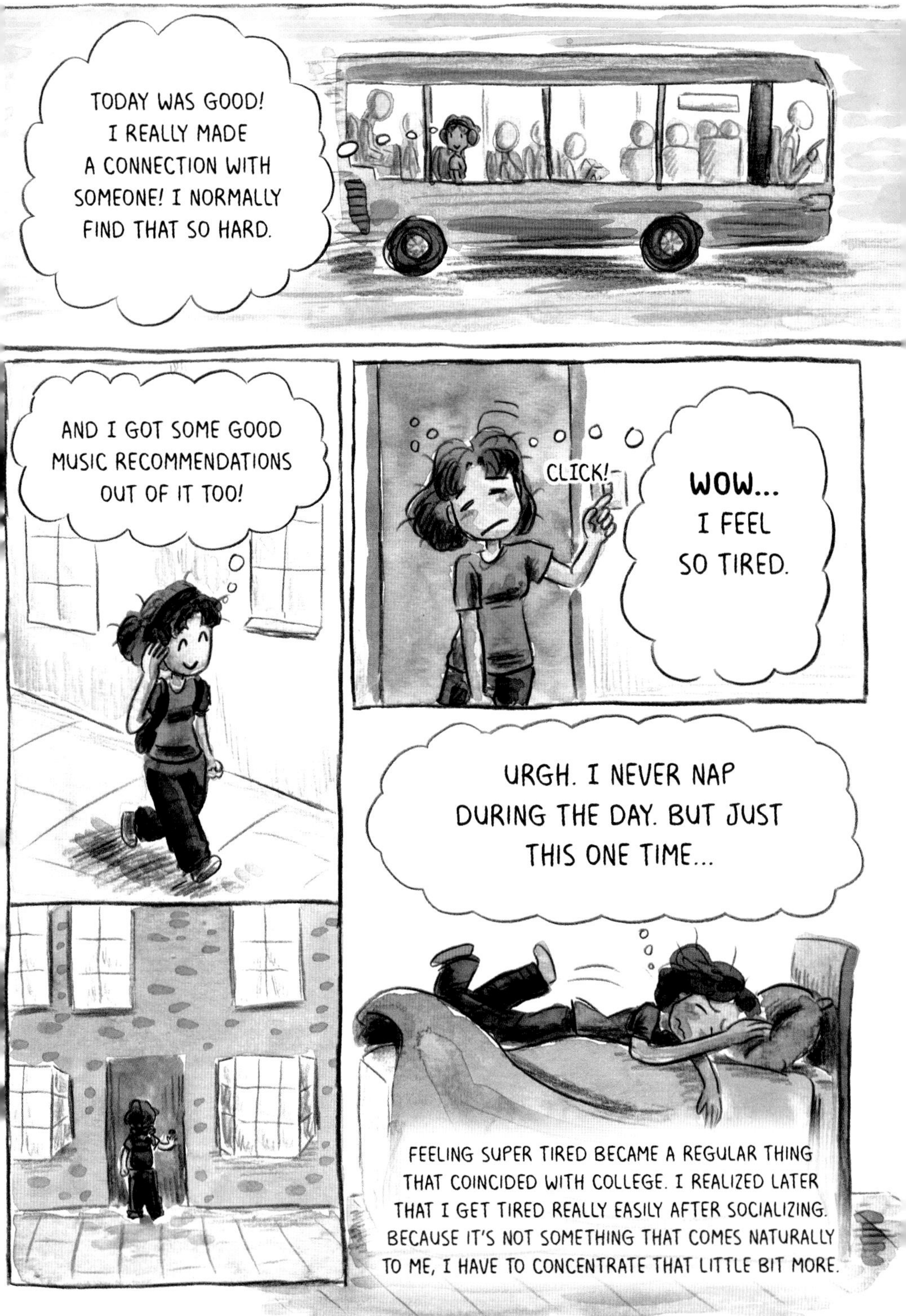
TODAY WAS GOOD! I REALLY MADE A CONNECTION WITH SOMEONE! I NORMALLY FIND THAT SO HARD.
AND I GOT SOME GOOD MUSIC RECOMMENDATIONS OUT OF IT TOO!
CLICK!
WOW... I FEEL SO TIRED.
URGH. I NEVER NAP DURING THE DAY. BUT JUST THIS ONE TIME...
FEELING SUPER TIRED BECAME A REGULAR THING THAT COINCIDED WITH COLLEGE. I REALIZED LATER THAT I GET TIRED REALLY EASILY AFTER SOCIALIZING. BECAUSE IT'S NOT SOMETHING THAT COMES NATURALLY TO ME, I HAVE TO CONCENTRATE THAT LITTLE BIT MORE.

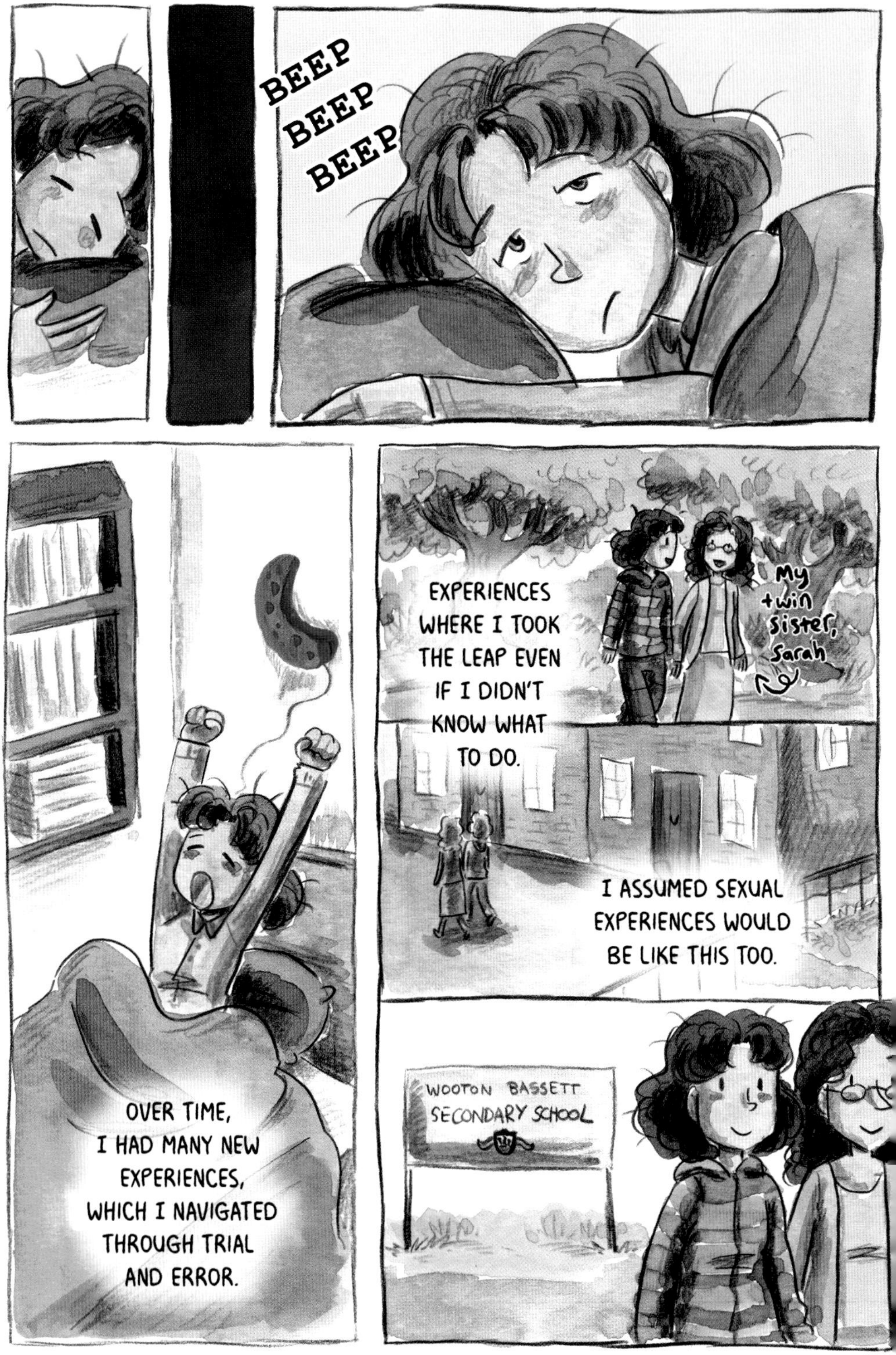
BEEP
BEEP
BEEP
OVER TIME, I HAD MANY NEW EXPERIENCES, WHICH I NAVIGATED THROUGH TRIAL AND ERROR.
EXPERIENCES WHERE I TOOK THE LEAP EVEN IF I DIDN'T KNOW WHAT TO DO.
My twin sister, Sarah
I ASSUMED SEXUAL EXPERIENCES WOULD BE LIKE THIS TOO.
WOOTON BASSETT SECONDARY SCHOOL

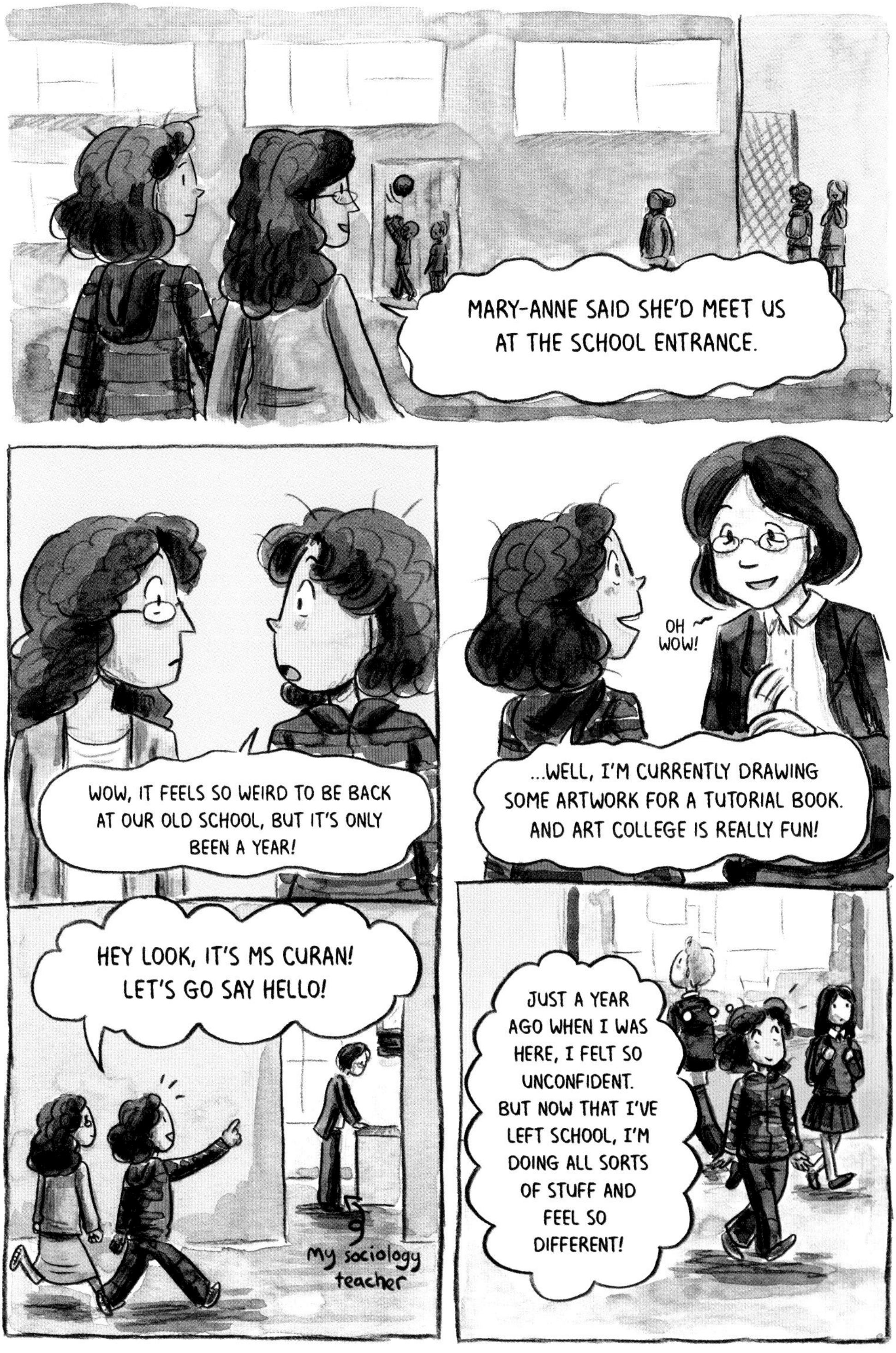
MARY-ANNE SAID SHE'D MEET US AT THE SCHOOL ENTRANCE.
WOW, IT FEELS SO WEIRD TO BE BACK AT OUR OLD SCHOOL, BUT IT'S ONLY BEEN A YEAR!
OH ~ WOW!
...WELL, I'M CURRENTLY DRAWING SOME ARTWORK FOR A TUTORIAL BOOK. AND ART COLLEGE IS REALLY FUN!
HEY LOOK, IT'S MS CURAN! LET'S GO SAY HELLO!
My sociology teacher
JUST A YEAR AGO WHEN I WAS HERE, I FELT SO UNCONFIDENT. BUT NOW THAT I'VE LEFT SCHOOL, I'M DOING ALL SORTS OF STUFF AND FEEL SO DIFFERENT!

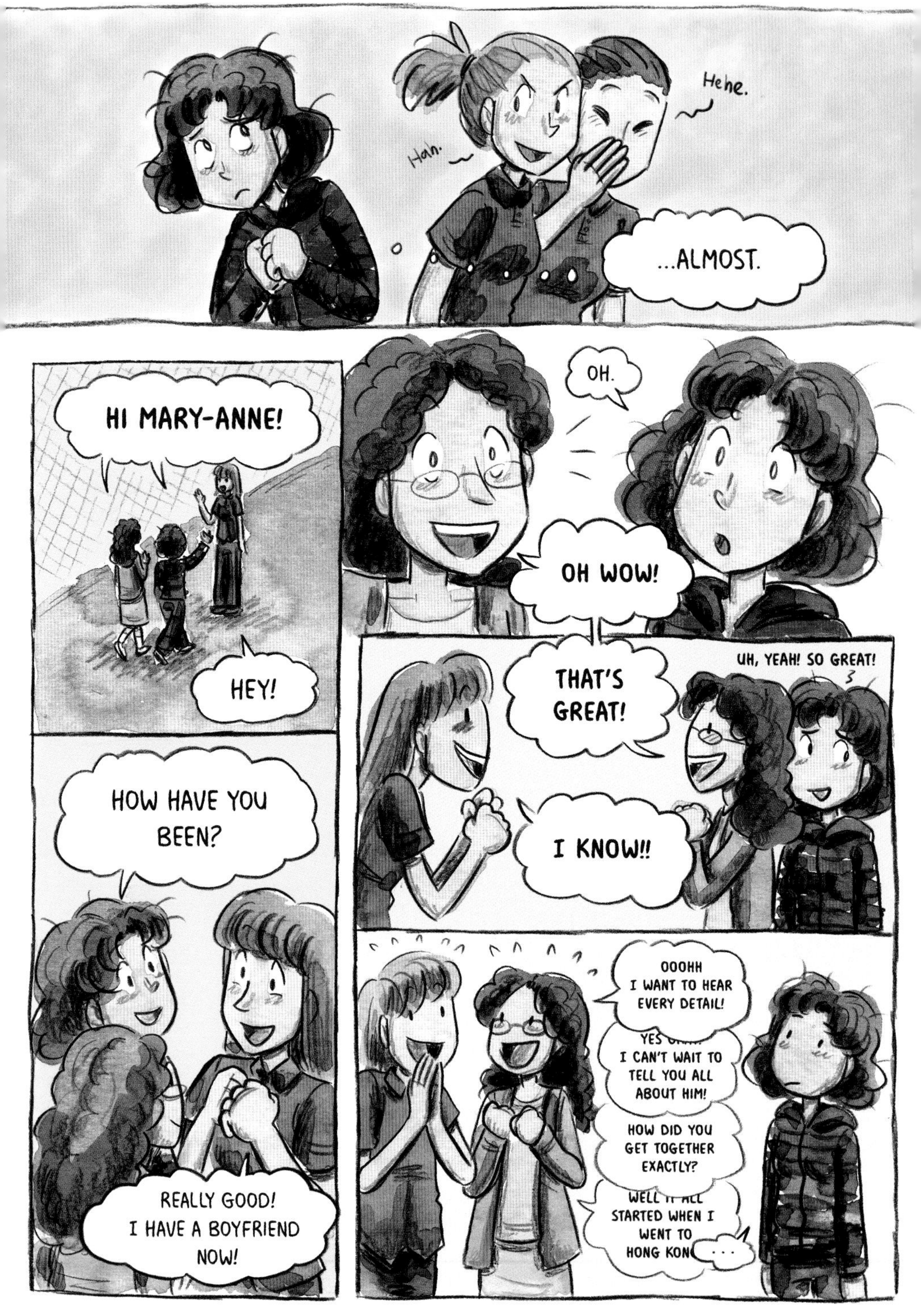
Hah.
Hehe.
...ALMOST.
HI MARY-ANNE!
HEY!
HOW HAVE YOU BEEN?
REALLY GOOD! I HAVE A BOYFRIEND NOW!
OH WOW!
OH.
THAT'S GREAT!
I KNOW!!
UH, YEAH! SO GREAT!
OOOHH I WANT TO HEAR EVERY DETAIL!
YES
I CAN'T WAIT TO TELL YOU ALL ABOUT HIM!
HOW DID YOU GET TOGETHER EXACTLY?
STARTED WHEN I WENT TO HONG KON
...

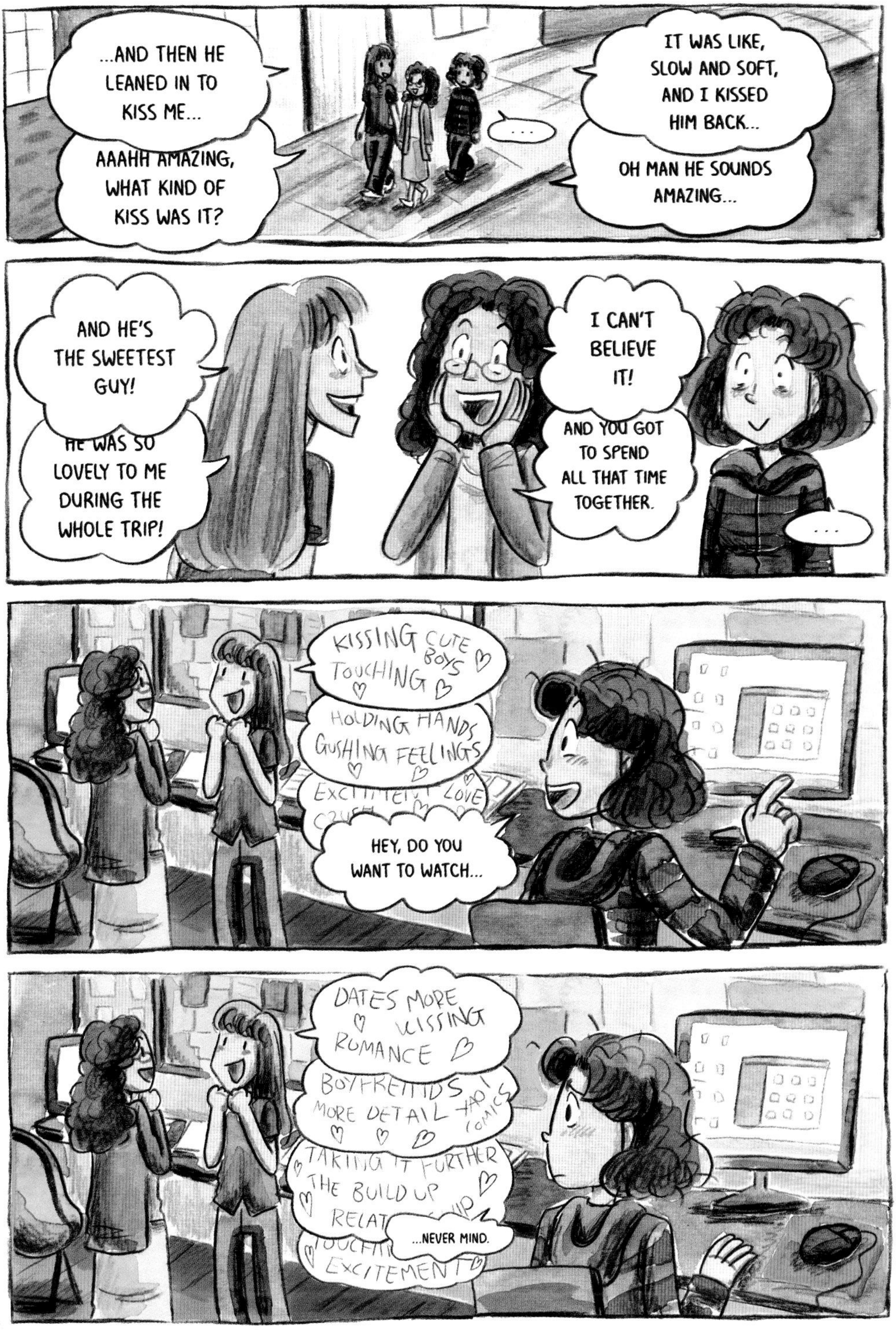
...AND THEN HE LEANED IN TO KISS ME...
AAAHH AMAZING, WHAT KIND OF KISS WAS IT?
. . .
IT WAS LIKE, SLOW AND SOFT, AND I KISSED HIM BACK...
OH MAN HE SOUNDS AMAZING...
AND HE'S THE SWEETEST GUY!
HE WAS SO LOVELY TO ME DURING THE WHOLE TRIP!
I CAN'T BELIEVE IT!
AND YOU GOT TO SPEND ALL THAT TIME TOGETHER.
. . .
KISSING CUTE BOYS TOUCHING
HOLDING HANDS GUSHING FEELINGS
EXCITEMENT LOVE
HEY, DO YOU WANT TO WATCH...
DATES MORE KISSING ROMANCE
BOYFRIENDS MORE DETAIL
TAKING IT FURTHER THE BUILD UP
...NEVER MIND.
EXCITEMENT

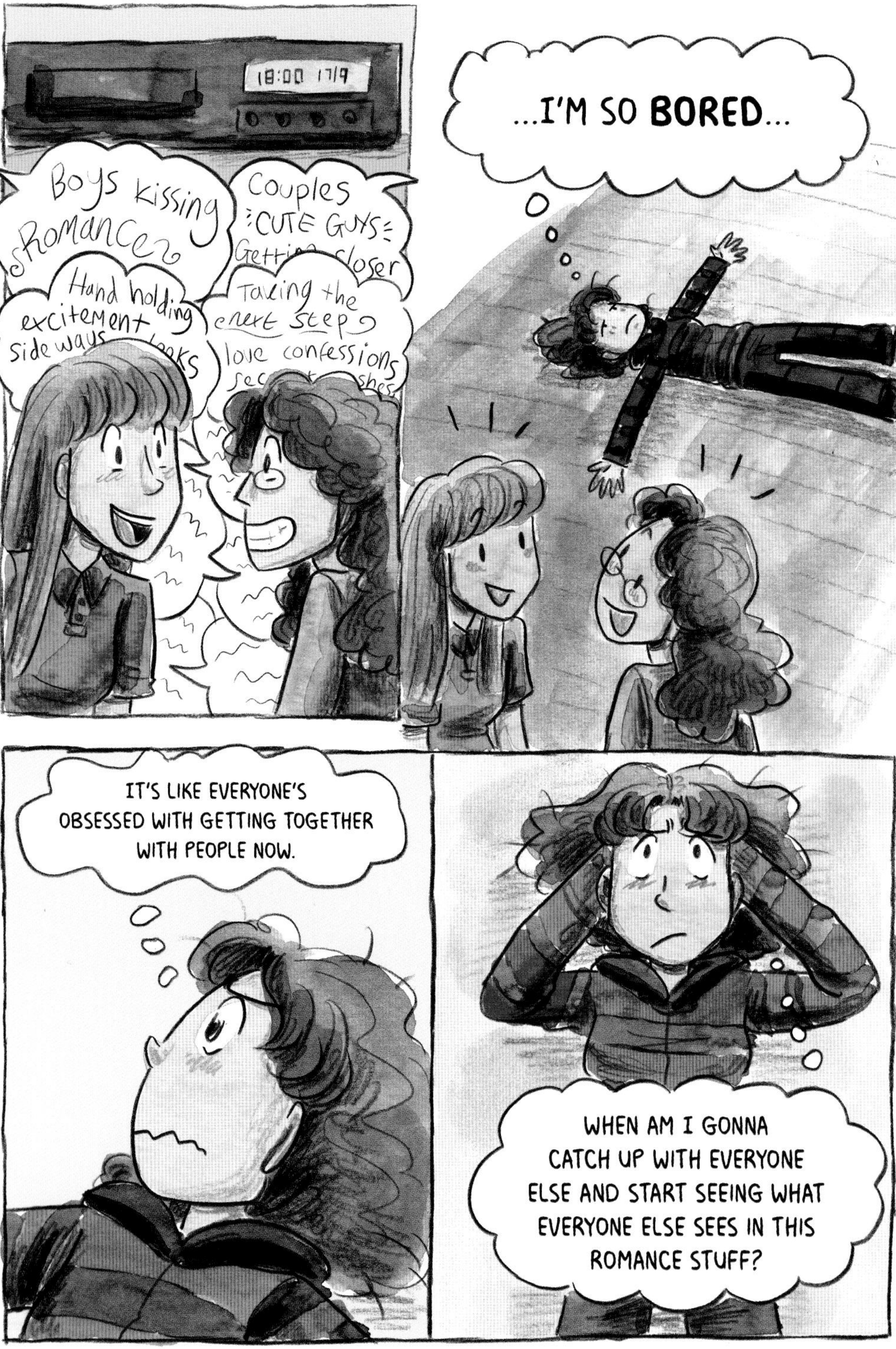
18:00 17/9
Boys kissing
Romance
Couples
CUTE GUYS
closer
Hand holding
excitement
sideways
Taking the
next step
love confessions
...I'M SO BORED...
IT'S LIKE EVERYONE'S OBSESSED WITH GETTING TOGETHER WITH PEOPLE NOW.
WHEN AM I GONNA CATCH UP WITH EVERYONE ELSE AND START SEEING WHAT EVERYONE ELSE SEES IN THIS ROMANCE STUFF?

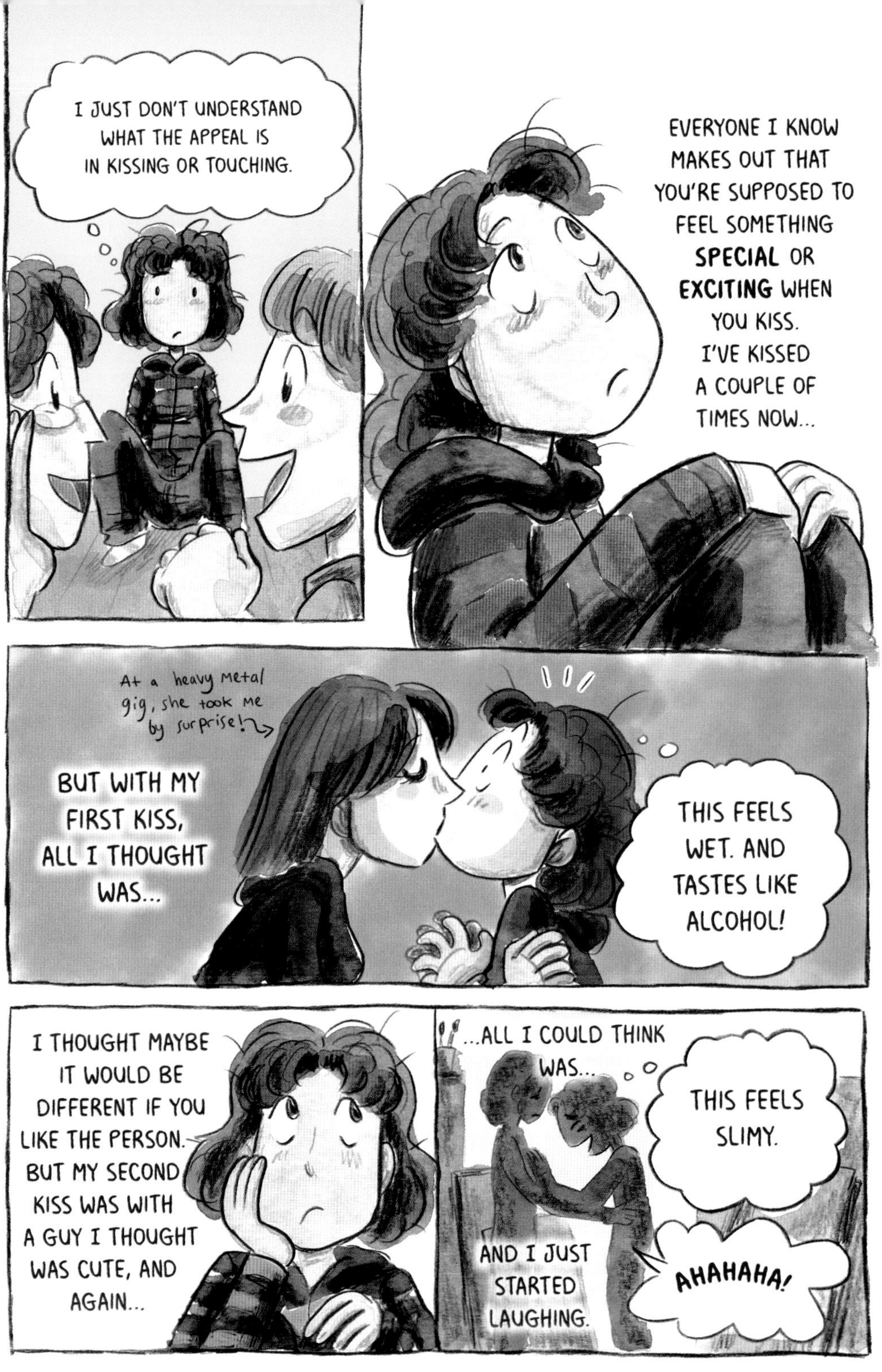
I JUST DON'T UNDERSTAND WHAT THE APPEAL IS IN KISSING OR TOUCHING.
EVERYONE I KNOW MAKES OUT THAT YOU'RE SUPPOSED TO FEEL SOMETHING **SPECIAL** OR **EXCITING** WHEN YOU KISS. I'VE KISSED A COUPLE OF TIMES NOW...
At a heavy metal gig, she took me by surprise!
BUT WITH MY FIRST KISS, ALL I THOUGHT WAS...
THIS FEELS WET. AND TASTES LIKE ALCOHOL!
I THOUGHT MAYBE IT WOULD BE DIFFERENT IF YOU LIKE THE PERSON. BUT MY SECOND KISS WAS WITH A GUY I THOUGHT WAS CUTE, AND AGAIN...
...ALL I COULD THINK WAS...
THIS FEELS SLIMY.
AND I JUST STARTED LAUGHING.
AHAHAHA!

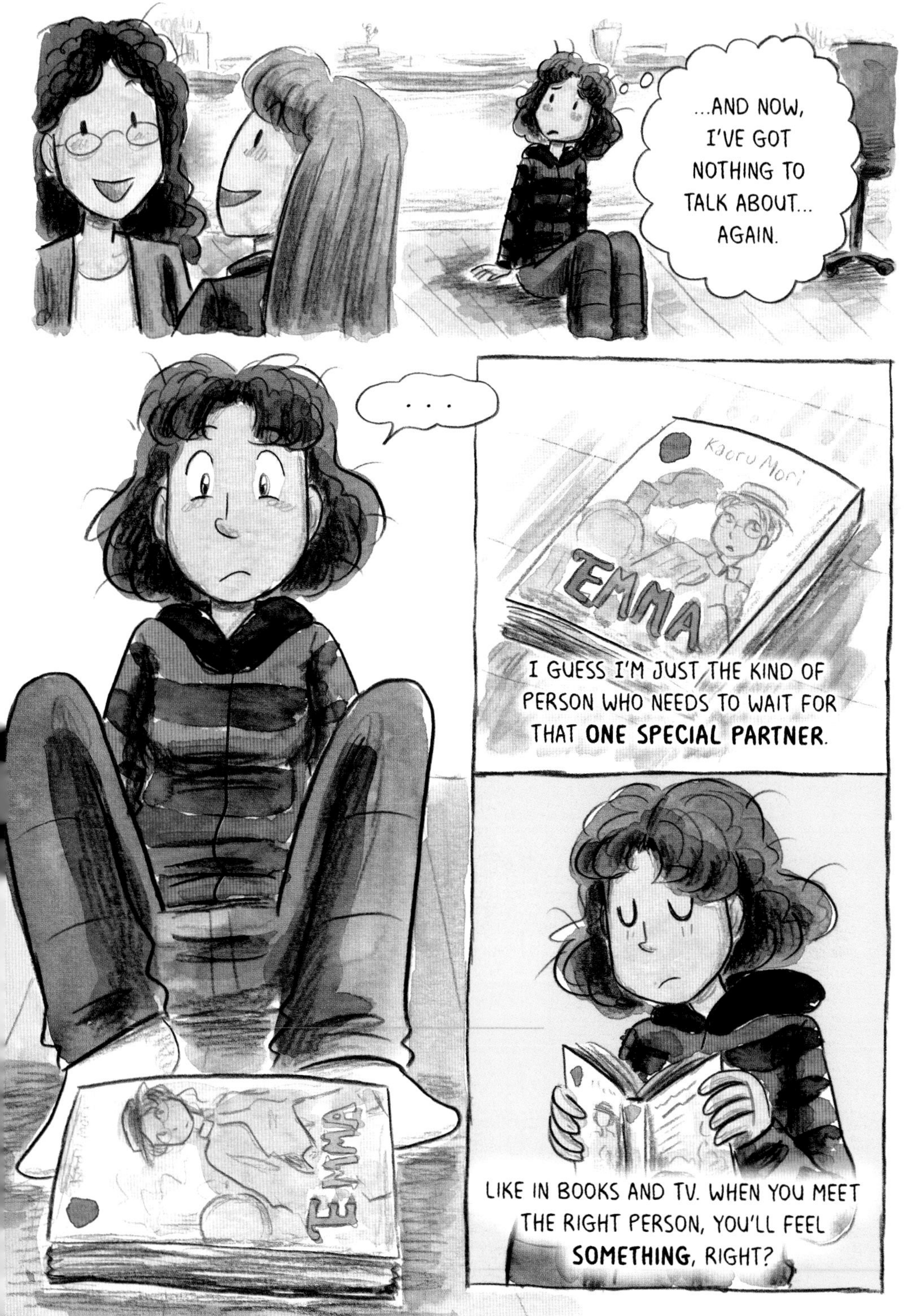
...AND NOW, I'VE GOT NOTHING TO TALK ABOUT... AGAIN.
. . .
Kaoru Mori
EMMA
I GUESS I'M JUST THE KIND OF PERSON WHO NEEDS TO WAIT FOR THAT **ONE SPECIAL PARTNER**.
EMMA
LIKE IN BOOKS AND TV. WHEN YOU MEET THE RIGHT PERSON, YOU'LL FEEL **SOMETHING**, RIGHT?

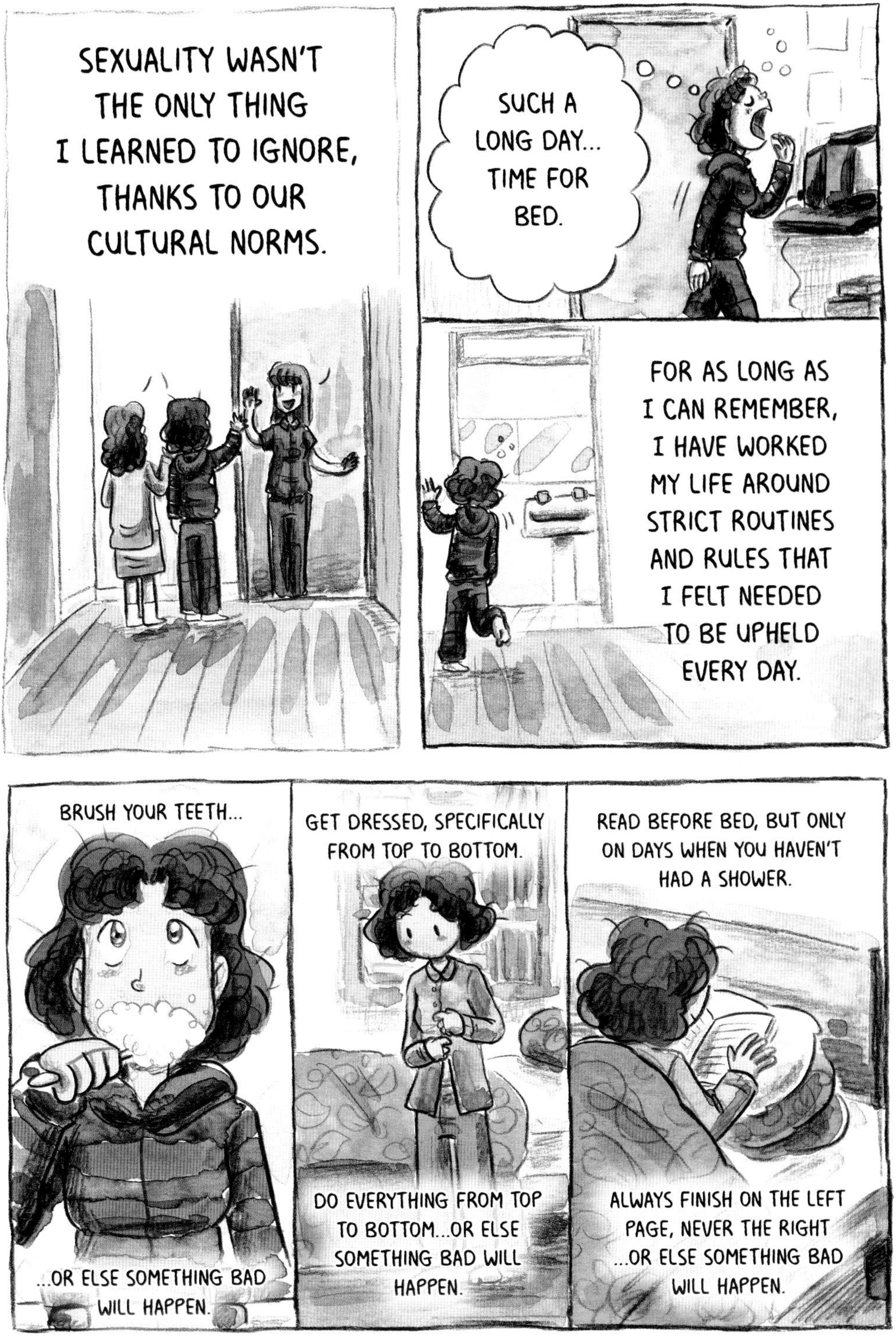
SEXUALITY WASN'T THE ONLY THING I LEARNED TO IGNORE, THANKS TO OUR CULTURAL NORMS.
SUCH A LONG DAY... TIME FOR BED.
FOR AS LONG AS I CAN REMEMBER, I HAVE WORKED MY LIFE AROUND STRICT ROUTINES AND RULES THAT I FELT NEEDED TO BE UPHELD EVERY DAY.
BRUSH YOUR TEETH...
...OR ELSE SOMETHING BAD WILL HAPPEN.
GET DRESSED, SPECIFICALLY FROM TOP TO BOTTOM.
DO EVERYTHING FROM TOP TO BOTTOM...OR ELSE SOMETHING BAD WILL HAPPEN.
READ BEFORE BED, BUT ONLY ON DAYS WHEN YOU HAVEN'T HAD A SHOWER.
ALWAYS FINISH ON THE LEFT PAGE, NEVER THE RIGHT ...OR ELSE SOMETHING BAD WILL HAPPEN.

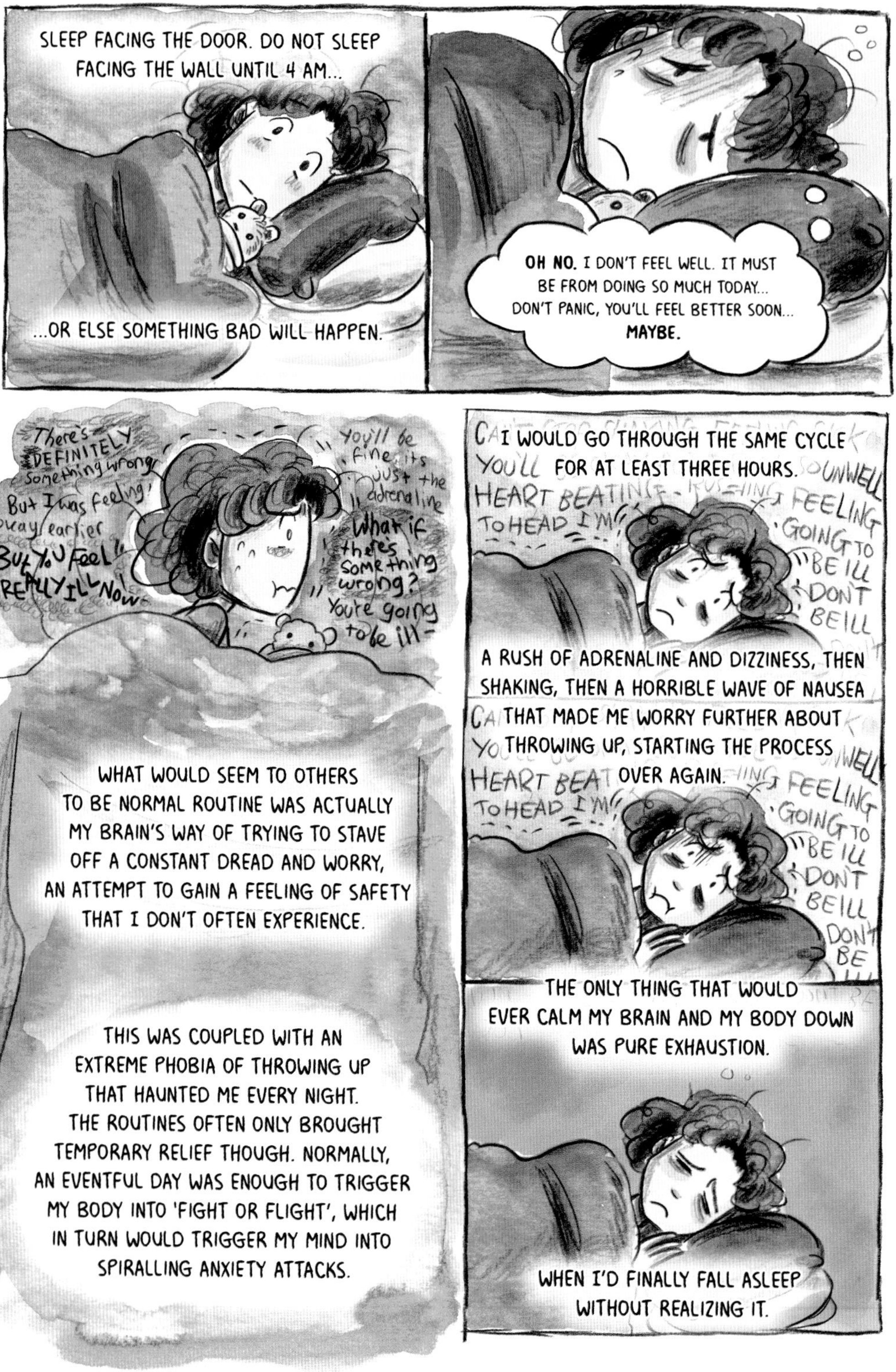
SLEEP FACING THE DOOR. DO NOT SLEEP FACING THE WALL UNTIL 4 AM...
...OR ELSE SOMETHING BAD WILL HAPPEN.
OH NO. I DON'T FEEL WELL. IT MUST BE FROM DOING SO MUCH TODAY... DON'T PANIC, YOU'LL FEEL BETTER SOON... MAYBE.
There's DEFINITELY something wrong
But I was feeling okay earlier
BUT YOU FEEL REALLY ILL NOW
You'll be fine its just the adrenaline
What if there's something wrong?
You're going to be ill
WHAT WOULD SEEM TO OTHERS TO BE NORMAL ROUTINE WAS ACTUALLY MY BRAIN'S WAY OF TRYING TO STAVE OFF A CONSTANT DREAD AND WORRY, AN ATTEMPT TO GAIN A FEELING OF SAFETY THAT I DON'T OFTEN EXPERIENCE.
THIS WAS COUPLED WITH AN EXTREME PHOBIA OF THROWING UP THAT HAUNTED ME EVERY NIGHT. THE ROUTINES OFTEN ONLY BROUGHT TEMPORARY RELIEF THOUGH. NORMALLY, AN EVENTFUL DAY WAS ENOUGH TO TRIGGER MY BODY INTO 'FIGHT OR FLIGHT', WHICH IN TURN WOULD TRIGGER MY MIND INTO SPIRALLING ANXIETY ATTACKS.
I WOULD GO THROUGH THE SAME CYCLE FOR AT LEAST THREE HOURS.
A RUSH OF ADRENALINE AND DIZZINESS, THEN SHAKING, THEN A HORRIBLE WAVE OF NAUSEA
THAT MADE ME WORRY FURTHER ABOUT THROWING UP, STARTING THE PROCESS OVER AGAIN.
THE ONLY THING THAT WOULD EVER CALM MY BRAIN AND MY BODY DOWN WAS PURE EXHAUSTION.
WHEN I'D FINALLY FALL ASLEEP WITHOUT REALIZING IT.

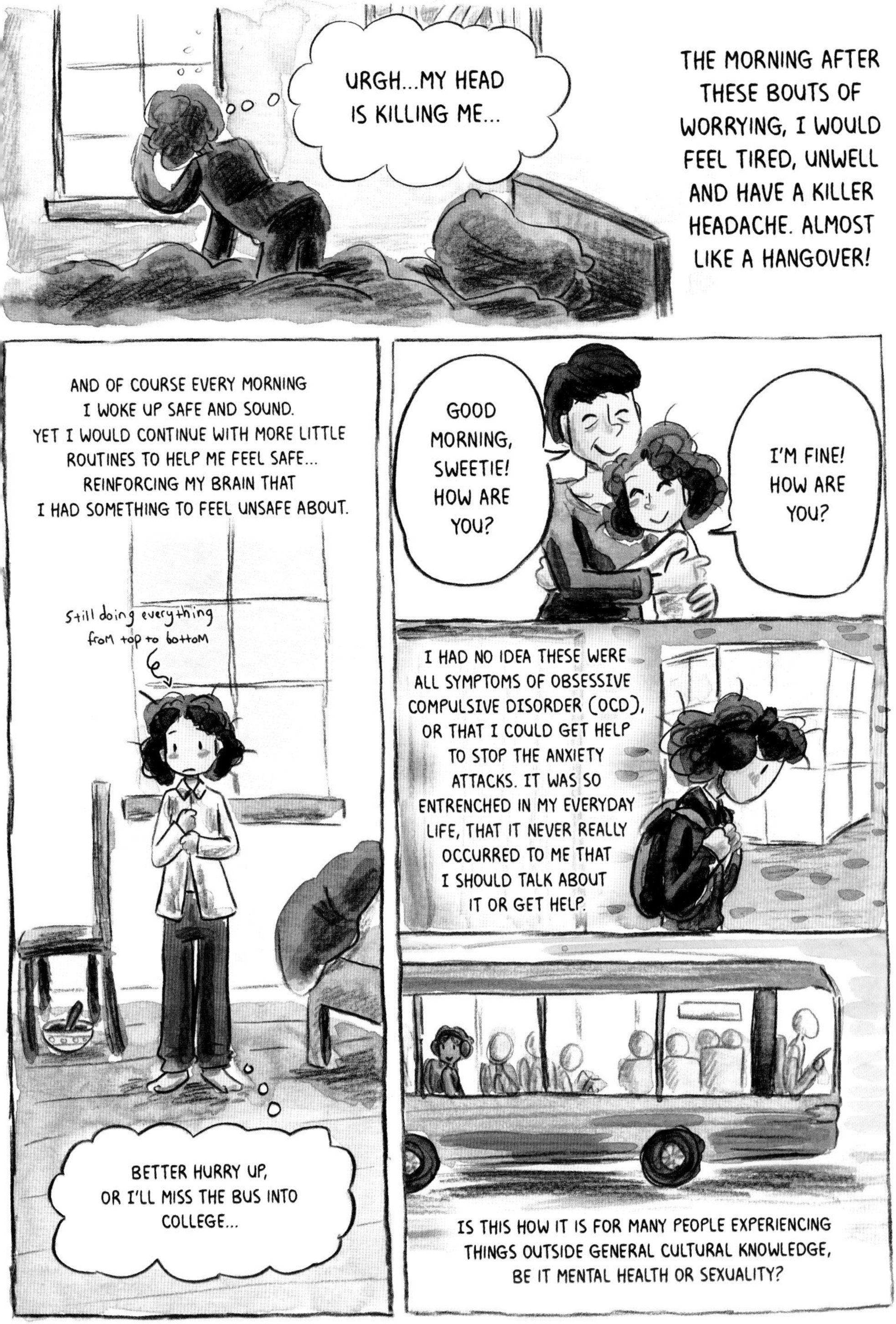
URGH...MY HEAD IS KILLING ME...
THE MORNING AFTER THESE BOUTS OF WORRYING, I WOULD FEEL TIRED, UNWELL AND HAVE A KILLER HEADACHE. ALMOST LIKE A HANGOVER!
AND OF COURSE EVERY MORNING I WOKE UP SAFE AND SOUND. YET I WOULD CONTINUE WITH MORE LITTLE ROUTINES TO HELP ME FEEL SAFE... REINFORCING MY BRAIN THAT I HAD SOMETHING TO FEEL UNSAFE ABOUT.
Still doing everything from top to bottom
BETTER HURRY UP, OR I'LL MISS THE BUS INTO COLLEGE...
GOOD MORNING, SWEETIE! HOW ARE YOU?
I'M FINE! HOW ARE YOU?
I HAD NO IDEA THESE WERE ALL SYMPTOMS OF OBSESSIVE COMPULSIVE DISORDER (OCD), OR THAT I COULD GET HELP TO STOP THE ANXIETY ATTACKS. IT WAS SO ENTRENCHED IN MY EVERYDAY LIFE, THAT IT NEVER REALLY OCCURRED TO ME THAT I SHOULD TALK ABOUT IT OR GET HELP.
IS THIS HOW IT IS FOR MANY PEOPLE EXPERIENCING THINGS OUTSIDE GENERAL CULTURAL KNOWLEDGE, BE IT MENTAL HEALTH OR SEXUALITY?

# SEXUAL ATTRACTION -and- ROMANTIC ATTRACTION

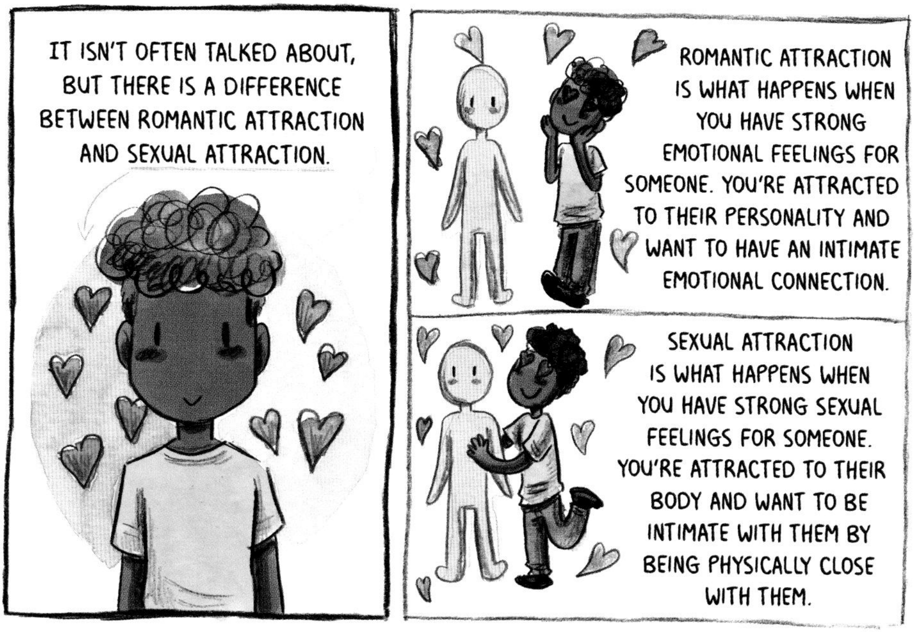
IT ISN'T OFTEN TALKED ABOUT, BUT THERE IS A DIFFERENCE BETWEEN ROMANTIC ATTRACTION AND SEXUAL ATTRACTION.
ROMANTIC ATTRACTION IS WHAT HAPPENS WHEN YOU HAVE STRONG EMOTIONAL FEELINGS FOR SOMEONE. YOU'RE ATTRACTED TO THEIR PERSONALITY AND WANT TO HAVE AN INTIMATE EMOTIONAL CONNECTION.
SEXUAL ATTRACTION IS WHAT HAPPENS WHEN YOU HAVE STRONG SEXUAL FEELINGS FOR SOMEONE. YOU'RE ATTRACTED TO THEIR BODY AND WANT TO BE INTIMATE WITH THEM BY BEING PHYSICALLY CLOSE WITH THEM.

FOR A LOT OF PEOPLE, THERE IS AN OVERLAP AND INTERWEAVING BETWEEN ROMANTIC AND SEXUAL ATTRACTION. THIS IS MAYBE WHY IT'S NOT COMMON KNOWLEDGE THAT THERE IS ACTUALLY A DIFFERENCE.

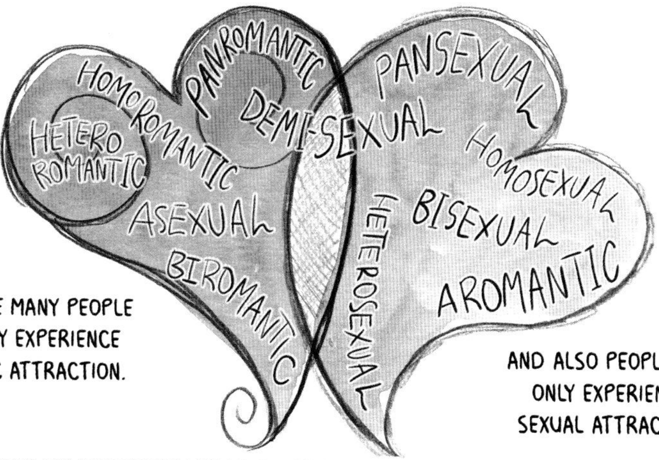
HOMOROMANTIC
PANROMANTIC
HETERO ROMANTIC
DEMI-SEXUAL
PANSEXUAL
ASEXUAL
BIROMANTIC
HETEROSEXUAL
HOMOSEXUAL
BISEXUAL
AROMANTIC

THERE ARE MANY PEOPLE WHO ONLY EXPERIENCE ROMANTIC ATTRACTION.

AND ALSO PEOPLE WHO ONLY EXPERIENCE SEXUAL ATTRACTION.

THERE ARE EVEN PEOPLE WHO HAVE DIFFERENT FEELINGS FOR DIFFERENT GENDERS (I.E. SOMEONE WHO IS ROMANTICALLY ATTRACTED TO ANY GENDER, BUT SEXUALLY ATTRACTED TO WOMEN).
**EVERYONE FALLS SOMEWHERE ON THIS SPECTRUM IN THEIR OWN WAY!**

# CHAPTER THREE

## HOW TO BREAK
## SOMEONE'S HEART

BEFORE I WENT TO UNI, I HAD A VERY SET IDEA IN MY HEAD ABOUT WHAT A UNI STUDENT WAS SUPPOSED TO DO.

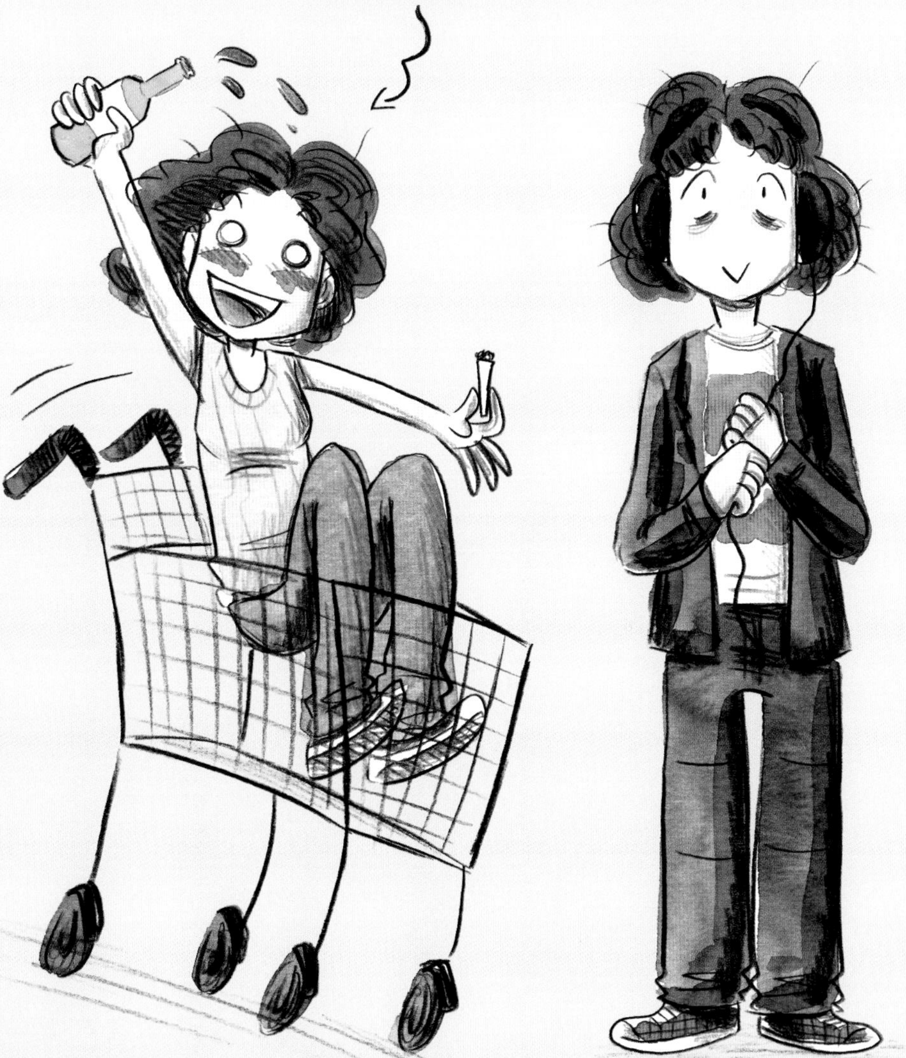

SOCIAL EXPECTATIONS TOLD ME THAT THE PERSON I **REALLY** WAS, WASN'T GOING TO LIVE LIFE TO THE FULL.

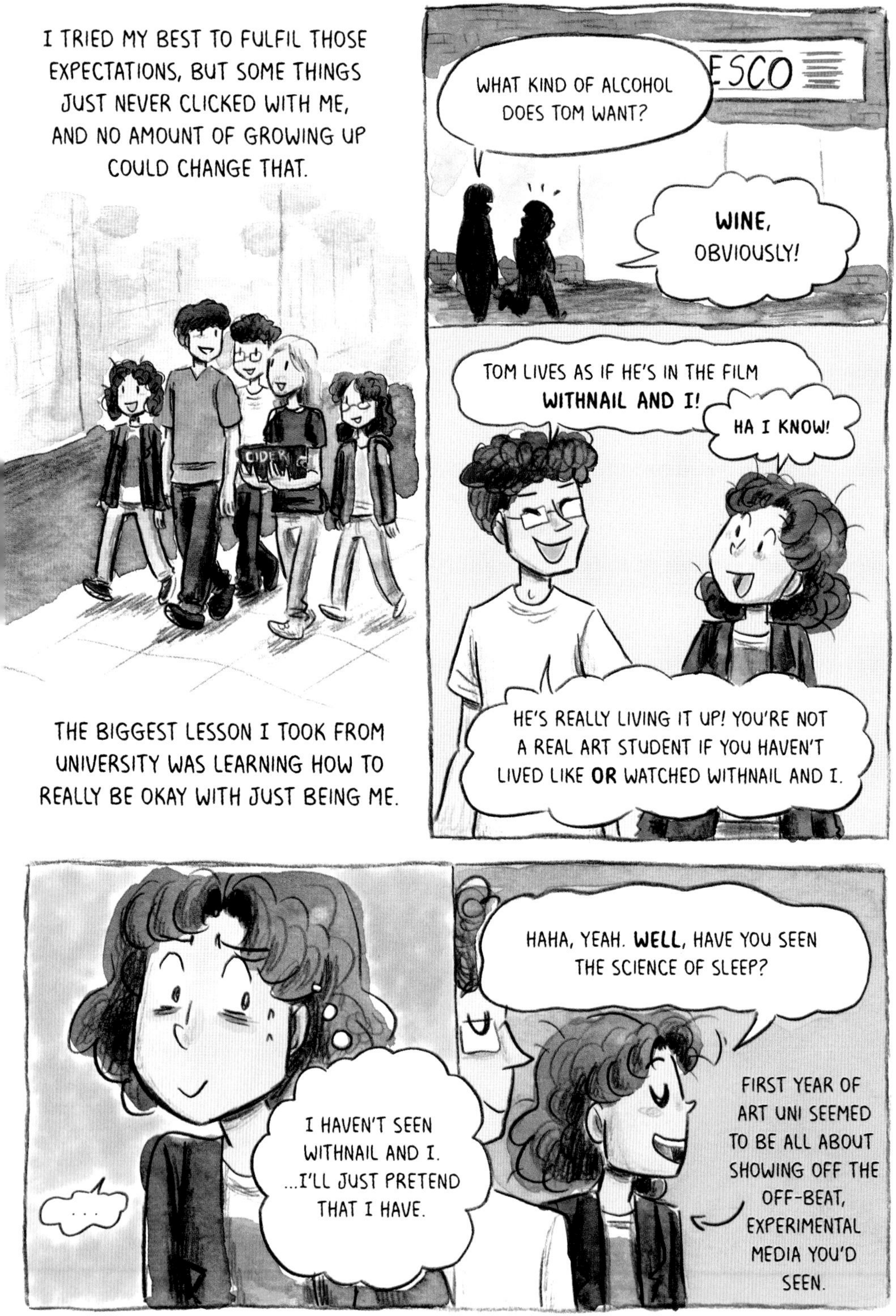
I TRIED MY BEST TO FULFIL THOSE EXPECTATIONS, BUT SOME THINGS JUST NEVER CLICKED WITH ME, AND NO AMOUNT OF GROWING UP COULD CHANGE THAT.
CIDER
THE BIGGEST LESSON I TOOK FROM UNIVERSITY WAS LEARNING HOW TO REALLY BE OKAY WITH JUST BEING ME.
ESCO
WHAT KIND OF ALCOHOL DOES TOM WANT?
WINE, OBVIOUSLY!
TOM LIVES AS IF HE'S IN THE FILM WITHNAIL AND I!
HA I KNOW!
HE'S REALLY LIVING IT UP! YOU'RE NOT A REAL ART STUDENT IF YOU HAVEN'T LIVED LIKE OR WATCHED WITHNAIL AND I.
...
I HAVEN'T SEEN WITHNAIL AND I. ...I'LL JUST PRETEND THAT I HAVE.
HAHA, YEAH. WELL, HAVE YOU SEEN THE SCIENCE OF SLEEP?
FIRST YEAR OF ART UNI SEEMED TO BE ALL ABOUT SHOWING OFF THE OFF-BEAT, EXPERIMENTAL MEDIA YOU'D SEEN.

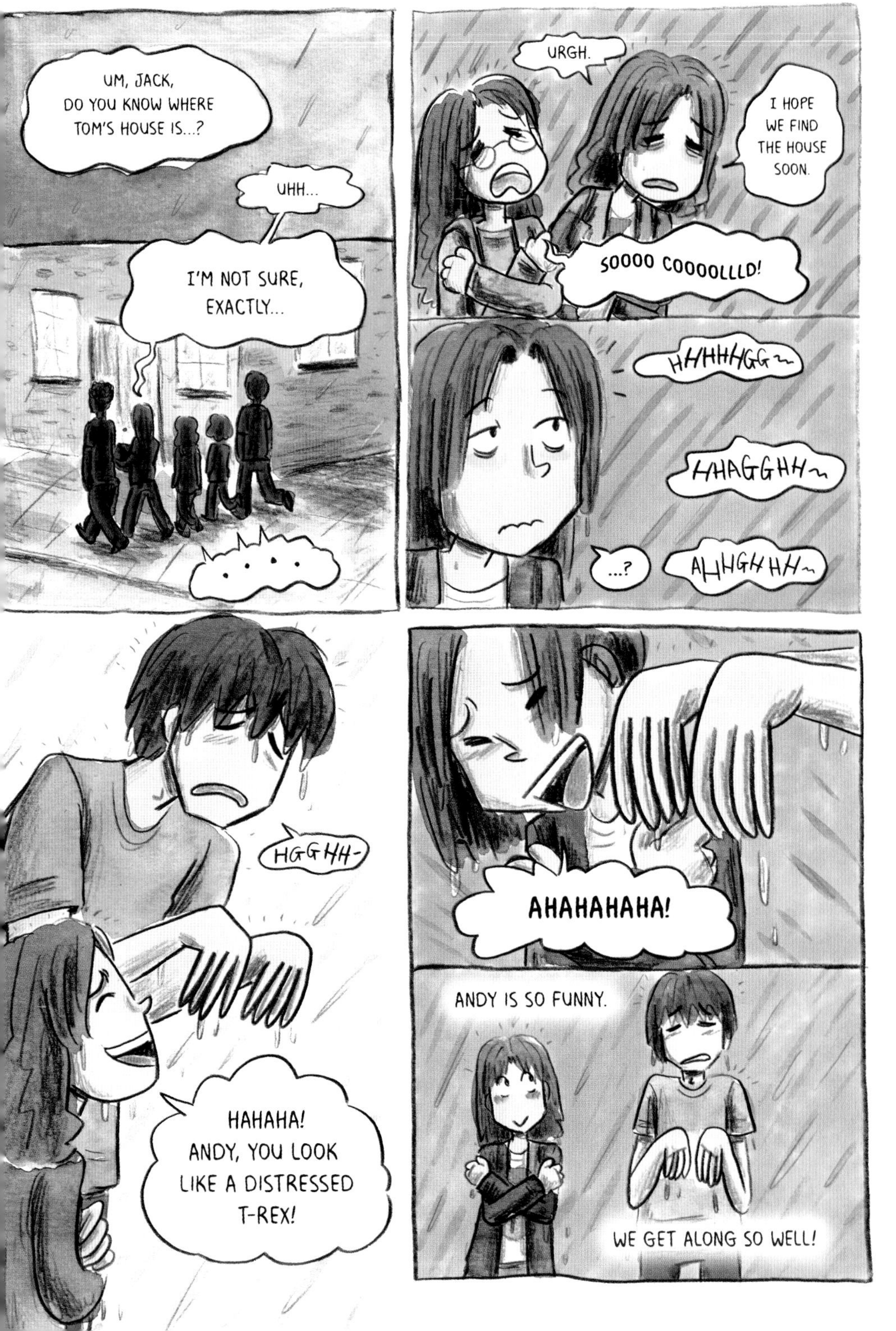
UM, JACK, DO YOU KNOW WHERE TOM'S HOUSE IS...?
UHH...
I'M NOT SURE, EXACTLY...
. . . .
URGH.
I HOPE WE FIND THE HOUSE SOON.
SOOOO COOOOLLLD!
HHHHHGG~
HHAGGHH~
...?
AHHGHHH~
HGGHH-
HAHAHA! ANDY, YOU LOOK LIKE A DISTRESSED T-REX!
AHAHAHAHA!
ANDY IS SO FUNNY.
WE GET ALONG SO WELL!

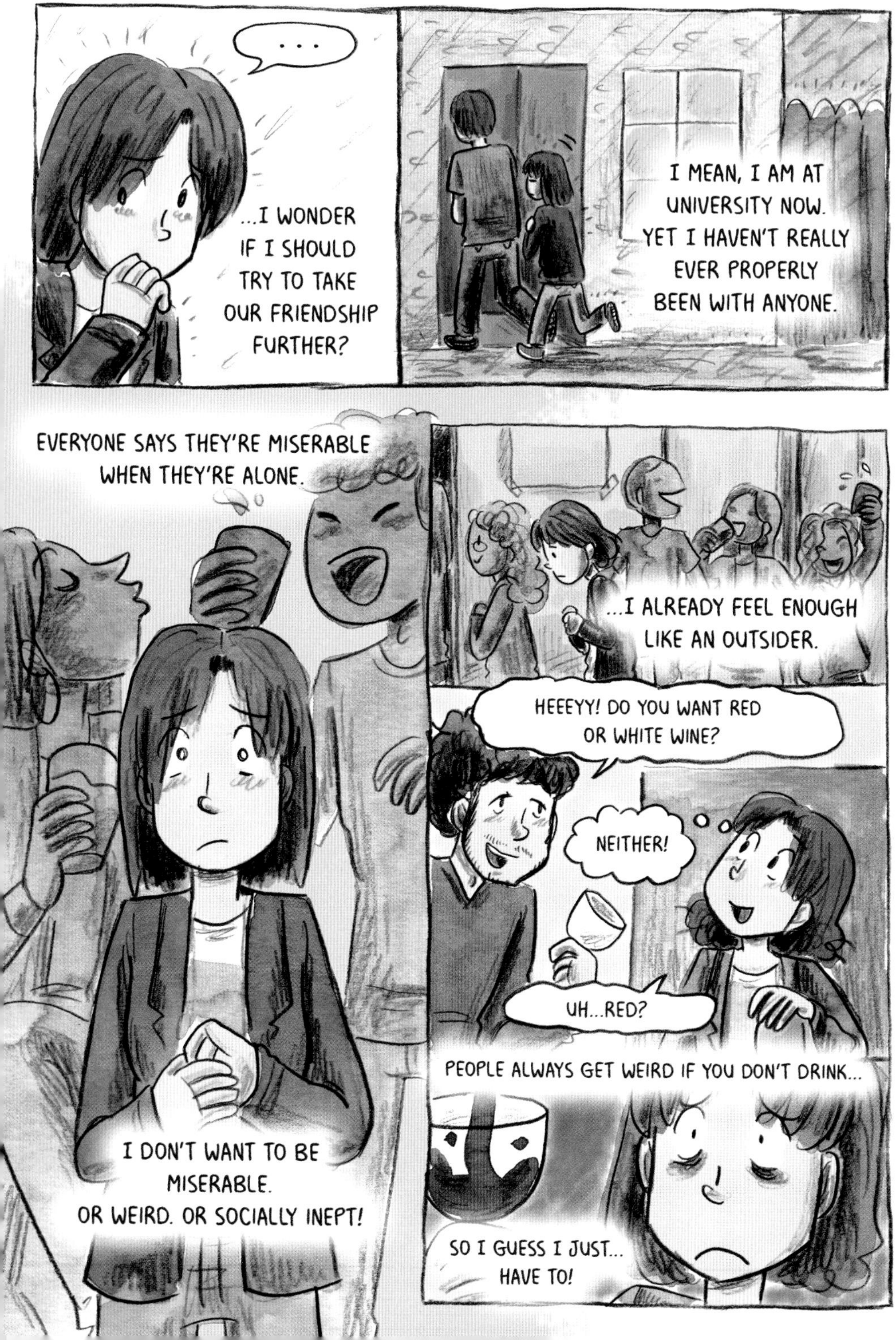
...
...I WONDER IF I SHOULD TRY TO TAKE OUR FRIENDSHIP FURTHER?
I MEAN, I AM AT UNIVERSITY NOW. YET I HAVEN'T REALLY EVER PROPERLY BEEN WITH ANYONE.
EVERYONE SAYS THEY'RE MISERABLE WHEN THEY'RE ALONE.
I DON'T WANT TO BE MISERABLE. OR WEIRD. OR SOCIALLY INEPT!
...I ALREADY FEEL ENOUGH LIKE AN OUTSIDER.
HEEEYY! DO YOU WANT RED OR WHITE WINE?
NEITHER!
UH...RED?
PEOPLE ALWAYS GET WEIRD IF YOU DON'T DRINK...
SO I GUESS I JUST... HAVE TO!

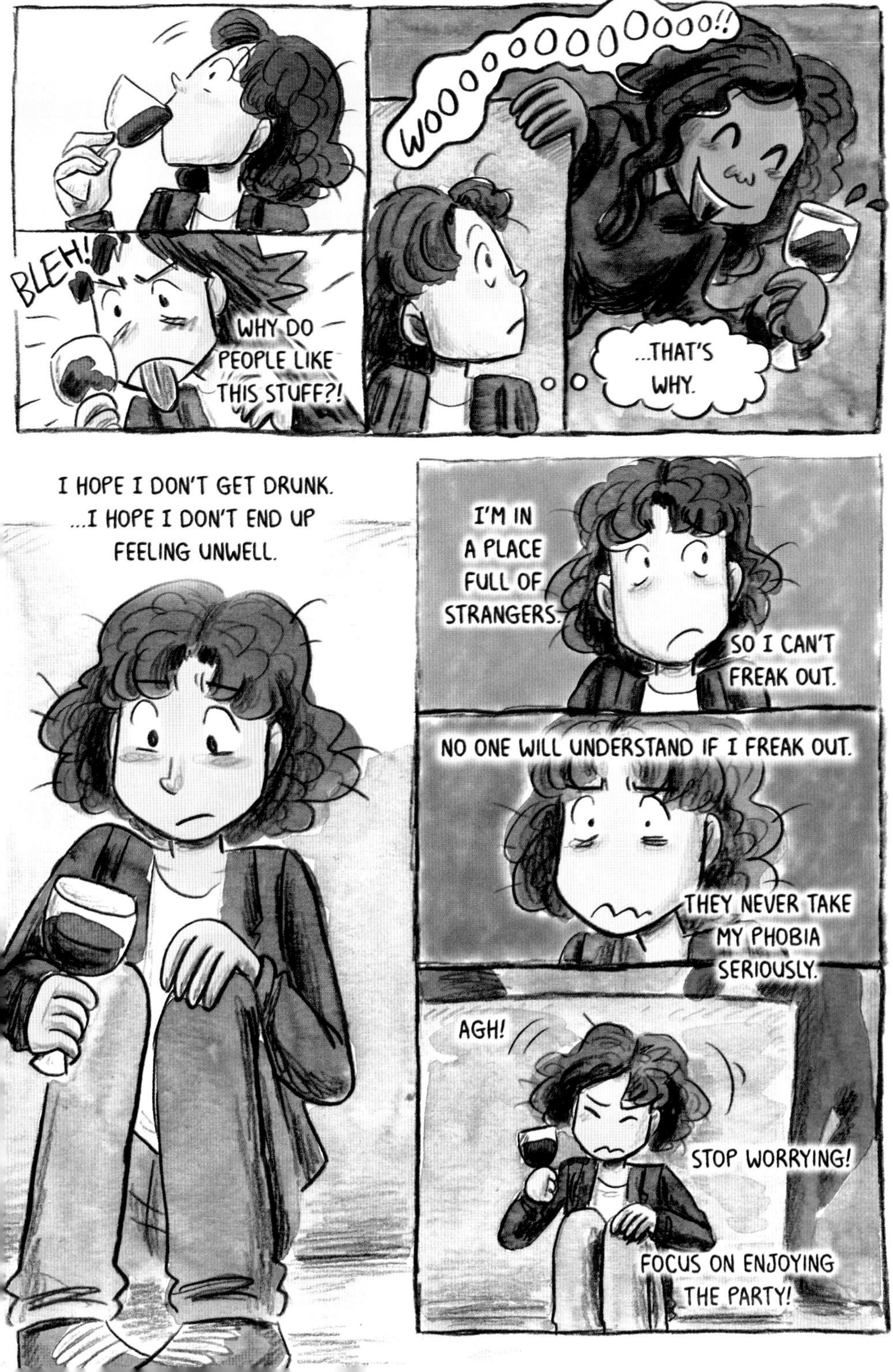
WOOOOOOOOOOOOOO!!
BLEH!
WHY DO PEOPLE LIKE THIS STUFF?!
...THAT'S WHY.
I HOPE I DON'T GET DRUNK.
...I HOPE I DON'T END UP FEELING UNWELL.
I'M IN A PLACE FULL OF STRANGERS.
SO I CAN'T FREAK OUT.
NO ONE WILL UNDERSTAND IF I FREAK OUT.
THEY NEVER TAKE MY PHOBIA SERIOUSLY.
AGH!
STOP WORRYING!
FOCUS ON ENJOYING THE PARTY!

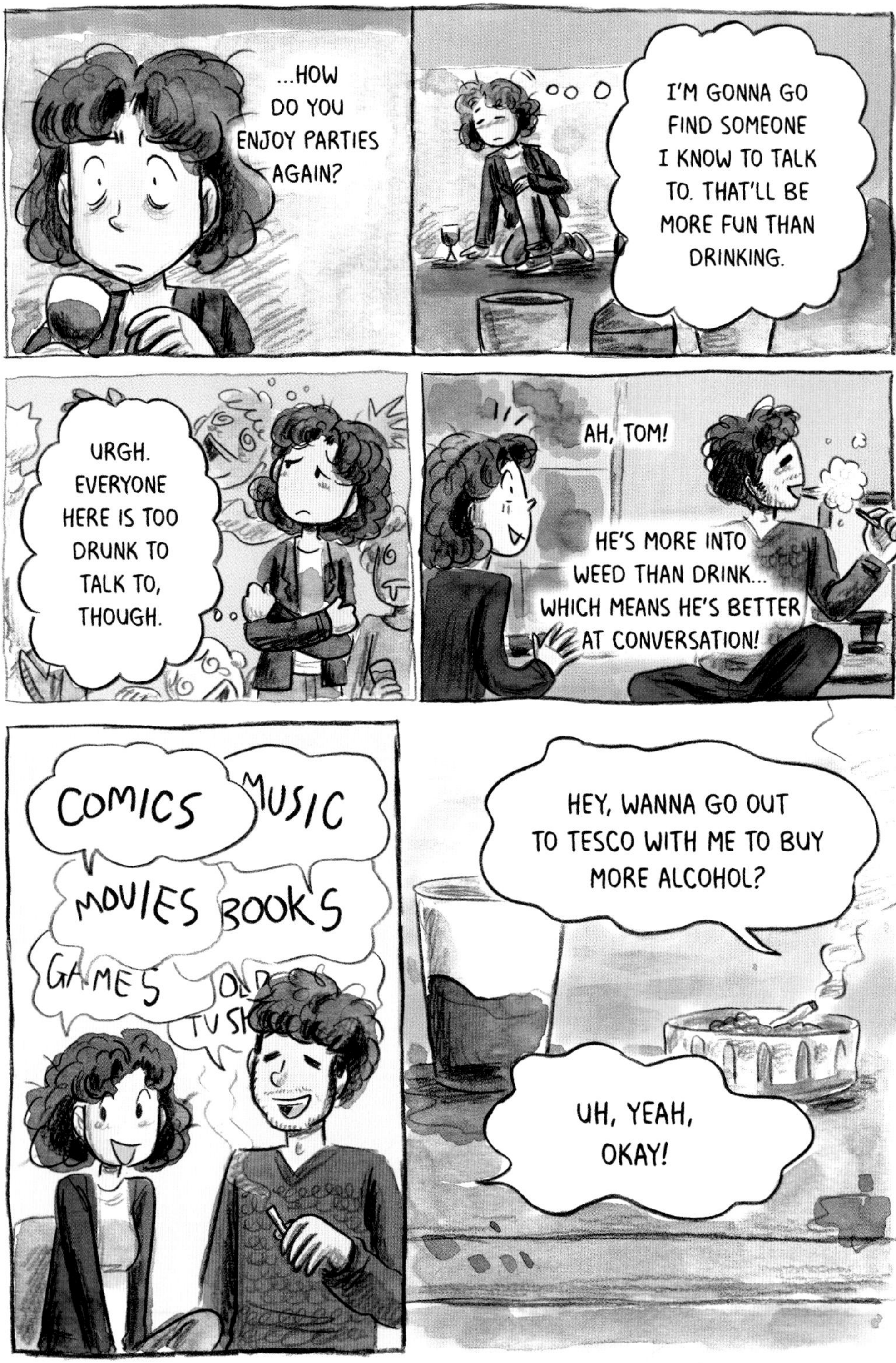
...HOW DO YOU ENJOY PARTIES AGAIN?
I'M GONNA GO FIND SOMEONE I KNOW TO TALK TO. THAT'LL BE MORE FUN THAN DRINKING.
URGH. EVERYONE HERE IS TOO DRUNK TO TALK TO, THOUGH.
AH, TOM!
HE'S MORE INTO WEED THAN DRINK... WHICH MEANS HE'S BETTER AT CONVERSATION!
COMICS
MUSIC
MOVIES
BOOKS
GAMES
HEY, WANNA GO OUT TO TESCO WITH ME TO BUY MORE ALCOHOL?
UH, YEAH, OKAY!

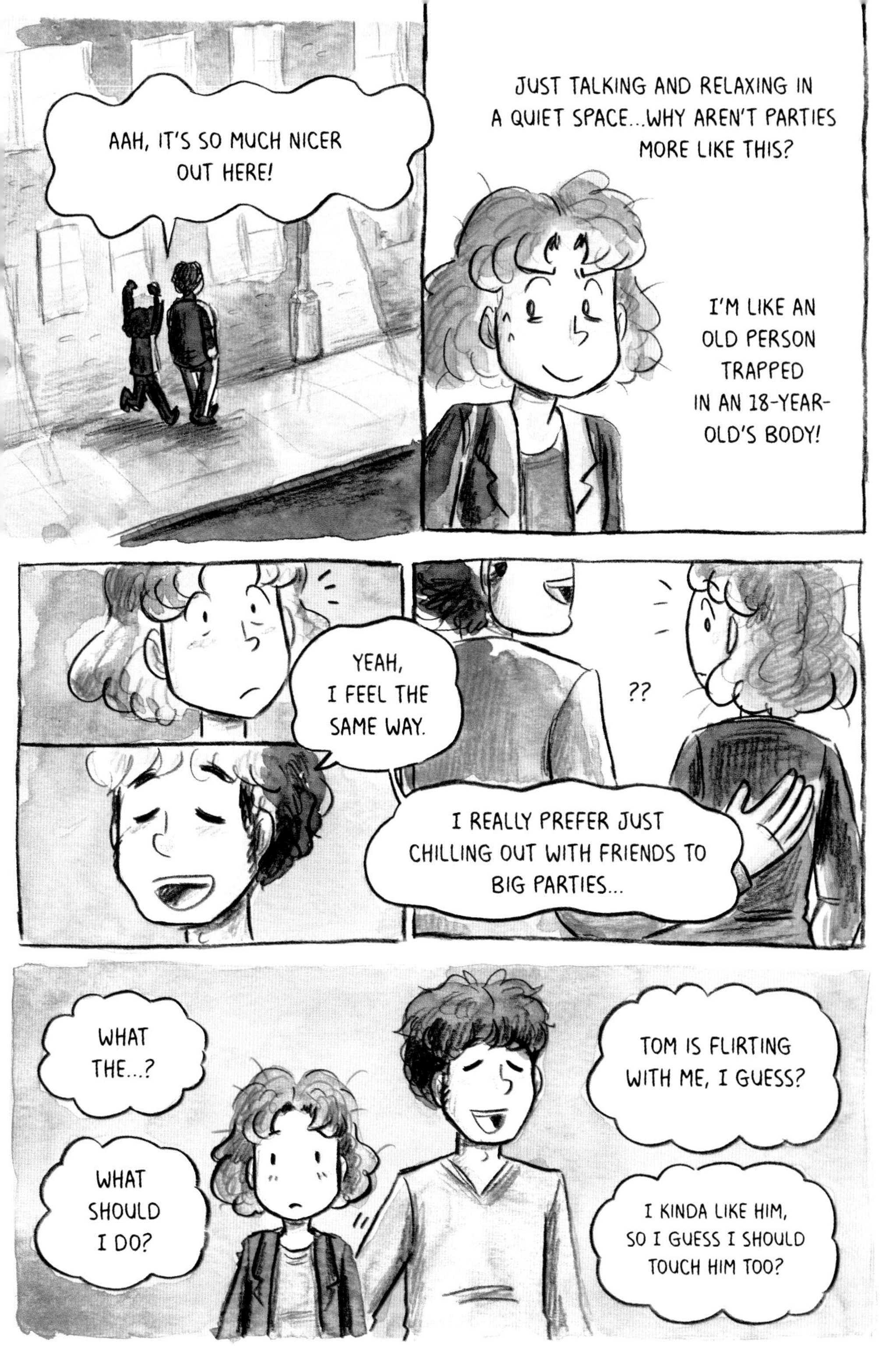

AAH, IT'S SO MUCH NICER OUT HERE!
JUST TALKING AND RELAXING IN A QUIET SPACE...WHY AREN'T PARTIES MORE LIKE THIS?
I'M LIKE AN OLD PERSON TRAPPED IN AN 18-YEAR-OLD'S BODY!
YEAH, I FEEL THE SAME WAY.
??
I REALLY PREFER JUST CHILLING OUT WITH FRIENDS TO BIG PARTIES...
WHAT THE...?
WHAT SHOULD I DO?
TOM IS FLIRTING WITH ME, I GUESS?
I KINDA LIKE HIM, SO I GUESS I SHOULD TOUCH HIM TOO?

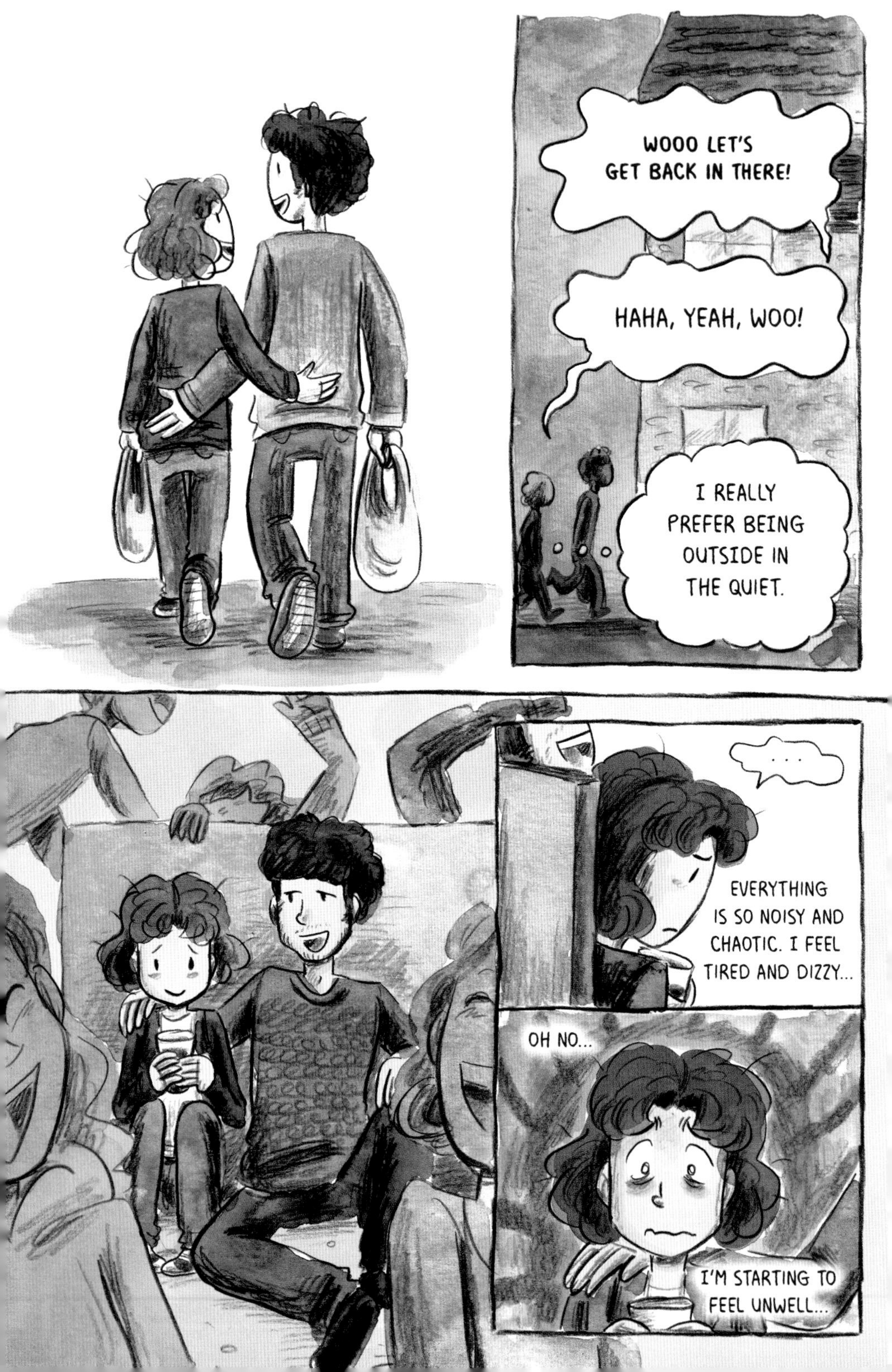
WOOO LET'S GET BACK IN THERE!
HAHA, YEAH, WOO!
I REALLY PREFER BEING OUTSIDE IN THE QUIET.
...
EVERYTHING IS SO NOISY AND CHAOTIC. I FEEL TIRED AND DIZZY...
OH NO...
I'M STARTING TO FEEL UNWELL...

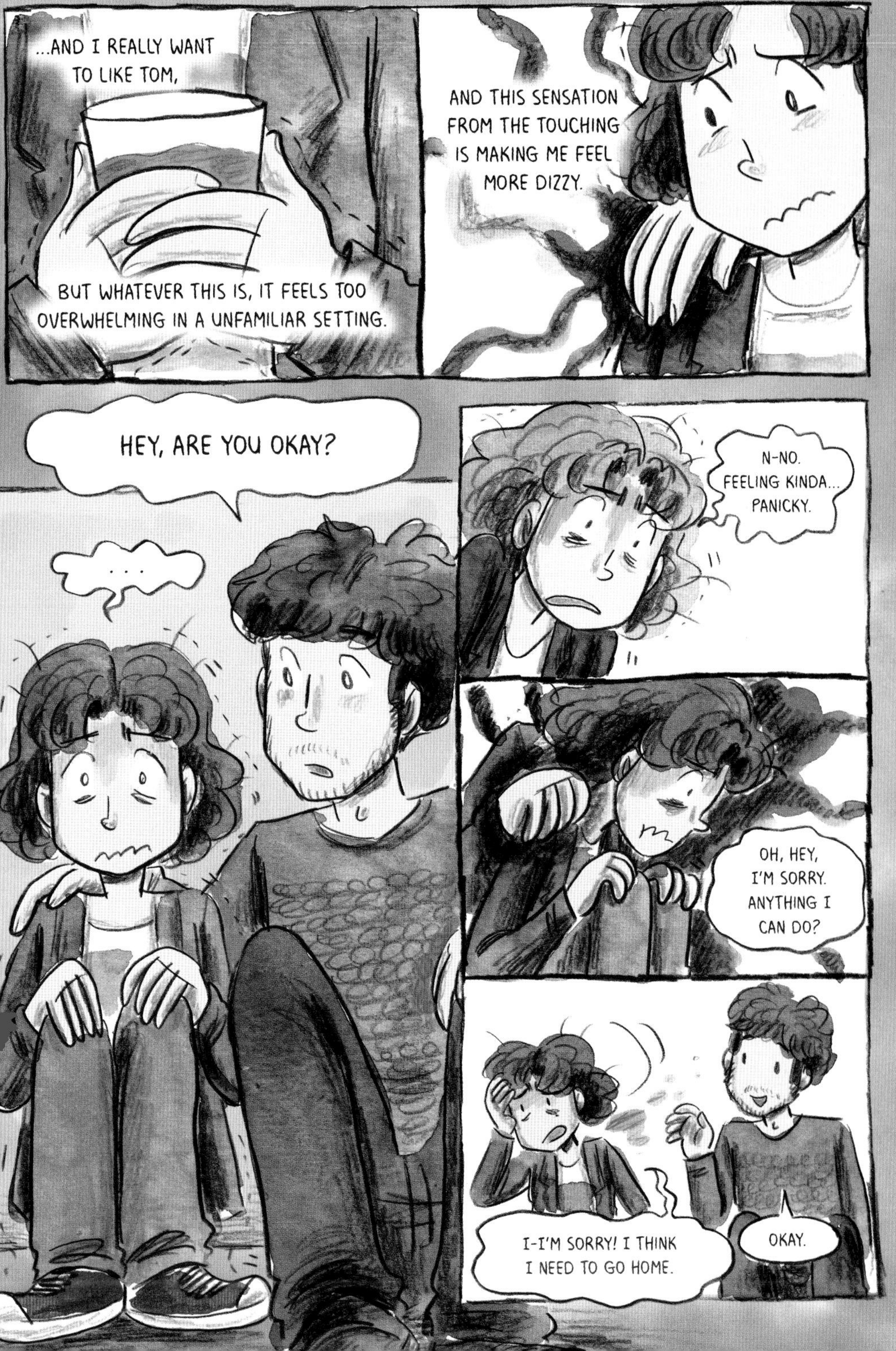
...AND I REALLY WANT TO LIKE TOM,
BUT WHATEVER THIS IS, IT FEELS TOO OVERWHELMING IN A UNFAMILIAR SETTING.
AND THIS SENSATION FROM THE TOUCHING IS MAKING ME FEEL MORE DIZZY.
HEY, ARE YOU OKAY?
...
N-NO. FEELING KINDA... PANICKY.
OH, HEY, I'M SORRY. ANYTHING I CAN DO?
I-I'M SORRY! I THINK I NEED TO GO HOME.
OKAY.

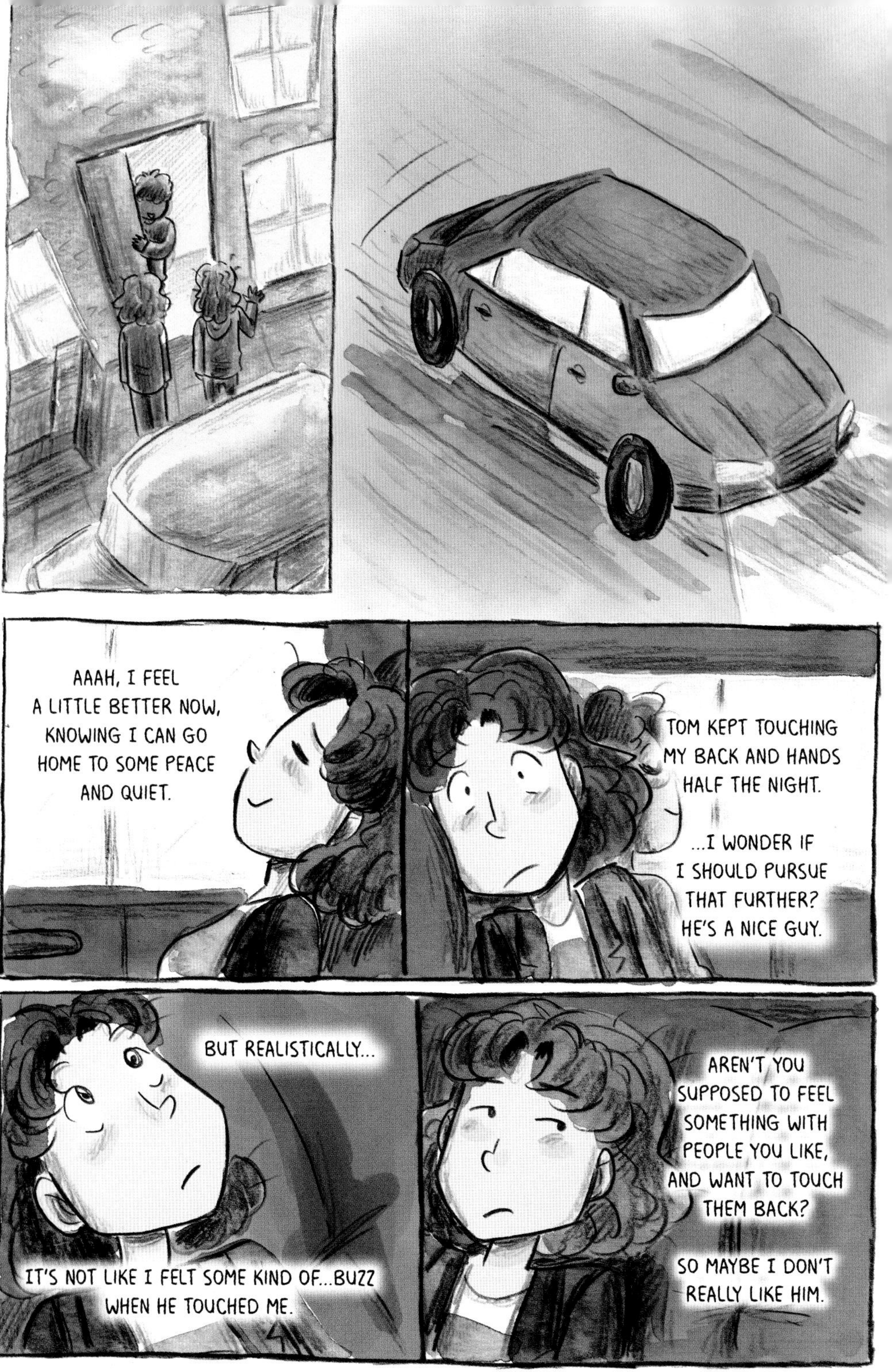
AAAH, I FEEL A LITTLE BETTER NOW, KNOWING I CAN GO HOME TO SOME PEACE AND QUIET.
TOM KEPT TOUCHING MY BACK AND HANDS HALF THE NIGHT.
...I WONDER IF I SHOULD PURSUE THAT FURTHER? HE'S A NICE GUY.
BUT REALISTICALLY...
IT'S NOT LIKE I FELT SOME KIND OF...BUZZ WHEN HE TOUCHED ME.
AREN'T YOU SUPPOSED TO FEEL SOMETHING WITH PEOPLE YOU LIKE, AND WANT TO TOUCH THEM BACK?
SO MAYBE I DON'T REALLY LIKE HIM.

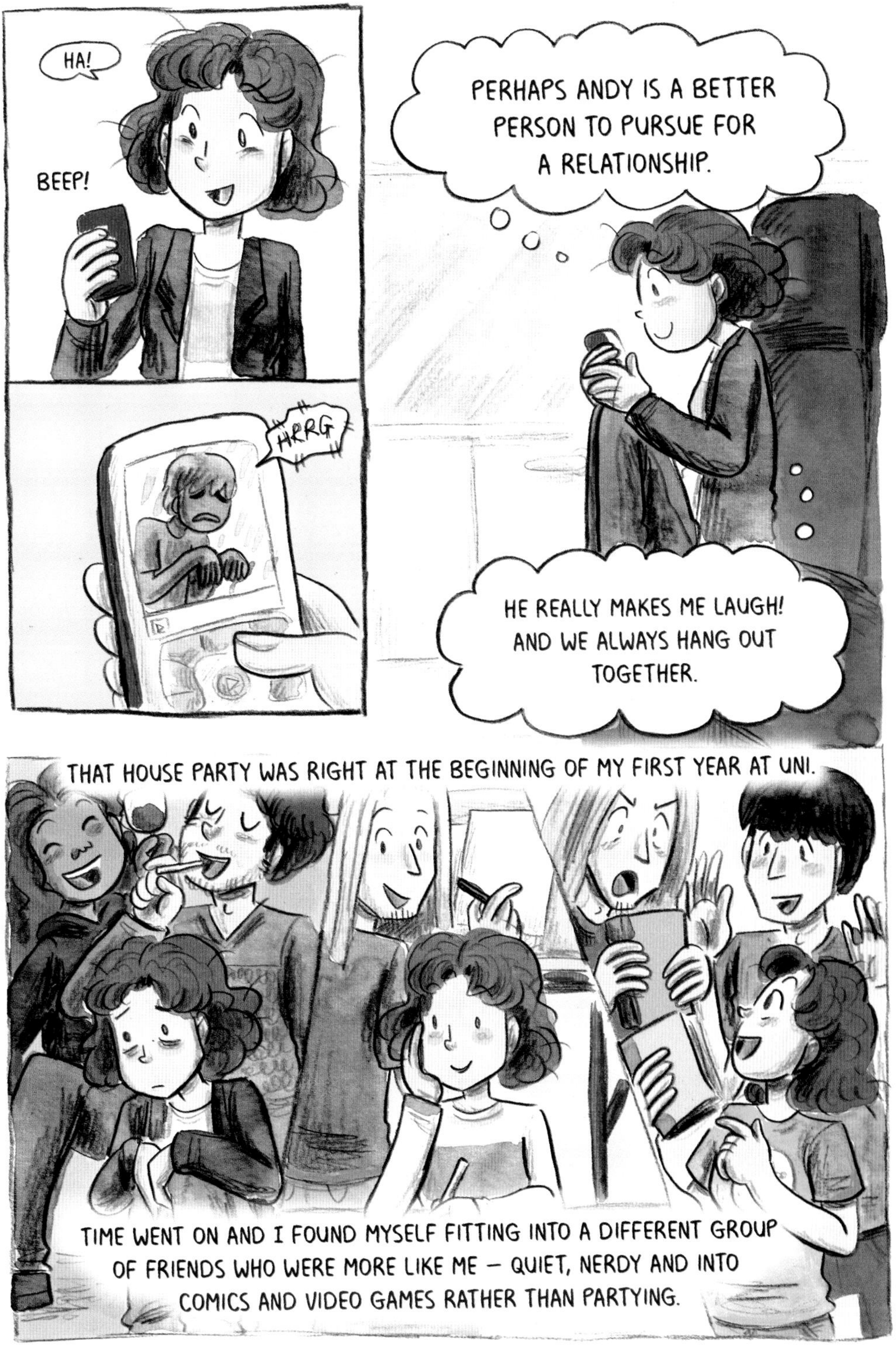
HA!
BEEP!
HRRG
PERHAPS ANDY IS A BETTER PERSON TO PURSUE FOR A RELATIONSHIP.
HE REALLY MAKES ME LAUGH! AND WE ALWAYS HANG OUT TOGETHER.
THAT HOUSE PARTY WAS RIGHT AT THE BEGINNING OF MY FIRST YEAR AT UNI.
TIME WENT ON AND I FOUND MYSELF FITTING INTO A DIFFERENT GROUP OF FRIENDS WHO WERE MORE LIKE ME – QUIET, NERDY AND INTO COMICS AND VIDEO GAMES RATHER THAN PARTYING.

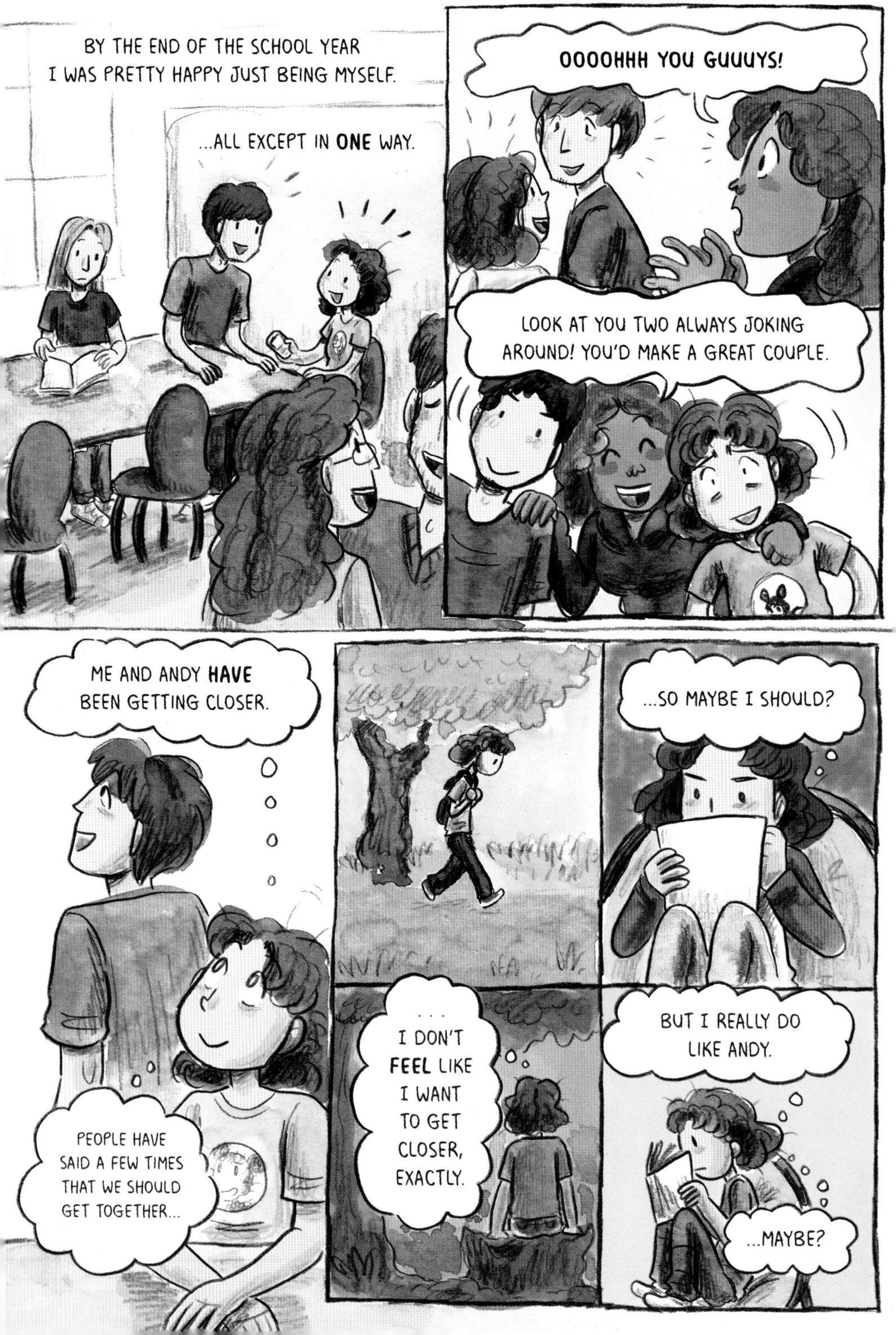
BY THE END OF THE SCHOOL YEAR I WAS PRETTY HAPPY JUST BEING MYSELF.
...ALL EXCEPT IN **ONE** WAY.
**OOOOHHH YOU GUUUYS!**
LOOK AT YOU TWO ALWAYS JOKING AROUND! YOU'D MAKE A GREAT COUPLE.
ME AND ANDY **HAVE** BEEN GETTING CLOSER.
PEOPLE HAVE SAID A FEW TIMES THAT WE SHOULD GET TOGETHER...
...SO MAYBE I SHOULD?
. . . I DON'T **FEEL** LIKE I WANT TO GET CLOSER, EXACTLY.
BUT I REALLY DO LIKE ANDY.
...MAYBE?

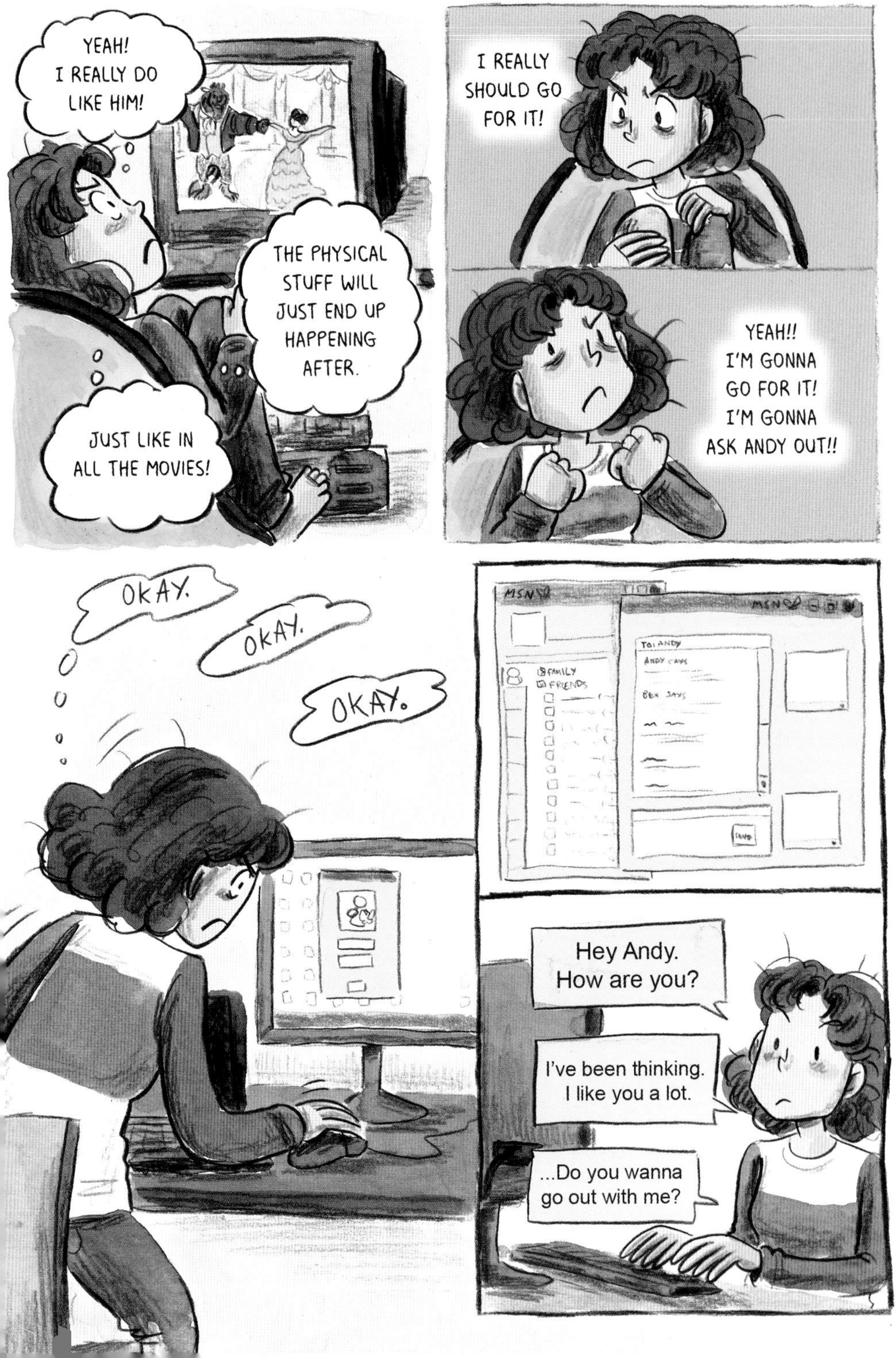
YEAH!
I REALLY DO
LIKE HIM!
THE PHYSICAL
STUFF WILL
JUST END UP
HAPPENING
AFTER.
JUST LIKE IN
ALL THE MOVIES!
I REALLY
SHOULD GO
FOR IT!
YEAH!!
I'M GONNA
GO FOR IT!
I'M GONNA
ASK ANDY OUT!!
OKAY.
OKAY.
OKAY.
MSN
MSN
FAMILY
FRIENDS
TO: ANDY
Hey Andy.
How are you?
I've been thinking.
I like you a lot.
...Do you wanna
go out with me?

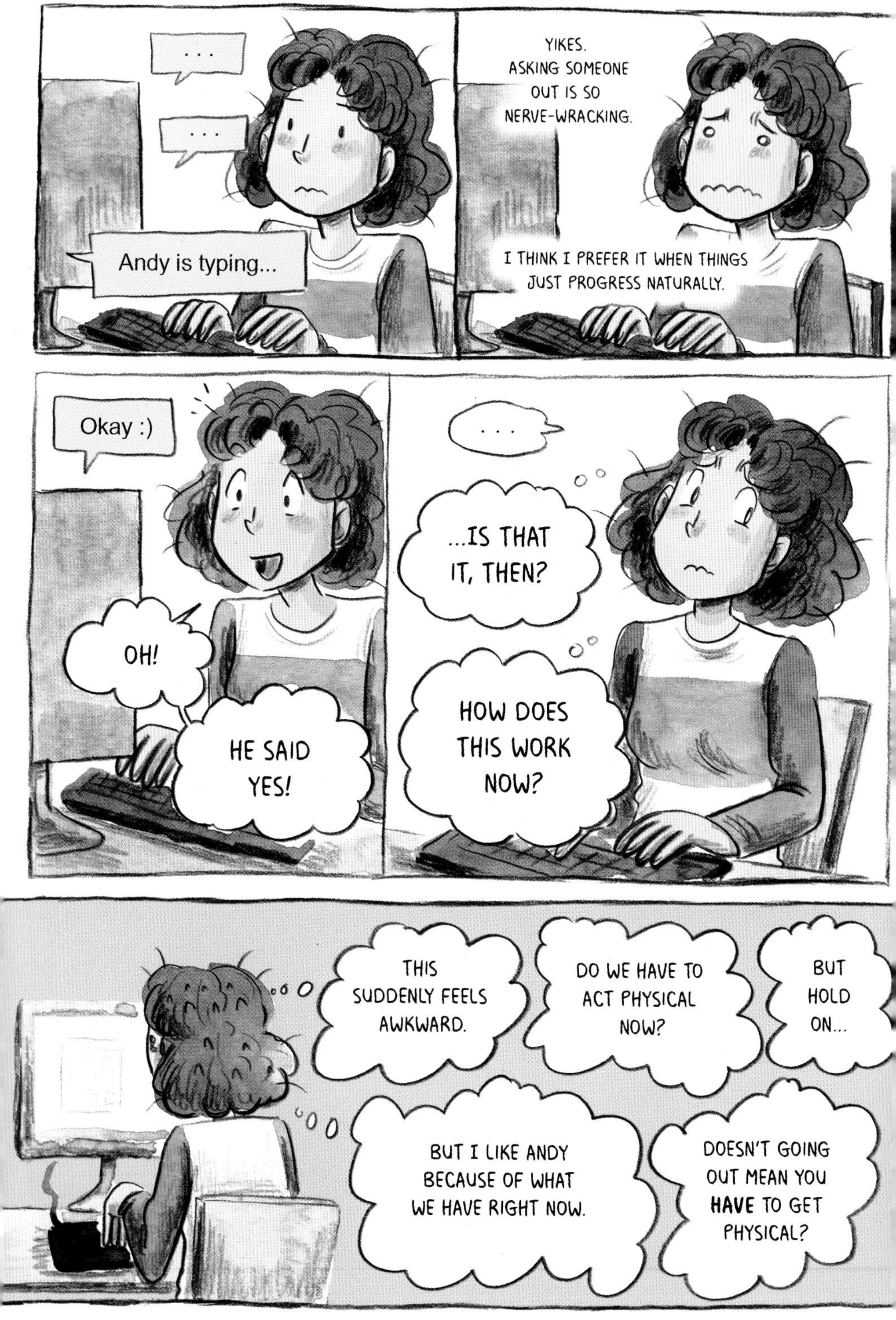
. . .
. . .
Andy is typing...
YIKES. ASKING SOMEONE OUT IS SO NERVE-WRACKING.
I THINK I PREFER IT WHEN THINGS JUST PROGRESS NATURALLY.
Okay :)
OH!
HE SAID YES!
. . .
...IS THAT IT, THEN?
HOW DOES THIS WORK NOW?
THIS SUDDENLY FEELS AWKWARD.
DO WE HAVE TO ACT PHYSICAL NOW?
BUT HOLD ON...
BUT I LIKE ANDY BECAUSE OF WHAT WE HAVE RIGHT NOW.
DOESN'T GOING OUT MEAN YOU **HAVE** TO GET PHYSICAL?

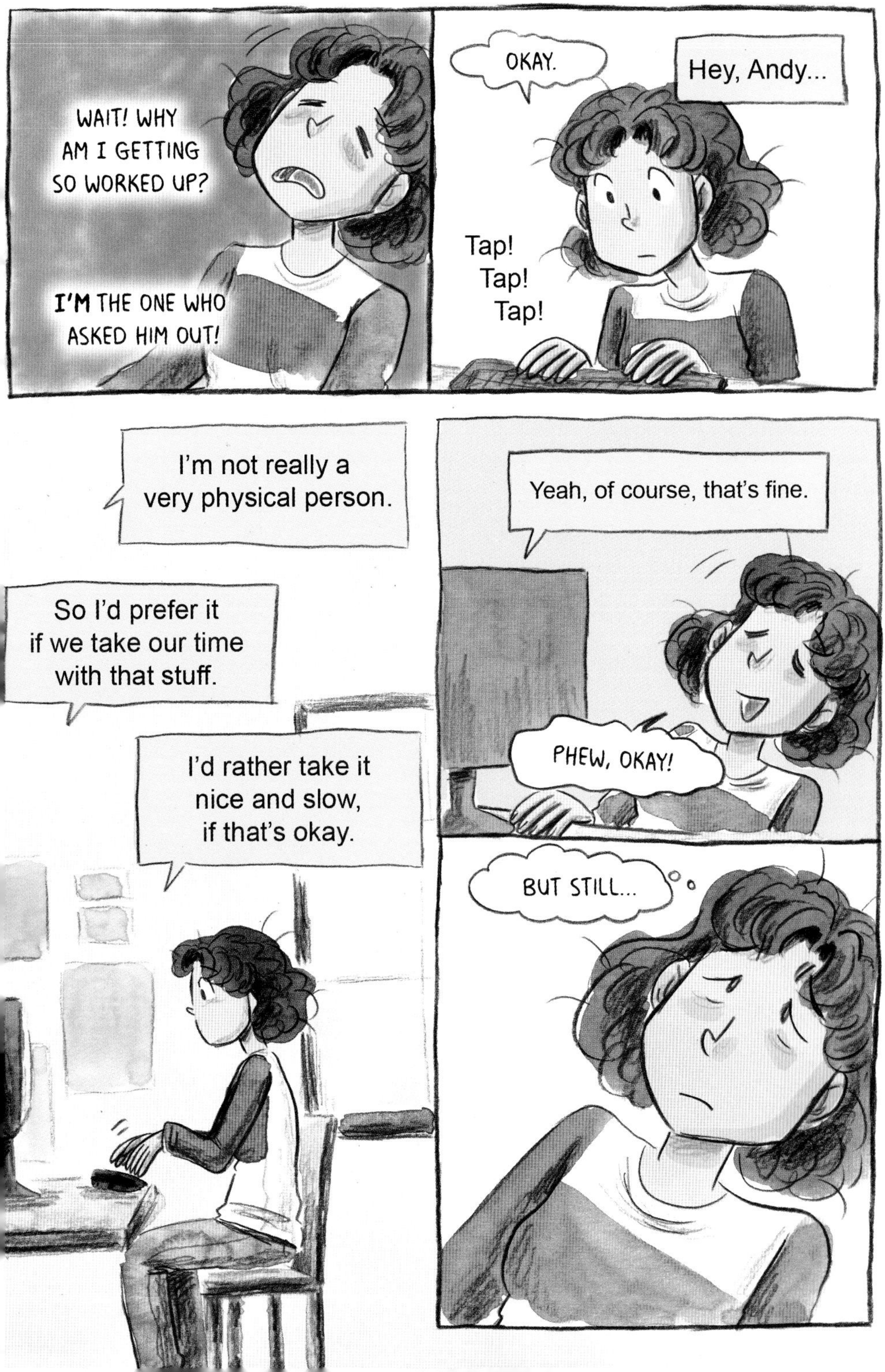

WAIT! WHY AM I GETTING SO WORKED UP?
I'M THE ONE WHO ASKED HIM OUT!
OKAY.
Hey, Andy...
Tap! Tap! Tap!
I'm not really a very physical person.
So I'd prefer it if we take our time with that stuff.
I'd rather take it nice and slow, if that's okay.
Yeah, of course, that's fine.
PHEW, OKAY!
BUT STILL...

EVEN THOUGH I WAS THE ONE WHO HAD SAID 'CAN WE TAKE OUR TIME?' IT DIDN'T MATTER THAT I HAD DECIDED THAT. IT DIDN'T MATTER THAT ANDY HAD SAID IT WAS FINE.

ALL THOSE MOVIES...

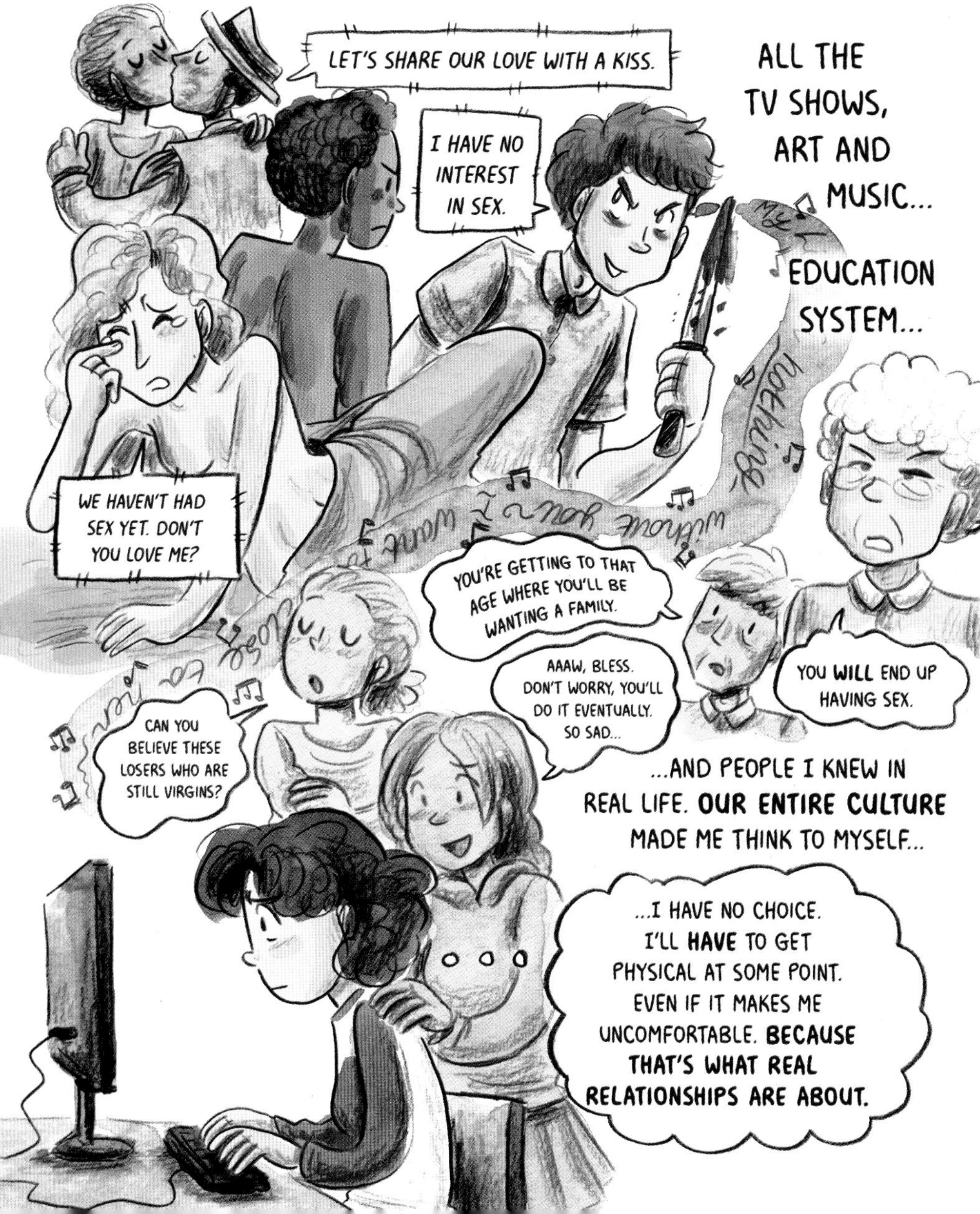
LET'S SHARE OUR LOVE WITH A KISS.
I HAVE NO INTEREST IN SEX.
ALL THE TV SHOWS, ART AND MUSIC...
EDUCATION SYSTEM...
WE HAVEN'T HAD SEX YET. DON'T YOU LOVE ME?
YOU'RE GETTING TO THAT AGE WHERE YOU'LL BE WANTING A FAMILY.
AAAW, BLESS. DON'T WORRY, YOU'LL DO IT EVENTUALLY. SO SAD...
YOU **WILL** END UP HAVING SEX.
CAN YOU BELIEVE THESE LOSERS WHO ARE STILL VIRGINS?
...AND PEOPLE I KNEW IN REAL LIFE. **OUR ENTIRE CULTURE** MADE ME THINK TO MYSELF...
...I HAVE NO CHOICE. I'LL **HAVE** TO GET PHYSICAL AT SOME POINT. EVEN IF IT MAKES ME UNCOMFORTABLE. **BECAUSE THAT'S WHAT REAL RELATIONSHIPS ARE ABOUT.**

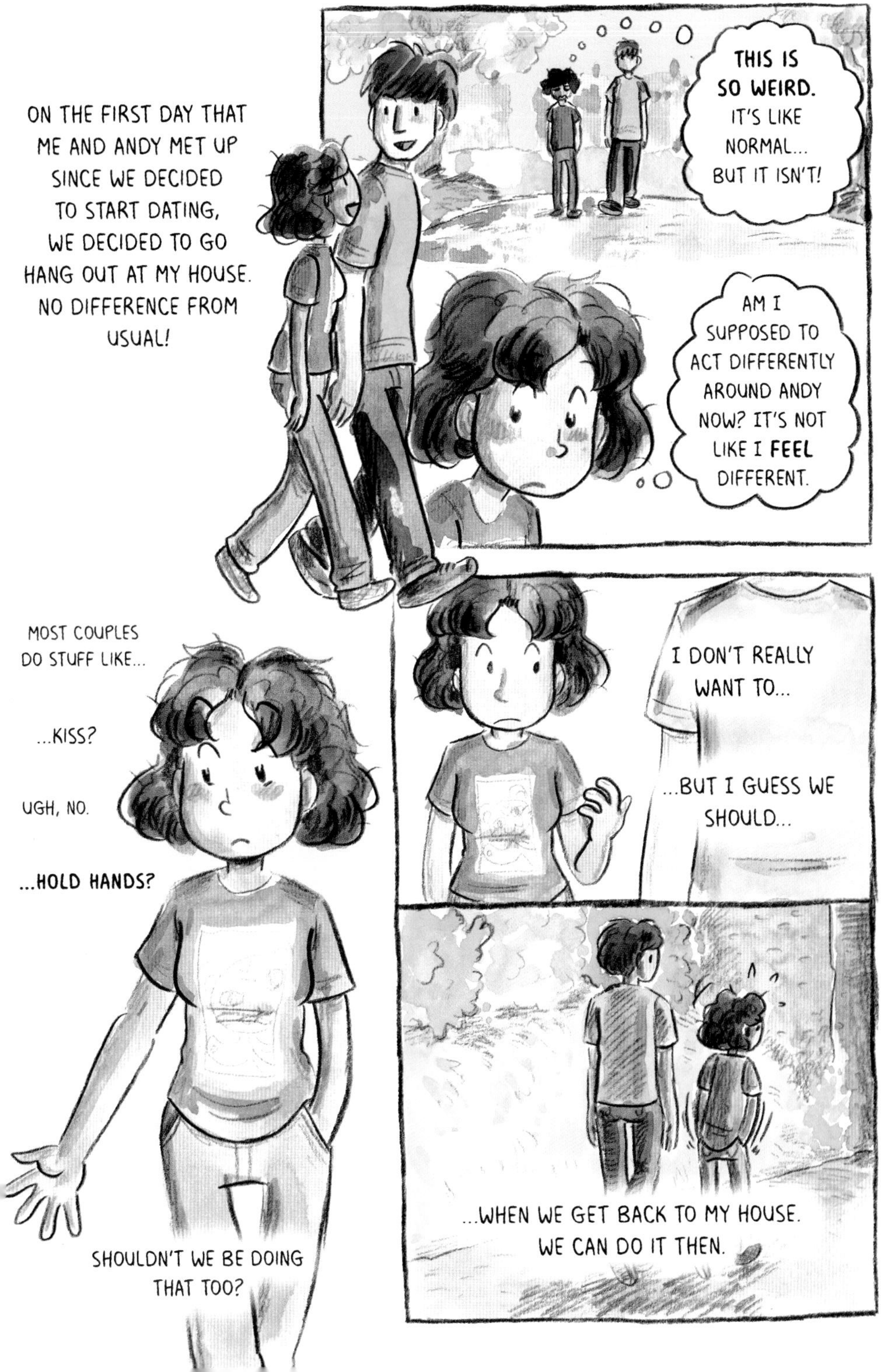
ON THE FIRST DAY THAT ME AND ANDY MET UP SINCE WE DECIDED TO START DATING, WE DECIDED TO GO HANG OUT AT MY HOUSE. NO DIFFERENCE FROM USUAL!
THIS IS SO WEIRD. IT'S LIKE NORMAL... BUT IT ISN'T!
AM I SUPPOSED TO ACT DIFFERENTLY AROUND ANDY NOW? IT'S NOT LIKE I FEEL DIFFERENT.
MOST COUPLES DO STUFF LIKE...
...KISS?
UGH, NO.
...HOLD HANDS?
SHOULDN'T WE BE DOING THAT TOO?
I DON'T REALLY WANT TO...
...BUT I GUESS WE SHOULD...
...WHEN WE GET BACK TO MY HOUSE. WE CAN DO IT THEN.

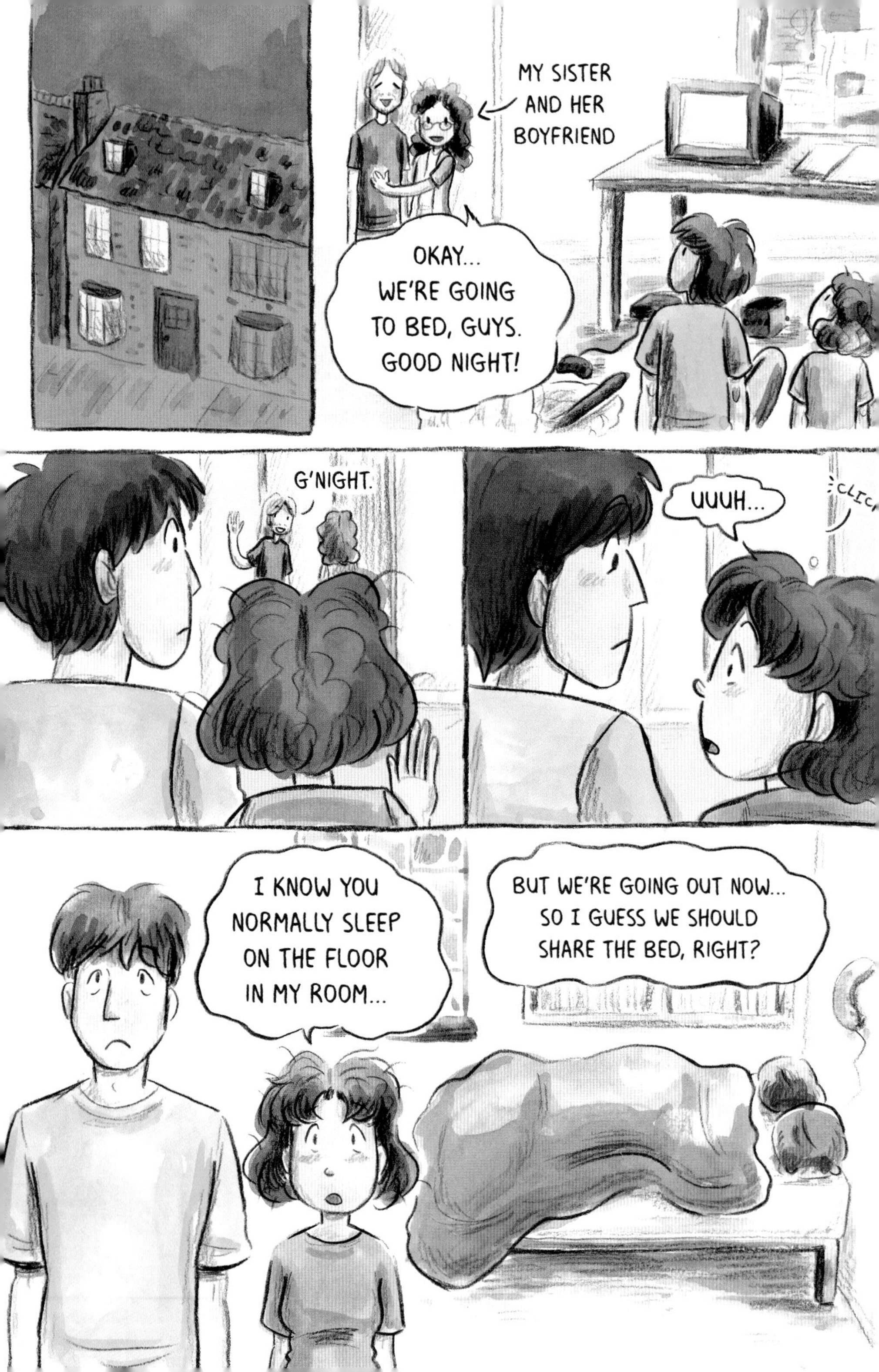
MY SISTER AND HER BOYFRIEND
OKAY... WE'RE GOING TO BED, GUYS. GOOD NIGHT!
G'NIGHT.
UUUH...
I KNOW YOU NORMALLY SLEEP ON THE FLOOR IN MY ROOM...
BUT WE'RE GOING OUT NOW... SO I GUESS WE SHOULD SHARE THE BED, RIGHT?

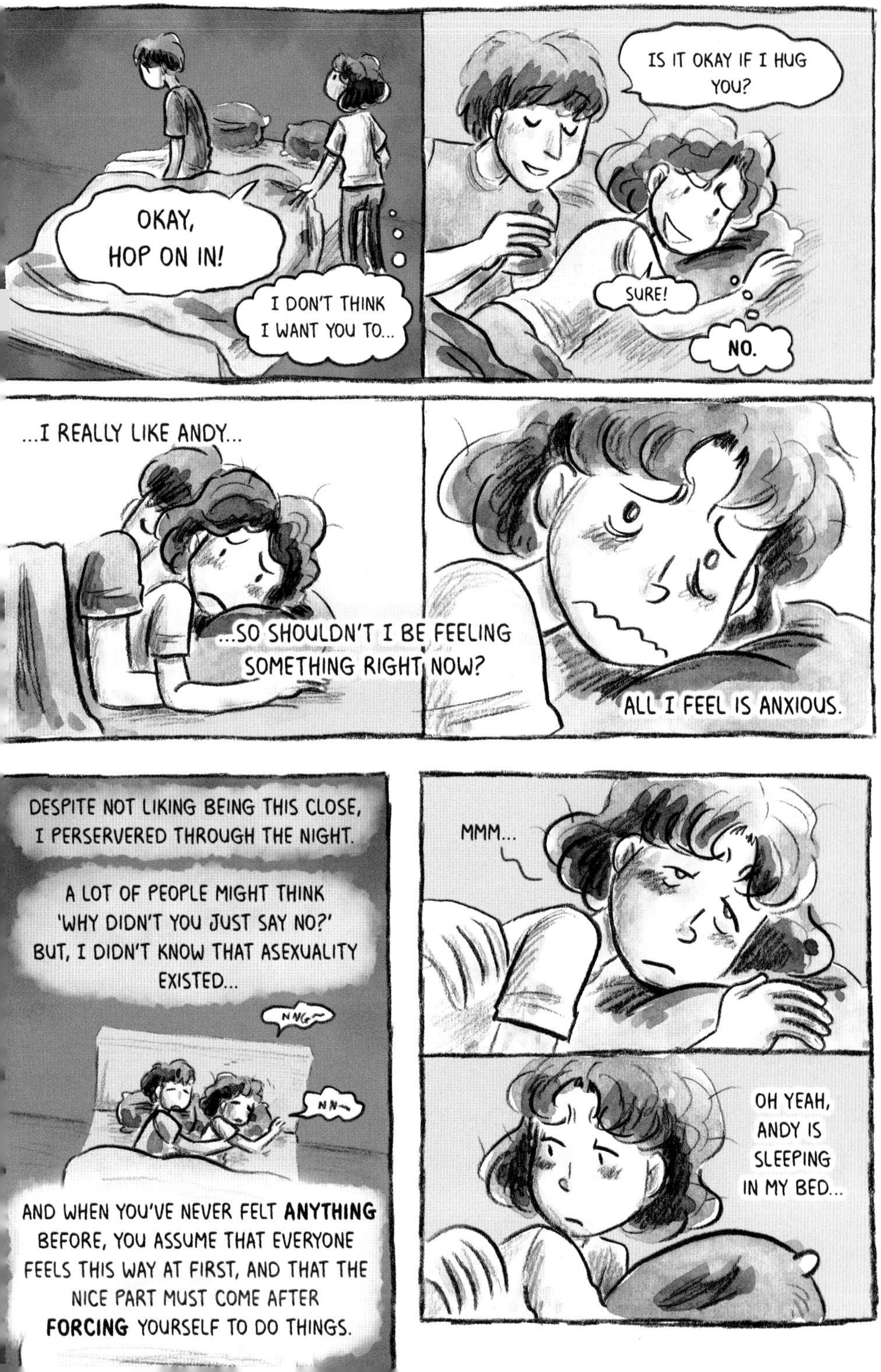
OKAY, HOP ON IN!
I DON'T THINK I WANT YOU TO...
IS IT OKAY IF I HUG YOU?
SURE!
NO.
...I REALLY LIKE ANDY...
...SO SHOULDN'T I BE FEELING SOMETHING RIGHT NOW?
ALL I FEEL IS ANXIOUS.
DESPITE NOT LIKING BEING THIS CLOSE, I PERSERVERED THROUGH THE NIGHT.
A LOT OF PEOPLE MIGHT THINK 'WHY DIDN'T YOU JUST SAY NO?' BUT, I DIDN'T KNOW THAT ASEXUALITY EXISTED...
NNG~
NN~
AND WHEN YOU'VE NEVER FELT **ANYTHING** BEFORE, YOU ASSUME THAT EVERYONE FEELS THIS WAY AT FIRST, AND THAT THE NICE PART MUST COME AFTER **FORCING** YOURSELF TO DO THINGS.
MMM...
OH YEAH, ANDY IS SLEEPING IN MY BED...

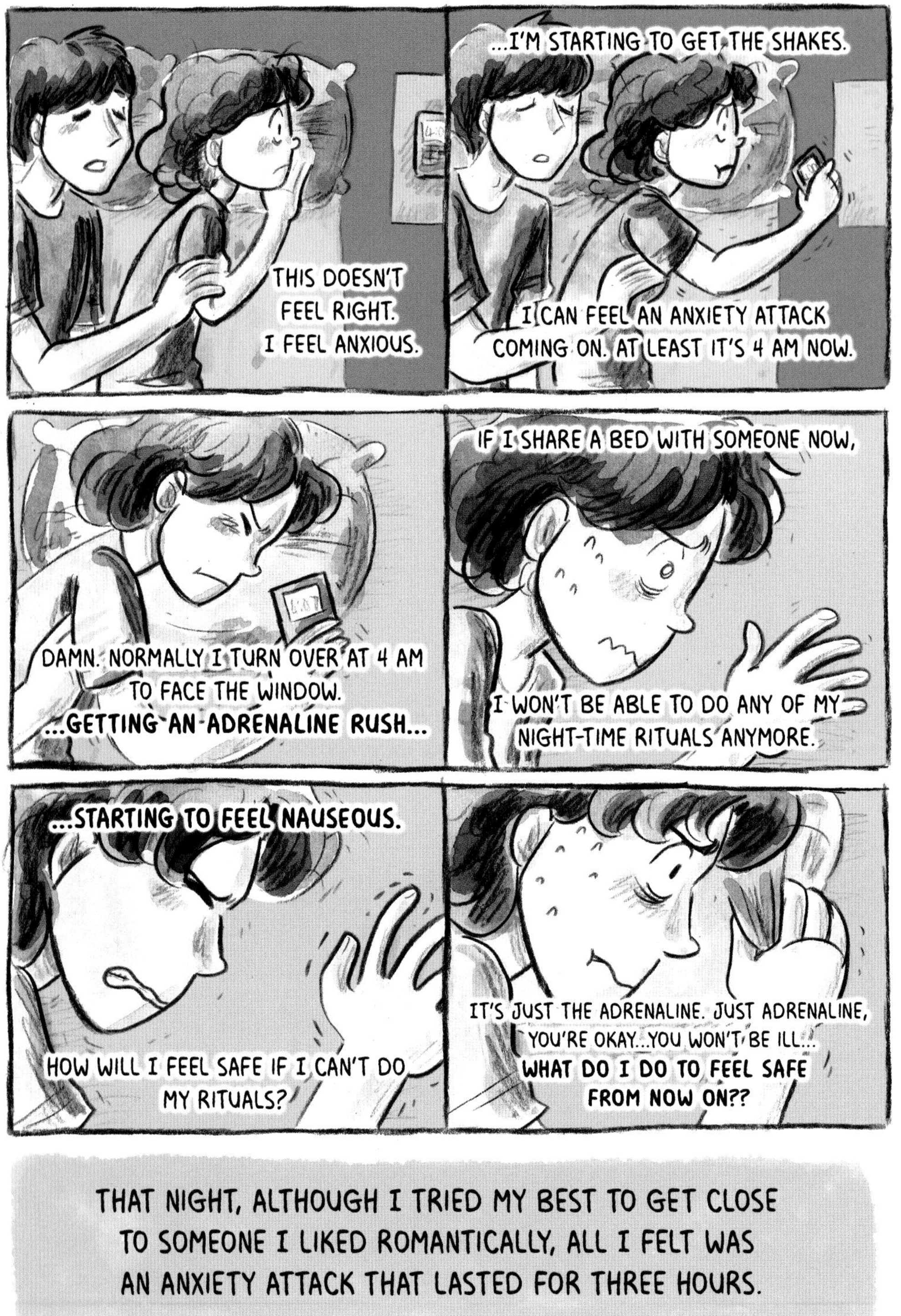
THIS DOESN'T FEEL RIGHT. I FEEL ANXIOUS.
...I'M STARTING TO GET THE SHAKES.
I CAN FEEL AN ANXIETY ATTACK COMING ON. AT LEAST IT'S 4 AM NOW.
DAMN. NORMALLY I TURN OVER AT 4 AM TO FACE THE WINDOW.
...GETTING AN ADRENALINE RUSH...
IF I SHARE A BED WITH SOMEONE NOW,
I WON'T BE ABLE TO DO ANY OF MY NIGHT-TIME RITUALS ANYMORE.
...STARTING TO FEEL NAUSEOUS.
HOW WILL I FEEL SAFE IF I CAN'T DO MY RITUALS?
IT'S JUST THE ADRENALINE. JUST ADRENALINE, YOU'RE OKAY...YOU WON'T BE ILL...
WHAT DO I DO TO FEEL SAFE FROM NOW ON??

THAT NIGHT, ALTHOUGH I TRIED MY BEST TO GET CLOSE TO SOMEONE I LIKED ROMANTICALLY, ALL I FELT WAS AN ANXIETY ATTACK THAT LASTED FOR THREE HOURS.

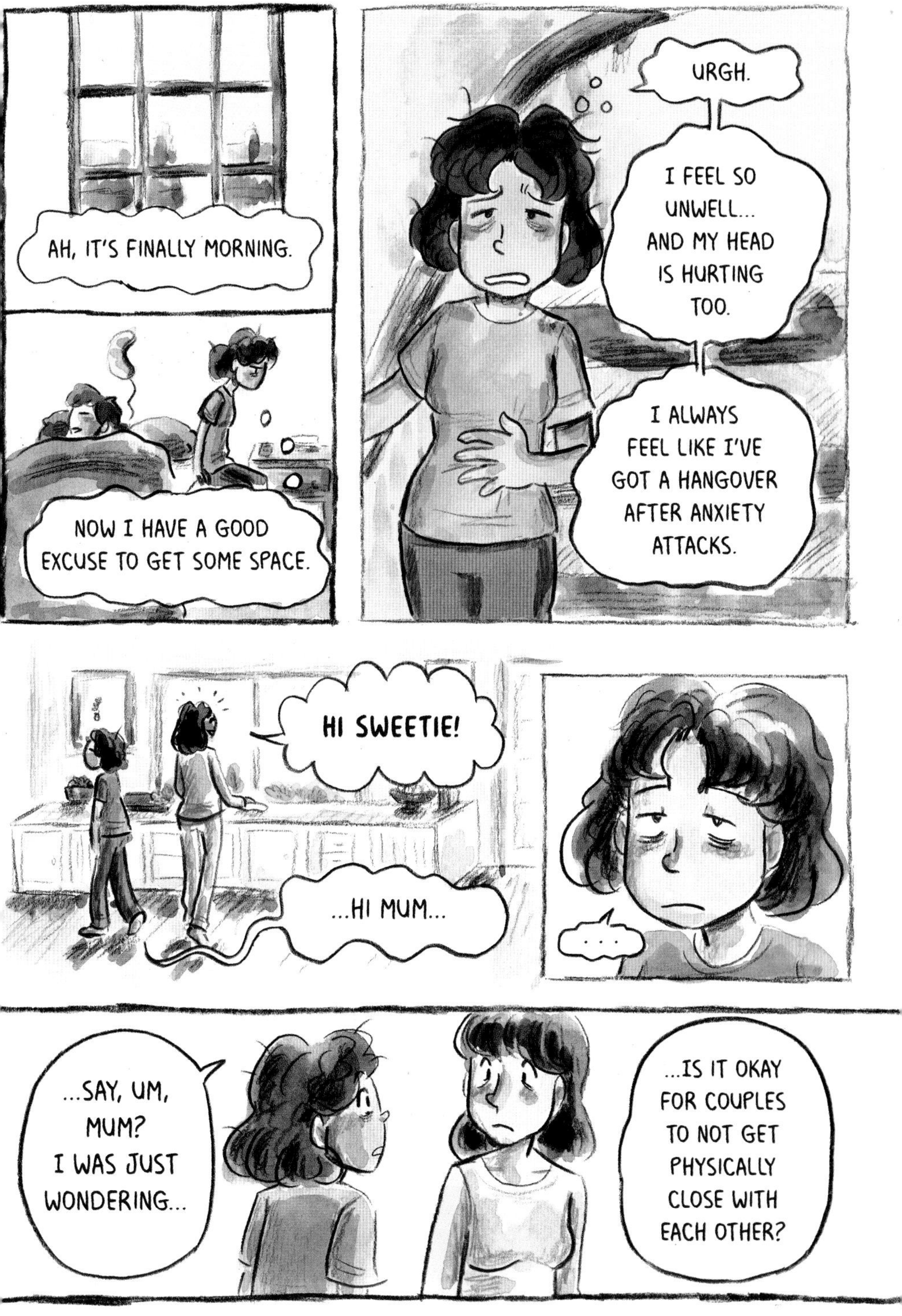
AH, IT'S FINALLY MORNING.
NOW I HAVE A GOOD EXCUSE TO GET SOME SPACE.
URGH.
I FEEL SO UNWELL... AND MY HEAD IS HURTING TOO.
I ALWAYS FEEL LIKE I'VE GOT A HANGOVER AFTER ANXIETY ATTACKS.
HI SWEETIE!
...HI MUM...
...
...SAY, UM, MUM? I WAS JUST WONDERING...
...IS IT OKAY FOR COUPLES TO NOT GET PHYSICALLY CLOSE WITH EACH OTHER?

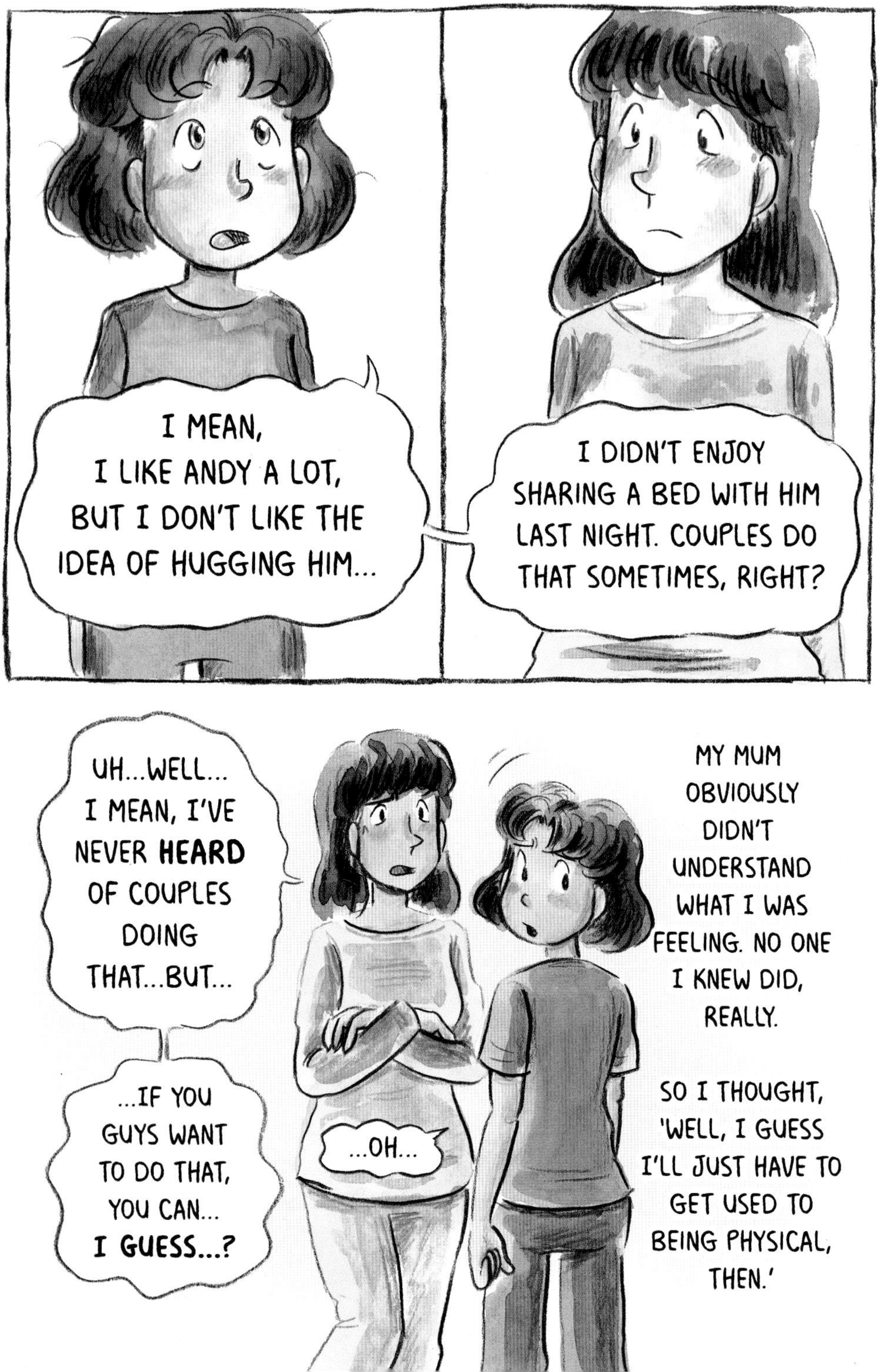
I MEAN, I LIKE ANDY A LOT, BUT I DON'T LIKE THE IDEA OF HUGGING HIM...
I DIDN'T ENJOY SHARING A BED WITH HIM LAST NIGHT. COUPLES DO THAT SOMETIMES, RIGHT?
UH...WELL... I MEAN, I'VE NEVER **HEARD** OF COUPLES DOING THAT...BUT...
...IF YOU GUYS WANT TO DO THAT, YOU CAN... **I GUESS...?**
...OH...
MY MUM OBVIOUSLY DIDN'T UNDERSTAND WHAT I WAS FEELING. NO ONE I KNEW DID, REALLY.
SO I THOUGHT, 'WELL, I GUESS I'LL JUST HAVE TO GET USED TO BEING PHYSICAL, THEN.'

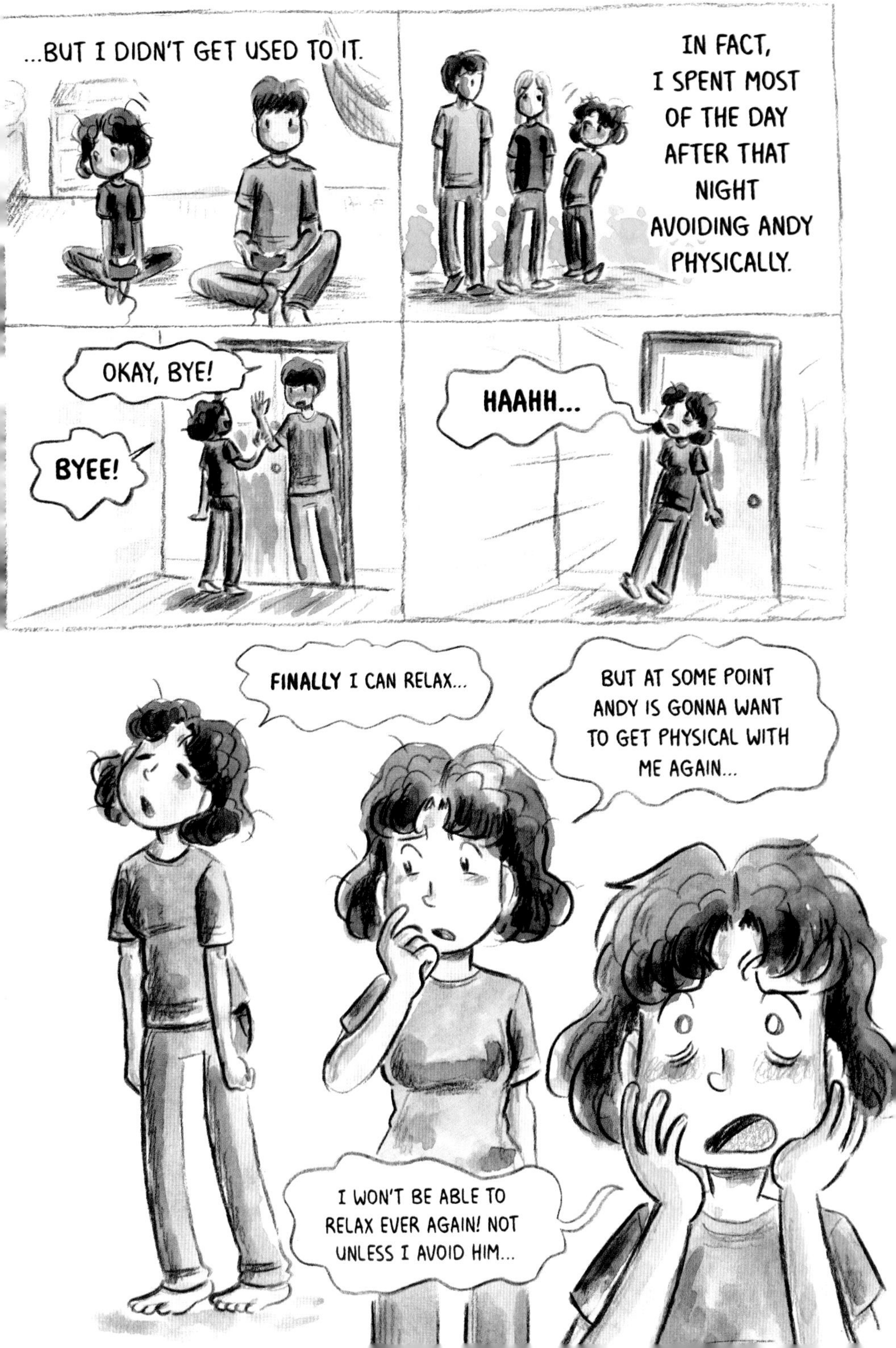

...BUT I DIDN'T GET USED TO IT.
IN FACT, I SPENT MOST OF THE DAY AFTER THAT NIGHT AVOIDING ANDY PHYSICALLY.
OKAY, BYE!
BYEE!
HAAHH...
FINALLY I CAN RELAX...
BUT AT SOME POINT ANDY IS GONNA WANT TO GET PHYSICAL WITH ME AGAIN...
I WON'T BE ABLE TO RELAX EVER AGAIN! NOT UNLESS I AVOID HIM...

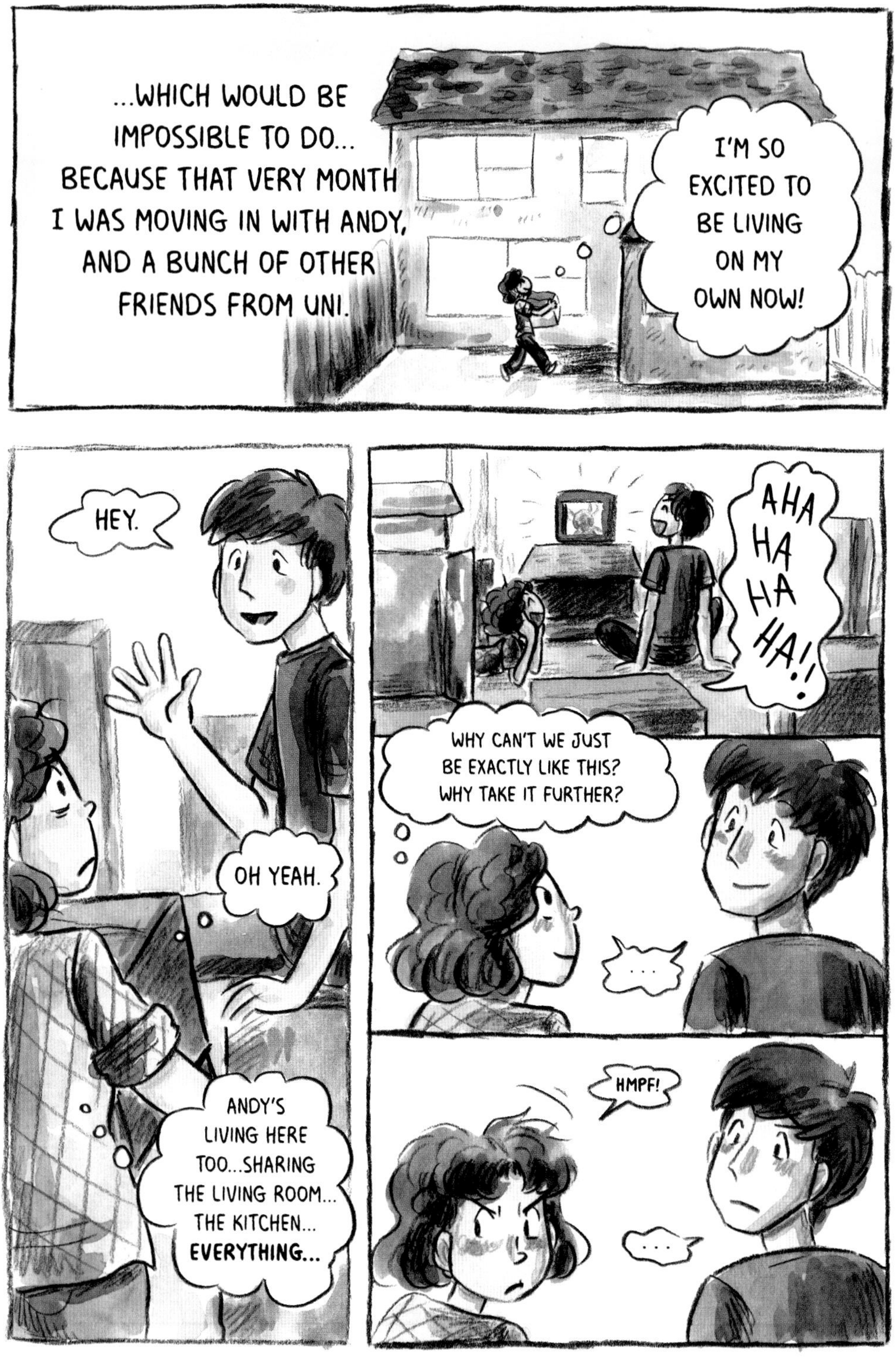
...WHICH WOULD BE IMPOSSIBLE TO DO... BECAUSE THAT VERY MONTH I WAS MOVING IN WITH ANDY, AND A BUNCH OF OTHER FRIENDS FROM UNI.
I'M SO EXCITED TO BE LIVING ON MY OWN NOW!
HEY.
OH YEAH.
ANDY'S LIVING HERE TOO...SHARING THE LIVING ROOM... THE KITCHEN... **EVERYTHING...**
AHA HA HA HA!!
WHY CAN'T WE JUST BE EXACTLY LIKE THIS? WHY TAKE IT FURTHER?
...
HMPF!
...

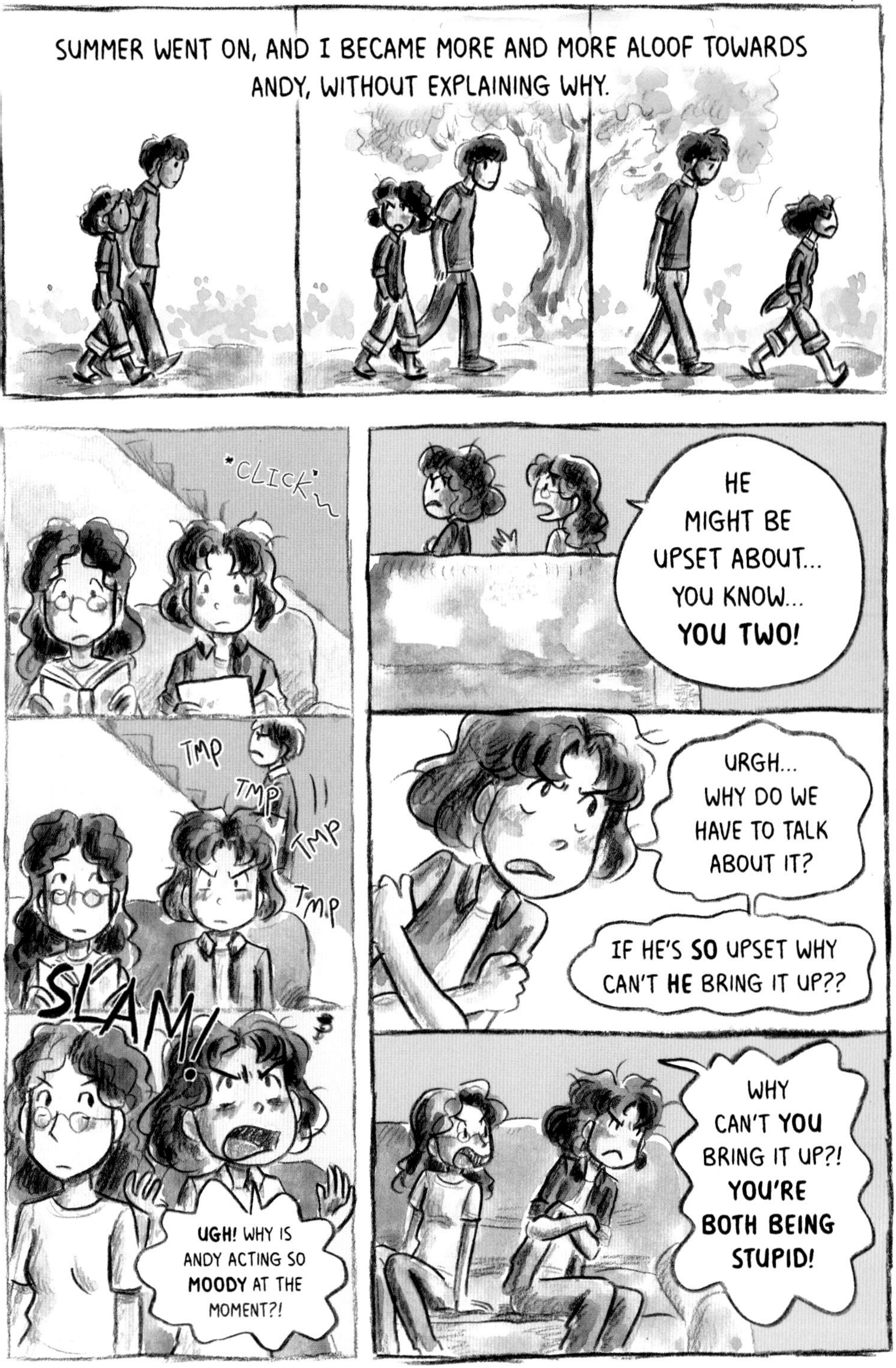
SUMMER WENT ON, AND I BECAME MORE AND MORE ALOOF TOWARDS ANDY, WITHOUT EXPLAINING WHY.
*CLICK*
TMP
TMP
TMP
TMP
SLAM!
UGH! WHY IS ANDY ACTING SO MOODY AT THE MOMENT?!
HE MIGHT BE UPSET ABOUT... YOU KNOW... YOU TWO!
URGH... WHY DO WE HAVE TO TALK ABOUT IT?
IF HE'S SO UPSET WHY CAN'T HE BRING IT UP??
WHY CAN'T YOU BRING IT UP?! YOU'RE BOTH BEING STUPID!

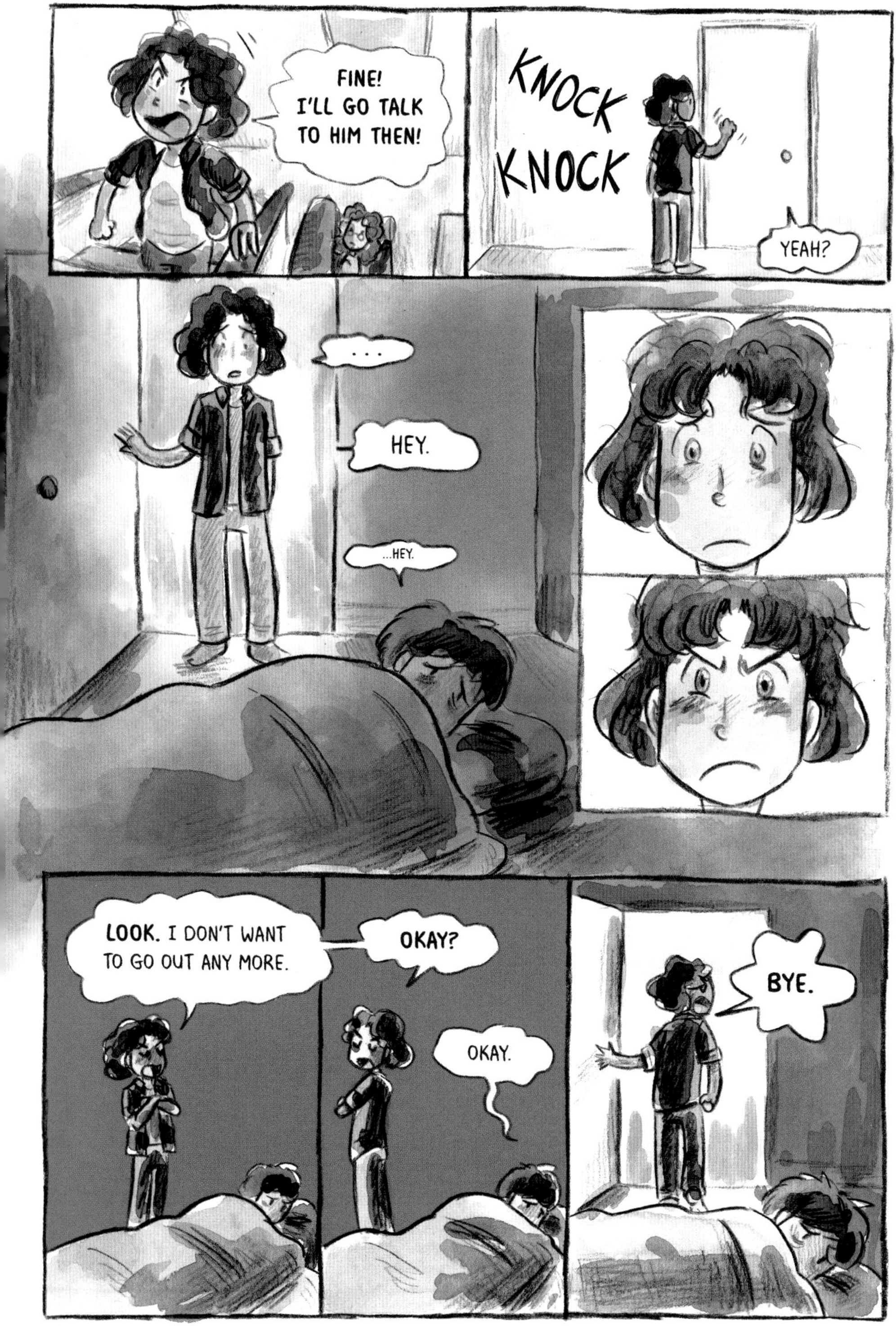
FINE!
I'LL GO TALK TO HIM THEN!
KNOCK
KNOCK
YEAH?
...
HEY.
...HEY.
LOOK. I DON'T WANT TO GO OUT ANY MORE.
OKAY?
OKAY.
BYE.

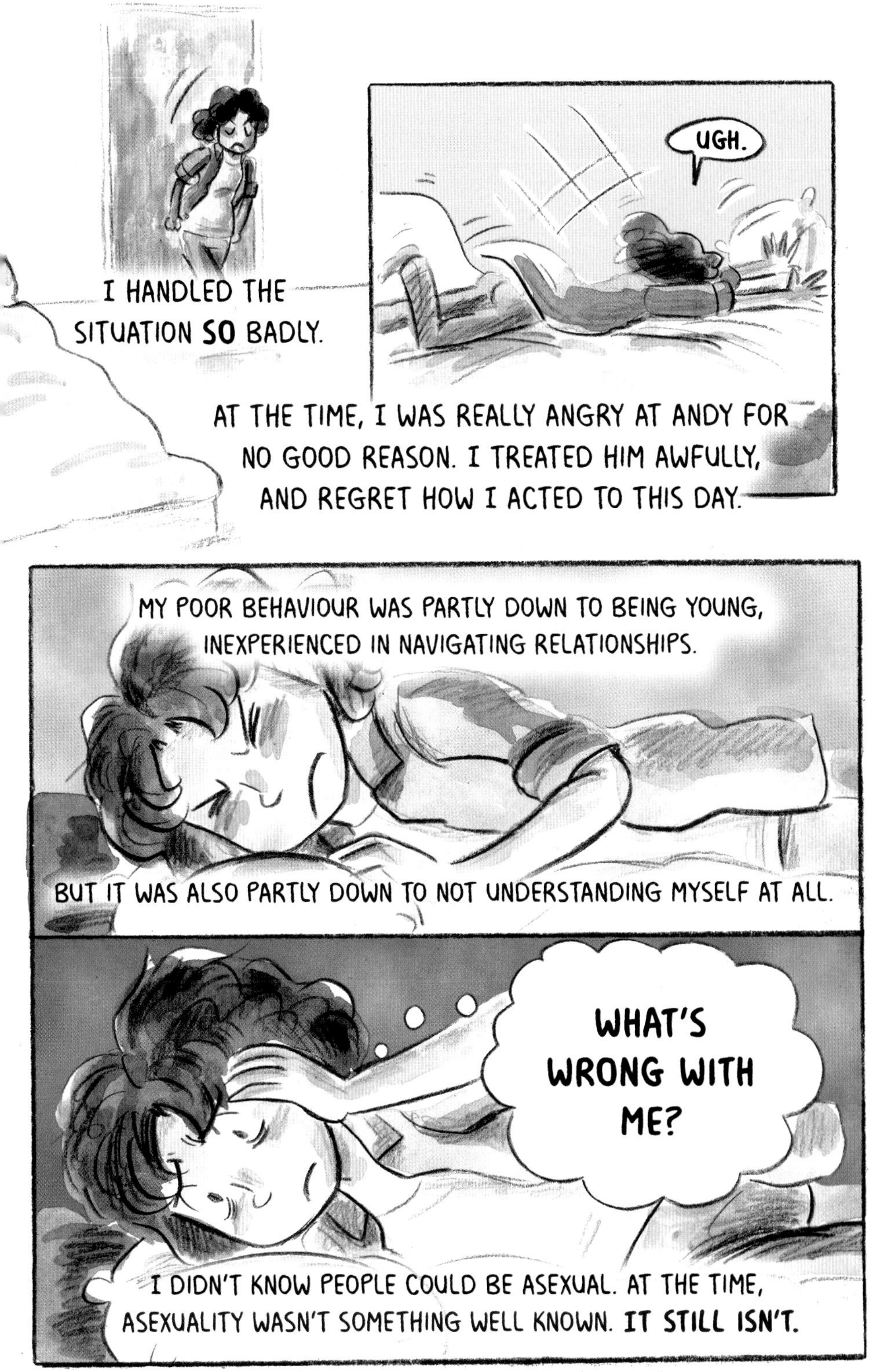
I HANDLED THE SITUATION SO BADLY.
UGH.
AT THE TIME, I WAS REALLY ANGRY AT ANDY FOR NO GOOD REASON. I TREATED HIM AWFULLY, AND REGRET HOW I ACTED TO THIS DAY.
MY POOR BEHAVIOUR WAS PARTLY DOWN TO BEING YOUNG, INEXPERIENCED IN NAVIGATING RELATIONSHIPS.
BUT IT WAS ALSO PARTLY DOWN TO NOT UNDERSTANDING MYSELF AT ALL.
WHAT'S WRONG WITH ME?
I DIDN'T KNOW PEOPLE COULD BE ASEXUAL. AT THE TIME, ASEXUALITY WASN'T SOMETHING WELL KNOWN. IT STILL ISN'T.

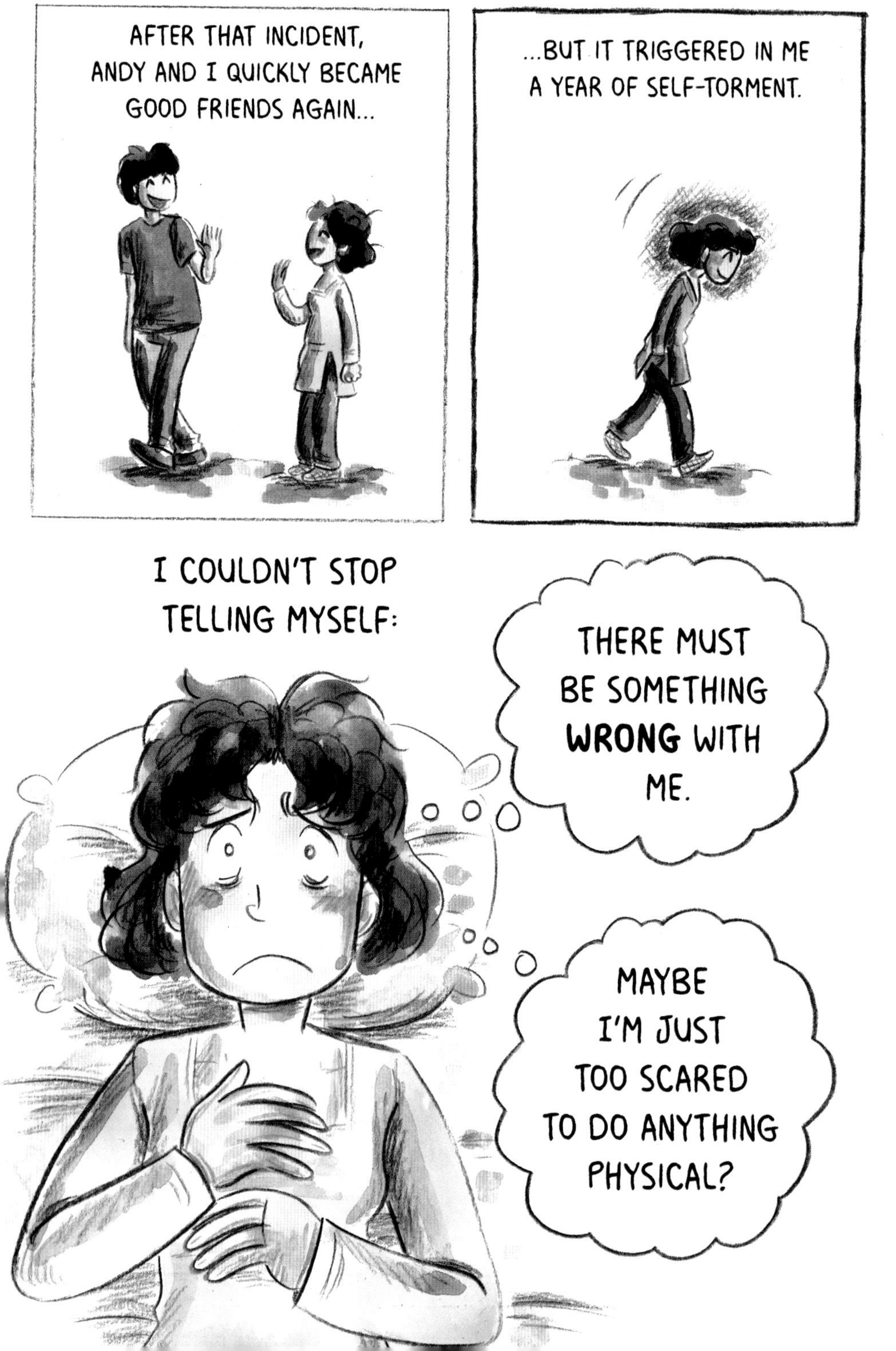
AFTER THAT INCIDENT, ANDY AND I QUICKLY BECAME GOOD FRIENDS AGAIN...
...BUT IT TRIGGERED IN ME A YEAR OF SELF-TORMENT.
I COULDN'T STOP TELLING MYSELF:
THERE MUST BE SOMETHING WRONG WITH ME.
MAYBE I'M JUST TOO SCARED TO DO ANYTHING PHYSICAL?

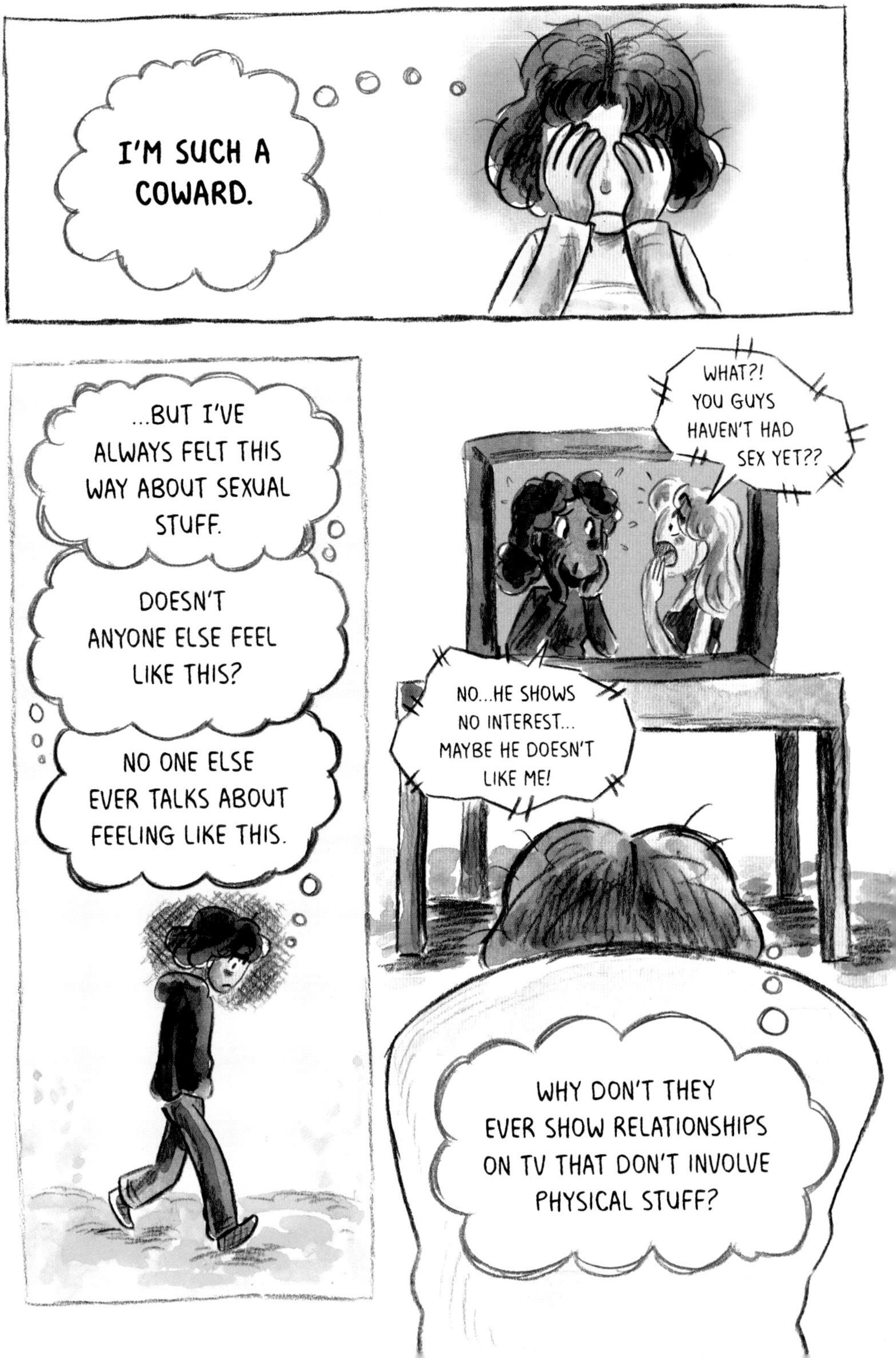
I'M SUCH A COWARD.
...BUT I'VE ALWAYS FELT THIS WAY ABOUT SEXUAL STUFF.
DOESN'T ANYONE ELSE FEEL LIKE THIS?
NO ONE ELSE EVER TALKS ABOUT FEELING LIKE THIS.
WHAT?! YOU GUYS HAVEN'T HAD SEX YET??
NO...HE SHOWS NO INTEREST... MAYBE HE DOESN'T LIKE ME!
WHY DON'T THEY EVER SHOW RELATIONSHIPS ON TV THAT DON'T INVOLVE PHYSICAL STUFF?

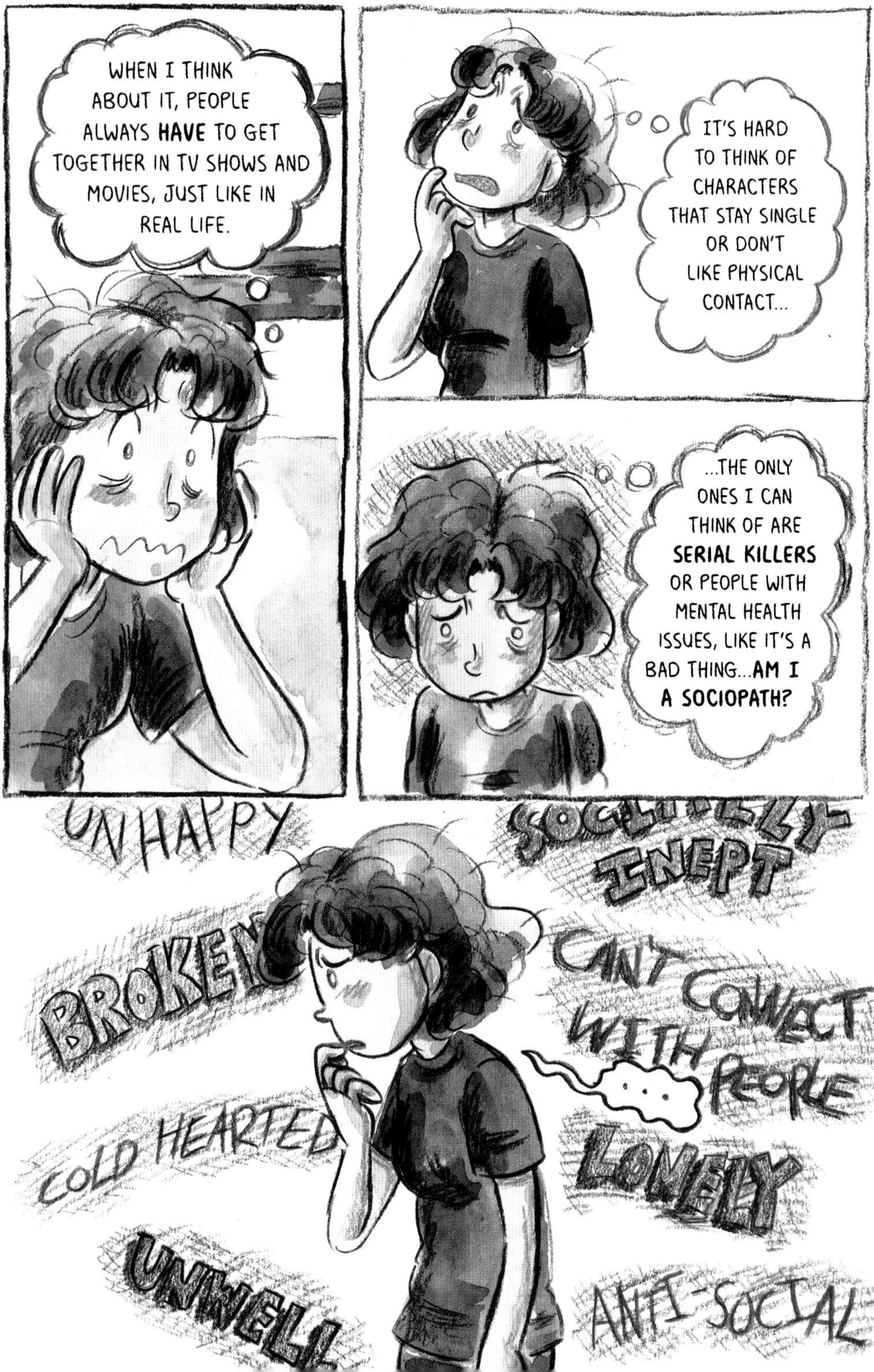

WHEN I THINK ABOUT IT, PEOPLE ALWAYS **HAVE** TO GET TOGETHER IN TV SHOWS AND MOVIES, JUST LIKE IN REAL LIFE.
IT'S HARD TO THINK OF CHARACTERS THAT STAY SINGLE OR DON'T LIKE PHYSICAL CONTACT...
...THE ONLY ONES I CAN THINK OF ARE **SERIAL KILLERS** OR PEOPLE WITH MENTAL HEALTH ISSUES, LIKE IT'S A BAD THING...**AM I A SOCIOPATH?**
UNHAPPY
SOCIALLY INEPT
BROKEN
CAN'T CONNECT WITH PEOPLE
...
COLD HEARTED
LONELY
UNWELL
ANTI-SOCIAL

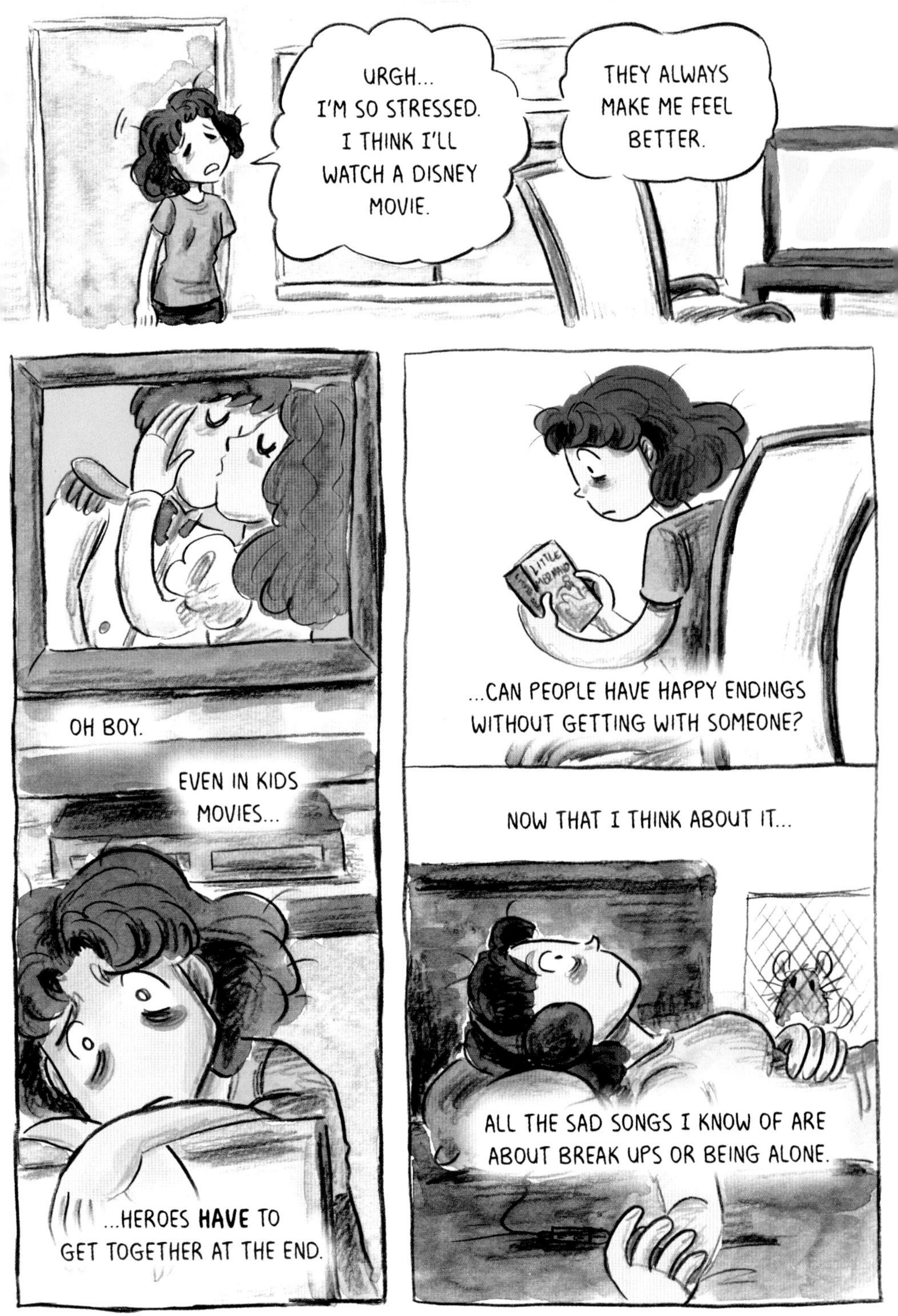
URGH... I'M SO STRESSED. I THINK I'LL WATCH A DISNEY MOVIE.
THEY ALWAYS MAKE ME FEEL BETTER.
OH BOY.
EVEN IN KIDS MOVIES...
...HEROES **HAVE** TO GET TOGETHER AT THE END.
LITTLE MERMAID
...CAN PEOPLE HAVE HAPPY ENDINGS WITHOUT GETTING WITH SOMEONE?
NOW THAT I THINK ABOUT IT...
ALL THE SAD SONGS I KNOW OF ARE ABOUT BREAK UPS OR BEING ALONE.

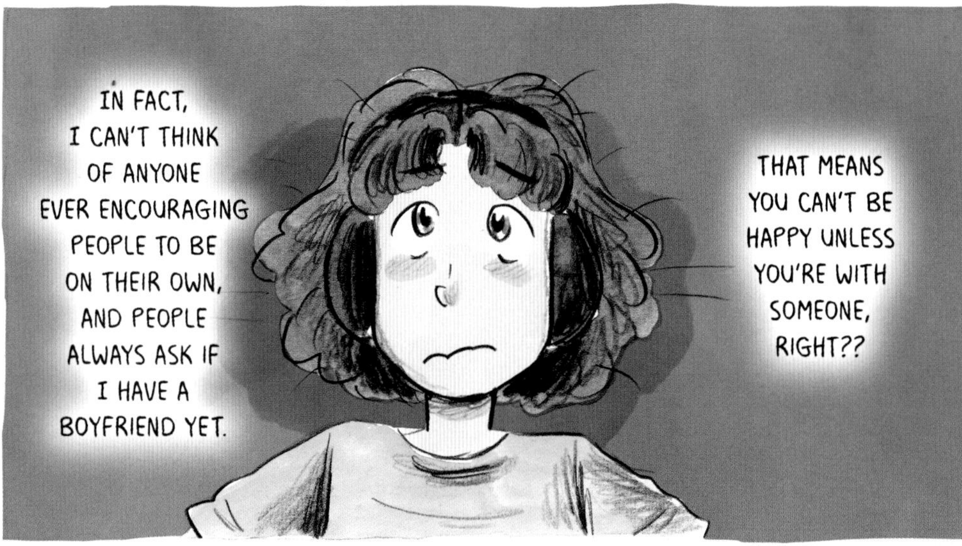
IN FACT, I CAN'T THINK OF ANYONE EVER ENCOURAGING PEOPLE TO BE ON THEIR OWN, AND PEOPLE ALWAYS ASK IF I HAVE A BOYFRIEND YET.
THAT MEANS YOU CAN'T BE HAPPY UNLESS YOU'RE WITH SOMEONE, RIGHT??

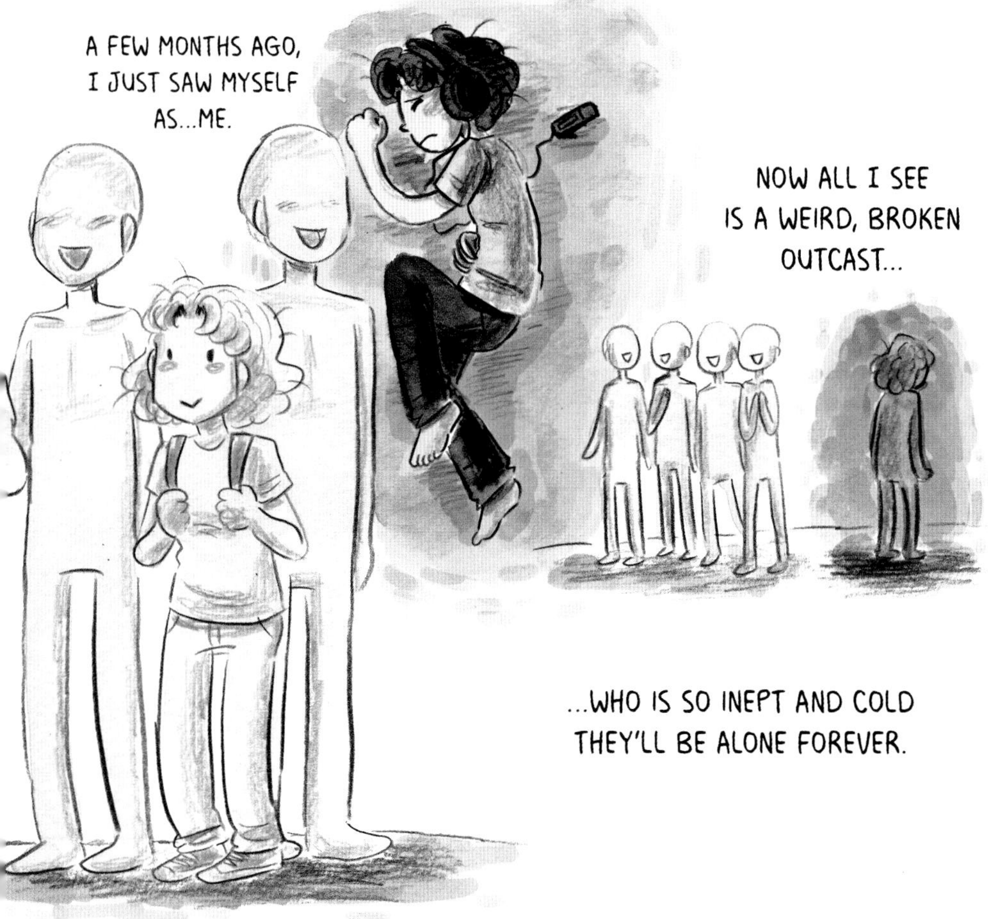
A FEW MONTHS AGO, I JUST SAW MYSELF AS...ME.
NOW ALL I SEE IS A WEIRD, BROKEN OUTCAST...
...WHO IS SO INEPT AND COLD THEY'LL BE ALONE FOREVER.

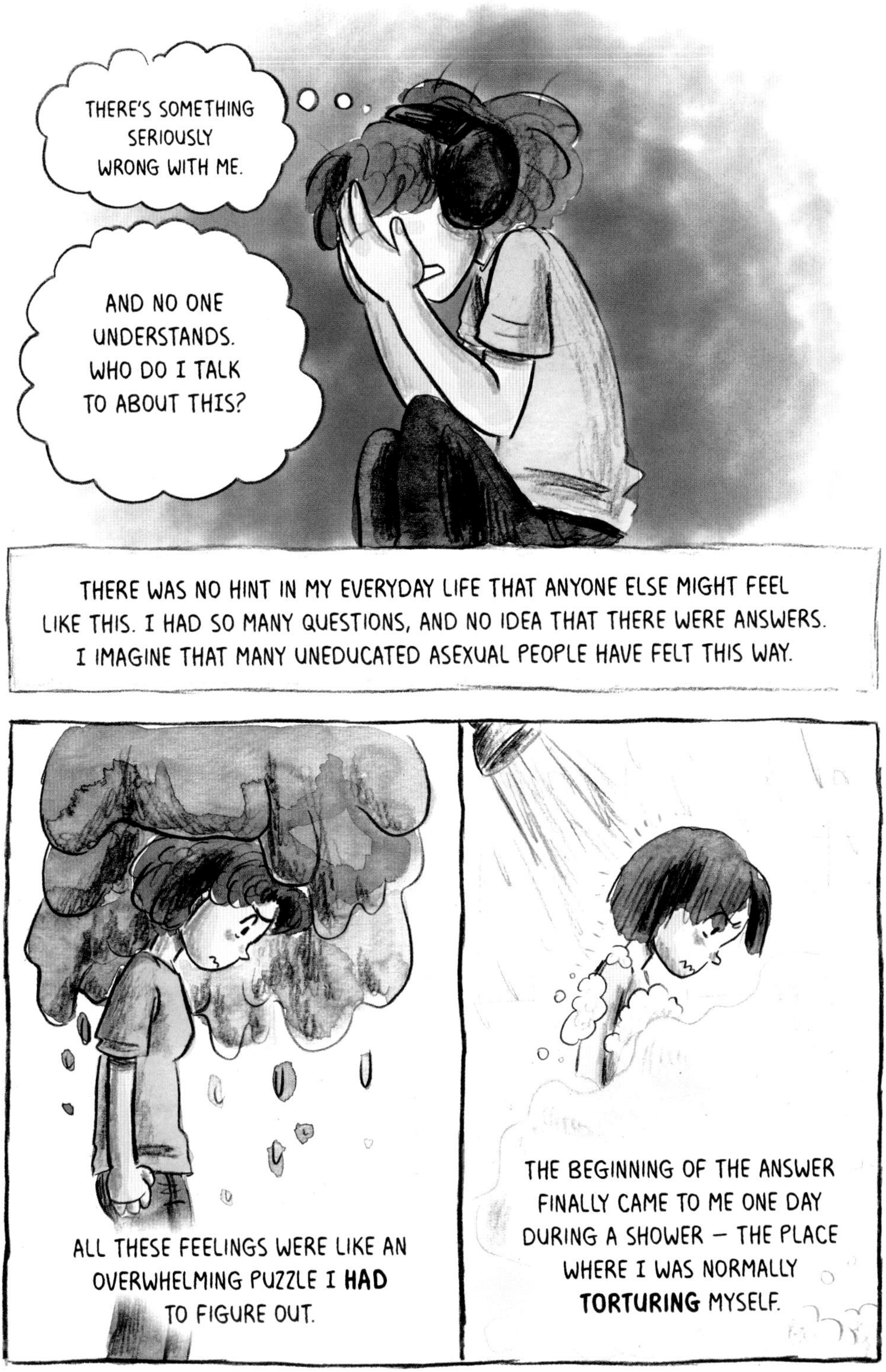
THERE'S SOMETHING SERIOUSLY WRONG WITH ME.
AND NO ONE UNDERSTANDS. WHO DO I TALK TO ABOUT THIS?
THERE WAS NO HINT IN MY EVERYDAY LIFE THAT ANYONE ELSE MIGHT FEEL LIKE THIS. I HAD SO MANY QUESTIONS, AND NO IDEA THAT THERE WERE ANSWERS. I IMAGINE THAT MANY UNEDUCATED ASEXUAL PEOPLE HAVE FELT THIS WAY.
ALL THESE FEELINGS WERE LIKE AN OVERWHELMING PUZZLE I **HAD** TO FIGURE OUT.
THE BEGINNING OF THE ANSWER FINALLY CAME TO ME ONE DAY DURING A SHOWER – THE PLACE WHERE I WAS NORMALLY **TORTURING** MYSELF.

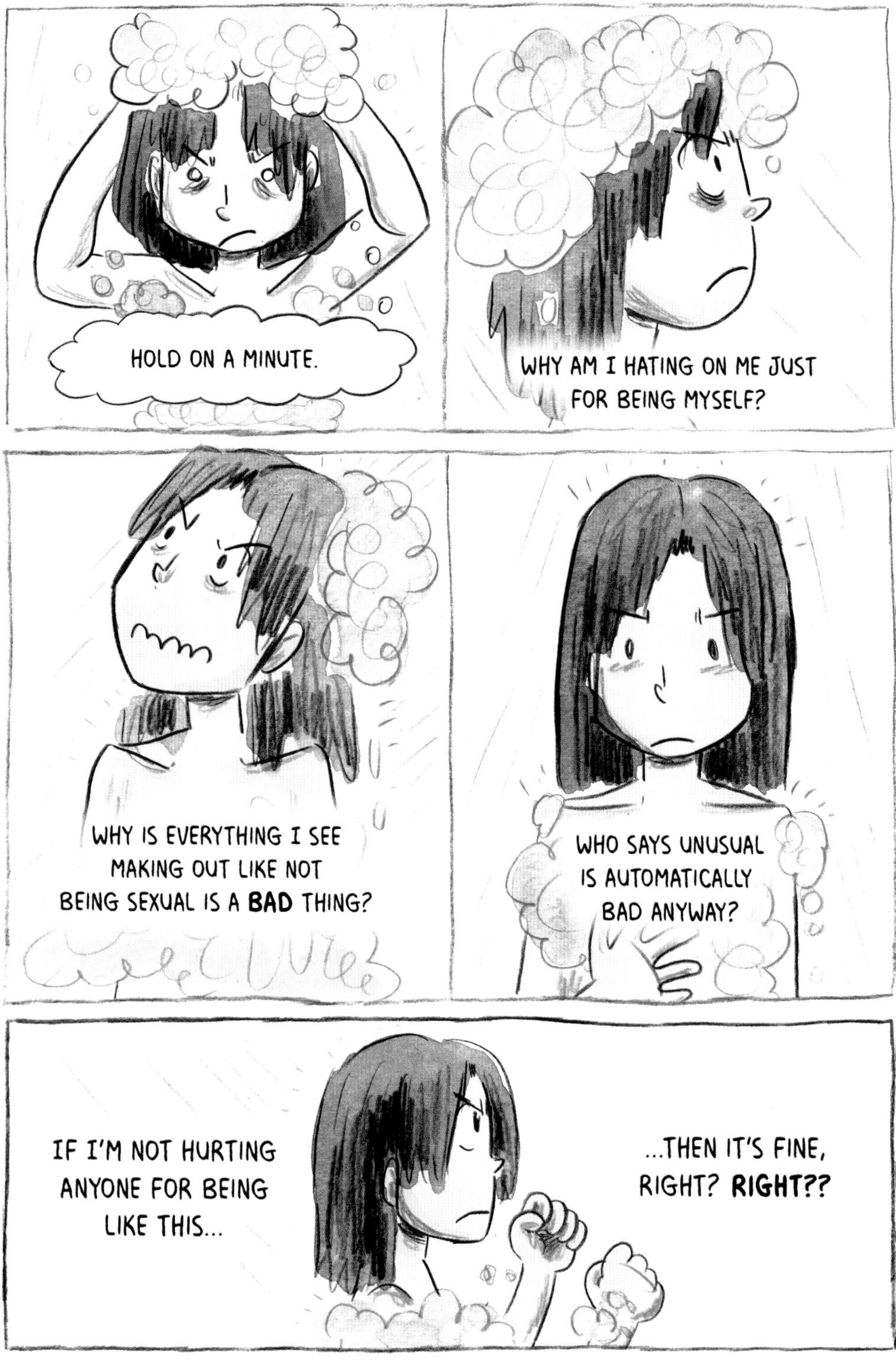
HOLD ON A MINUTE.
WHY AM I HATING ON ME JUST FOR BEING MYSELF?
WHY IS EVERYTHING I SEE MAKING OUT LIKE NOT BEING SEXUAL IS A **BAD** THING?
WHO SAYS UNUSUAL IS AUTOMATICALLY BAD ANYWAY?
IF I'M NOT HURTING ANYONE FOR BEING LIKE THIS...
...THEN IT'S FINE, RIGHT? **RIGHT??**

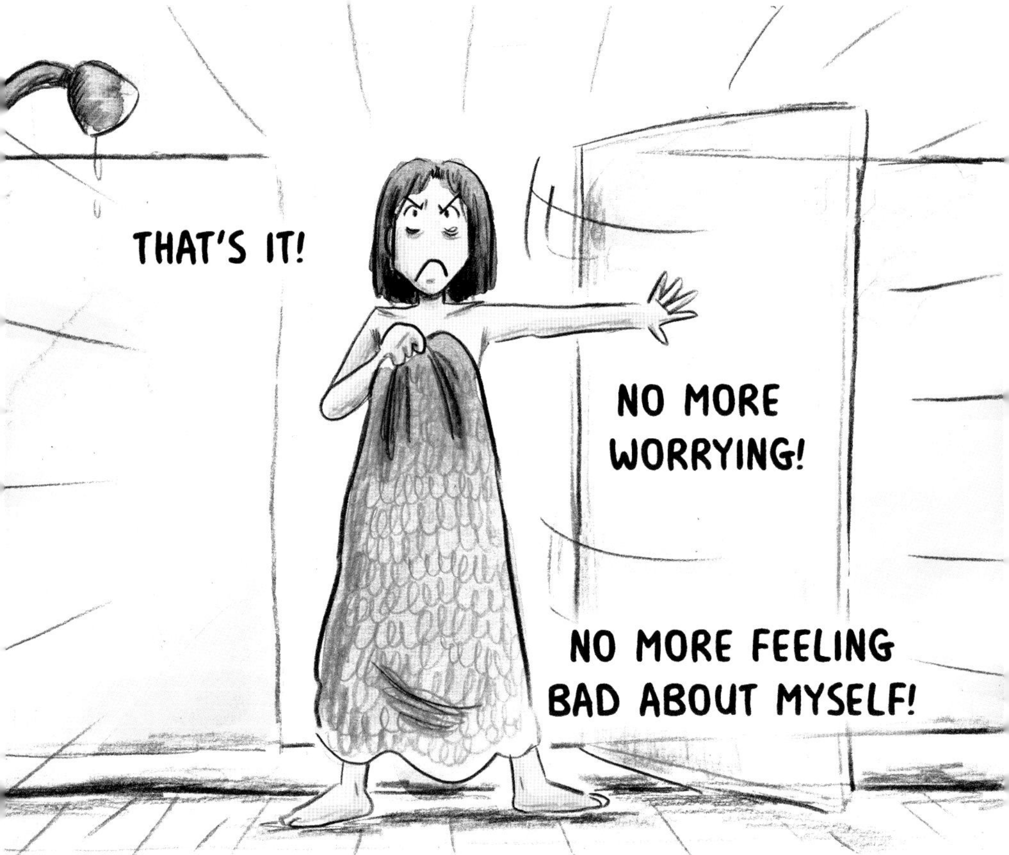
THAT'S IT!
NO MORE WORRYING!
NO MORE FEELING BAD ABOUT MYSELF!

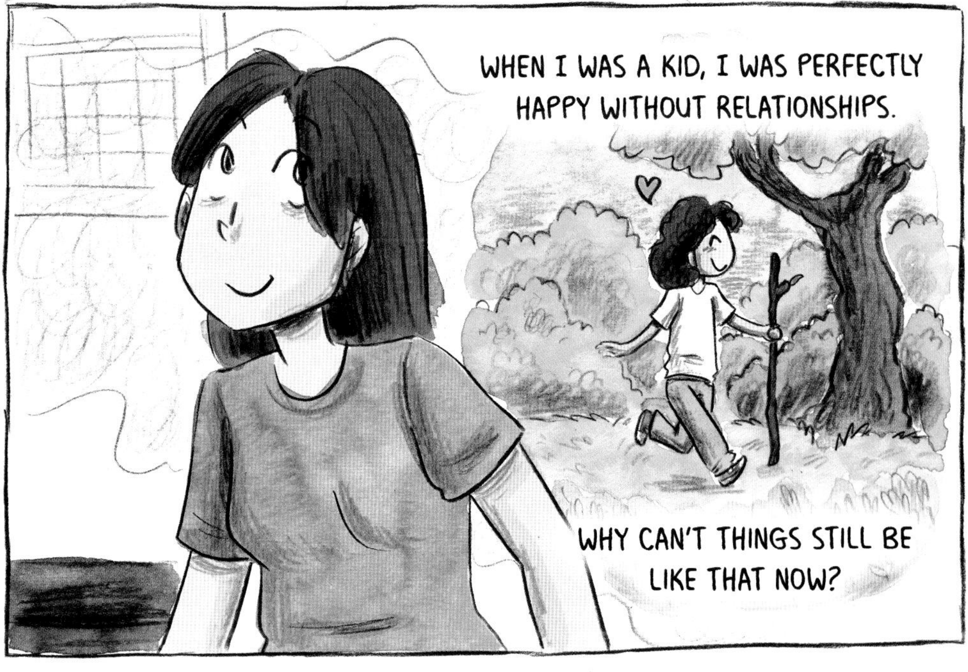
WHEN I WAS A KID, I WAS PERFECTLY HAPPY WITHOUT RELATIONSHIPS.
WHY CAN'T THINGS STILL BE LIKE THAT NOW?

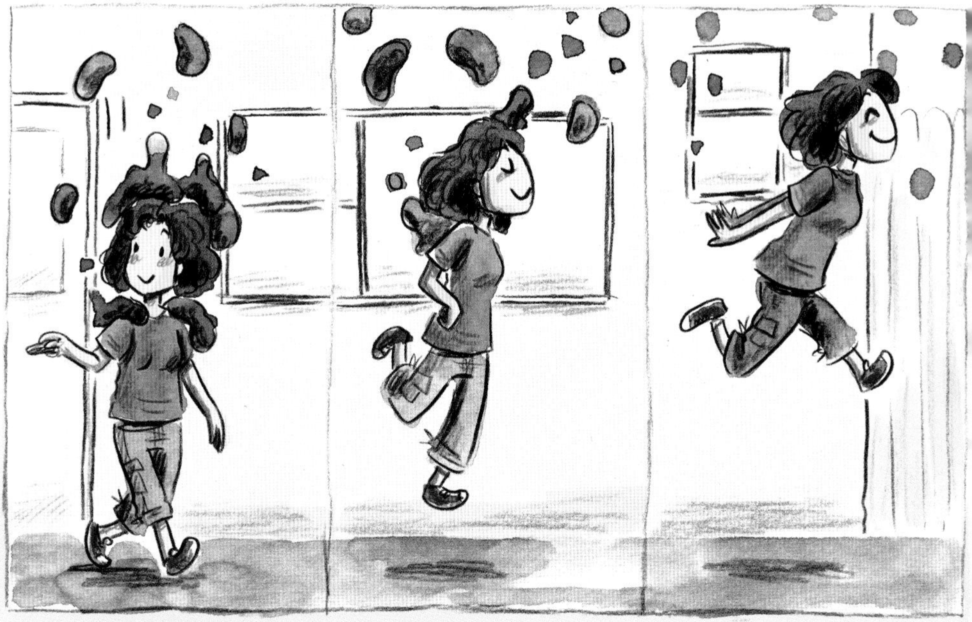

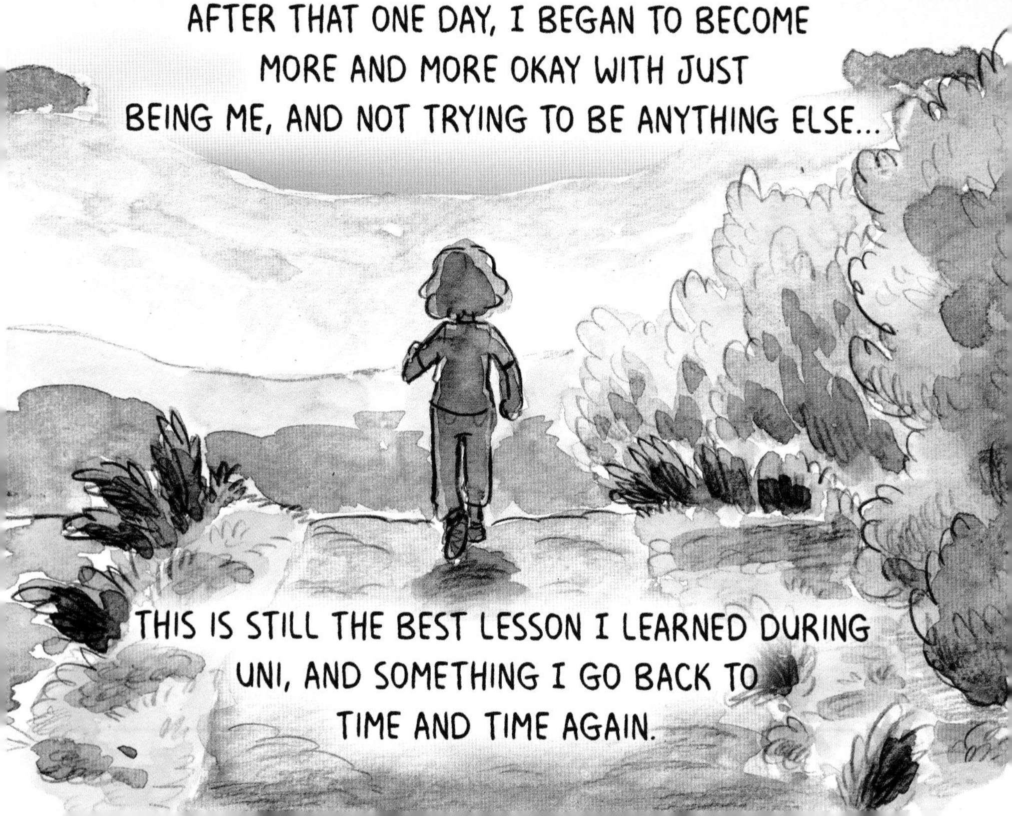
AFTER THAT ONE DAY, I BEGAN TO BECOME MORE AND MORE OKAY WITH JUST BEING ME, AND NOT TRYING TO BE ANYTHING ELSE...
THIS IS STILL THE BEST LESSON I LEARNED DURING UNI, AND SOMETHING I GO BACK TO TIME AND TIME AGAIN.

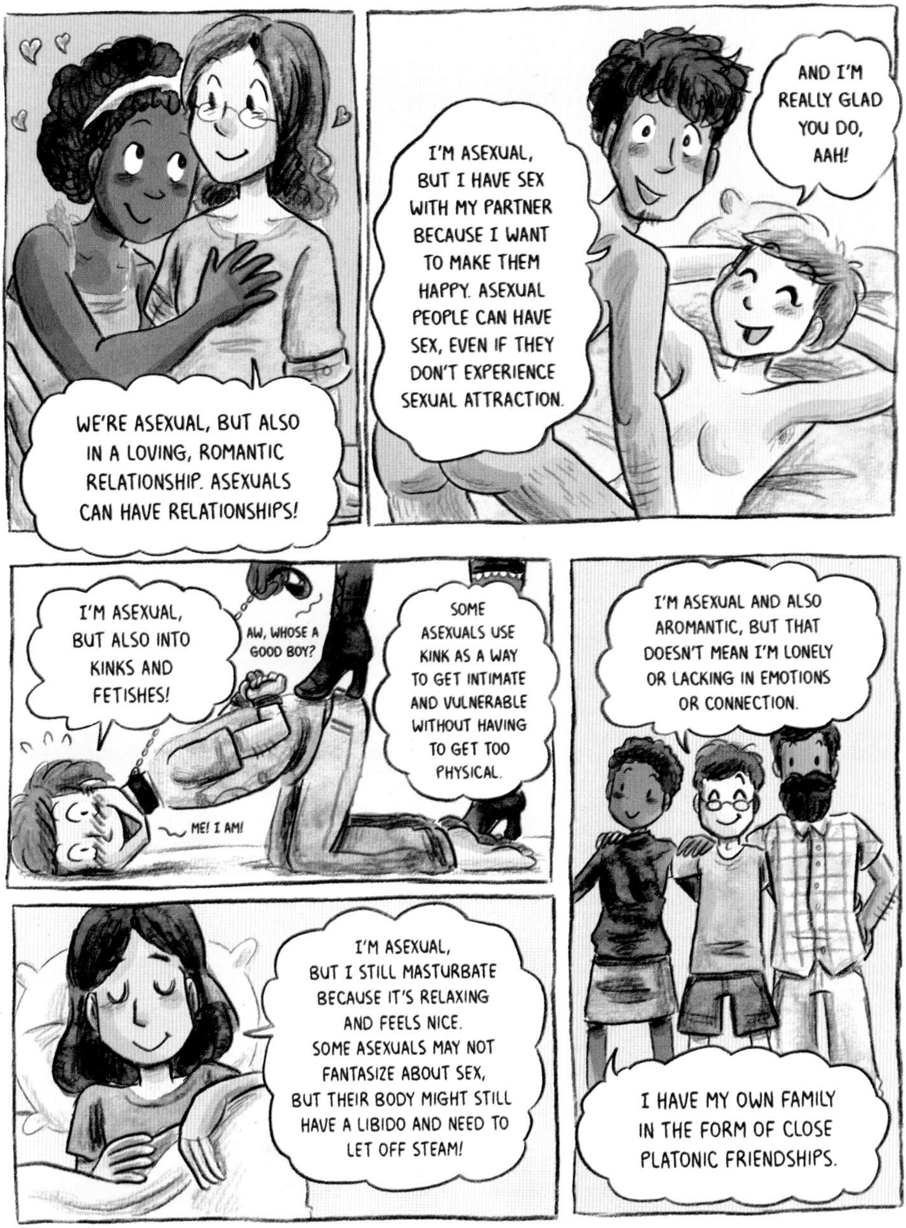
WE'RE ASEXUAL, BUT ALSO IN A LOVING, ROMANTIC RELATIONSHIP. ASEXUALS CAN HAVE RELATIONSHIPS!
I'M ASEXUAL, BUT I HAVE SEX WITH MY PARTNER BECAUSE I WANT TO MAKE THEM HAPPY. ASEXUAL PEOPLE CAN HAVE SEX, EVEN IF THEY DON'T EXPERIENCE SEXUAL ATTRACTION.
AND I'M REALLY GLAD YOU DO, AAH!
I'M ASEXUAL, BUT ALSO INTO KINKS AND FETISHES!
AW, WHOSE A GOOD BOY?
ME! I AM!
SOME ASEXUALS USE KINK AS A WAY TO GET INTIMATE AND VULNERABLE WITHOUT HAVING TO GET TOO PHYSICAL.
I'M ASEXUAL AND ALSO AROMANTIC, BUT THAT DOESN'T MEAN I'M LONELY OR LACKING IN EMOTIONS OR CONNECTION.
I HAVE MY OWN FAMILY IN THE FORM OF CLOSE PLATONIC FRIENDSHIPS.
I'M ASEXUAL, BUT I STILL MASTURBATE BECAUSE IT'S RELAXING AND FEELS NICE. SOME ASEXUALS MAY NOT FANTASIZE ABOUT SEX, BUT THEIR BODY MIGHT STILL HAVE A LIBIDO AND NEED TO LET OFF STEAM!

LIKE **EVERY OTHER** SEXUALITY, ASEXUALITY IS JUST A SIMPLE, SHORTHAND LABEL TO HELP SOMEONE EXPRESS THEIR MUCH MORE INDIVIDUAL AND UNIQUE EXPERIENCE!

# CHAPTER FOUR

## HOW TO BE OKAY
## WITH BEING ALONE FOREVER

WHEN I WAS 19 YEARS OLD, I HAD THE NEXT TEN YEARS OF MY LIFE ALL PLANNED OUT IN MY HEAD, LIKE A SIMPLE MAP, WHERE IF I FOLLOWED THE PLAN IT WOULD JUST HAPPEN.

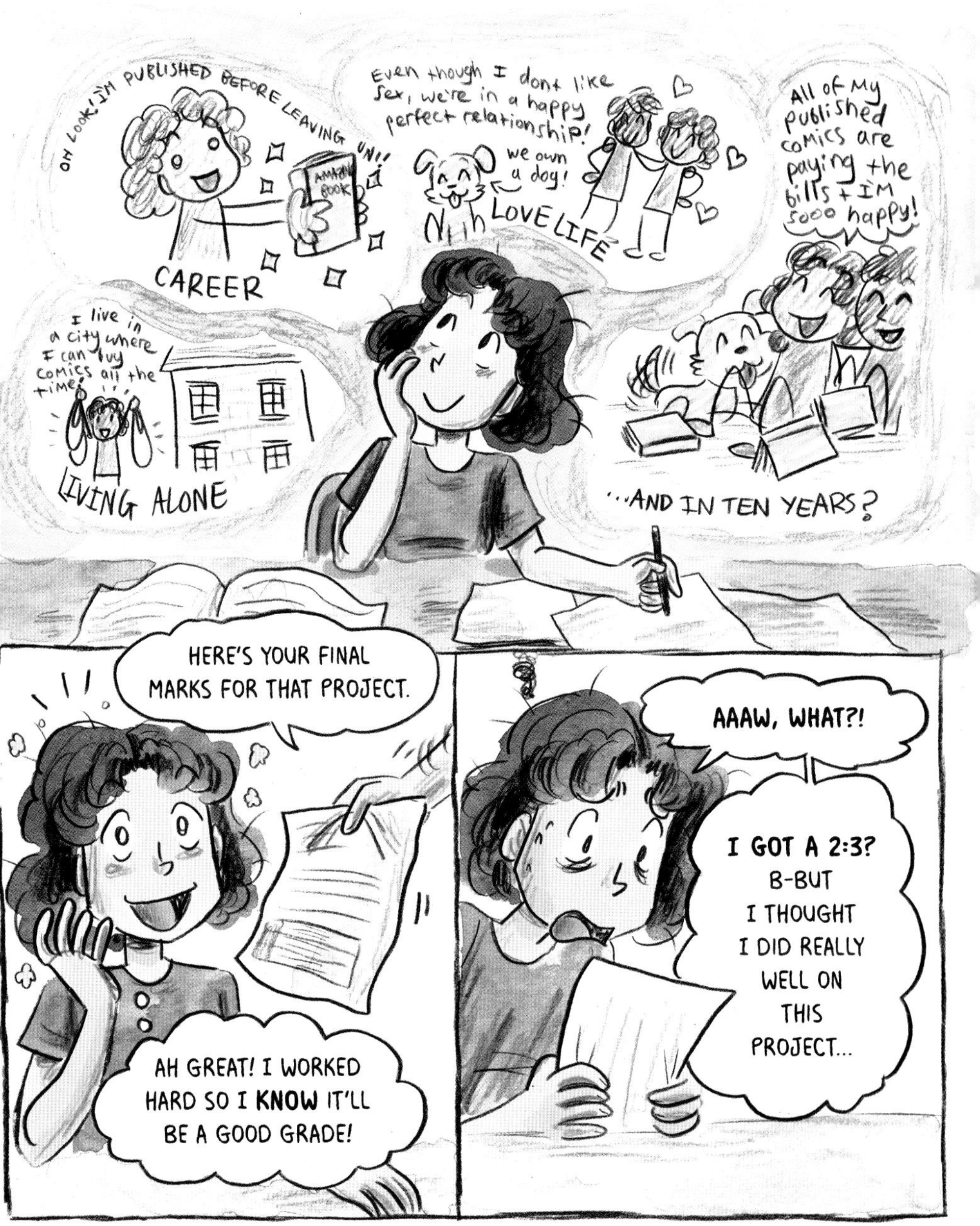
OH LOOK! I'M PUBLISHED BEFORE LEAVING UNI!!
AMAZING BOOK
CAREER
Even though I don't like sex, we're in a happy perfect relationship!
we own a dog!
LOVE LIFE
All of My published comics are paying the bills + I'M sooo happy!
I live in a city where I can buy comics all the time!
LIVING ALONE
...AND IN TEN YEARS?
HERE'S YOUR FINAL MARKS FOR THAT PROJECT.
AH GREAT! I WORKED HARD SO I KNOW IT'LL BE A GOOD GRADE!
AAAW, WHAT?!
I GOT A 2:3? B-BUT I THOUGHT I DID REALLY WELL ON THIS PROJECT...

OF COURSE, THE REALITY IS THAT JUST BECAUSE YOU REALLY WANT SOMETHING TO HAPPEN, IT DOESN'T MEAN THAT IT WILL.

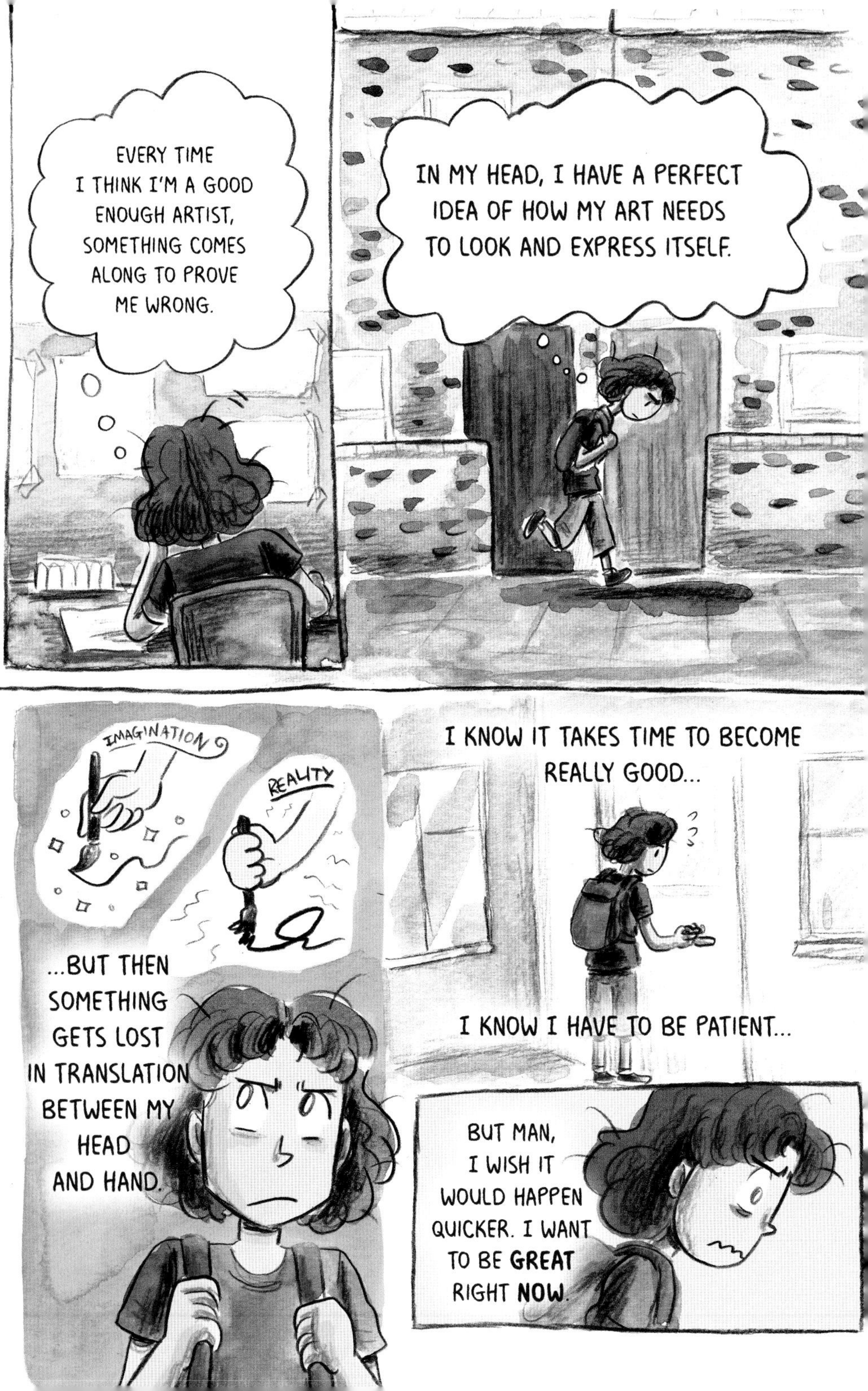
EVERY TIME I THINK I'M A GOOD ENOUGH ARTIST, SOMETHING COMES ALONG TO PROVE ME WRONG.
IN MY HEAD, I HAVE A PERFECT IDEA OF HOW MY ART NEEDS TO LOOK AND EXPRESS ITSELF.
IMAGINATION
REALITY
...BUT THEN SOMETHING GETS LOST IN TRANSLATION BETWEEN MY HEAD AND HAND.
I KNOW IT TAKES TIME TO BECOME REALLY GOOD...
I KNOW I HAVE TO BE PATIENT...
BUT MAN, I WISH IT WOULD HAPPEN QUICKER. I WANT TO BE **GREAT** RIGHT **NOW**.

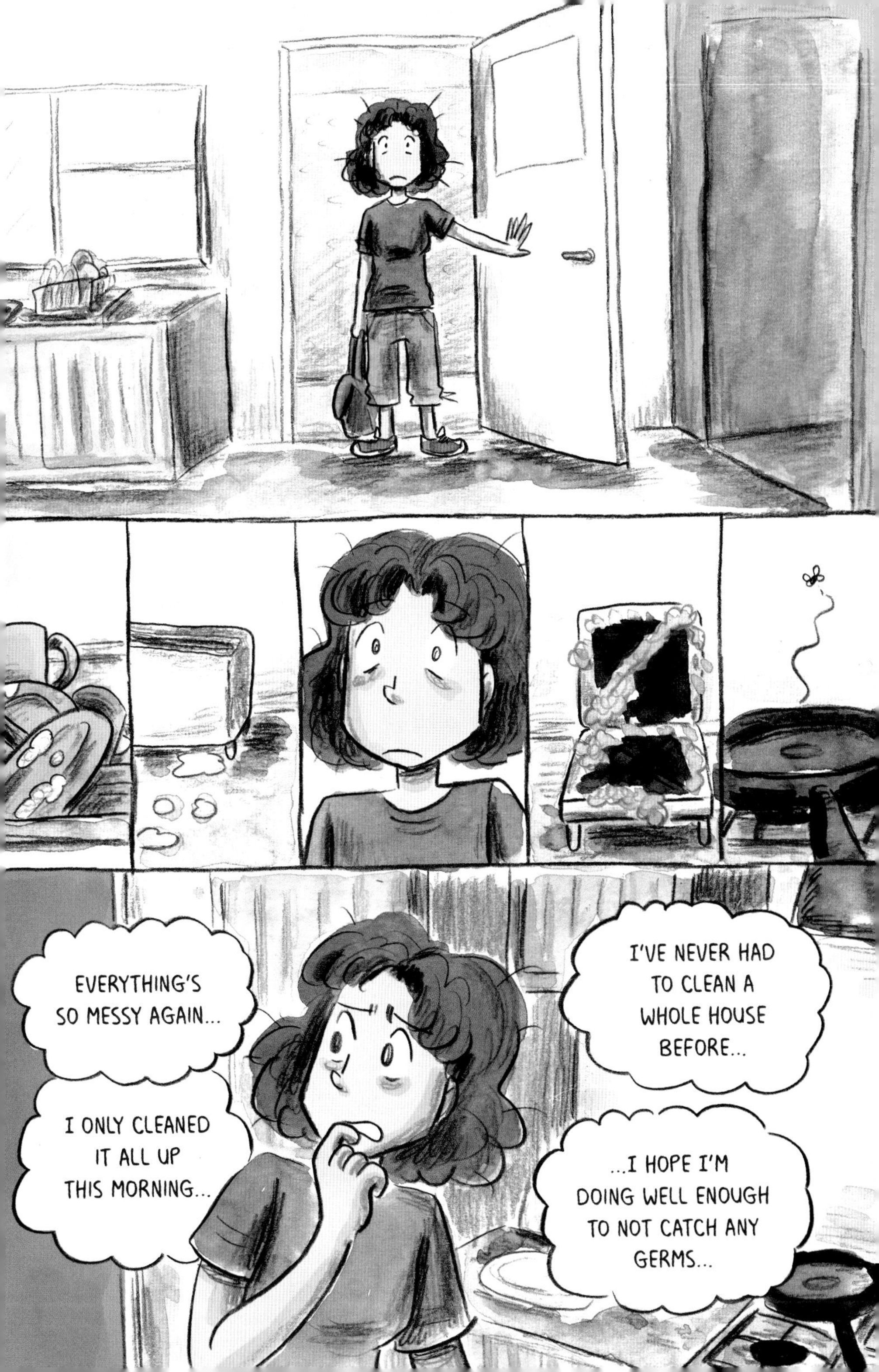
EVERYTHING'S SO MESSY AGAIN...
I ONLY CLEANED IT ALL UP THIS MORNING...
I'VE NEVER HAD TO CLEAN A WHOLE HOUSE BEFORE...
...I HOPE I'M DOING WELL ENOUGH TO NOT CATCH ANY GERMS...

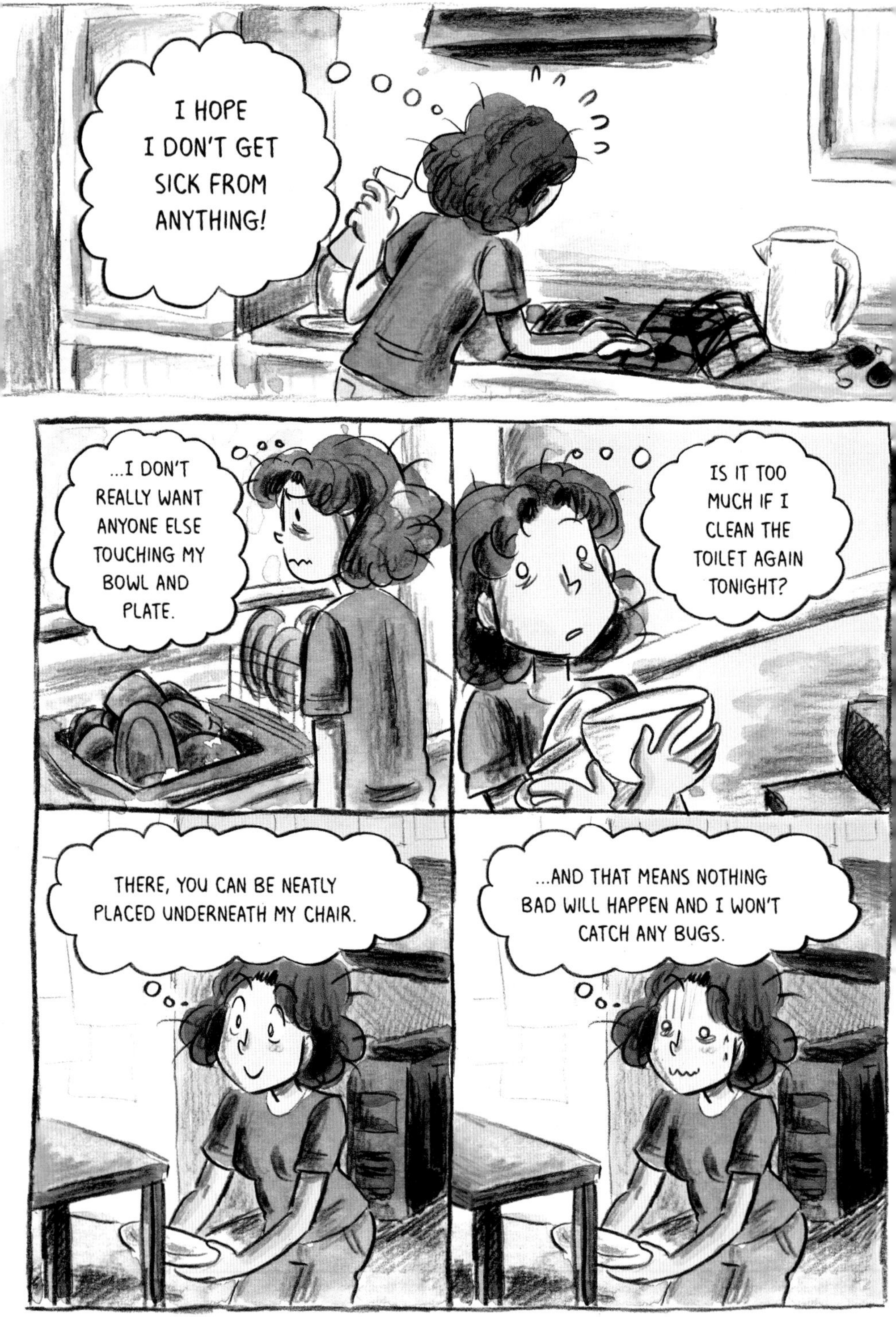
I HOPE I DON'T GET SICK FROM ANYTHING!
...I DON'T REALLY WANT ANYONE ELSE TOUCHING MY BOWL AND PLATE.
IS IT TOO MUCH IF I CLEAN THE TOILET AGAIN TONIGHT?
THERE, YOU CAN BE NEATLY PLACED UNDERNEATH MY CHAIR.
...AND THAT MEANS NOTHING BAD WILL HAPPEN AND I WON'T CATCH ANY BUGS.

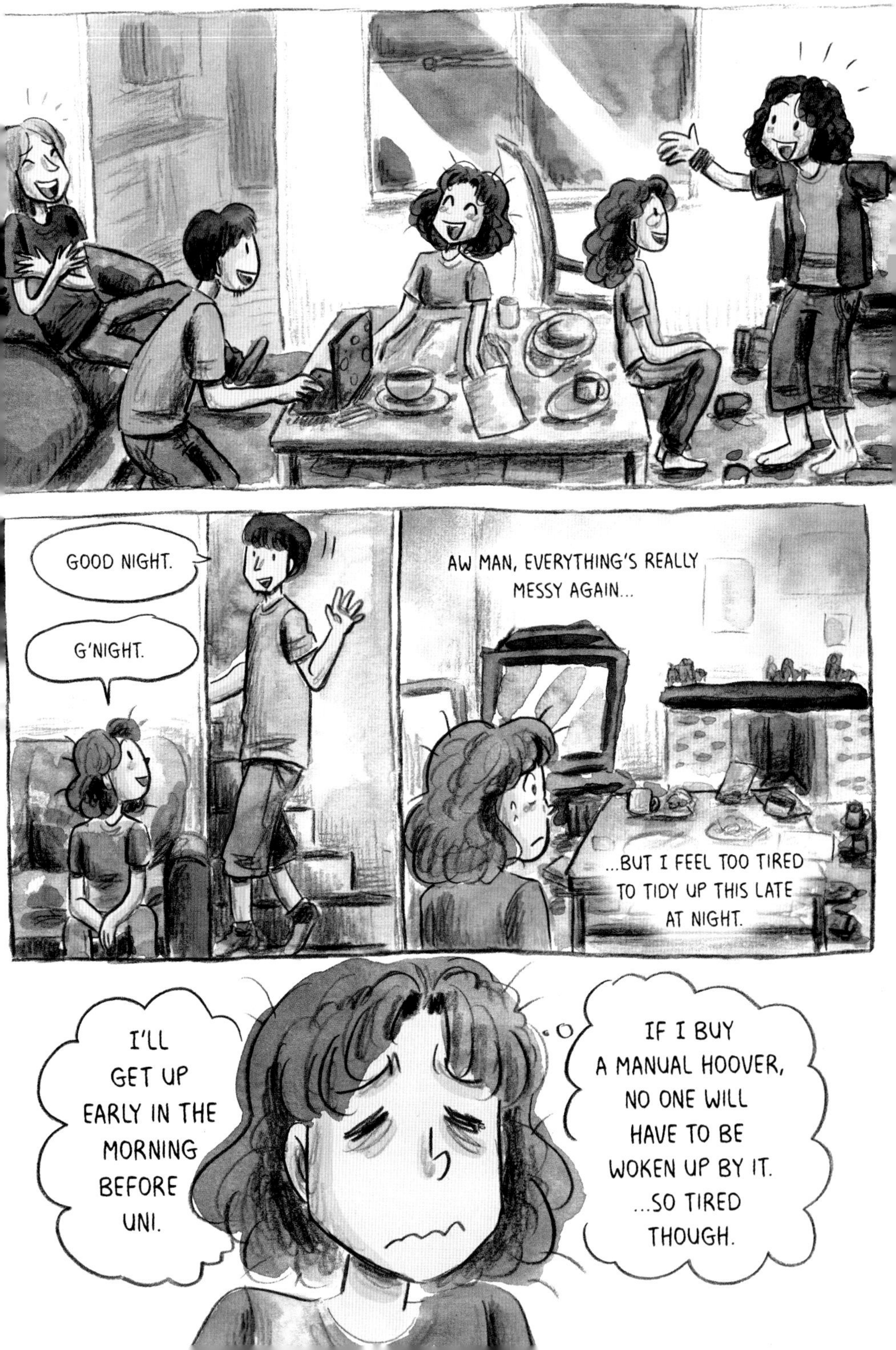
GOOD NIGHT.
G'NIGHT.
AW MAN, EVERYTHING'S REALLY MESSY AGAIN...
...BUT I FEEL TOO TIRED TO TIDY UP THIS LATE AT NIGHT.
I'LL GET UP EARLY IN THE MORNING BEFORE UNI.
IF I BUY A MANUAL HOOVER, NO ONE WILL HAVE TO BE WOKEN UP BY IT. ...SO TIRED THOUGH.

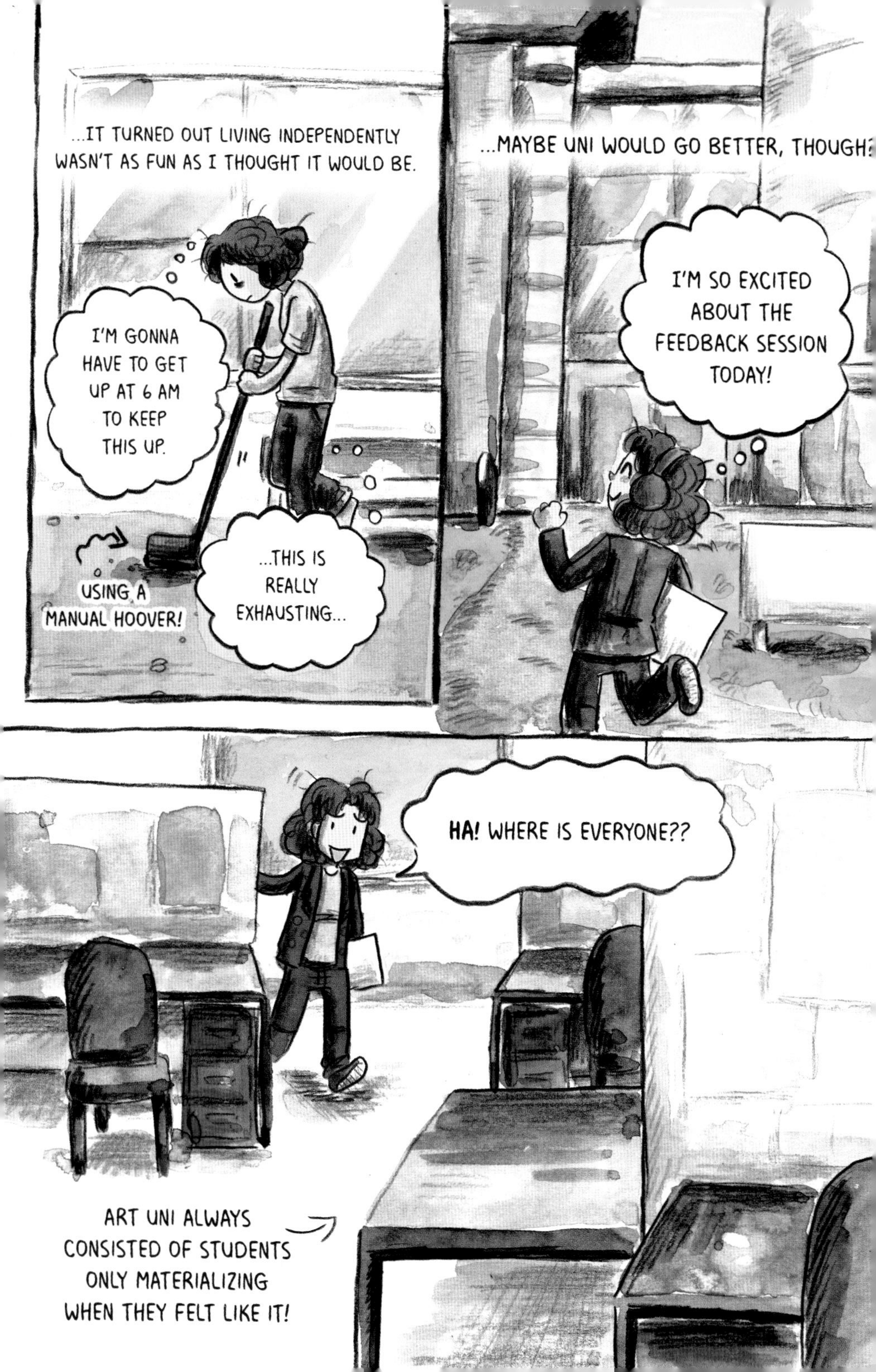
...IT TURNED OUT LIVING INDEPENDENTLY WASN'T AS FUN AS I THOUGHT IT WOULD BE.
I'M GONNA HAVE TO GET UP AT 6 AM TO KEEP THIS UP.
USING A MANUAL HOOVER!
...THIS IS REALLY EXHAUSTING...
...MAYBE UNI WOULD GO BETTER, THOUGH?
I'M SO EXCITED ABOUT THE FEEDBACK SESSION TODAY!
HA! WHERE IS EVERYONE??
ART UNI ALWAYS CONSISTED OF STUDENTS ONLY MATERIALIZING WHEN THEY FELT LIKE IT!

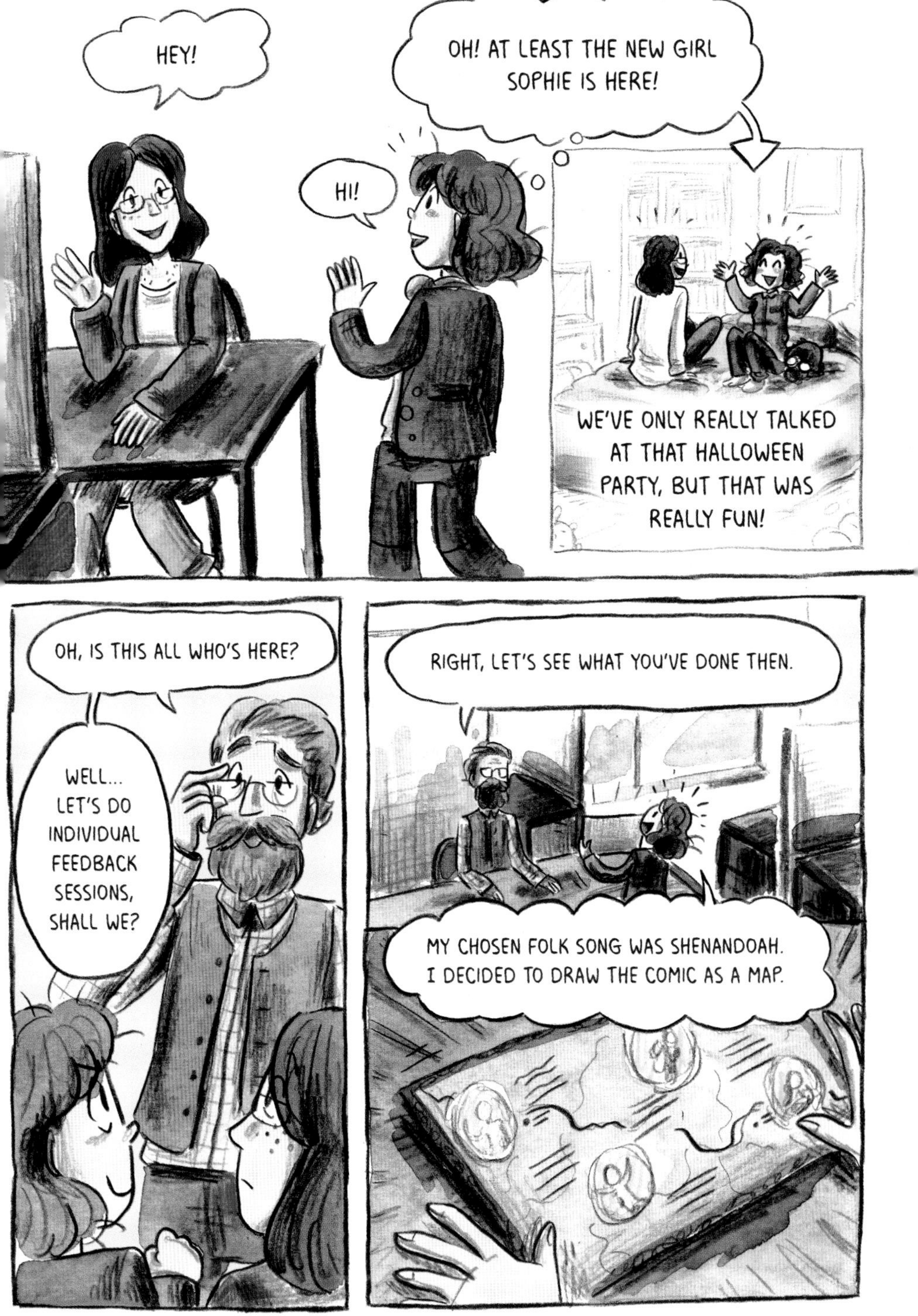
HEY!
OH! AT LEAST THE NEW GIRL SOPHIE IS HERE!
HI!
WE'VE ONLY REALLY TALKED AT THAT HALLOWEEN PARTY, BUT THAT WAS REALLY FUN!
OH, IS THIS ALL WHO'S HERE?
WELL... LET'S DO INDIVIDUAL FEEDBACK SESSIONS, SHALL WE?
RIGHT, LET'S SEE WHAT YOU'VE DONE THEN.
MY CHOSEN FOLK SONG WAS SHENANDOAH. I DECIDED TO DRAW THE COMIC AS A MAP.

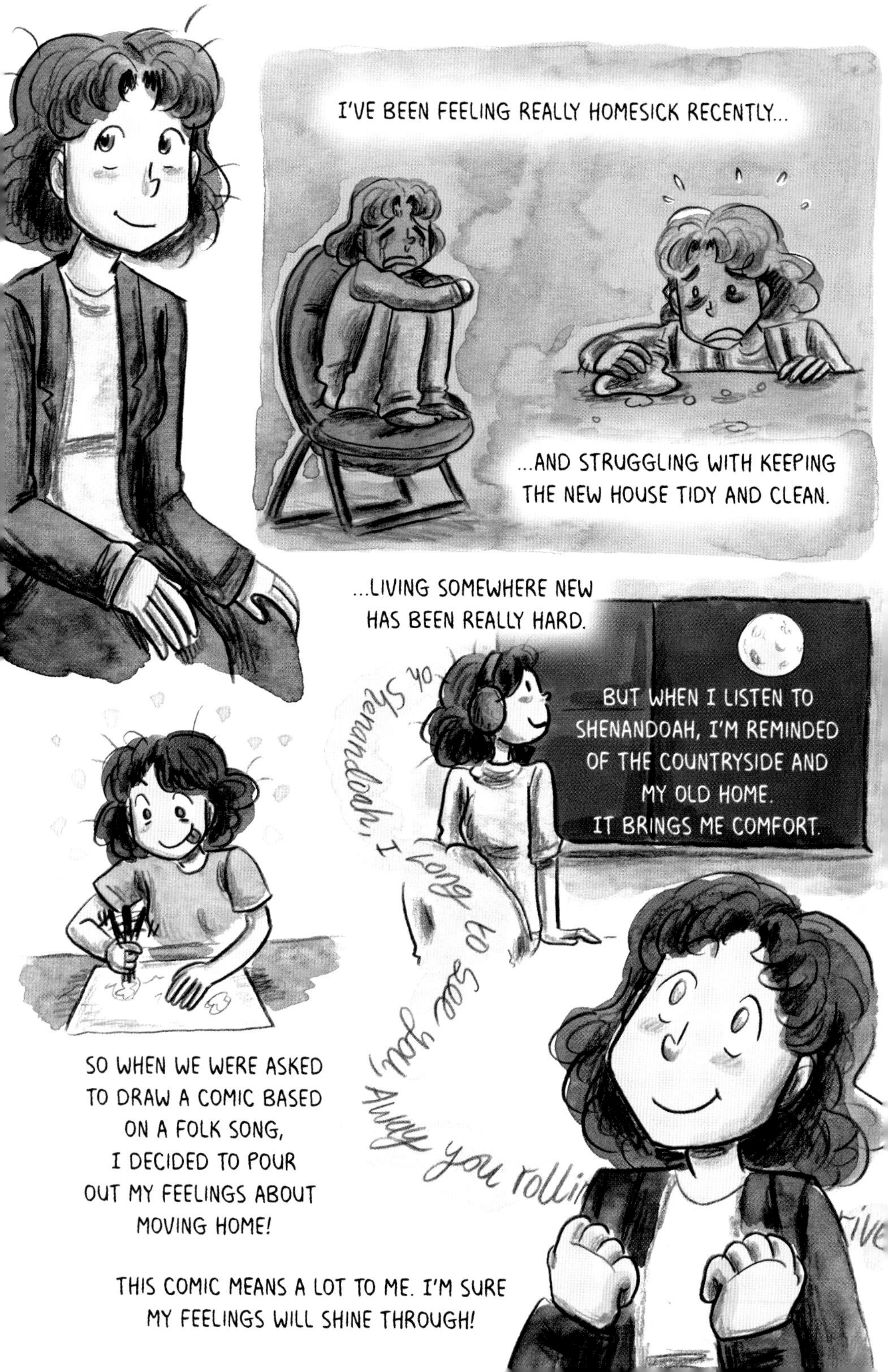
I'VE BEEN FEELING REALLY HOMESICK RECENTLY...
...AND STRUGGLING WITH KEEPING THE NEW HOUSE TIDY AND CLEAN.
...LIVING SOMEWHERE NEW HAS BEEN REALLY HARD.
BUT WHEN I LISTEN TO SHENANDOAH, I'M REMINDED OF THE COUNTRYSIDE AND MY OLD HOME. IT BRINGS ME COMFORT.
Oh Shenandoah, I long to see you, Away you rolli
rive
SO WHEN WE WERE ASKED TO DRAW A COMIC BASED ON A FOLK SONG, I DECIDED TO POUR OUT MY FEELINGS ABOUT MOVING HOME!
THIS COMIC MEANS A LOT TO ME. I'M SURE MY FEELINGS WILL SHINE THROUGH!

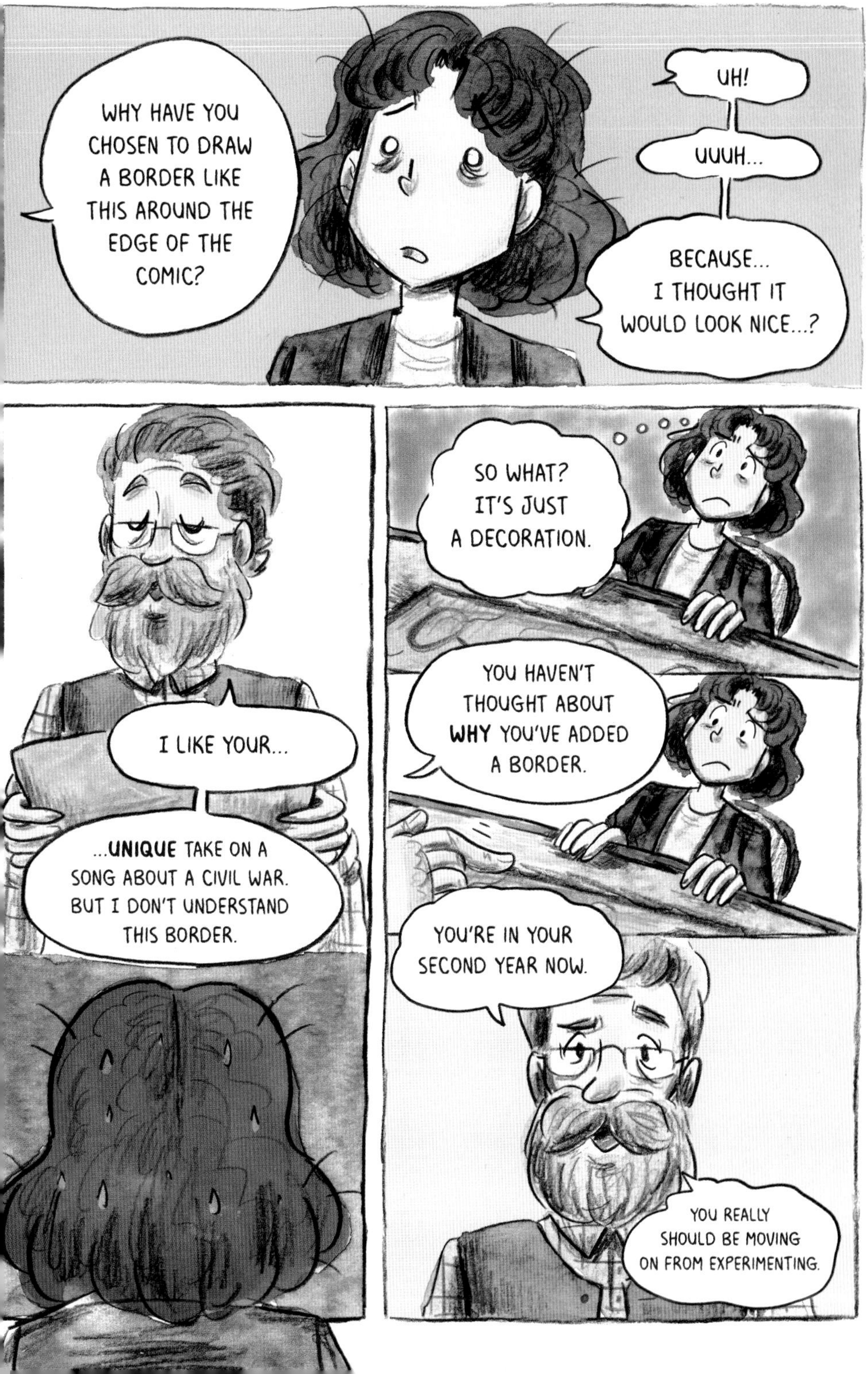
WHY HAVE YOU CHOSEN TO DRAW A BORDER LIKE THIS AROUND THE EDGE OF THE COMIC?
UH!
UUUH...
BECAUSE... I THOUGHT IT WOULD LOOK NICE...?
I LIKE YOUR...
...**UNIQUE** TAKE ON A SONG ABOUT A CIVIL WAR. BUT I DON'T UNDERSTAND THIS BORDER.
SO WHAT? IT'S JUST A DECORATION.
YOU HAVEN'T THOUGHT ABOUT **WHY** YOU'VE ADDED A BORDER.
YOU'RE IN YOUR SECOND YEAR NOW.
YOU REALLY SHOULD BE MOVING ON FROM EXPERIMENTING.

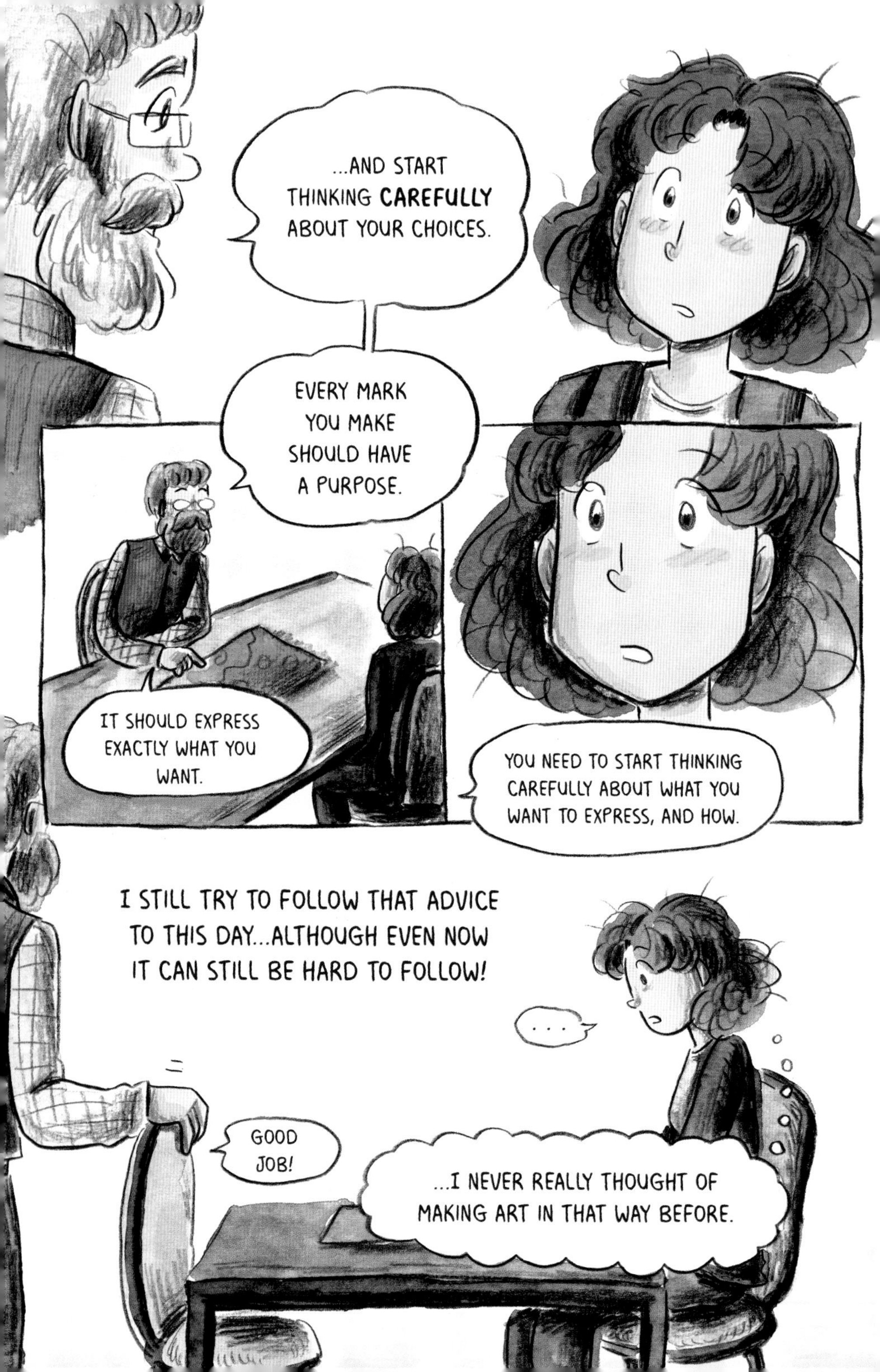
...AND START THINKING **CAREFULLY** ABOUT YOUR CHOICES.
EVERY MARK YOU MAKE SHOULD HAVE A PURPOSE.
IT SHOULD EXPRESS EXACTLY WHAT YOU WANT.
YOU NEED TO START THINKING CAREFULLY ABOUT WHAT YOU WANT TO EXPRESS, AND HOW.
I STILL TRY TO FOLLOW THAT ADVICE TO THIS DAY...ALTHOUGH EVEN NOW IT CAN STILL BE HARD TO FOLLOW!
. . .
GOOD JOB!
...I NEVER REALLY THOUGHT OF MAKING ART IN THAT WAY BEFORE.

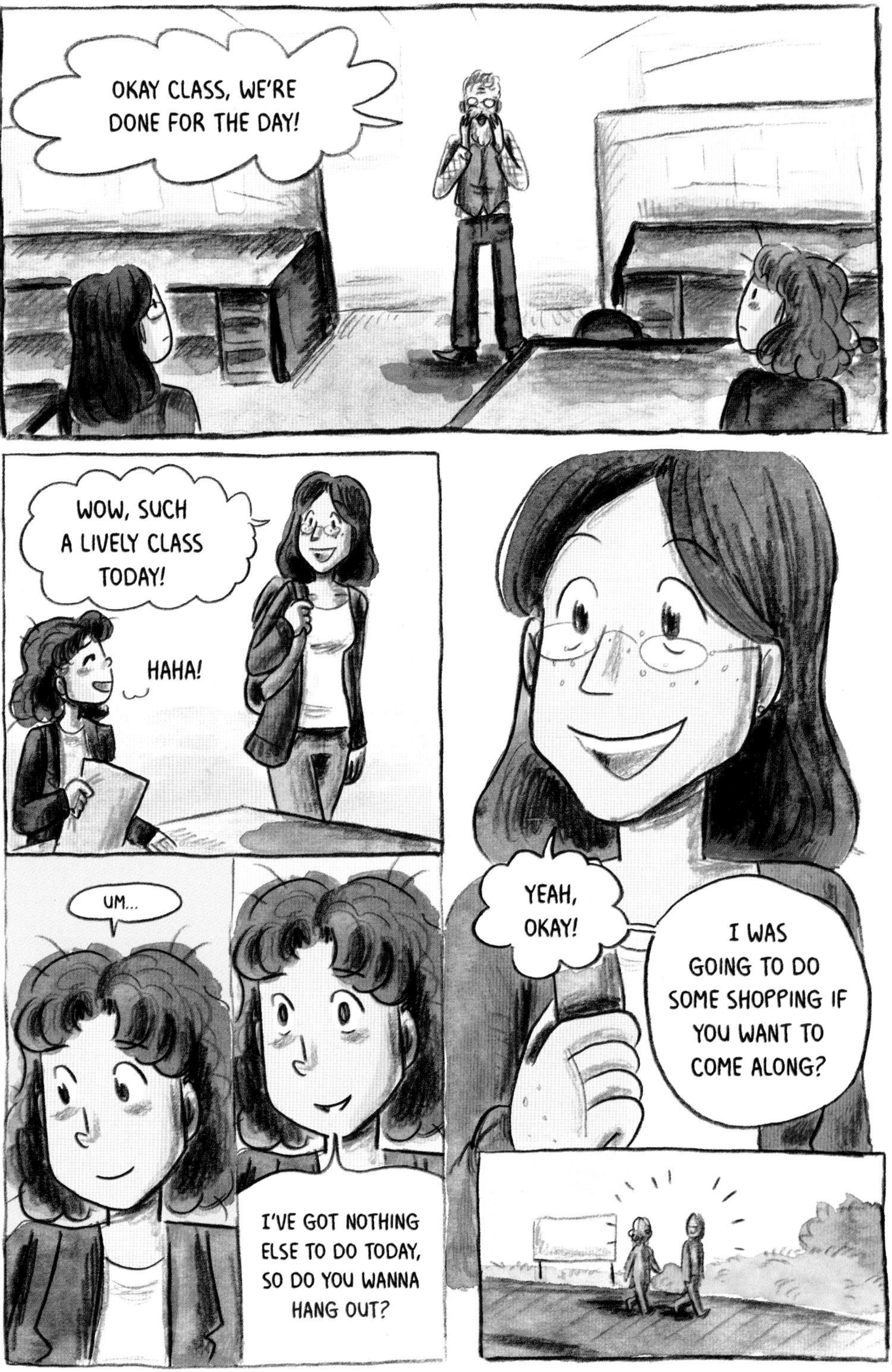
OKAY CLASS, WE'RE DONE FOR THE DAY!
WOW, SUCH A LIVELY CLASS TODAY!
HAHA!
YEAH, OKAY!
I WAS GOING TO DO SOME SHOPPING IF YOU WANT TO COME ALONG?
UM...
I'VE GOT NOTHING ELSE TO DO TODAY, SO DO YOU WANNA HANG OUT?

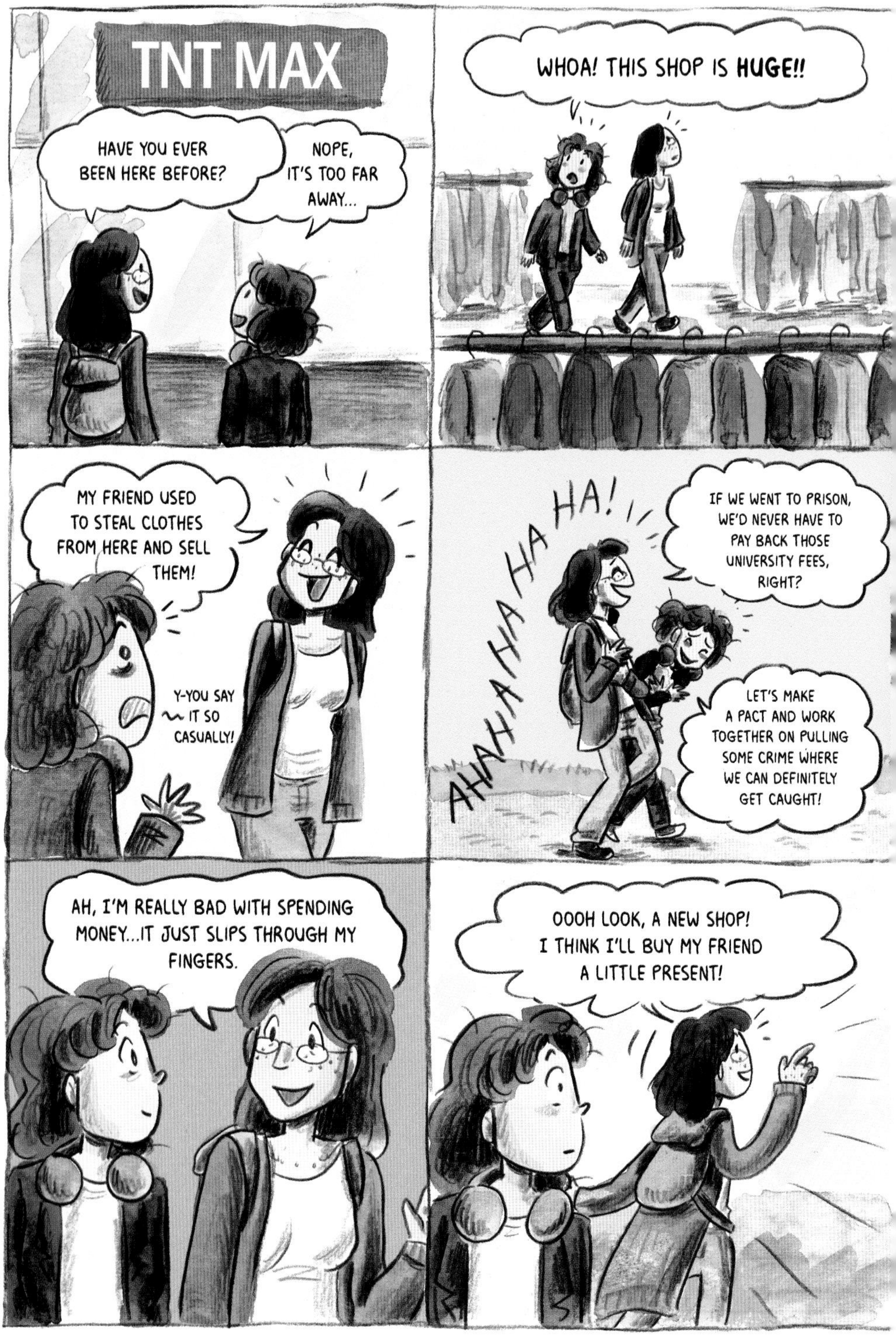
TNT MAX
HAVE YOU EVER BEEN HERE BEFORE?
NOPE, IT'S TOO FAR AWAY...
WHOA! THIS SHOP IS **HUGE!!**
MY FRIEND USED TO STEAL CLOTHES FROM HERE AND SELL THEM!
Y-YOU SAY IT SO CASUALLY!
AHAHAHAHA HA!
IF WE WENT TO PRISON, WE'D NEVER HAVE TO PAY BACK THOSE UNIVERSITY FEES, RIGHT?
LET'S MAKE A PACT AND WORK TOGETHER ON PULLING SOME CRIME WHERE WE CAN DEFINITELY GET CAUGHT!
AH, I'M REALLY BAD WITH SPENDING MONEY...IT JUST SLIPS THROUGH MY FINGERS.
OOOH LOOK, A NEW SHOP! I THINK I'LL BUY MY FRIEND A LITTLE PRESENT!

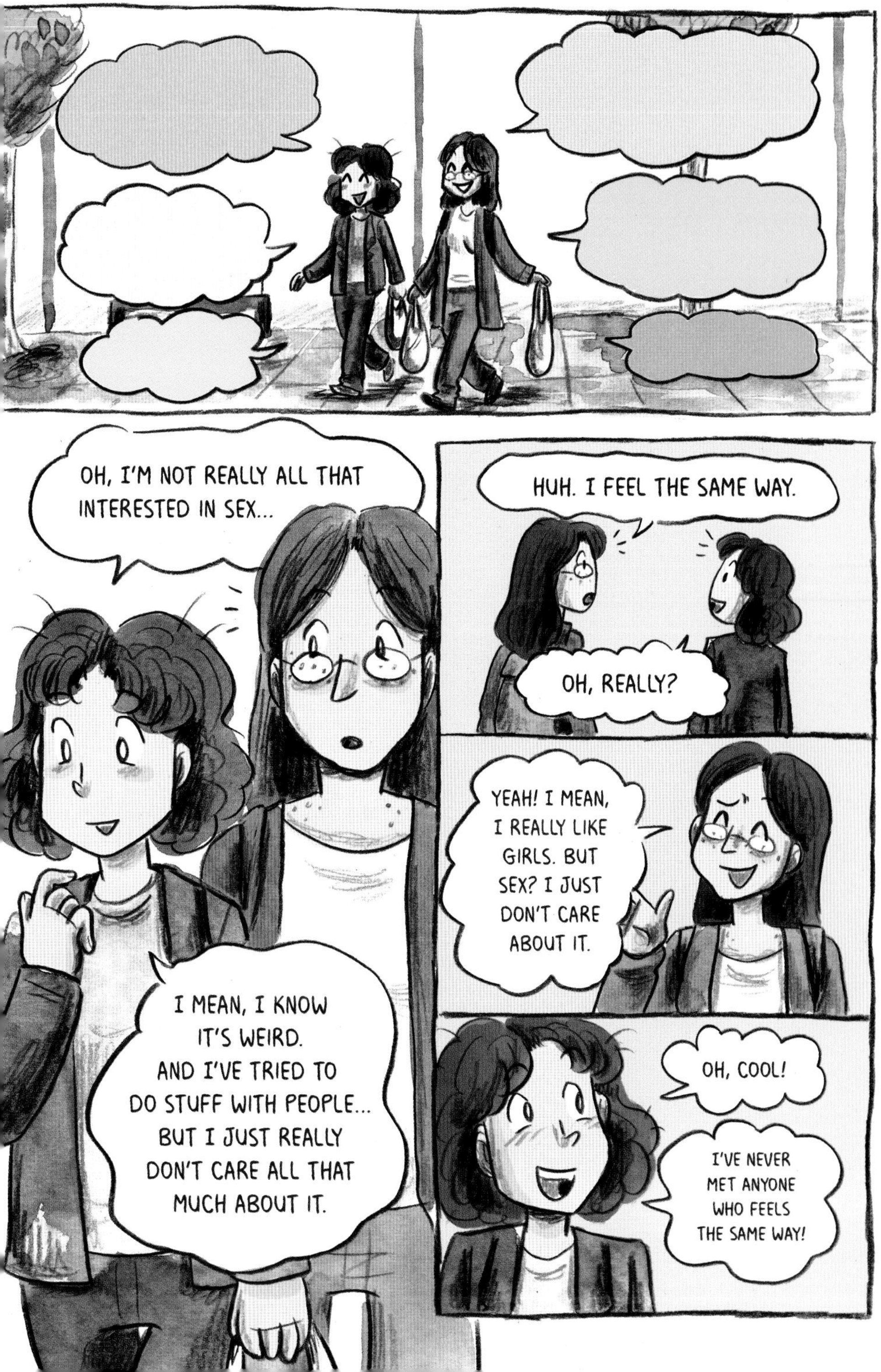
OH, I'M NOT REALLY ALL THAT INTERESTED IN SEX...
I MEAN, I KNOW IT'S WEIRD. AND I'VE TRIED TO DO STUFF WITH PEOPLE... BUT I JUST REALLY DON'T CARE ALL THAT MUCH ABOUT IT.
HUH. I FEEL THE SAME WAY.
OH, REALLY?
YEAH! I MEAN, I REALLY LIKE GIRLS. BUT SEX? I JUST DON'T CARE ABOUT IT.
OH, COOL!
I'VE NEVER MET ANYONE WHO FEELS THE SAME WAY!

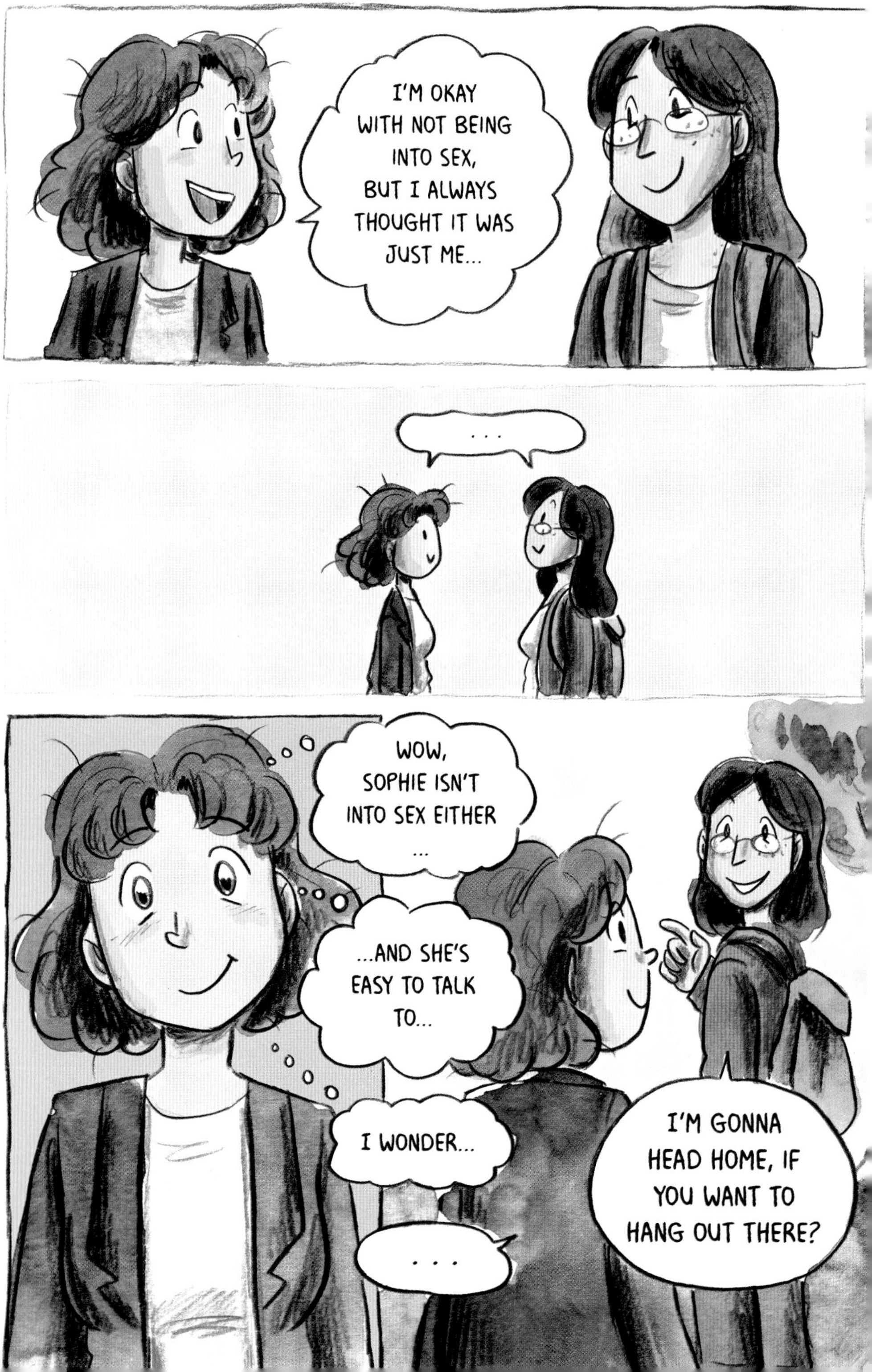
I'M OKAY WITH NOT BEING INTO SEX, BUT I ALWAYS THOUGHT IT WAS JUST ME...
. . .
WOW, SOPHIE ISN'T INTO SEX EITHER ...
...AND SHE'S EASY TO TALK TO...
I WONDER...
I'M GONNA HEAD HOME, IF YOU WANT TO HANG OUT THERE?
. . .

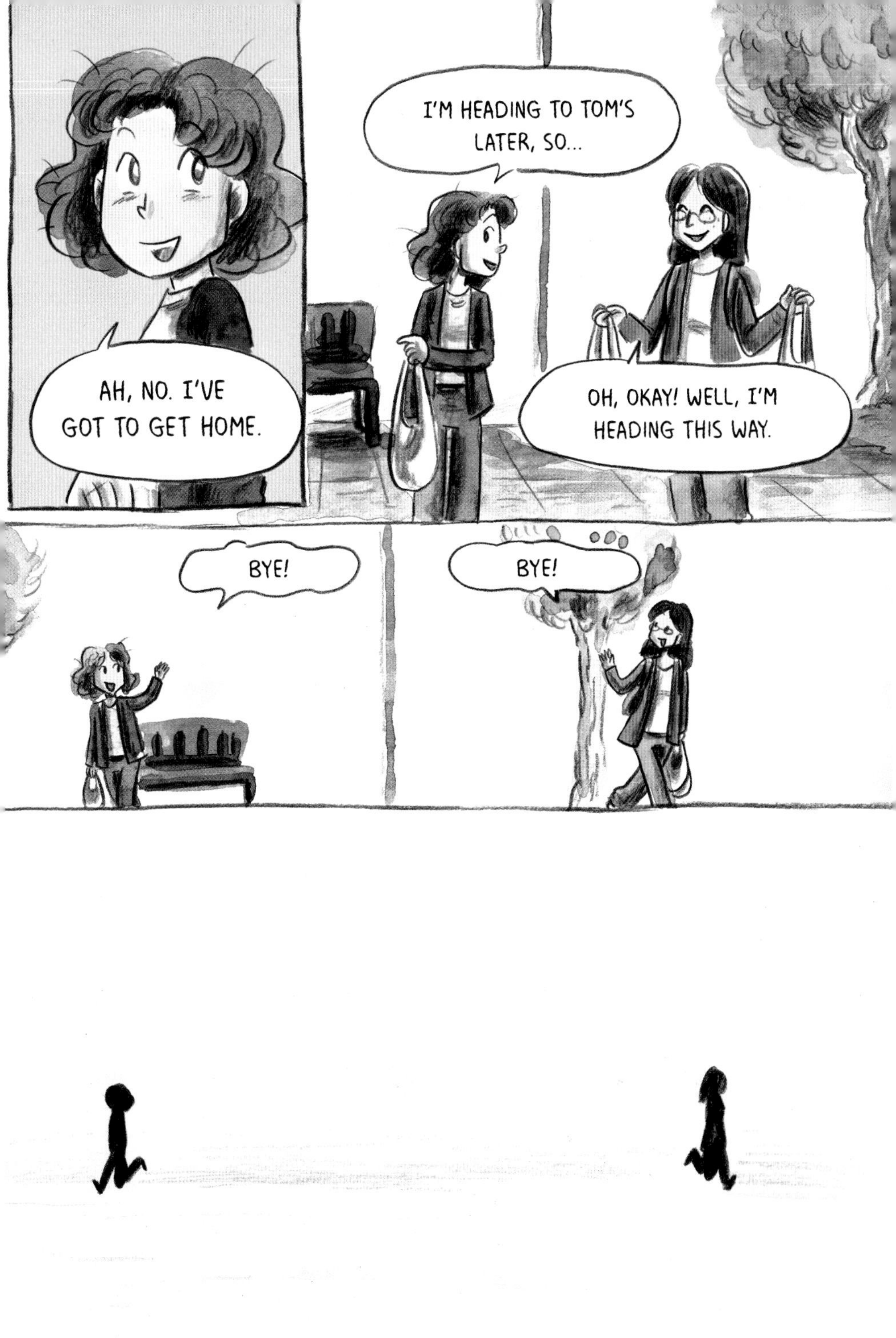
AH, NO. I'VE GOT TO GET HOME.
I'M HEADING TO TOM'S LATER, SO...
OH, OKAY! WELL, I'M HEADING THIS WAY.
BYE!
BYE!

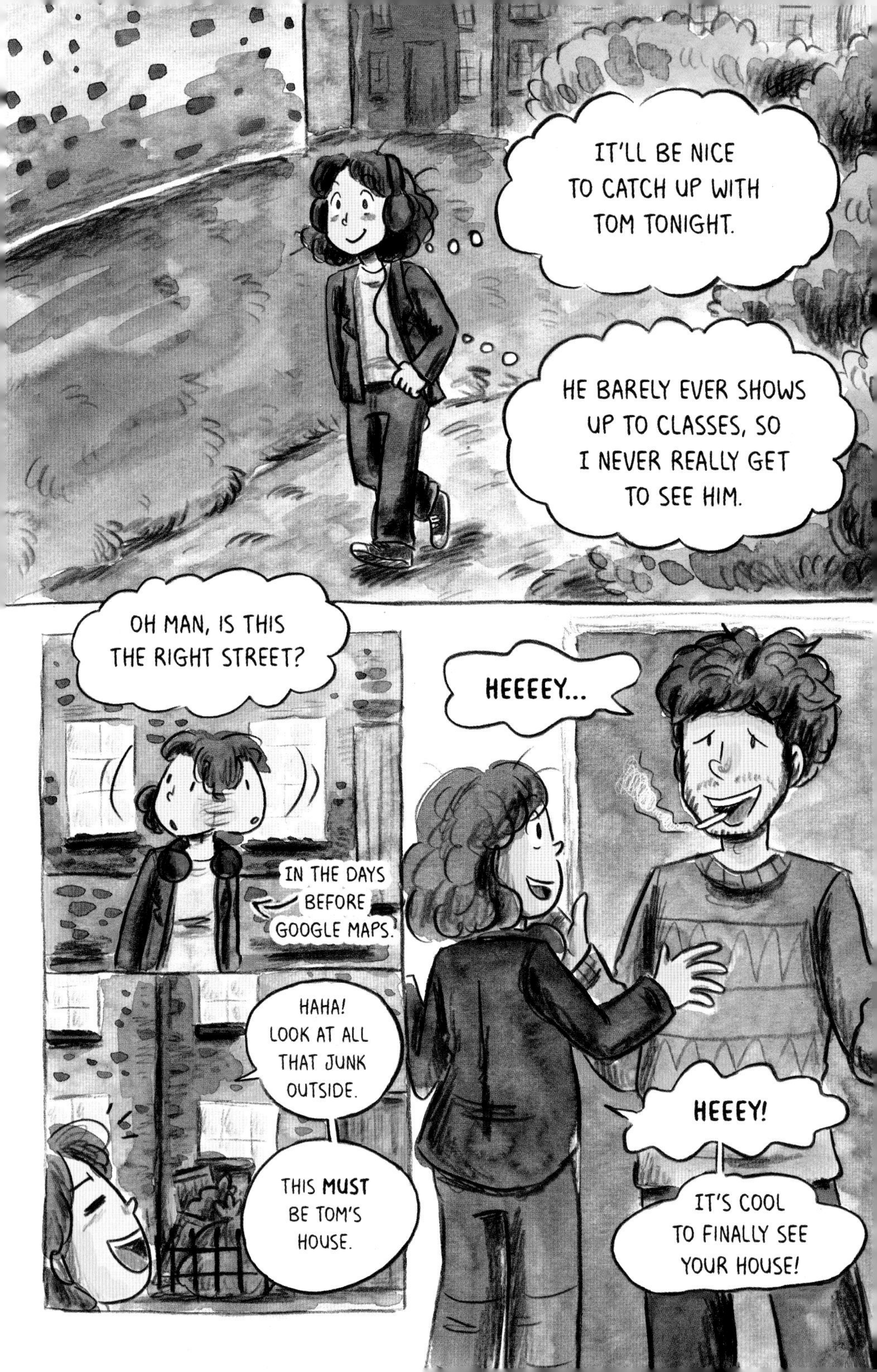
IT'LL BE NICE TO CATCH UP WITH TOM TONIGHT.
HE BARELY EVER SHOWS UP TO CLASSES, SO I NEVER REALLY GET TO SEE HIM.
OH MAN, IS THIS THE RIGHT STREET?
IN THE DAYS BEFORE GOOGLE MAPS.
HAHA! LOOK AT ALL THAT JUNK OUTSIDE.
THIS **MUST** BE TOM'S HOUSE.
**HEEEEY...**
**HEEEY!**
IT'S COOL TO FINALLY SEE YOUR HOUSE!

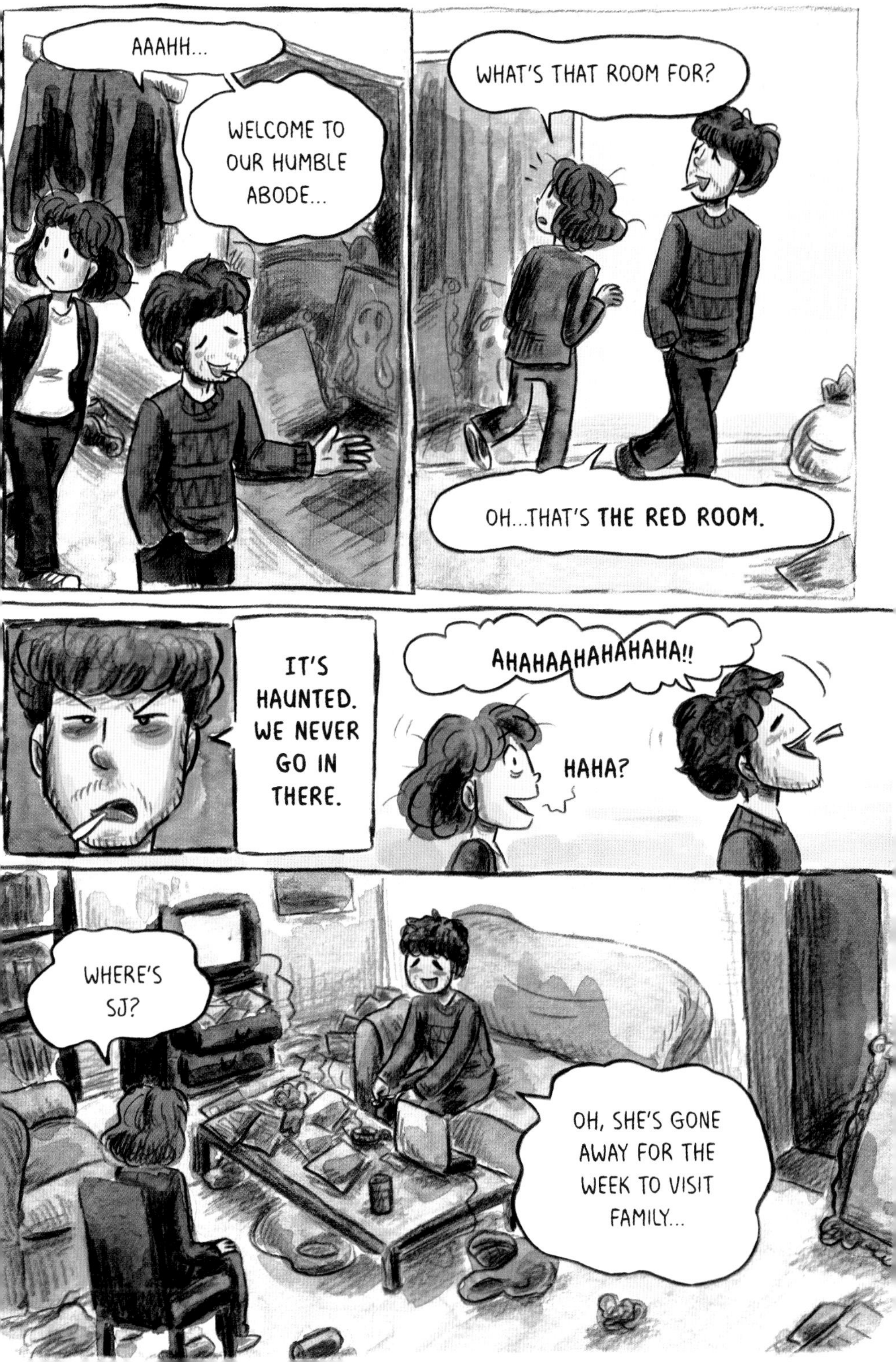
AAAHH...
WELCOME TO OUR HUMBLE ABODE...
WHAT'S THAT ROOM FOR?
OH...THAT'S **THE RED ROOM.**
IT'S HAUNTED. WE NEVER GO IN THERE.
AHAHAAHAHAHAHA!!
HAHA?
WHERE'S SJ?
OH, SHE'S GONE AWAY FOR THE WEEK TO VISIT FAMILY...

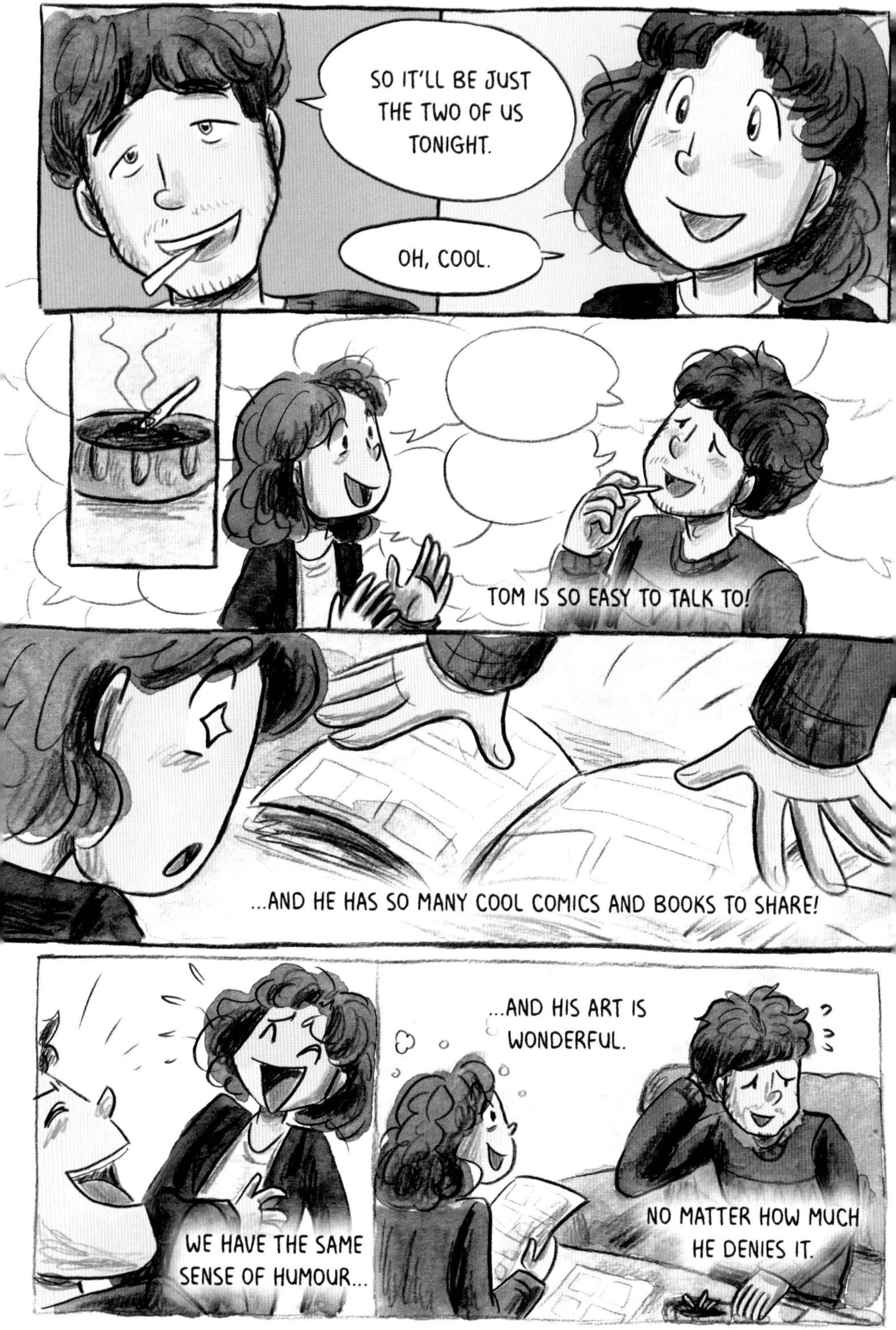
SO IT'LL BE JUST THE TWO OF US TONIGHT.
OH, COOL.
TOM IS SO EASY TO TALK TO!
...AND HE HAS SO MANY COOL COMICS AND BOOKS TO SHARE!
WE HAVE THE SAME SENSE OF HUMOUR...
...AND HIS ART IS WONDERFUL.
NO MATTER HOW MUCH HE DENIES IT.

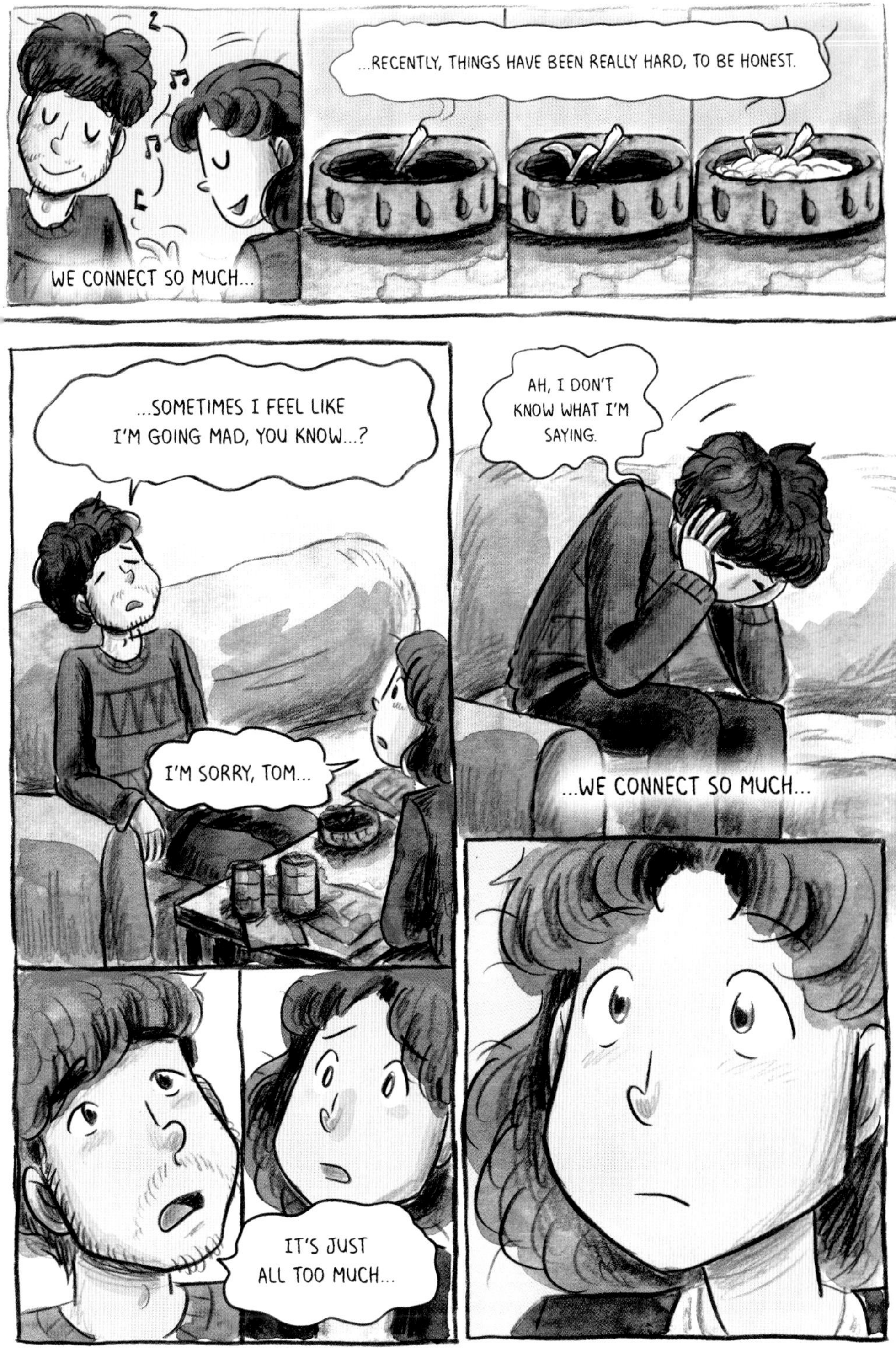
WE CONNECT SO MUCH...
...RECENTLY, THINGS HAVE BEEN REALLY HARD, TO BE HONEST.
...SOMETIMES I FEEL LIKE I'M GOING MAD, YOU KNOW...?
I'M SORRY, TOM...
AH, I DON'T KNOW WHAT I'M SAYING.
...WE CONNECT SO MUCH...
IT'S JUST ALL TOO MUCH...

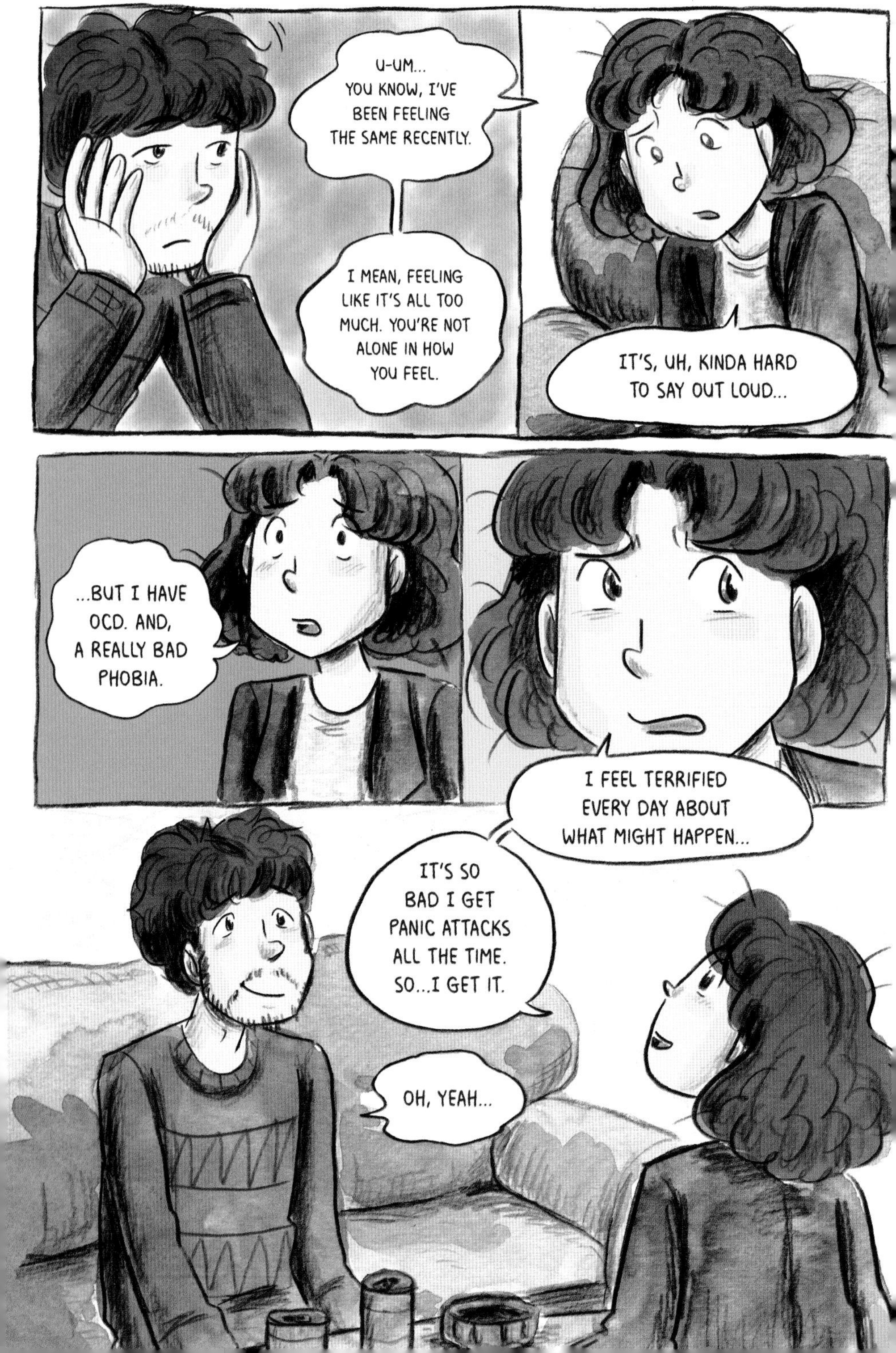
U-UM... YOU KNOW, I'VE BEEN FEELING THE SAME RECENTLY.
I MEAN, FEELING LIKE IT'S ALL TOO MUCH. YOU'RE NOT ALONE IN HOW YOU FEEL.
IT'S, UH, KINDA HARD TO SAY OUT LOUD...
...BUT I HAVE OCD. AND, A REALLY BAD PHOBIA.
I FEEL TERRIFIED EVERY DAY ABOUT WHAT MIGHT HAPPEN...
IT'S SO BAD I GET PANIC ATTACKS ALL THE TIME. SO...I GET IT.
OH, YEAH...

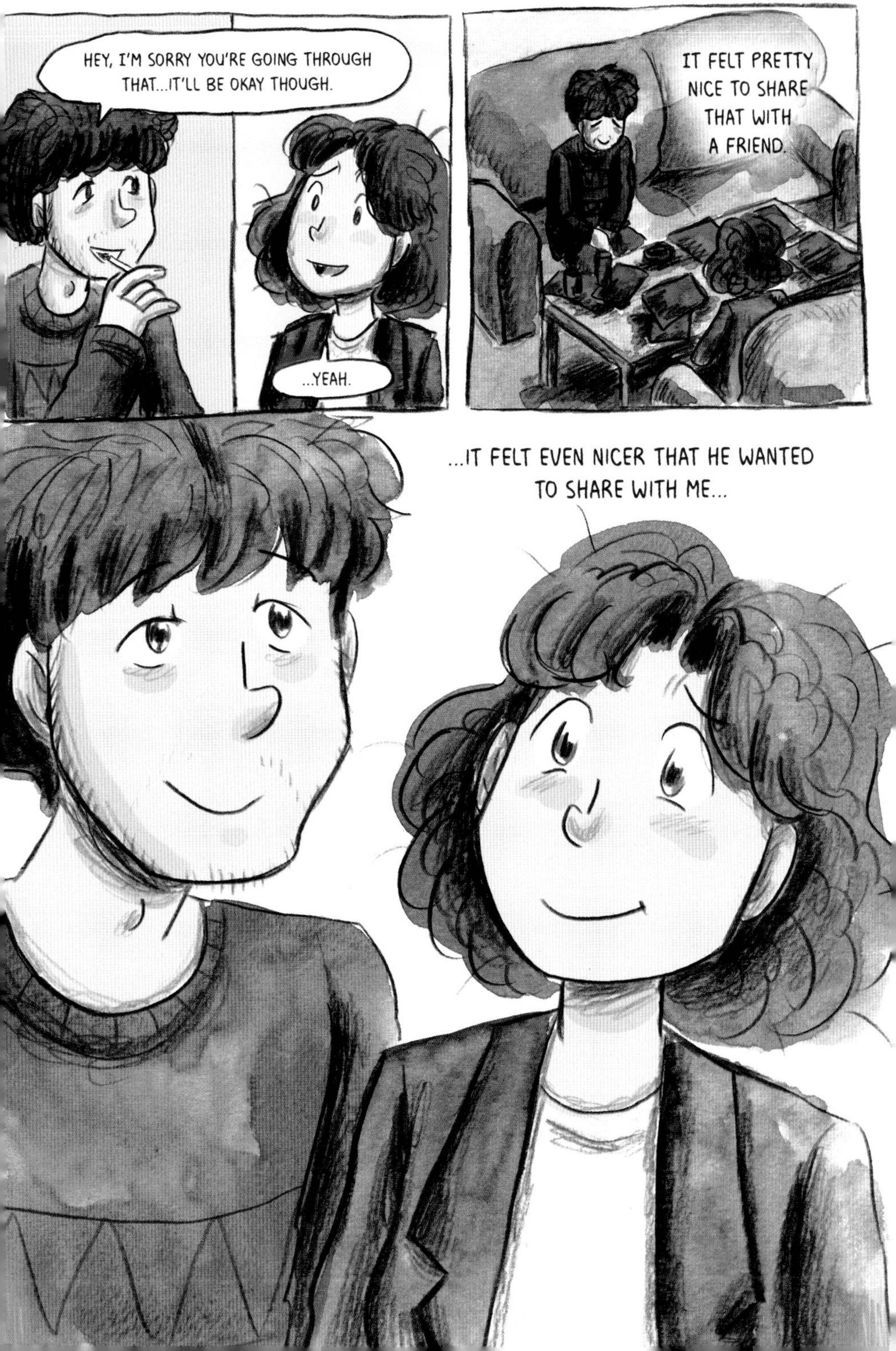
HEY, I'M SORRY YOU'RE GOING THROUGH THAT...IT'LL BE OKAY THOUGH.
...YEAH.
IT FELT PRETTY NICE TO SHARE THAT WITH A FRIEND.
...IT FELT EVEN NICER THAT HE WANTED TO SHARE WITH ME...

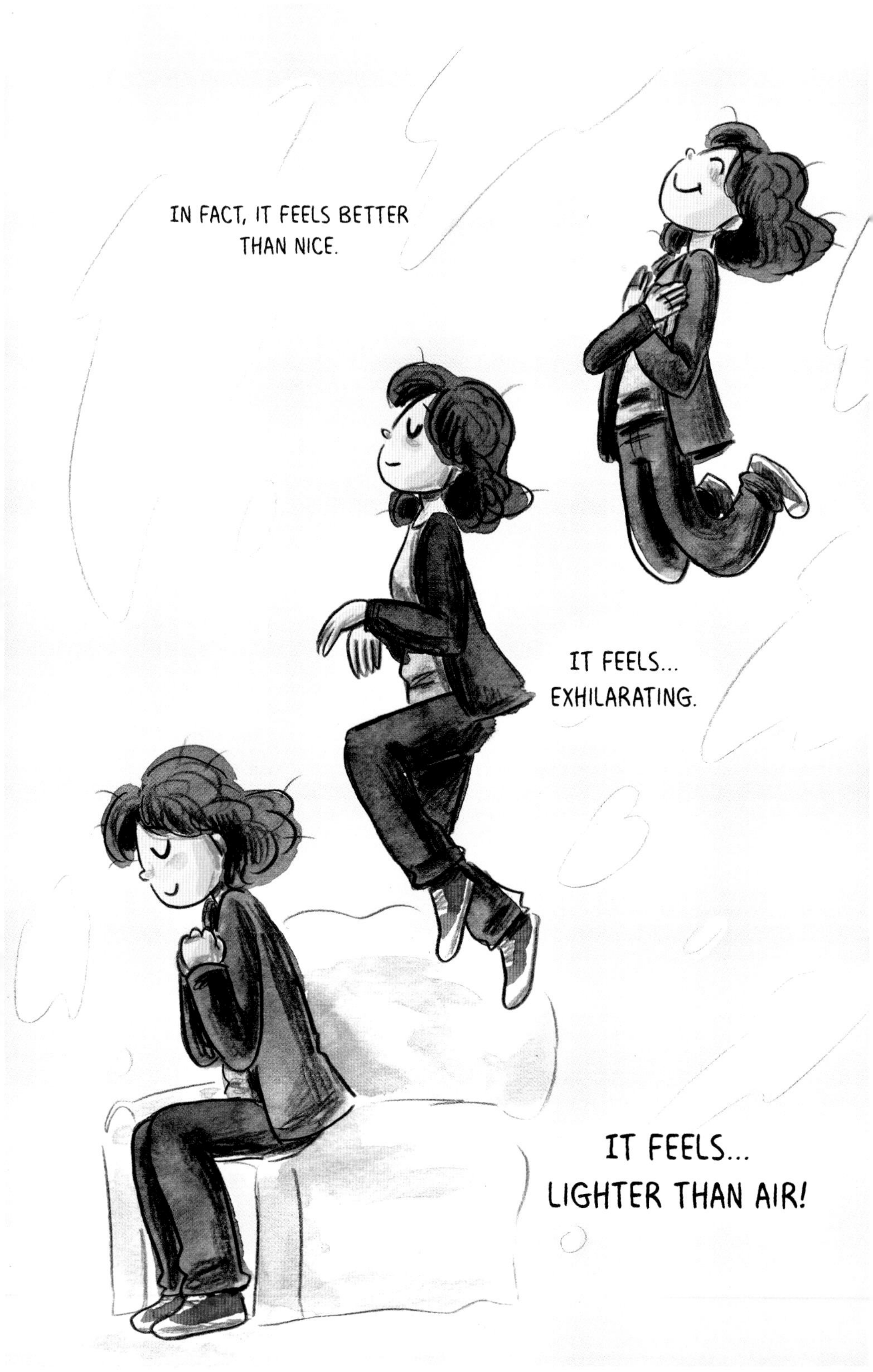
IN FACT, IT FEELS BETTER THAN NICE.
IT FEELS... EXHILARATING.
IT FEELS... LIGHTER THAN AIR!

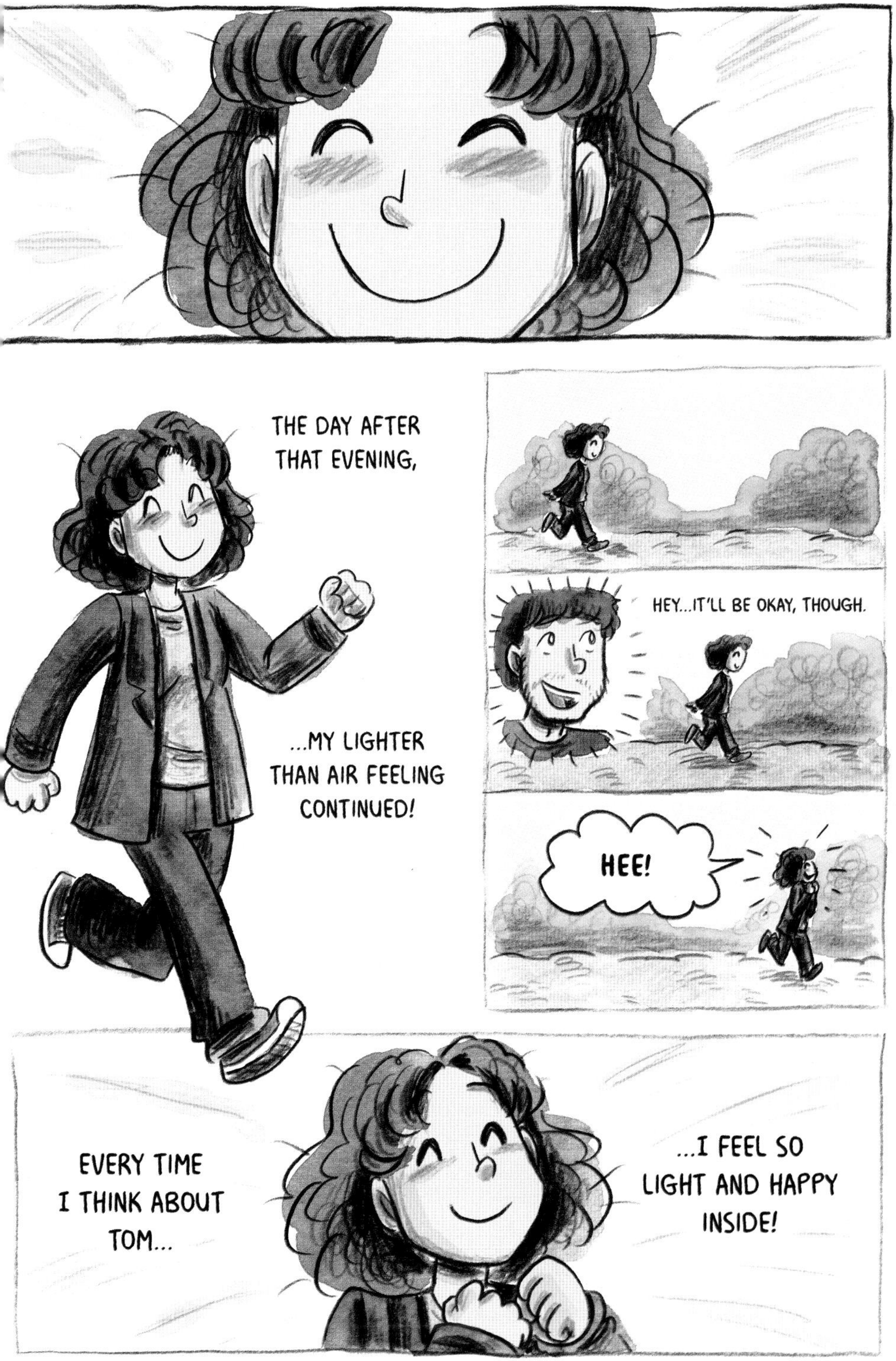
THE DAY AFTER THAT EVENING,
...MY LIGHTER THAN AIR FEELING CONTINUED!
HEY...IT'LL BE OKAY, THOUGH.
HEE!
EVERY TIME I THINK ABOUT TOM...
...I FEEL SO LIGHT AND HAPPY INSIDE!

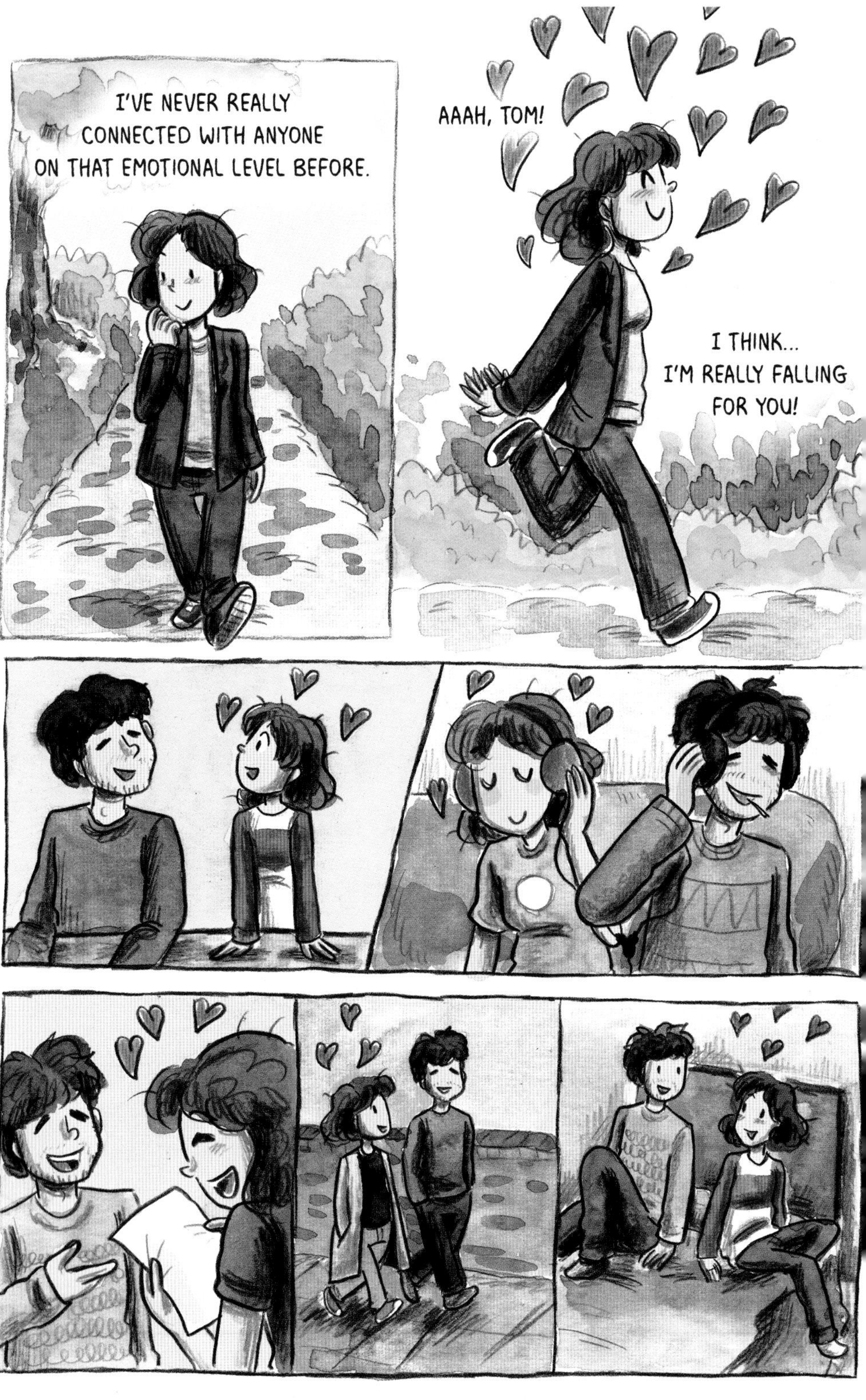
I'VE NEVER REALLY CONNECTED WITH ANYONE ON THAT EMOTIONAL LEVEL BEFORE.
AAAH, TOM!
I THINK... I'M REALLY FALLING FOR YOU!

AH...

HEY, WHY DON'T...

...YOU COME HERE...

UUH.

...LET'S BE A LITTLE CLOSER, YEAH?

THERE.

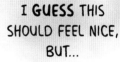

I **GUESS** THIS SHOULD FEEL NICE, BUT...

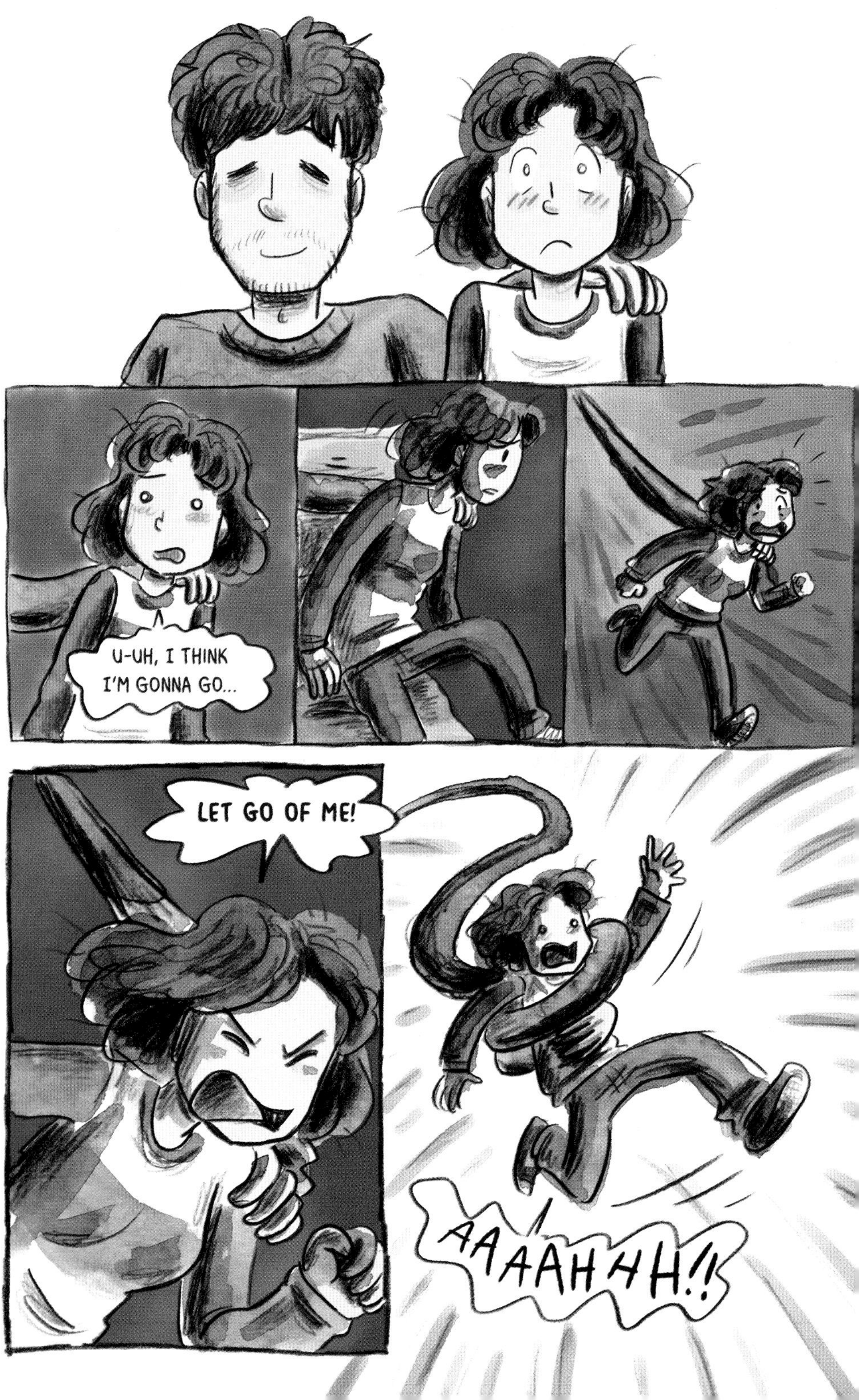
U-UH, I THINK I'M GONNA GO...
LET GO OF ME!
AAAAHHH!!

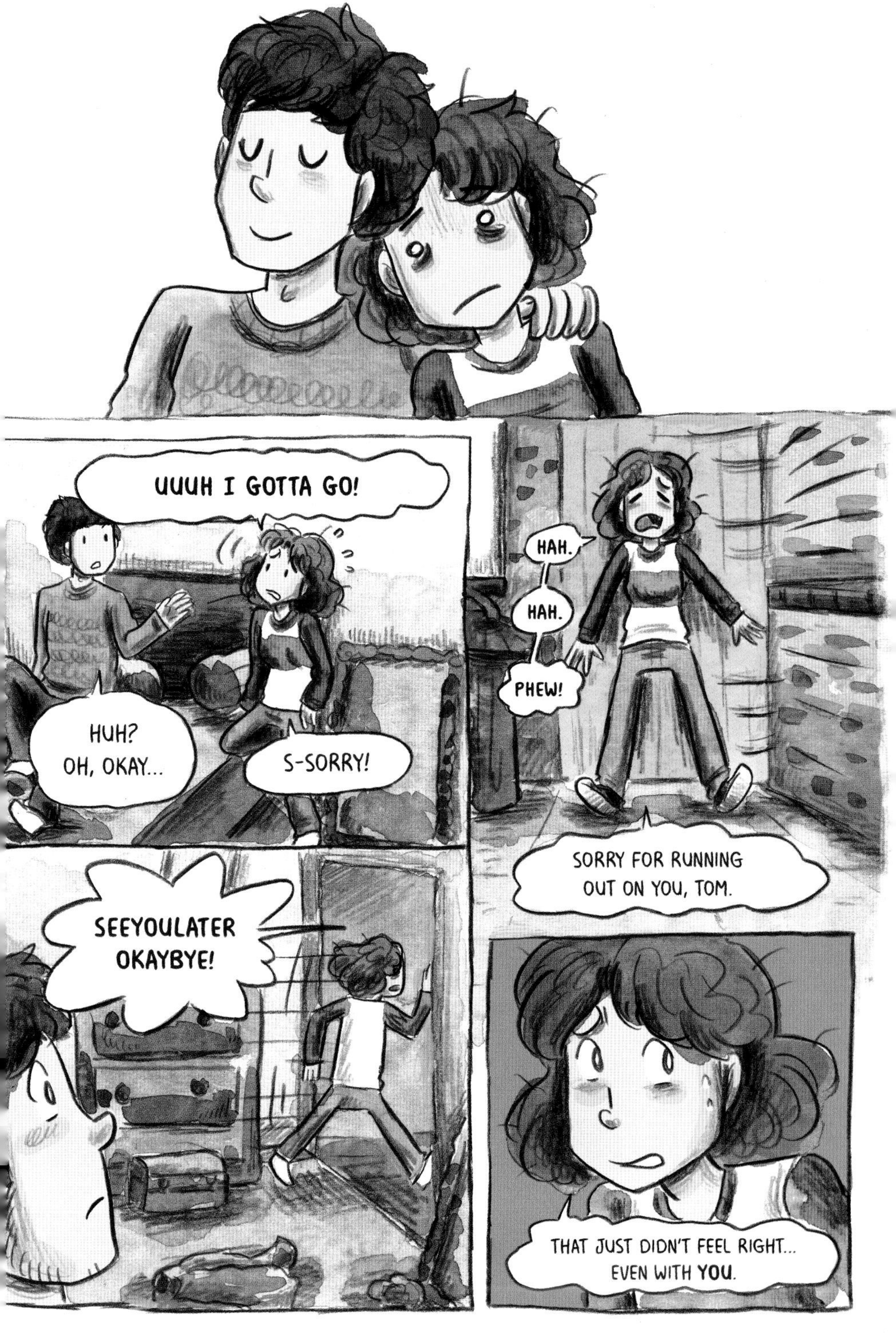
UUUH I GOTTA GO!
HUH?
OH, OKAY...
S-SORRY!
HAH.
HAH.
PHEW!
SORRY FOR RUNNING OUT ON YOU, TOM.
SEEYOULATER OKAYBYE!
THAT JUST DIDN'T FEEL RIGHT... EVEN WITH **YOU**.

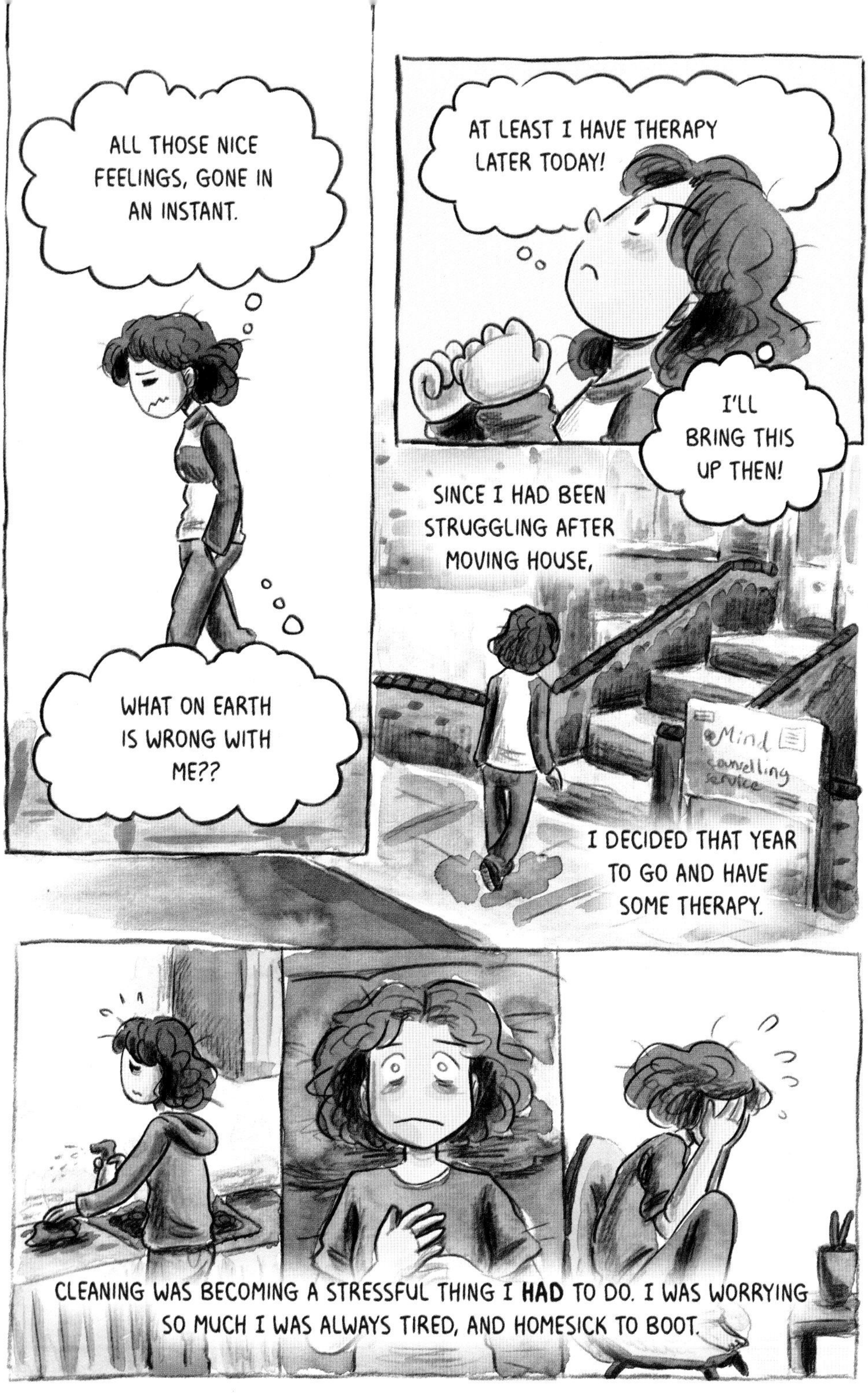

ALL THOSE NICE FEELINGS, GONE IN AN INSTANT.
WHAT ON EARTH IS WRONG WITH ME??
AT LEAST I HAVE THERAPY LATER TODAY!
I'LL BRING THIS UP THEN!
SINCE I HAD BEEN STRUGGLING AFTER MOVING HOUSE,
Mind counselling service
I DECIDED THAT YEAR TO GO AND HAVE SOME THERAPY.
CLEANING WAS BECOMING A STRESSFUL THING I **HAD** TO DO. I WAS WORRYING SO MUCH I WAS ALWAYS TIRED, AND HOMESICK TO BOOT.

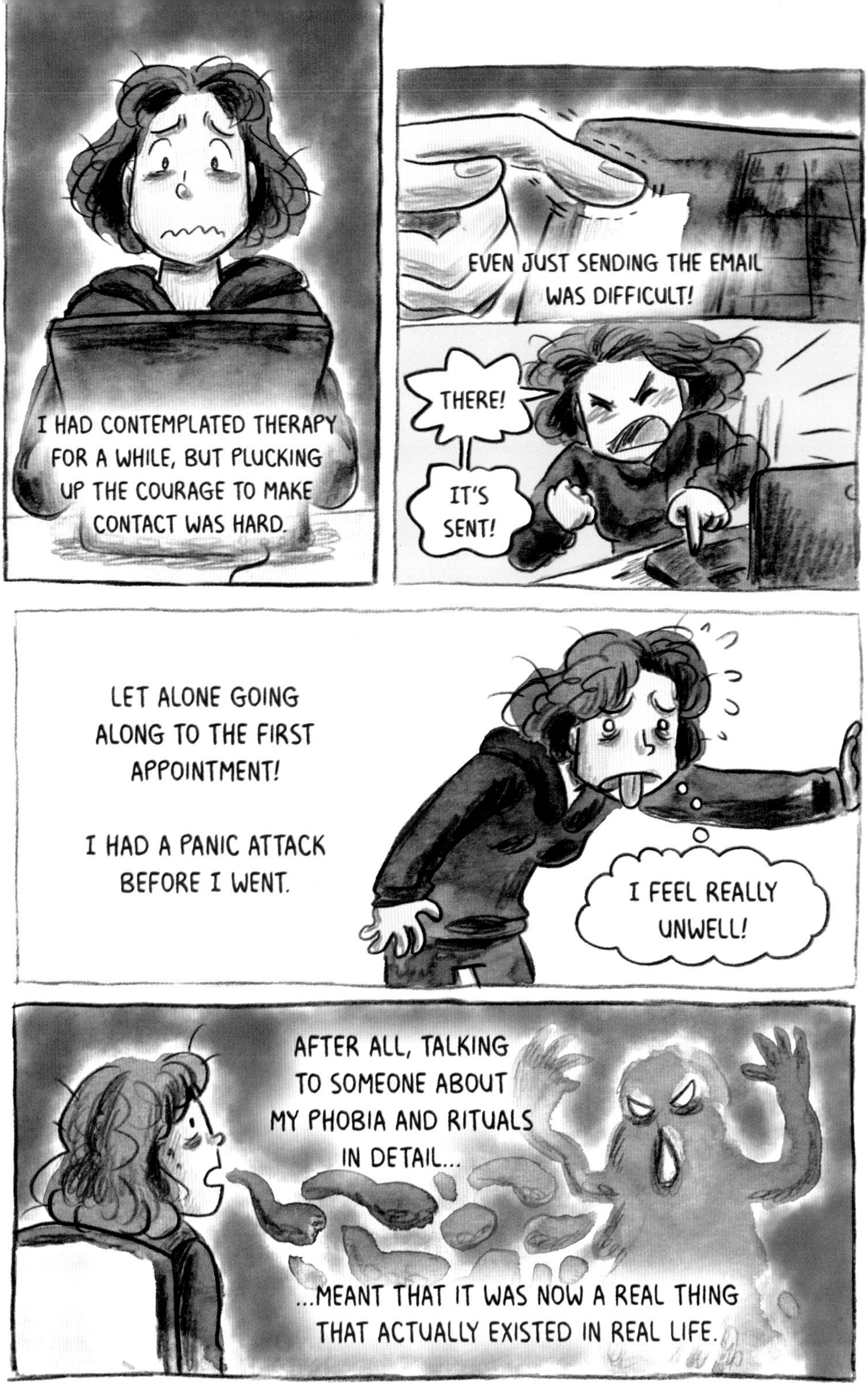

I HAD CONTEMPLATED THERAPY FOR A WHILE, BUT PLUCKING UP THE COURAGE TO MAKE CONTACT WAS HARD.
EVEN JUST SENDING THE EMAIL WAS DIFFICULT!
THERE!
IT'S SENT!
LET ALONE GOING ALONG TO THE FIRST APPOINTMENT!
I HAD A PANIC ATTACK BEFORE I WENT.
I FEEL REALLY UNWELL!
AFTER ALL, TALKING TO SOMEONE ABOUT MY PHOBIA AND RITUALS IN DETAIL...
...MEANT THAT IT WAS NOW A REAL THING THAT ACTUALLY EXISTED IN REAL LIFE.

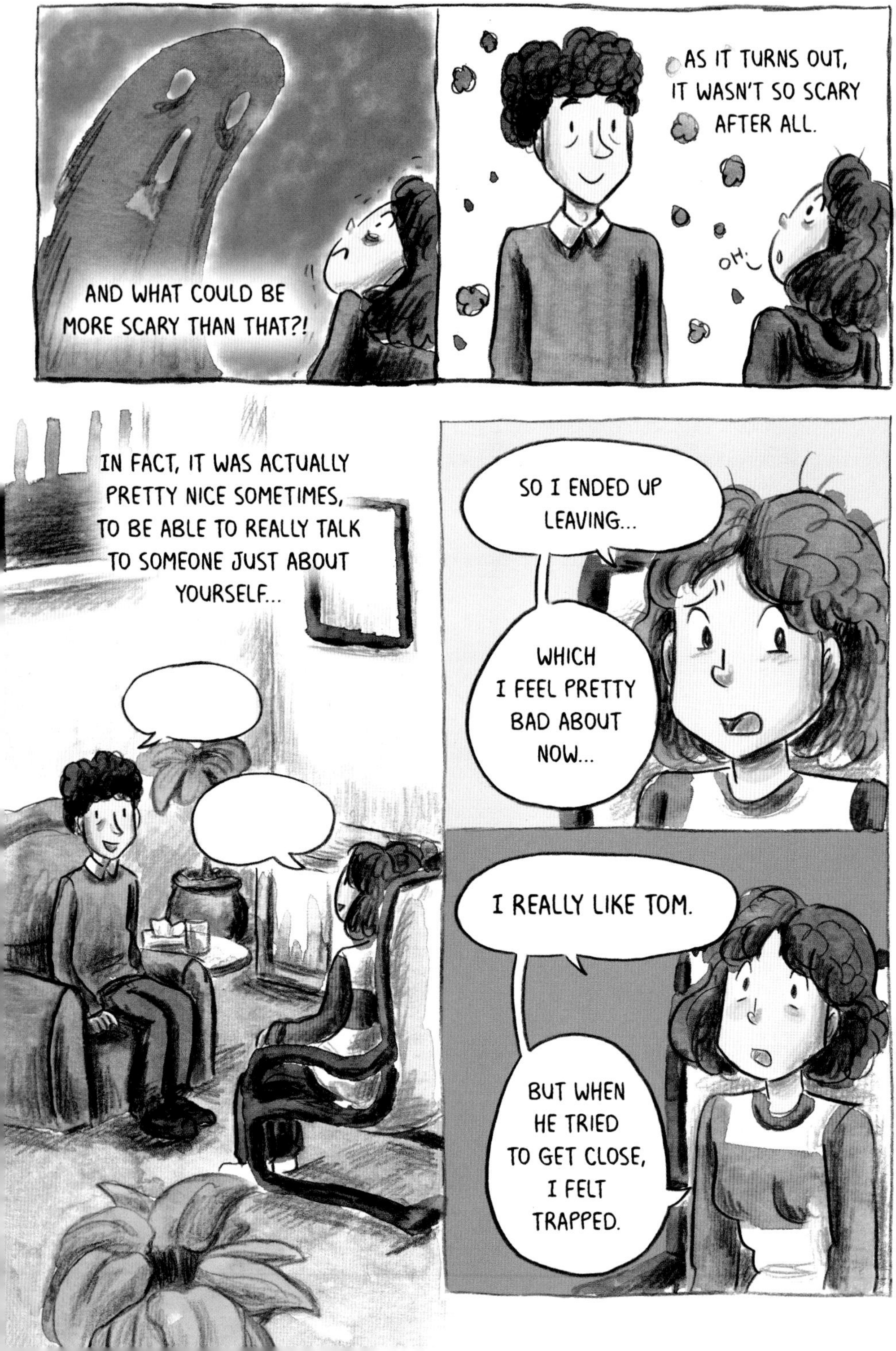
AND WHAT COULD BE MORE SCARY THAN THAT?!
AS IT TURNS OUT, IT WASN'T SO SCARY AFTER ALL.
OH!
IN FACT, IT WAS ACTUALLY PRETTY NICE SOMETIMES, TO BE ABLE TO REALLY TALK TO SOMEONE JUST ABOUT YOURSELF...
SO I ENDED UP LEAVING...
WHICH I FEEL PRETTY BAD ABOUT NOW...
I REALLY LIKE TOM.
BUT WHEN HE TRIED TO GET CLOSE, I FELT TRAPPED.

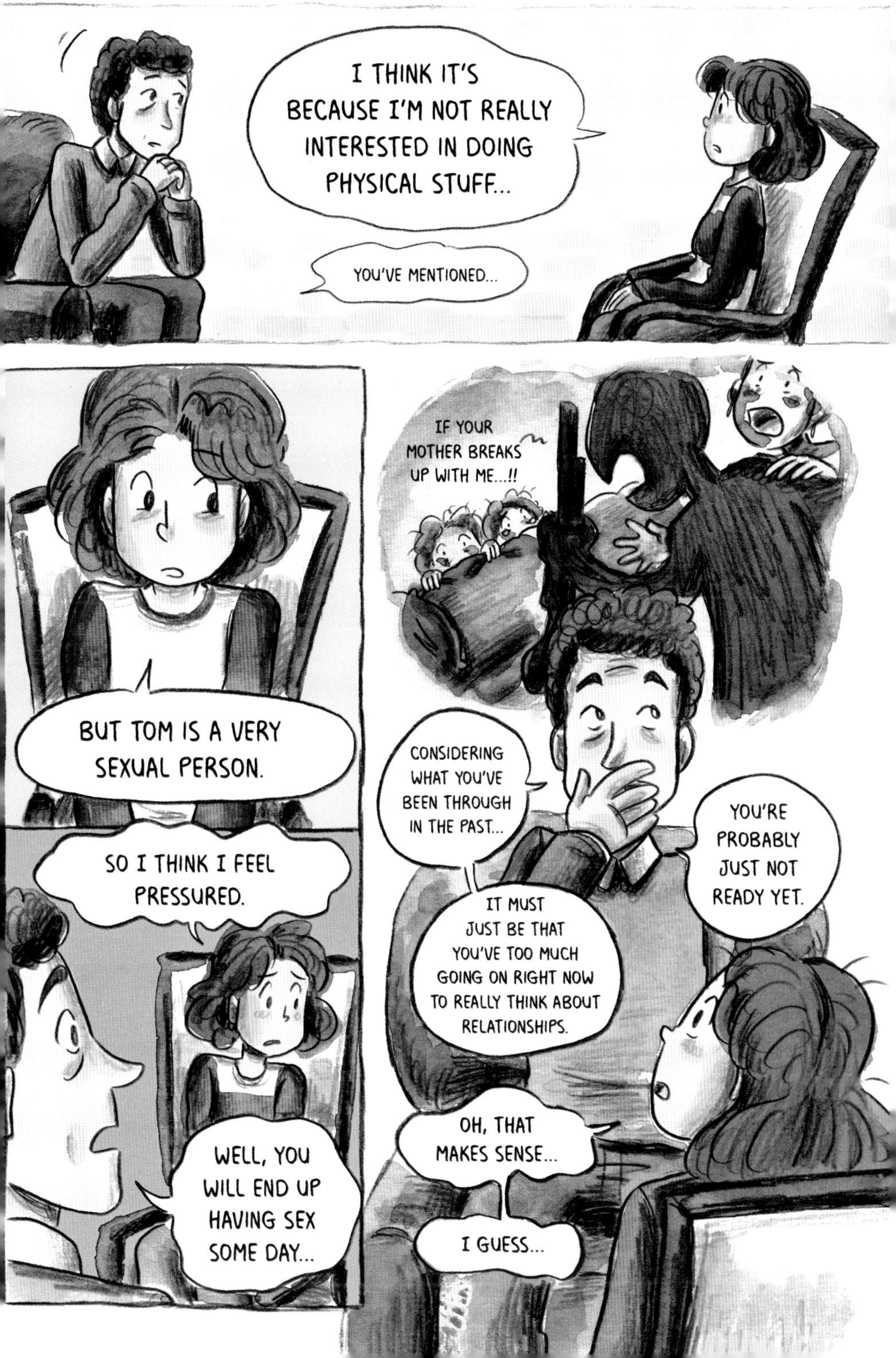
I THINK IT'S BECAUSE I'M NOT REALLY INTERESTED IN DOING PHYSICAL STUFF...
YOU'VE MENTIONED...
BUT TOM IS A VERY SEXUAL PERSON.
SO I THINK I FEEL PRESSURED.
WELL, YOU WILL END UP HAVING SEX SOME DAY...
IF YOUR MOTHER BREAKS UP WITH ME...!!
CONSIDERING WHAT YOU'VE BEEN THROUGH IN THE PAST...
IT MUST JUST BE THAT YOU'VE TOO MUCH GOING ON RIGHT NOW TO REALLY THINK ABOUT RELATIONSHIPS.
YOU'RE PROBABLY JUST NOT READY YET.
OH, THAT MAKES SENSE...
I GUESS...

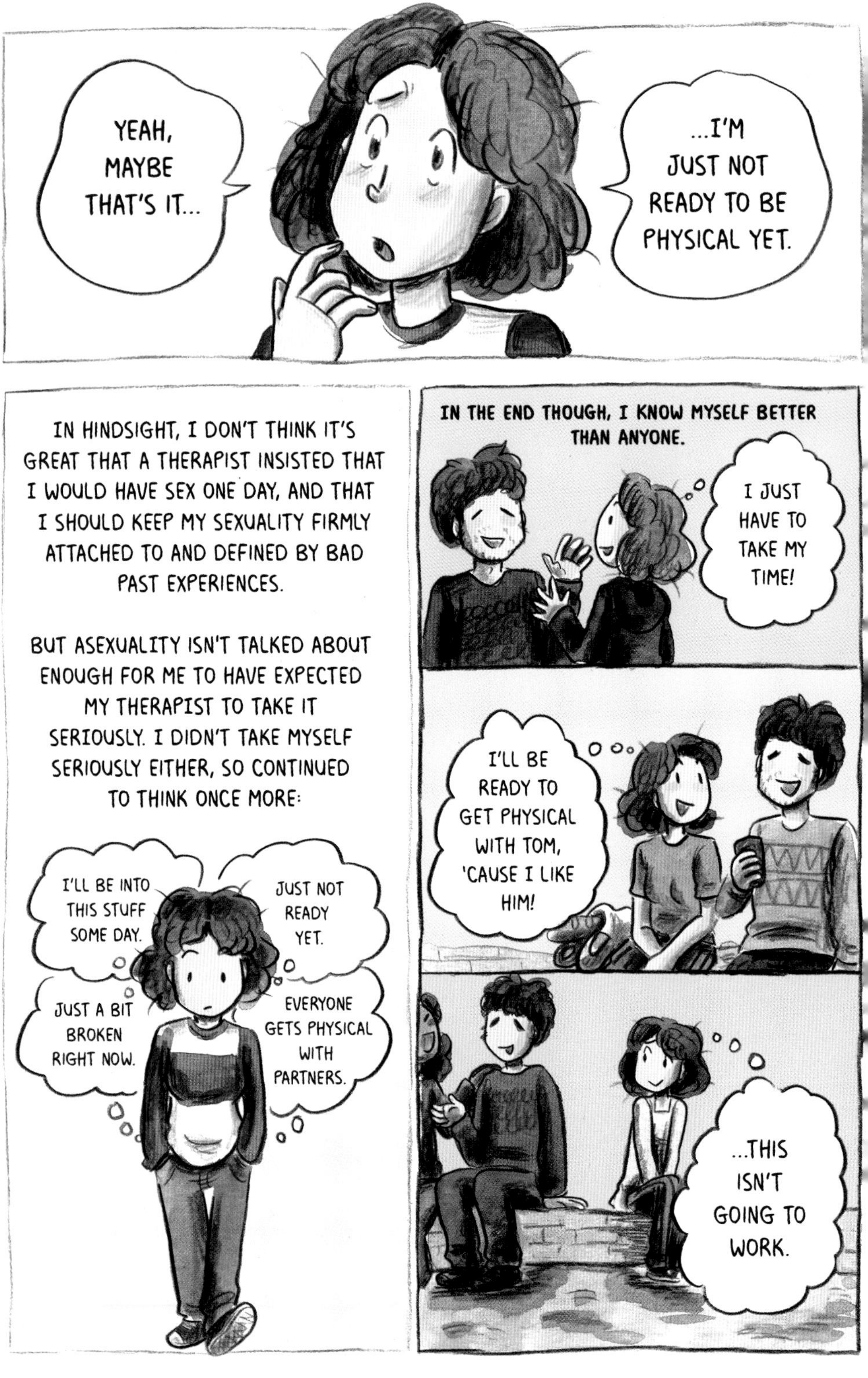
YEAH, MAYBE THAT'S IT...
...I'M JUST NOT READY TO BE PHYSICAL YET.
IN HINDSIGHT, I DON'T THINK IT'S GREAT THAT A THERAPIST INSISTED THAT I WOULD HAVE SEX ONE DAY, AND THAT I SHOULD KEEP MY SEXUALITY FIRMLY ATTACHED TO AND DEFINED BY BAD PAST EXPERIENCES.
BUT ASEXUALITY ISN'T TALKED ABOUT ENOUGH FOR ME TO HAVE EXPECTED MY THERAPIST TO TAKE IT SERIOUSLY. I DIDN'T TAKE MYSELF SERIOUSLY EITHER, SO CONTINUED TO THINK ONCE MORE:
I'LL BE INTO THIS STUFF SOME DAY.
JUST NOT READY YET.
JUST A BIT BROKEN RIGHT NOW.
EVERYONE GETS PHYSICAL WITH PARTNERS.
IN THE END THOUGH, I KNOW MYSELF BETTER THAN ANYONE.
I JUST HAVE TO TAKE MY TIME!
I'LL BE READY TO GET PHYSICAL WITH TOM, 'CAUSE I LIKE HIM!
...THIS ISN'T GOING TO WORK.

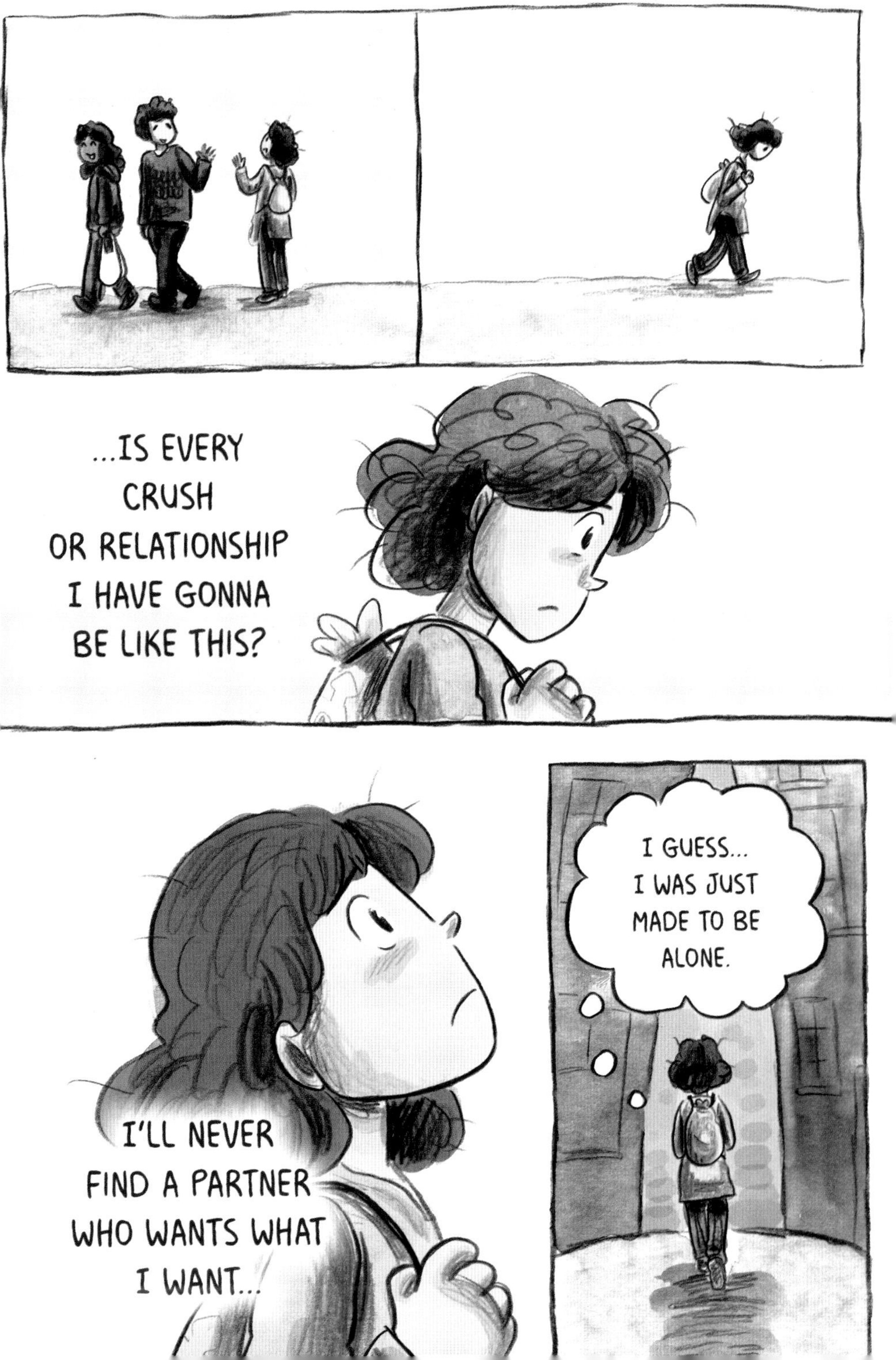
...IS EVERY CRUSH OR RELATIONSHIP I HAVE GONNA BE LIKE THIS?
I'LL NEVER FIND A PARTNER WHO WANTS WHAT I WANT...
I GUESS... I WAS JUST MADE TO BE ALONE.

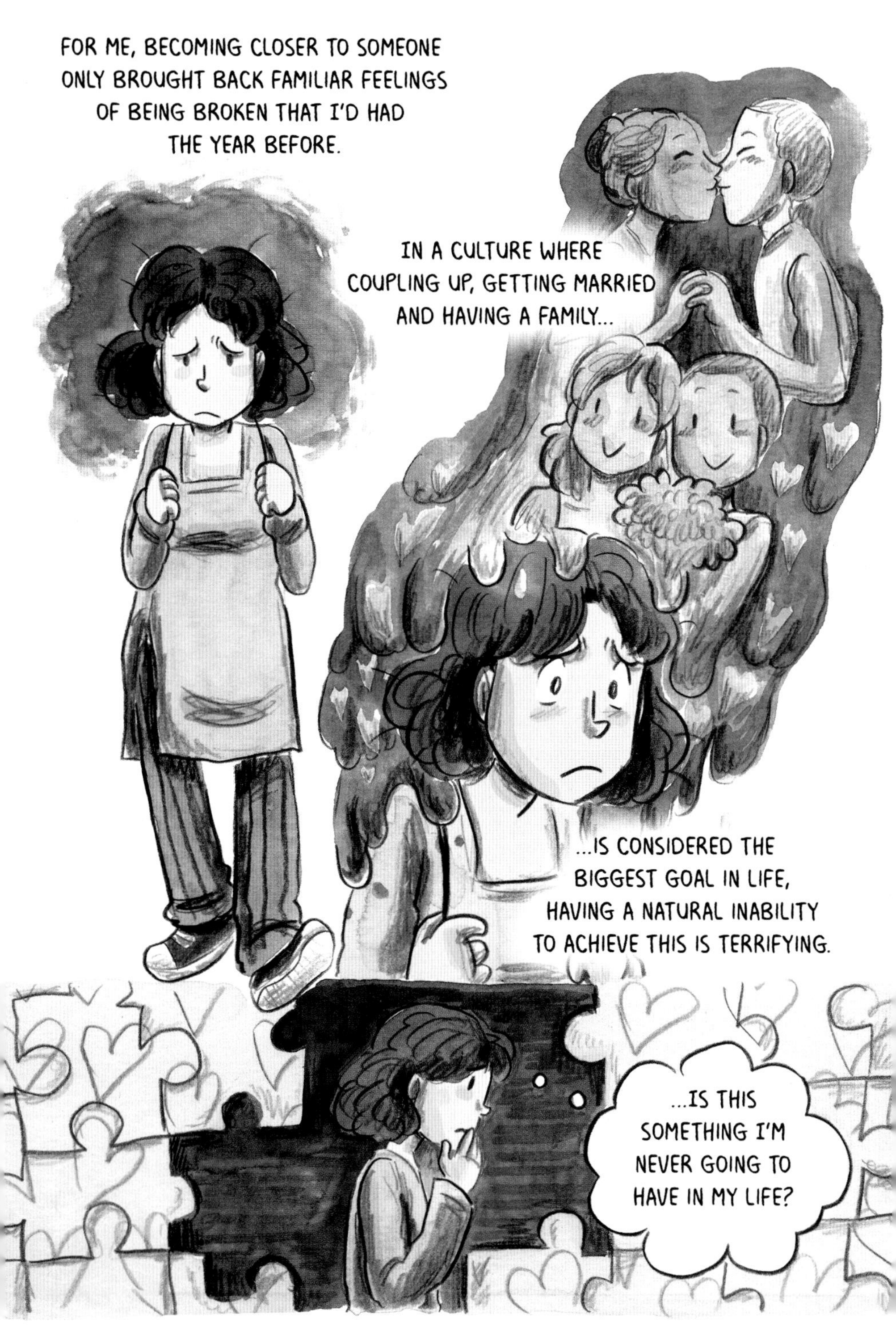
FOR ME, BECOMING CLOSER TO SOMEONE ONLY BROUGHT BACK FAMILIAR FEELINGS OF BEING BROKEN THAT I'D HAD THE YEAR BEFORE.
IN A CULTURE WHERE COUPLING UP, GETTING MARRIED AND HAVING A FAMILY...
...IS CONSIDERED THE BIGGEST GOAL IN LIFE, HAVING A NATURAL INABILITY TO ACHIEVE THIS IS TERRIFYING.
...IS THIS SOMETHING I'M NEVER GOING TO HAVE IN MY LIFE?

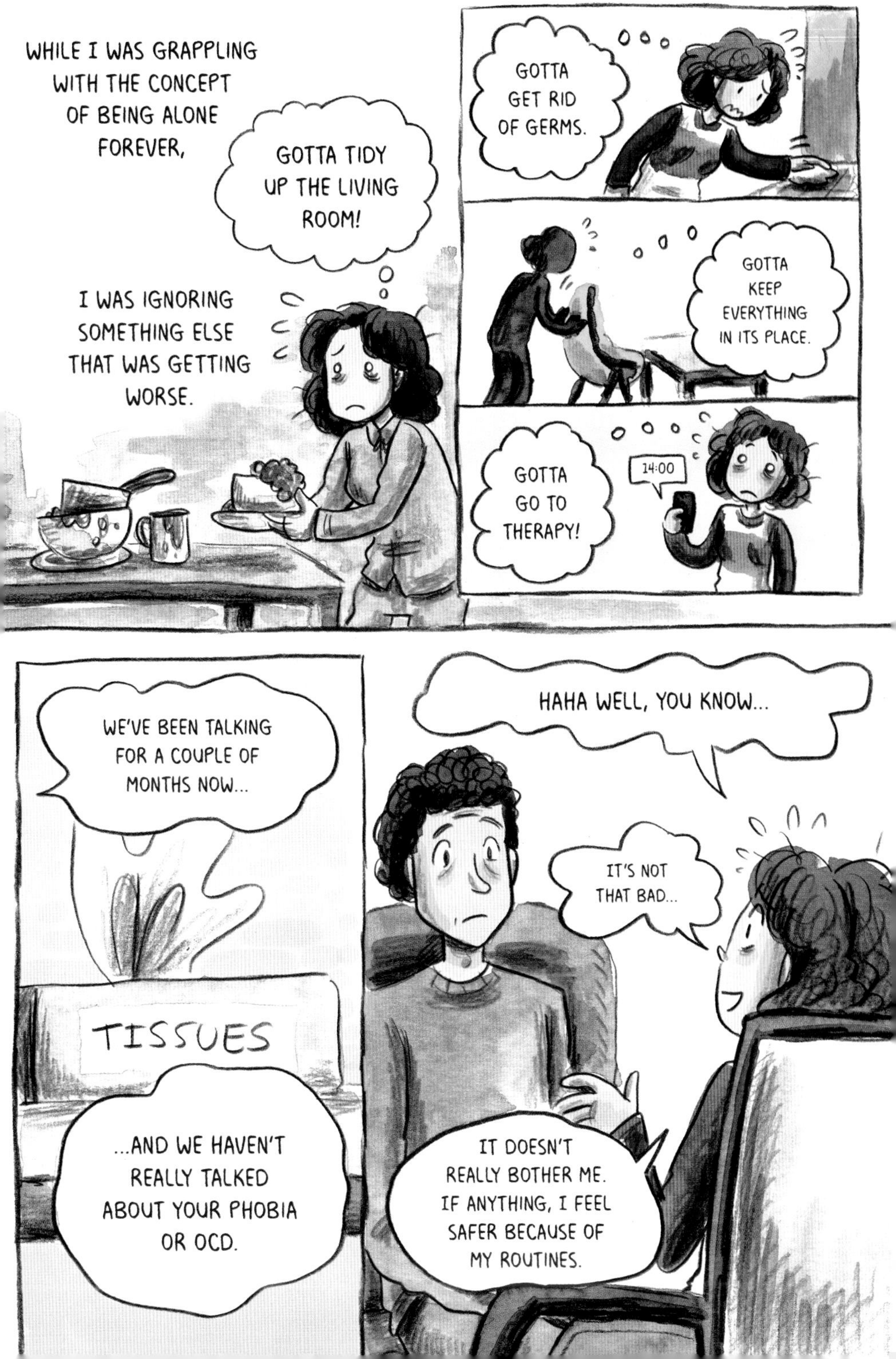
WHILE I WAS GRAPPLING WITH THE CONCEPT OF BEING ALONE FOREVER,
GOTTA TIDY UP THE LIVING ROOM!
I WAS IGNORING SOMETHING ELSE THAT WAS GETTING WORSE.
GOTTA GET RID OF GERMS.
GOTTA KEEP EVERYTHING IN ITS PLACE.
14:00
GOTTA GO TO THERAPY!
WE'VE BEEN TALKING FOR A COUPLE OF MONTHS NOW...
TISSUES
...AND WE HAVEN'T REALLY TALKED ABOUT YOUR PHOBIA OR OCD.
HAHA WELL, YOU KNOW...
IT'S NOT THAT BAD...
IT DOESN'T REALLY BOTHER ME. IF ANYTHING, I FEEL SAFER BECAUSE OF MY ROUTINES.

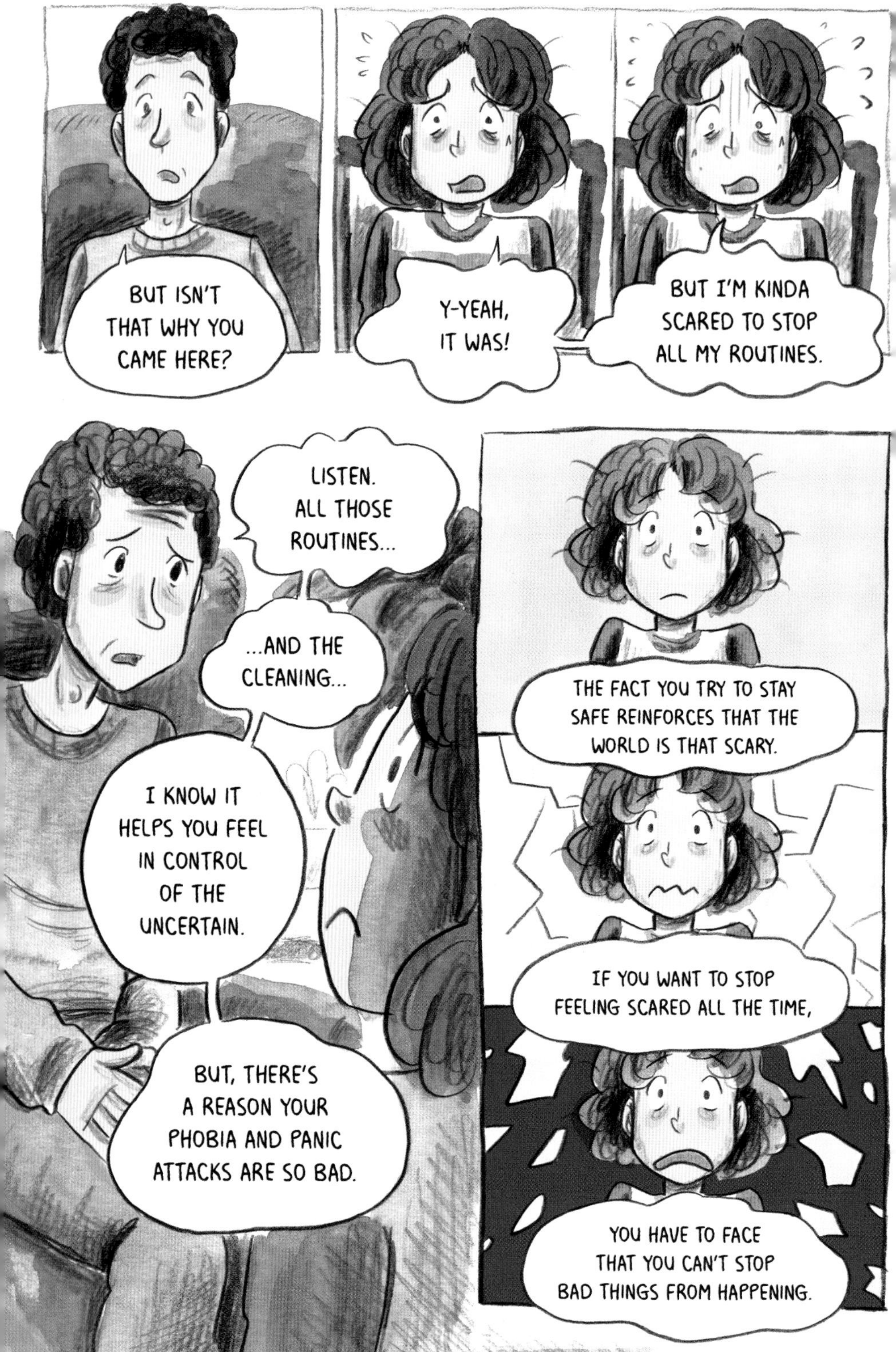
BUT ISN'T THAT WHY YOU CAME HERE?
Y-YEAH, IT WAS!
BUT I'M KINDA SCARED TO STOP ALL MY ROUTINES.
LISTEN. ALL THOSE ROUTINES...
...AND THE CLEANING...
I KNOW IT HELPS YOU FEEL IN CONTROL OF THE UNCERTAIN.
BUT, THERE'S A REASON YOUR PHOBIA AND PANIC ATTACKS ARE SO BAD.
THE FACT YOU TRY TO STAY SAFE REINFORCES THAT THE WORLD IS THAT SCARY.
IF YOU WANT TO STOP FEELING SCARED ALL THE TIME,
YOU HAVE TO FACE THAT YOU CAN'T STOP BAD THINGS FROM HAPPENING.

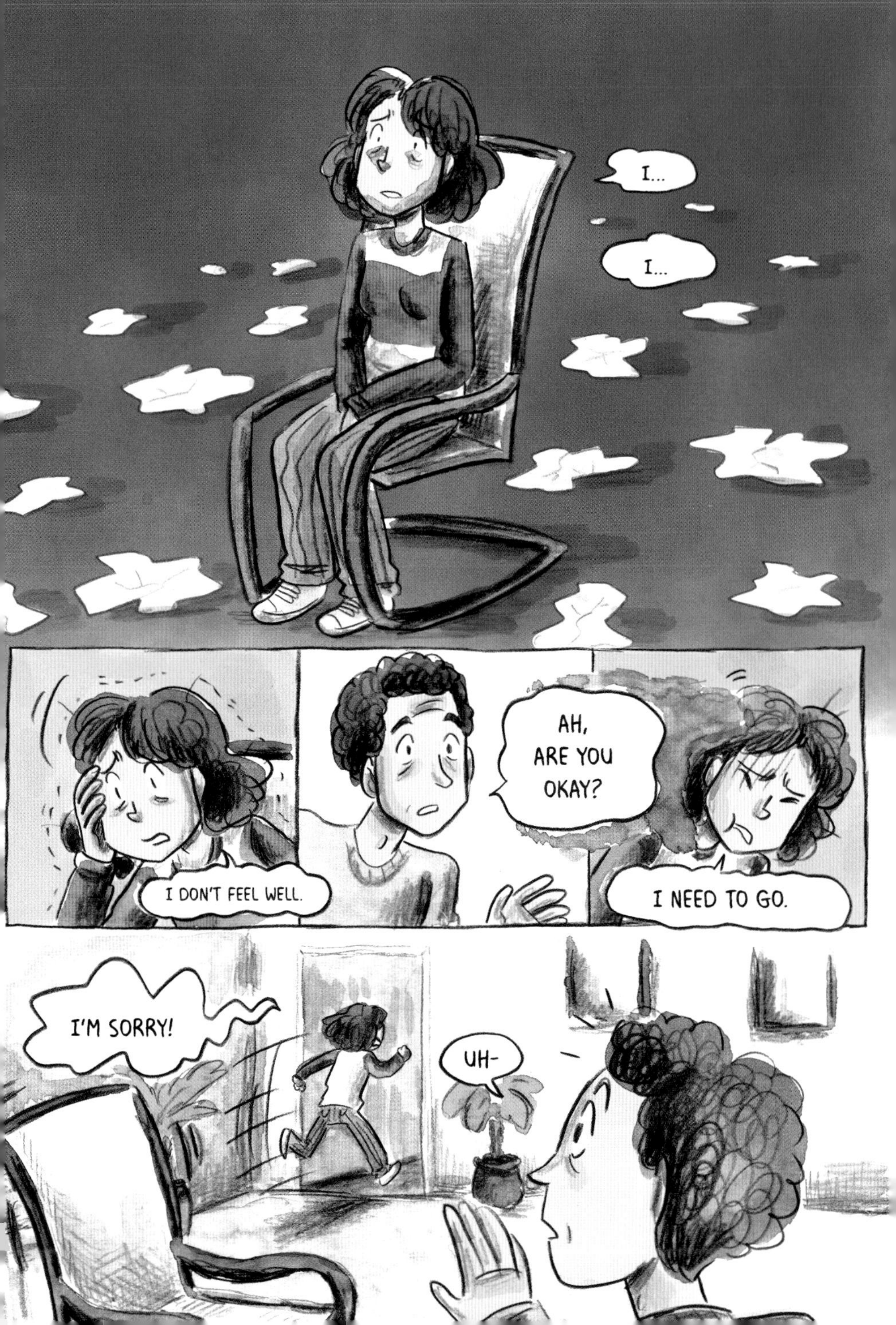
I...
I...
I DON'T FEEL WELL.
AH,
ARE YOU
OKAY?
I NEED TO GO.
I'M SORRY!
UH-

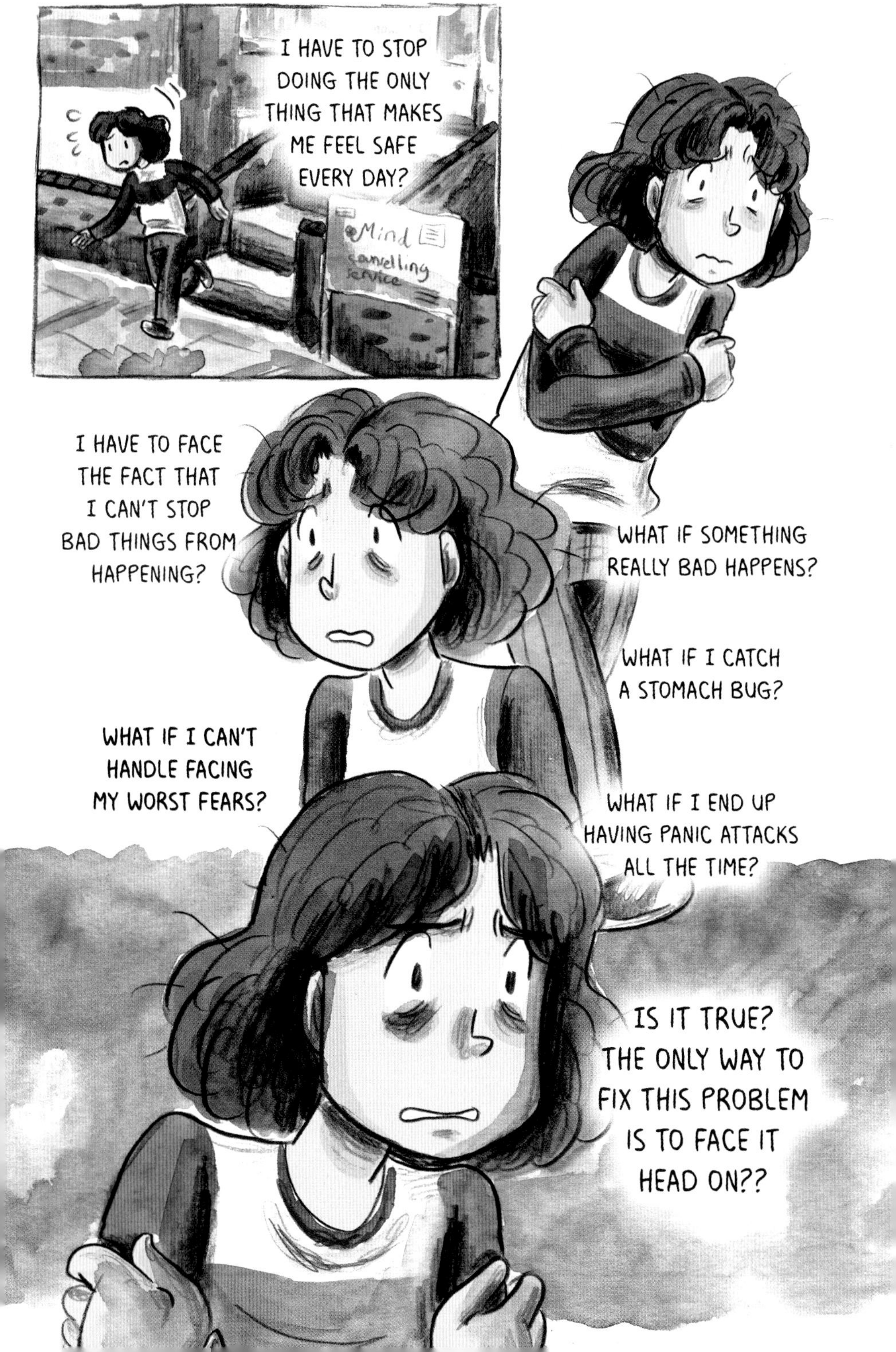
I HAVE TO STOP DOING THE ONLY THING THAT MAKES ME FEEL SAFE EVERY DAY?
Mind
counselling service
I HAVE TO FACE THE FACT THAT I CAN'T STOP BAD THINGS FROM HAPPENING?
WHAT IF SOMETHING REALLY BAD HAPPENS?
WHAT IF I CATCH A STOMACH BUG?
WHAT IF I CAN'T HANDLE FACING MY WORST FEARS?
WHAT IF I END UP HAVING PANIC ATTACKS ALL THE TIME?
IS IT TRUE? THE ONLY WAY TO FIX THIS PROBLEM IS TO FACE IT HEAD ON??

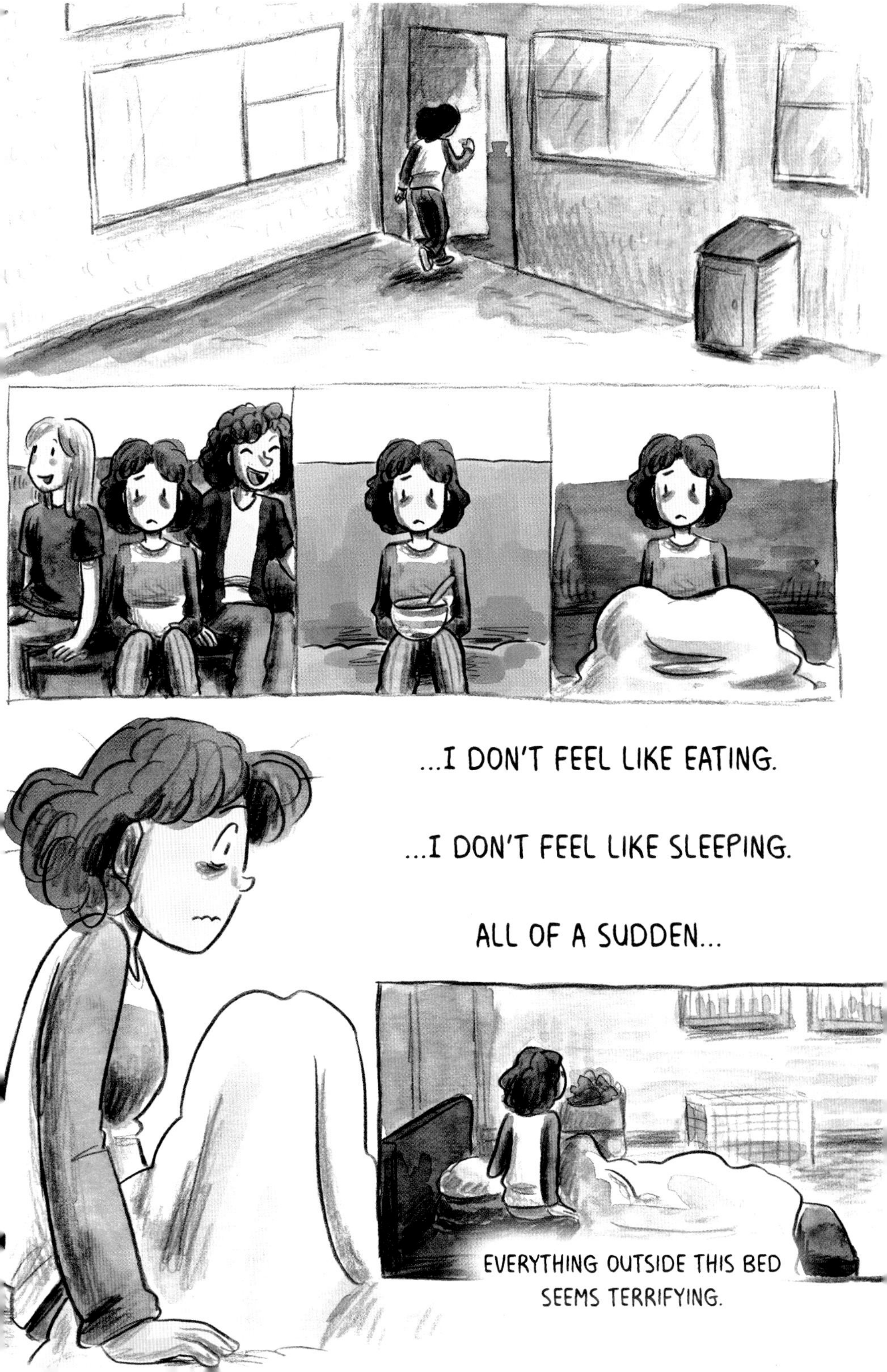
...I DON'T FEEL LIKE EATING.
...I DON'T FEEL LIKE SLEEPING.
ALL OF A SUDDEN...
EVERYTHING OUTSIDE THIS BED SEEMS TERRIFYING.

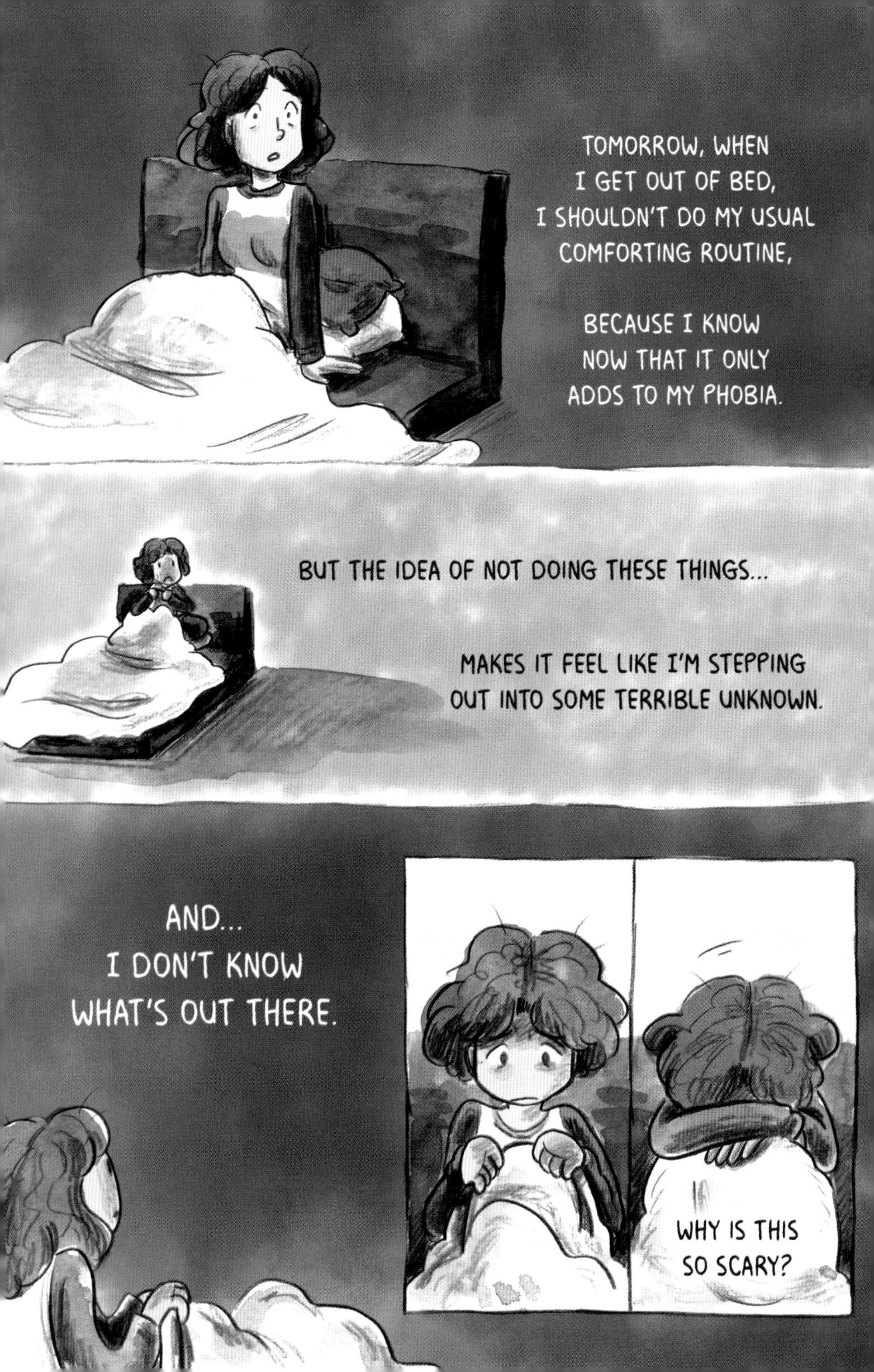
TOMORROW, WHEN I GET OUT OF BED, I SHOULDN'T DO MY USUAL COMFORTING ROUTINE,
BECAUSE I KNOW NOW THAT IT ONLY ADDS TO MY PHOBIA.
BUT THE IDEA OF NOT DOING THESE THINGS...
MAKES IT FEEL LIKE I'M STEPPING OUT INTO SOME TERRIBLE UNKNOWN.
AND... I DON'T KNOW WHAT'S OUT THERE.
WHY IS THIS SO SCARY?

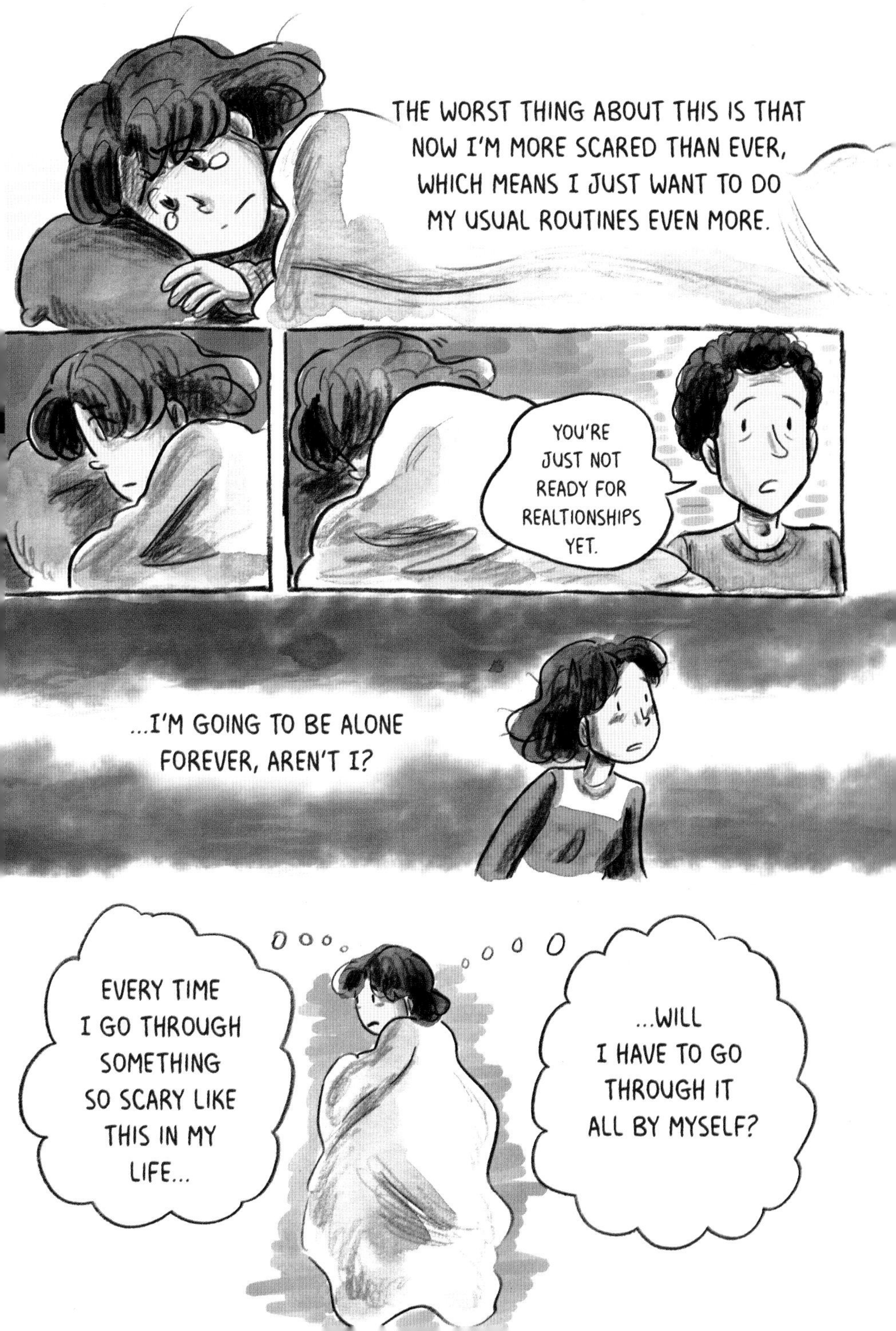
THE WORST THING ABOUT THIS IS THAT NOW I'M MORE SCARED THAN EVER, WHICH MEANS I JUST WANT TO DO MY USUAL ROUTINES EVEN MORE.
YOU'RE JUST NOT READY FOR REALTIONSHIPS YET.
...I'M GOING TO BE ALONE FOREVER, AREN'T I?
EVERY TIME I GO THROUGH SOMETHING SO SCARY LIKE THIS IN MY LIFE...
...WILL I HAVE TO GO THROUGH IT ALL BY MYSELF?

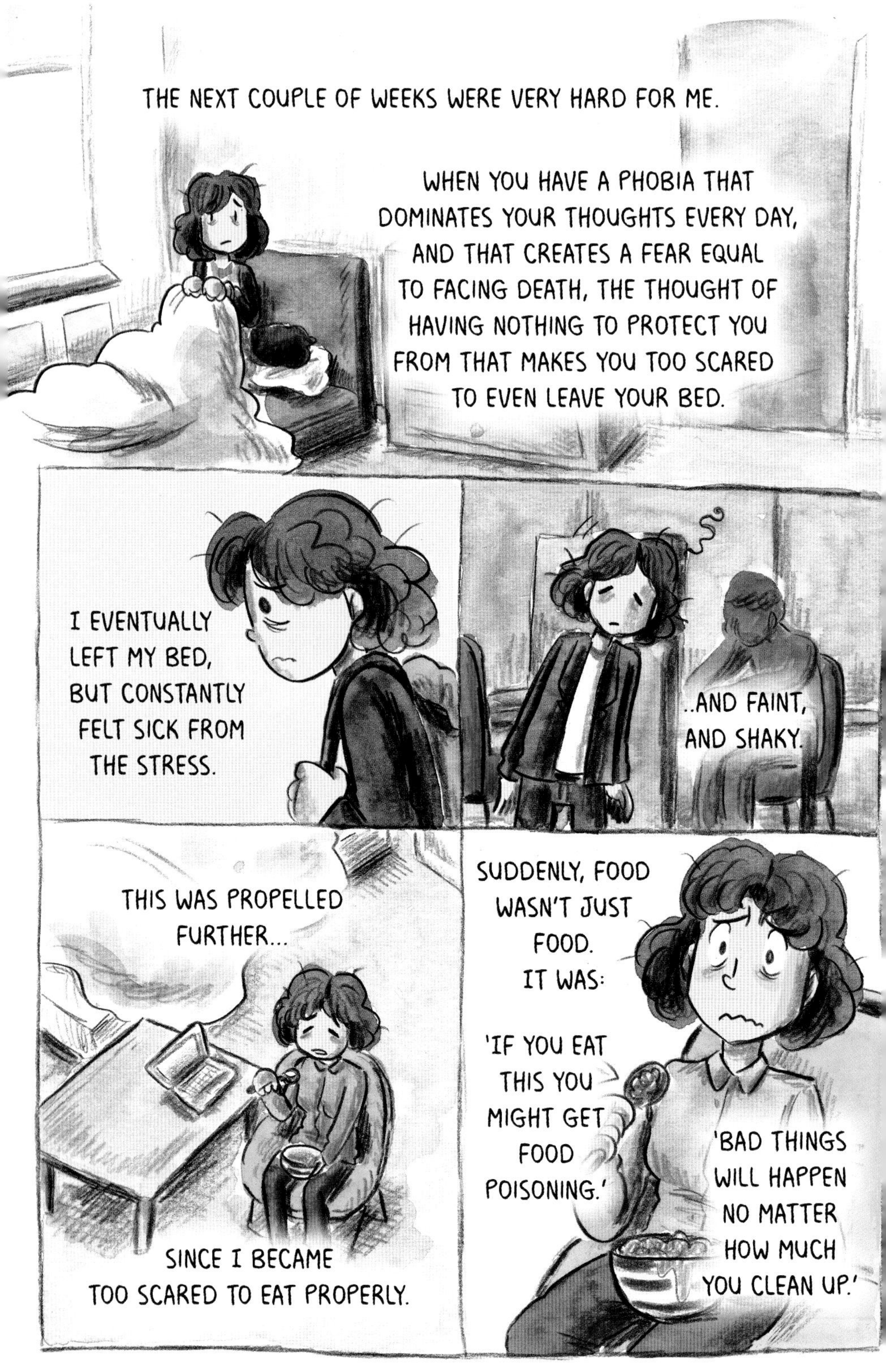
THE NEXT COUPLE OF WEEKS WERE VERY HARD FOR ME.
WHEN YOU HAVE A PHOBIA THAT DOMINATES YOUR THOUGHTS EVERY DAY, AND THAT CREATES A FEAR EQUAL TO FACING DEATH, THE THOUGHT OF HAVING NOTHING TO PROTECT YOU FROM THAT MAKES YOU TOO SCARED TO EVEN LEAVE YOUR BED.
I EVENTUALLY LEFT MY BED, BUT CONSTANTLY FELT SICK FROM THE STRESS.
..AND FAINT, AND SHAKY.
THIS WAS PROPELLED FURTHER...
SINCE I BECAME TOO SCARED TO EAT PROPERLY.
SUDDENLY, FOOD WASN'T JUST FOOD. IT WAS:
'IF YOU EAT THIS YOU MIGHT GET FOOD POISONING.'
'BAD THINGS WILL HAPPEN NO MATTER HOW MUCH YOU CLEAN UP.'

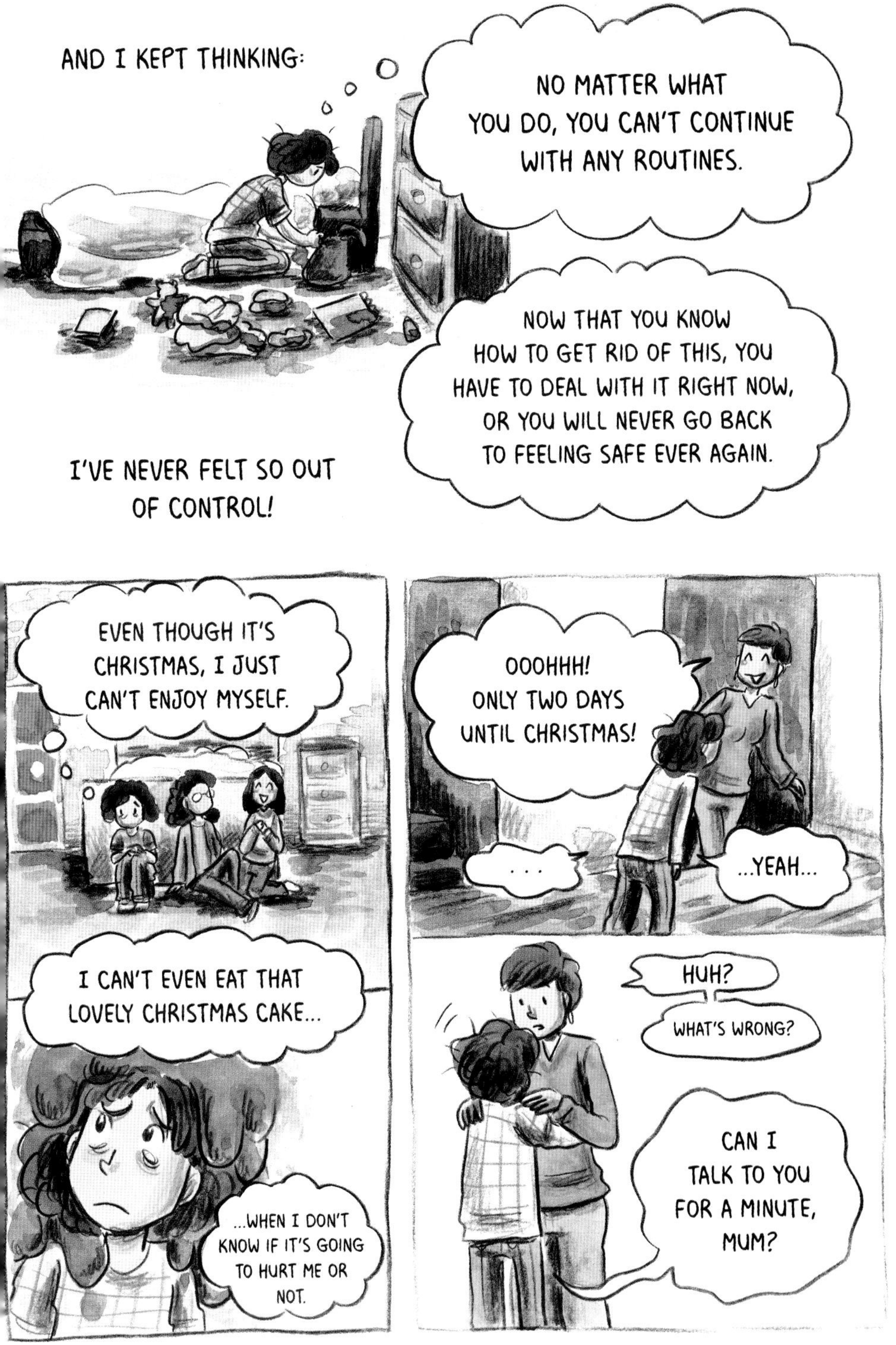
AND I KEPT THINKING:
NO MATTER WHAT YOU DO, YOU CAN'T CONTINUE WITH ANY ROUTINES.
NOW THAT YOU KNOW HOW TO GET RID OF THIS, YOU HAVE TO DEAL WITH IT RIGHT NOW, OR YOU WILL NEVER GO BACK TO FEELING SAFE EVER AGAIN.
I'VE NEVER FELT SO OUT OF CONTROL!
EVEN THOUGH IT'S CHRISTMAS, I JUST CAN'T ENJOY MYSELF.
I CAN'T EVEN EAT THAT LOVELY CHRISTMAS CAKE...
...WHEN I DON'T KNOW IF IT'S GOING TO HURT ME OR NOT.
OOOHHH! ONLY TWO DAYS UNTIL CHRISTMAS!
. . .
...YEAH...
HUH?
WHAT'S WRONG?
CAN I TALK TO YOU FOR A MINUTE, MUM?

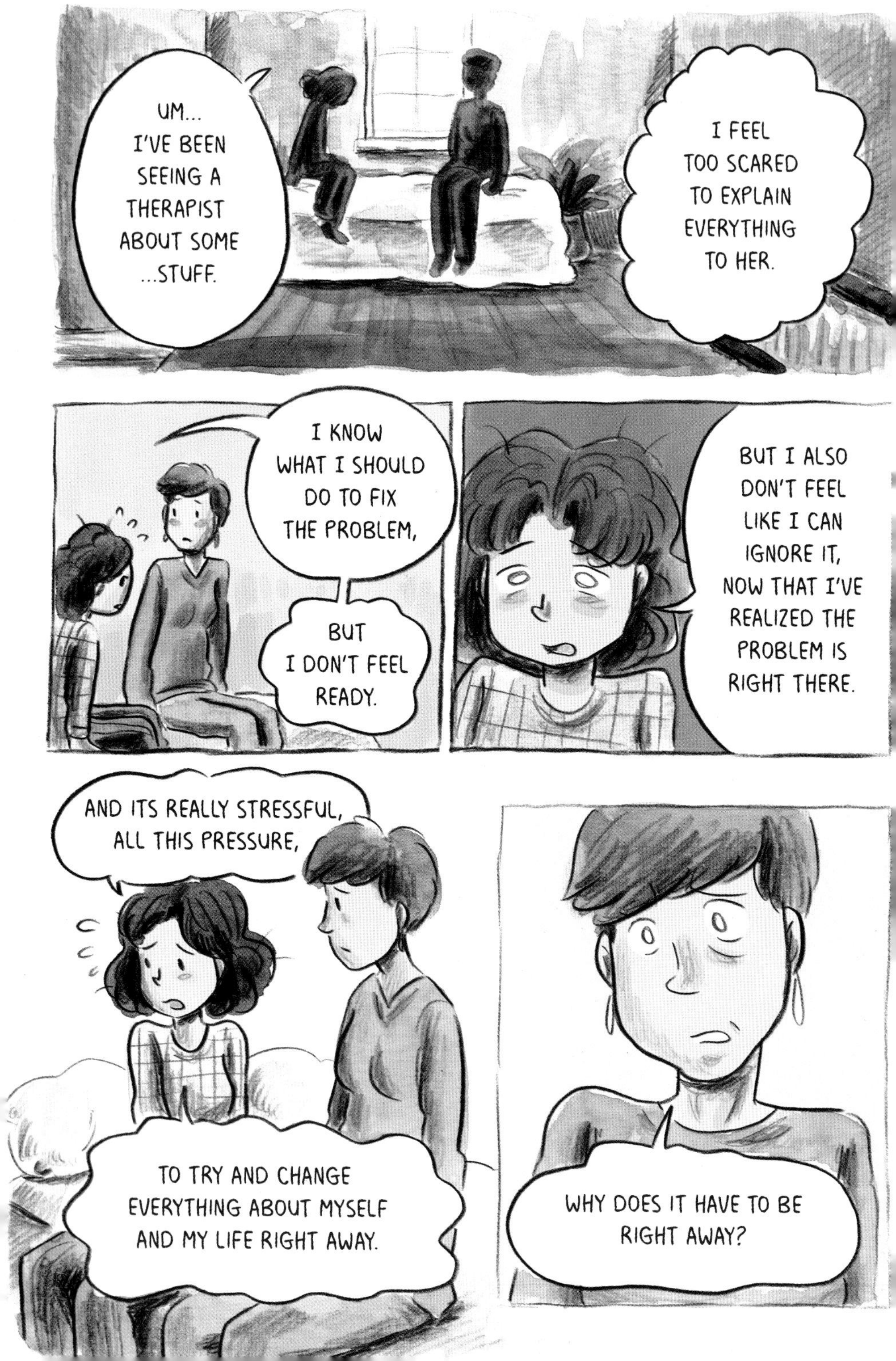
UM...
I'VE BEEN SEEING A THERAPIST ABOUT SOME ...STUFF.
I FEEL TOO SCARED TO EXPLAIN EVERYTHING TO HER.
I KNOW WHAT I SHOULD DO TO FIX THE PROBLEM,
BUT I DON'T FEEL READY.
BUT I ALSO DON'T FEEL LIKE I CAN IGNORE IT, NOW THAT I'VE REALIZED THE PROBLEM IS RIGHT THERE.
AND ITS REALLY STRESSFUL, ALL THIS PRESSURE,
TO TRY AND CHANGE EVERYTHING ABOUT MYSELF AND MY LIFE RIGHT AWAY.
WHY DOES IT HAVE TO BE RIGHT AWAY?

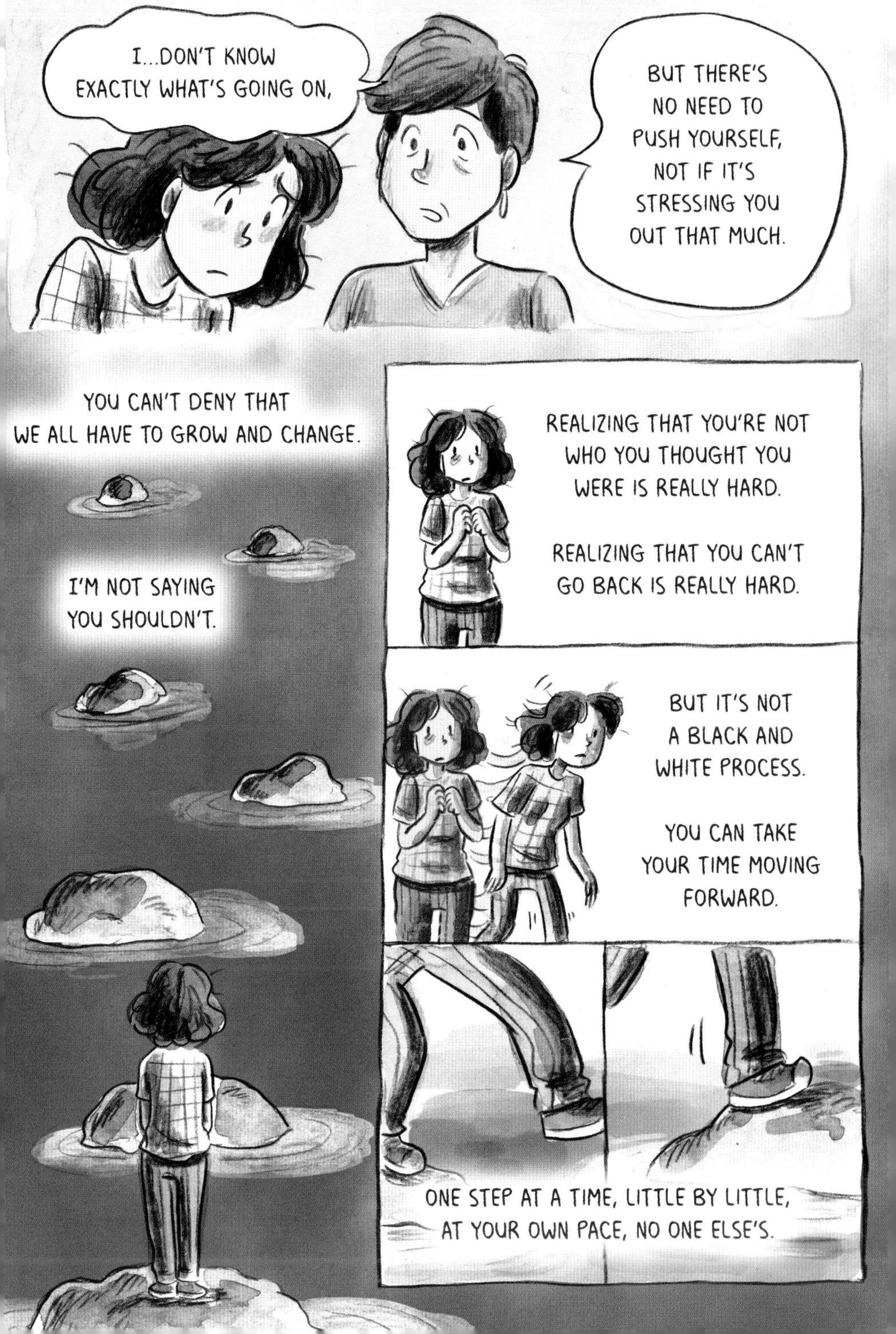
I...DON'T KNOW EXACTLY WHAT'S GOING ON,
BUT THERE'S NO NEED TO PUSH YOURSELF, NOT IF IT'S STRESSING YOU OUT THAT MUCH.
YOU CAN'T DENY THAT WE ALL HAVE TO GROW AND CHANGE.
I'M NOT SAYING YOU SHOULDN'T.
REALIZING THAT YOU'RE NOT WHO YOU THOUGHT YOU WERE IS REALLY HARD.
REALIZING THAT YOU CAN'T GO BACK IS REALLY HARD.
BUT IT'S NOT A BLACK AND WHITE PROCESS.
YOU CAN TAKE YOUR TIME MOVING FORWARD.
ONE STEP AT A TIME, LITTLE BY LITTLE, AT YOUR OWN PACE, NO ONE ELSE'S.

THE IMPORTANT PART IS ACCEPTING THAT YOU HAVE TO MOVE FORWARD.

FROM THAT POINT OF UNDERSTANDING, YOU BEGIN TO MOVE ON, NO MATTER WHAT.

THE THING IS, ALTHOUGH YOU CAN'T CONTROL THE WORLD AROUND YOU, YOU CAN CONTROL HOW MUCH YOU WANT TO DO AT ANY TIME.

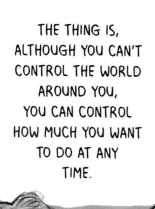

IT'S YOUR LIFE, NOT ANYONE ELSE'S. AS LONG AS YOU REMEMBER THAT, YOU CAN TAKE YOUR TIME.

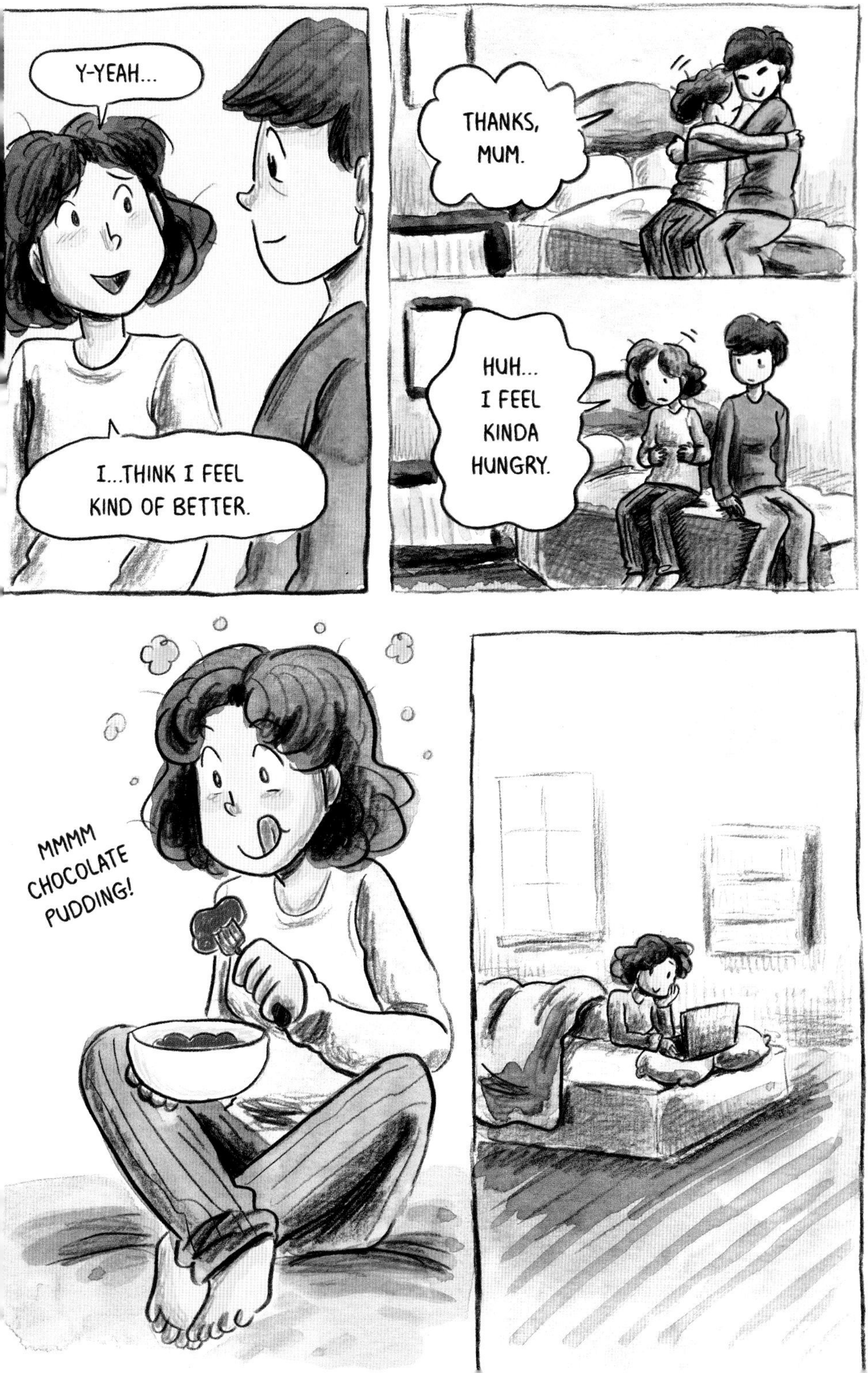
Y-YEAH...
I...THINK I FEEL KIND OF BETTER.
THANKS, MUM.
HUH... I FEEL KINDA HUNGRY.
MMMM CHOCOLATE PUDDING!

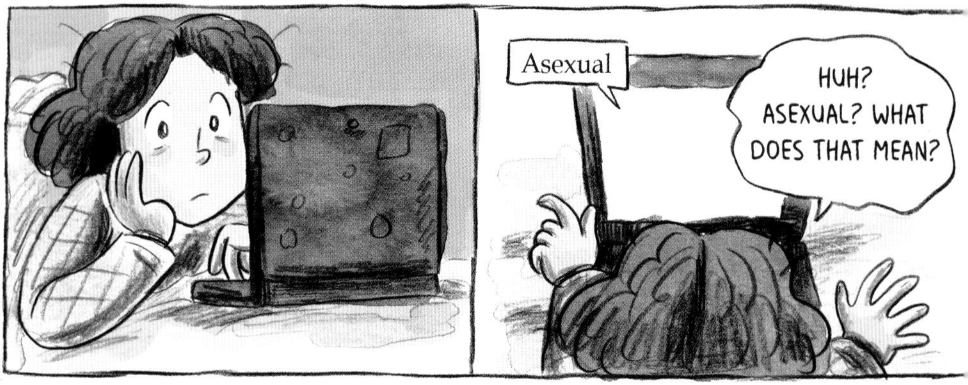
Asexual
HUH? ASEXUAL? WHAT DOES THAT MEAN?

Asexuality is the lack of sexual attraction to others, or low or absent interest in or desire for sexual activity. It may be considered a sexual orientation or the lack thereof. It may also be categorized more widely to include a broad spectrum of asexual sub-identities.

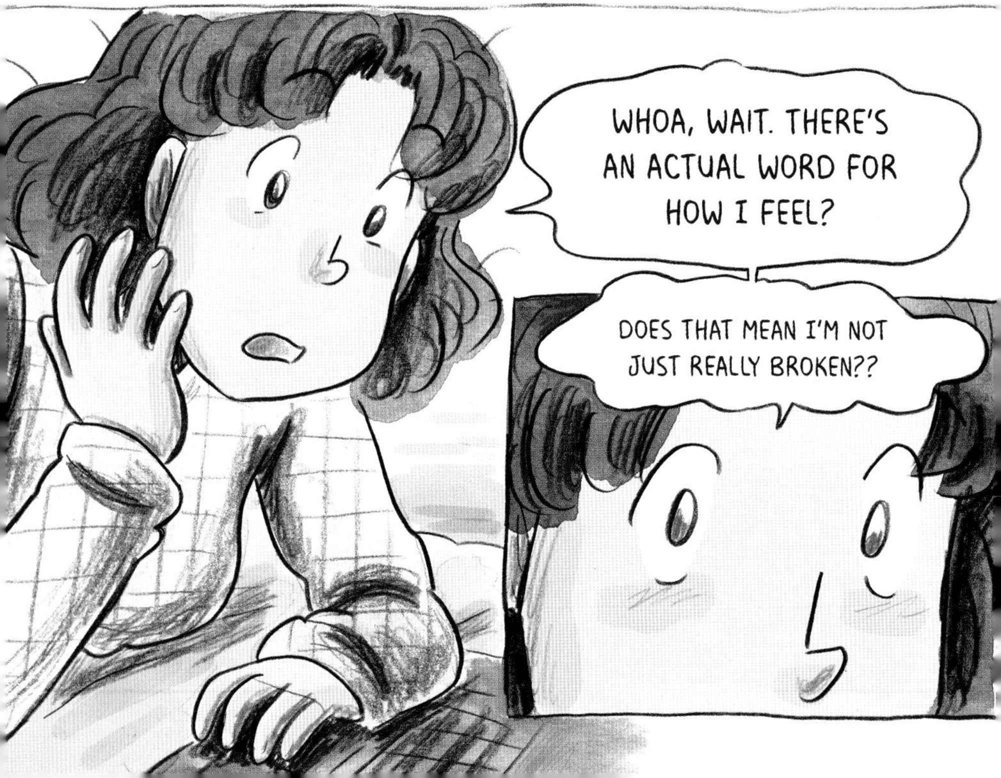
WHOA, WAIT. THERE'S AN ACTUAL WORD FOR HOW I FEEL?
DOES THAT MEAN I'M NOT JUST REALLY BROKEN??

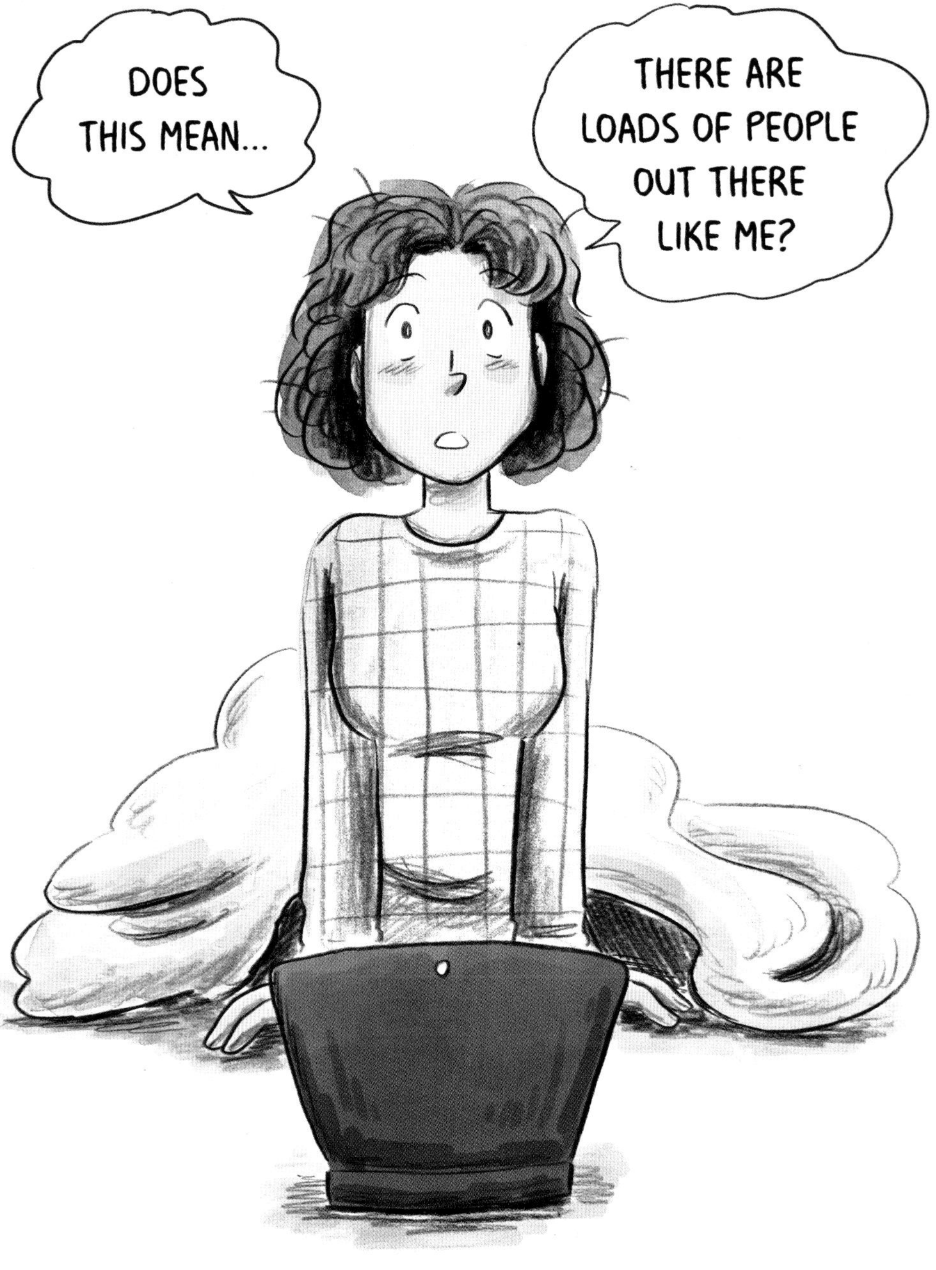
DOES THIS MEAN...
THERE ARE LOADS OF PEOPLE OUT THERE LIKE ME?

'...FROM THAT POINT OF UNDERSTANDING, YOU BEGIN TO MOVE ON, NO MATTER WHAT.'

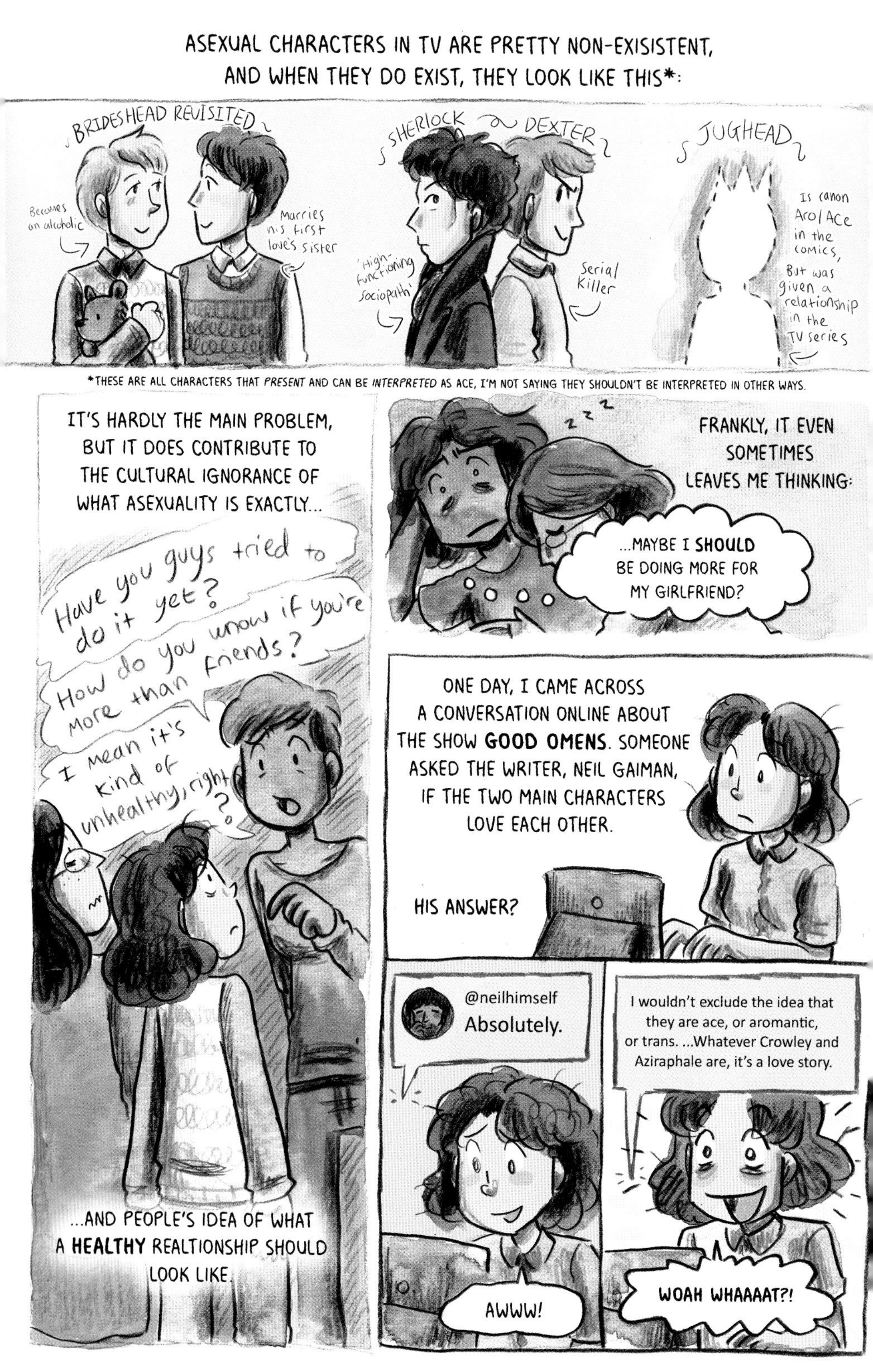

ASEXUAL CHARACTERS IN TV ARE PRETTY NON-EXISISTENT, AND WHEN THEY DO EXIST, THEY LOOK LIKE THIS*:
BRIDESHEAD REVISITED
Becomes an alcoholic
Marries his first love's sister
SHERLOCK
DEXTER
'High-functioning sociopath'
Serial Killer
JUGHEAD
Is canon Aro/Ace in the comics, But was given a relationship in the TV series
*THESE ARE ALL CHARACTERS THAT PRESENT AND CAN BE INTERPRETED AS ACE, I'M NOT SAYING THEY SHOULDN'T BE INTERPRETED IN OTHER WAYS.
IT'S HARDLY THE MAIN PROBLEM, BUT IT DOES CONTRIBUTE TO THE CULTURAL IGNORANCE OF WHAT ASEXUALITY IS EXACTLY...
Have you guys tried to do it yet?
How do you know if you're more than friends?
I mean it's kind of unhealthy, right?
...AND PEOPLE'S IDEA OF WHAT A HEALTHY REALTIONSHIP SHOULD LOOK LIKE.
FRANKLY, IT EVEN SOMETIMES LEAVES ME THINKING:
z z z
...MAYBE I SHOULD BE DOING MORE FOR MY GIRLFRIEND?
ONE DAY, I CAME ACROSS A CONVERSATION ONLINE ABOUT THE SHOW GOOD OMENS. SOMEONE ASKED THE WRITER, NEIL GAIMAN, IF THE TWO MAIN CHARACTERS LOVE EACH OTHER.
HIS ANSWER?
@neilhimself
Absolutely.
AWWW!
I wouldn't exclude the idea that they are ace, or aromantic, or trans. ...Whatever Crowley and Aziraphale are, it's a love story.
WOAH WHAAAAT?!

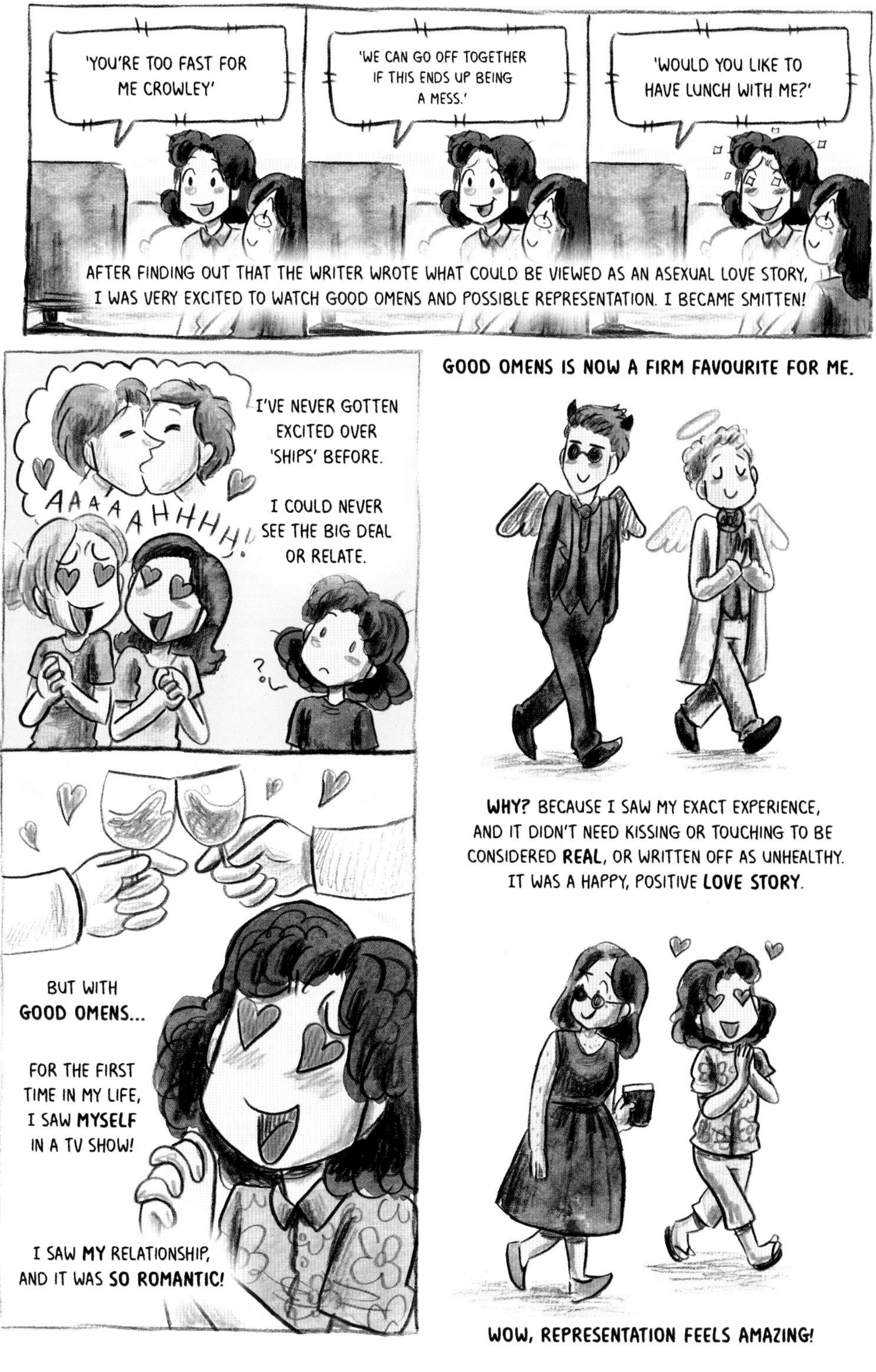
'YOU'RE TOO FAST FOR ME CROWLEY'
'WE CAN GO OFF TOGETHER IF THIS ENDS UP BEING A MESS.'
'WOULD YOU LIKE TO HAVE LUNCH WITH ME?'
AFTER FINDING OUT THAT THE WRITER WROTE WHAT COULD BE VIEWED AS AN ASEXUAL LOVE STORY, I WAS VERY EXCITED TO WATCH GOOD OMENS AND POSSIBLE REPRESENTATION. I BECAME SMITTEN!
I'VE NEVER GOTTEN EXCITED OVER 'SHIPS' BEFORE.
AAAAAHHHHH!
I COULD NEVER SEE THE BIG DEAL OR RELATE.
BUT WITH GOOD OMENS...
FOR THE FIRST TIME IN MY LIFE, I SAW MYSELF IN A TV SHOW!
I SAW MY RELATIONSHIP, AND IT WAS SO ROMANTIC!
GOOD OMENS IS NOW A FIRM FAVOURITE FOR ME.
WHY? BECAUSE I SAW MY EXACT EXPERIENCE, AND IT DIDN'T NEED KISSING OR TOUCHING TO BE CONSIDERED REAL, OR WRITTEN OFF AS UNHEALTHY. IT WAS A HAPPY, POSITIVE LOVE STORY.
WOW, REPRESENTATION FEELS AMAZING!

# CHAPTER FIVE

## HOW TO FALL IN LOVE

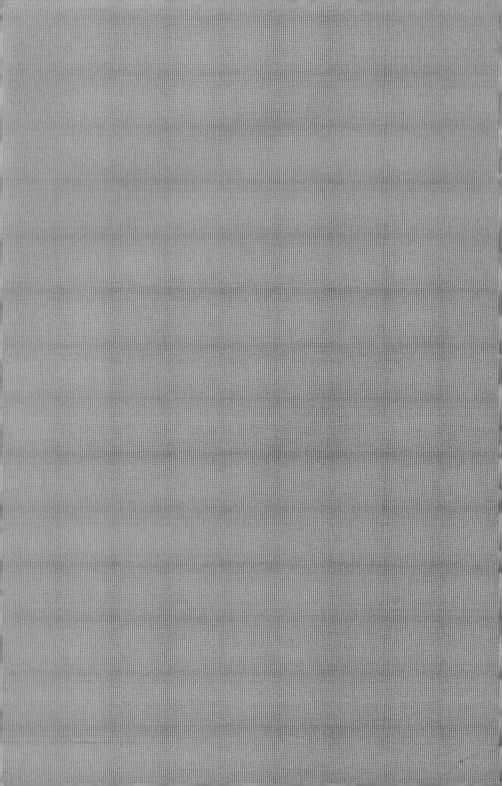

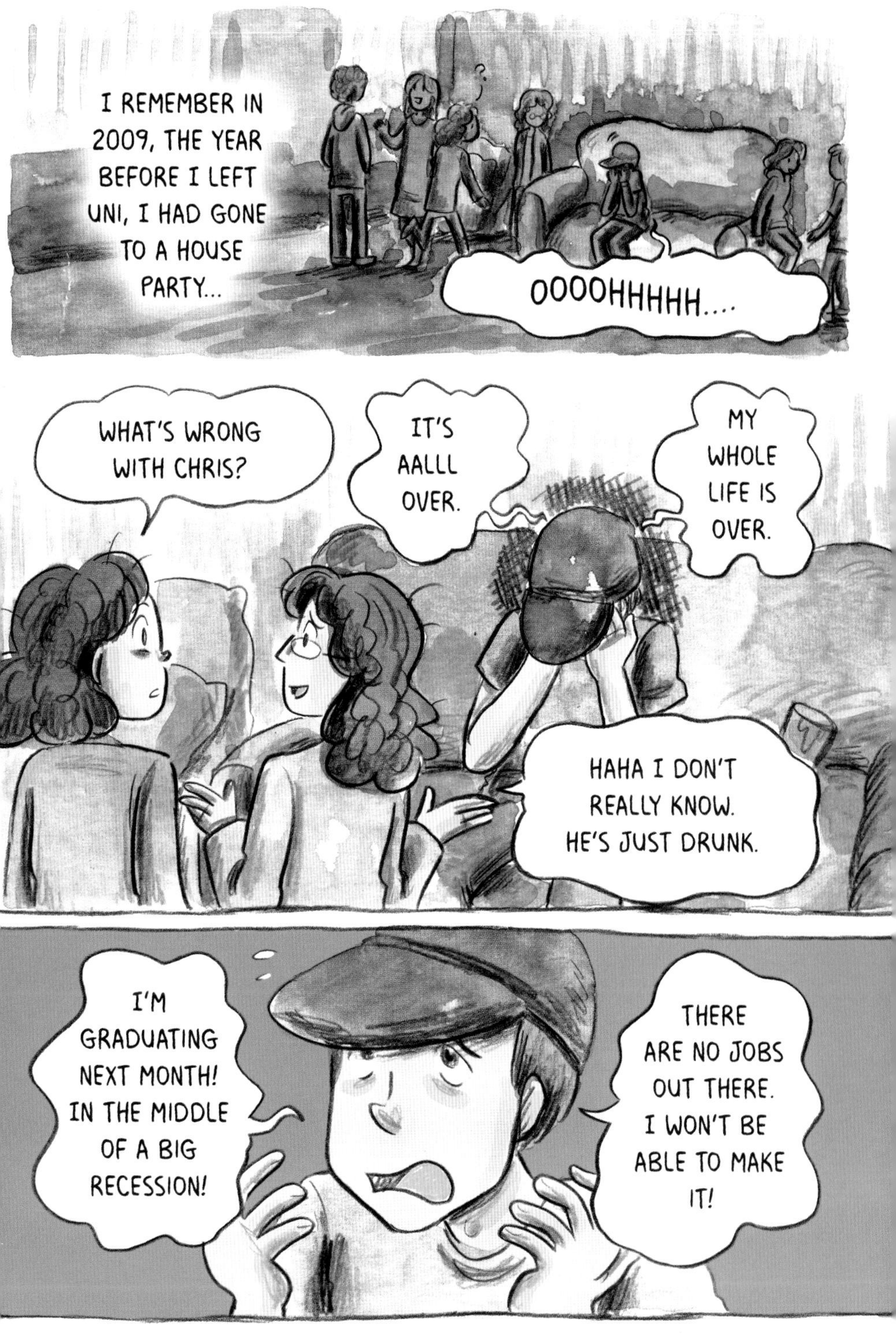
I REMEMBER IN 2009, THE YEAR BEFORE I LEFT UNI, I HAD GONE TO A HOUSE PARTY...
OOOOHHHHH....
WHAT'S WRONG WITH CHRIS?
IT'S AALLL OVER.
MY WHOLE LIFE IS OVER.
HAHA I DON'T REALLY KNOW. HE'S JUST DRUNK.
I'M GRADUATING NEXT MONTH! IN THE MIDDLE OF A BIG RECESSION!
THERE ARE NO JOBS OUT THERE. I WON'T BE ABLE TO MAKE IT!

UUURGH. LIFE IS TERRIBLE. WHY CAN'T I STAY AT UNI?

AHAHA!

YOU'LL BE FINE, CHRIS!!

IT'S NOT LIKE I HADN'T HEARD ABOUT THE RECESSION OR MARKET CRASH IN 2008...

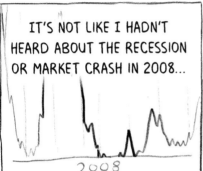

2008

BUT IT STARTED WHILE I WAS STILL IN FULL-TIME EDUCATION.

WOW, IT'S SO CHEAP NOW!

WHEN A STUDENT LOAN PAYS YOUR RENT AND BILLS, IT'S PRETTY GREAT THAT TAX HAS BEEN LIFTED FROM FOOD SO THAT THE POOR CAN EAT.

THAT IDIOT GOT ELECTED MAYOR?!

BORIS ELECTED MAYOR

POLITICS DIDN'T AFFECT ME, SO IT WAS JUST SOMETHING I LAUGHED AT.

THE ECONOMY WAS A BORING THING I DIDN'T NEED TO UNDERSTAND...

...NOT WHEN I HAD FUN CARTOONS TO WATCH!

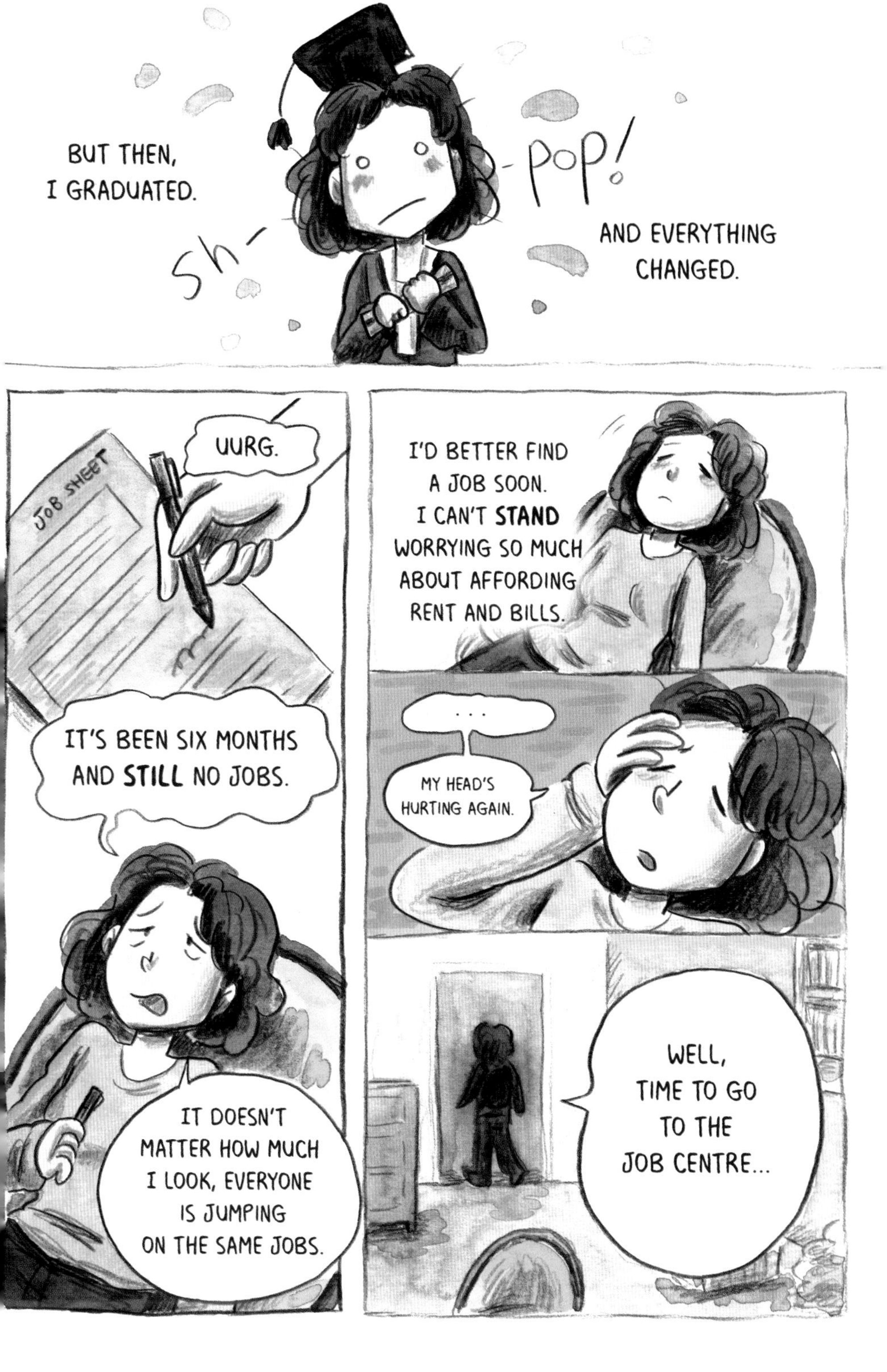

BUT THEN, I GRADUATED.
SH- POP!
AND EVERYTHING CHANGED.
JOB SHEET
UURG.
IT'S BEEN SIX MONTHS AND STILL NO JOBS.
IT DOESN'T MATTER HOW MUCH I LOOK, EVERYONE IS JUMPING ON THE SAME JOBS.
I'D BETTER FIND A JOB SOON. I CAN'T STAND WORRYING SO MUCH ABOUT AFFORDING RENT AND BILLS.
. . .
MY HEAD'S HURTING AGAIN.
WELL, TIME TO GO TO THE JOB CENTRE...

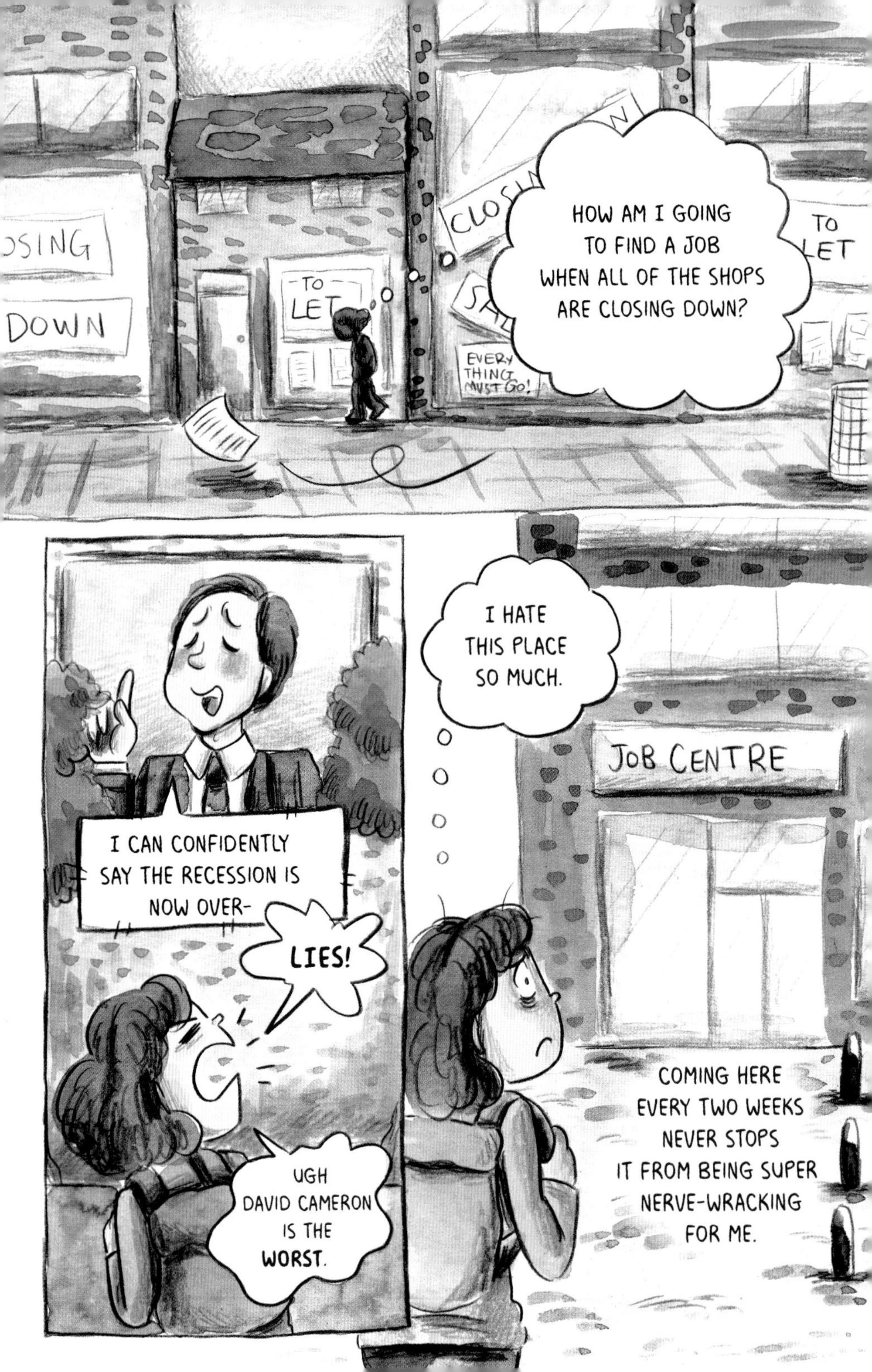

CLOSING DOWN
TO LET
CLOSING DOWN SALE
EVERY THING MUST GO!
TO LET
HOW AM I GOING TO FIND A JOB WHEN ALL OF THE SHOPS ARE CLOSING DOWN?
I CAN CONFIDENTLY SAY THE RECESSION IS NOW OVER-
LIES!
UGH DAVID CAMERON IS THE WORST.
I HATE THIS PLACE SO MUCH.
JOB CENTRE
COMING HERE EVERY TWO WEEKS NEVER STOPS IT FROM BEING SUPER NERVE-WRACKING FOR ME.

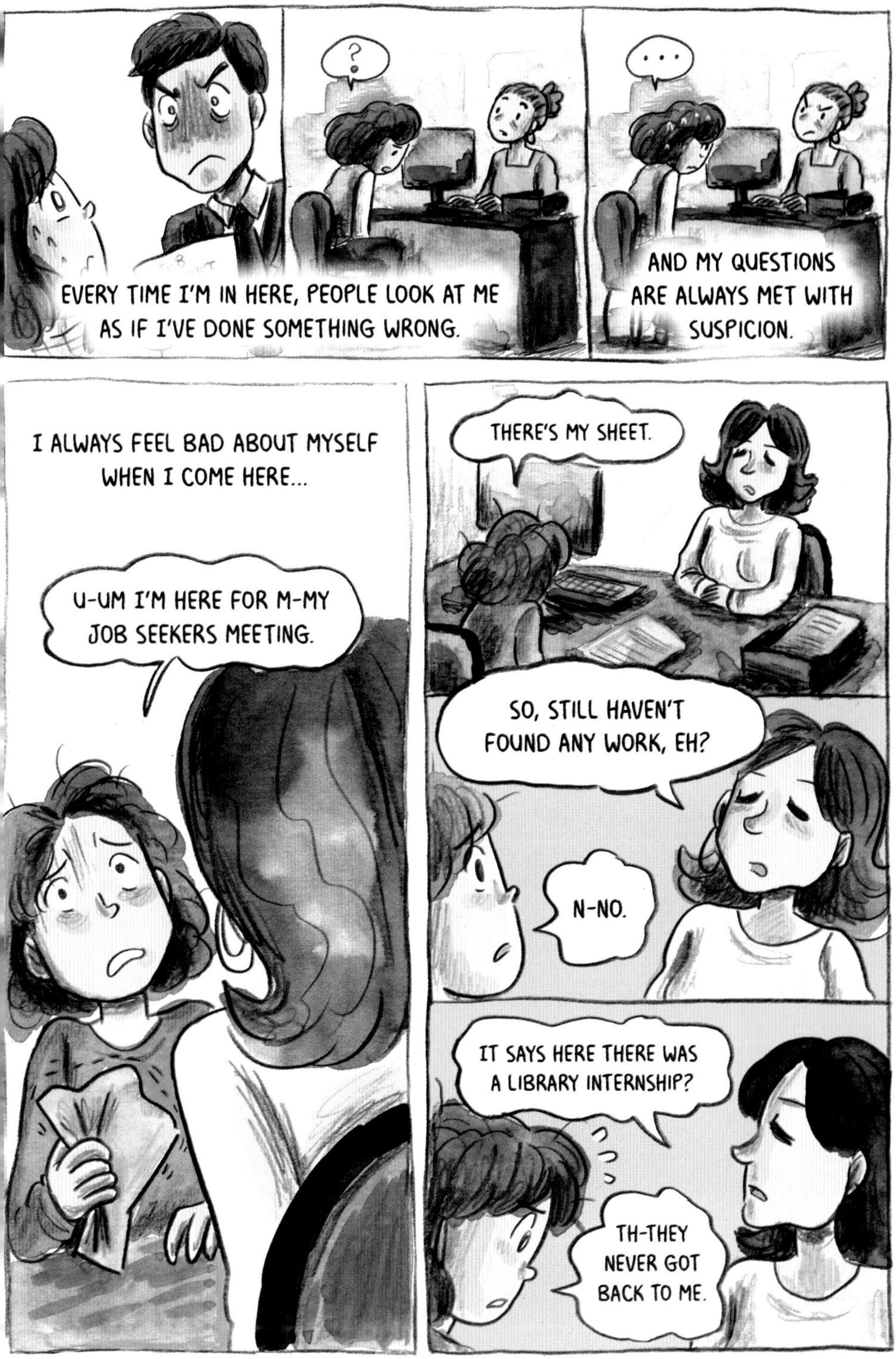
EVERY TIME I'M IN HERE, PEOPLE LOOK AT ME AS IF I'VE DONE SOMETHING WRONG.
?
...
AND MY QUESTIONS ARE ALWAYS MET WITH SUSPICION.
I ALWAYS FEEL BAD ABOUT MYSELF WHEN I COME HERE...
U-UM I'M HERE FOR M-MY JOB SEEKERS MEETING.
THERE'S MY SHEET.
SO, STILL HAVEN'T FOUND ANY WORK, EH?
N-NO.
IT SAYS HERE THERE WAS A LIBRARY INTERNSHIP?
TH-THEY NEVER GOT BACK TO ME.

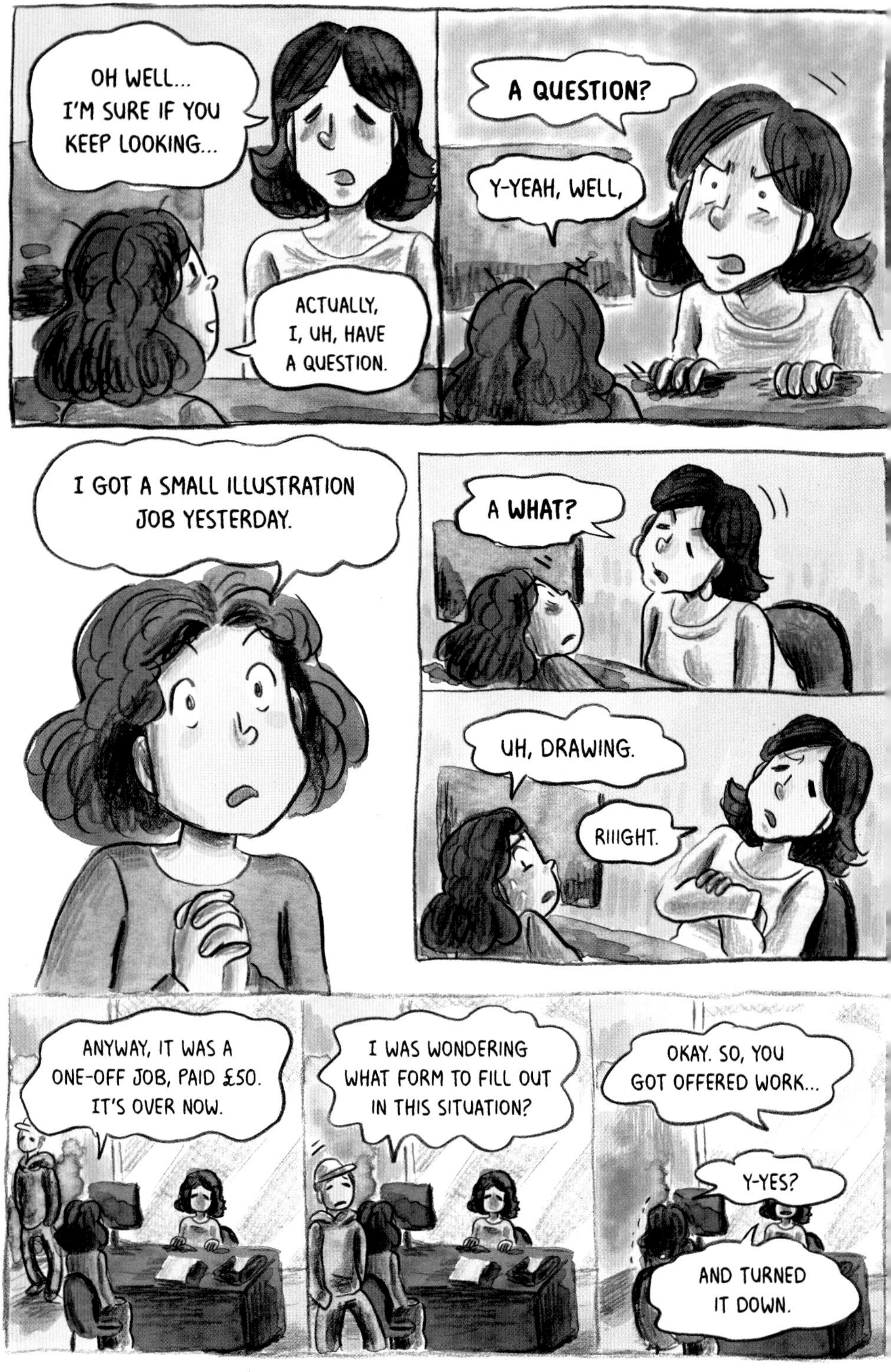
OH WELL... I'M SURE IF YOU KEEP LOOKING...
ACTUALLY, I, UH, HAVE A QUESTION.
A QUESTION?
Y-YEAH, WELL,
I GOT A SMALL ILLUSTRATION JOB YESTERDAY.
A WHAT?
UH, DRAWING.
RIIIGHT.
ANYWAY, IT WAS A ONE-OFF JOB, PAID £50. IT'S OVER NOW.
I WAS WONDERING WHAT FORM TO FILL OUT IN THIS SITUATION?
OKAY. SO, YOU GOT OFFERED WORK...
Y-YES?
AND TURNED IT DOWN.

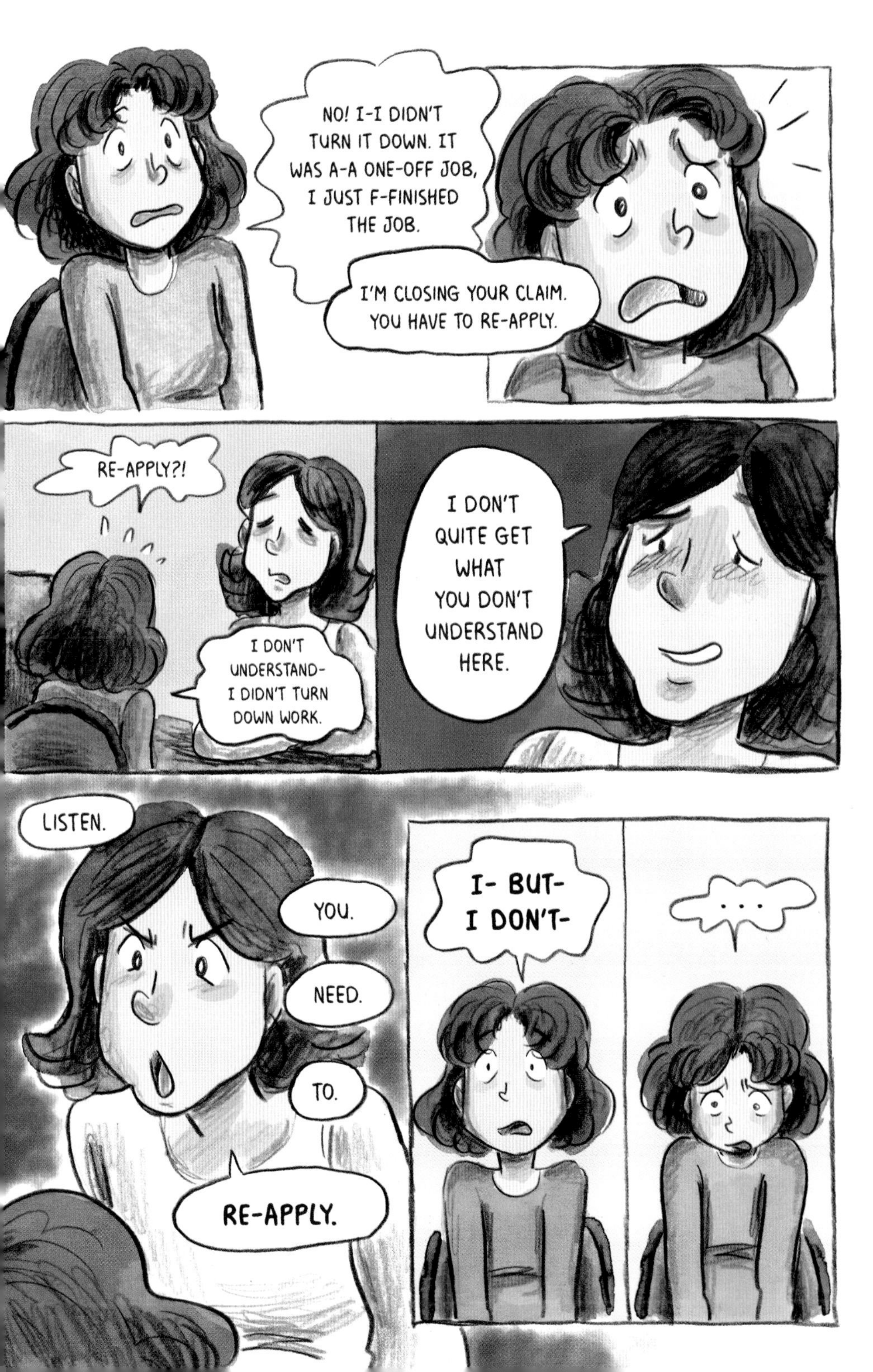
NO! I-I DIDN'T TURN IT DOWN. IT WAS A-A ONE-OFF JOB, I JUST F-FINISHED THE JOB.
I'M CLOSING YOUR CLAIM. YOU HAVE TO RE-APPLY.
RE-APPLY?!
I DON'T UNDERSTAND- I DIDN'T TURN DOWN WORK.
I DON'T QUITE GET WHAT YOU DON'T UNDERSTAND HERE.
LISTEN.
YOU.
NEED.
TO.
RE-APPLY.
I- BUT- I DON'T-
. . .

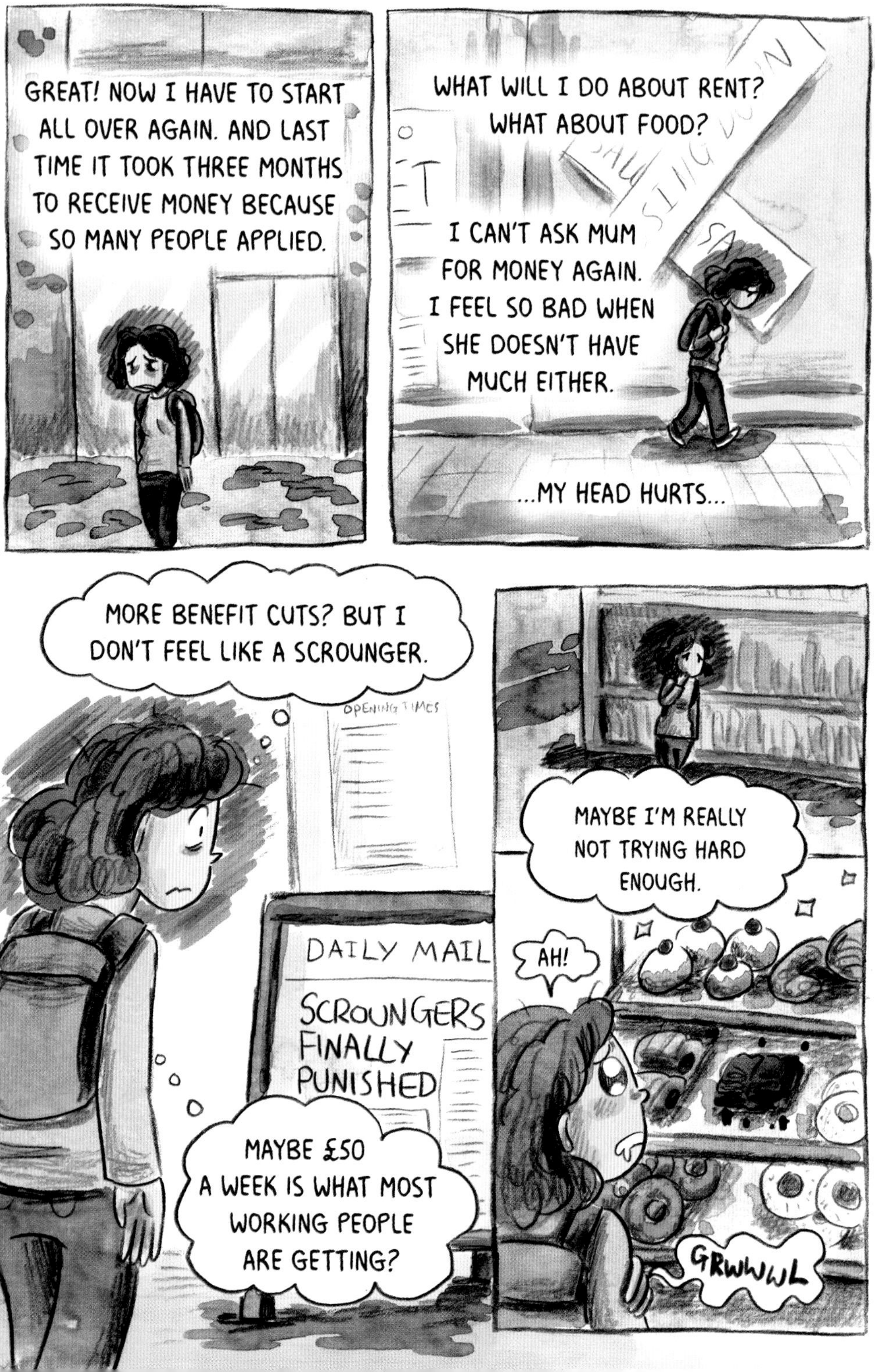
GREAT! NOW I HAVE TO START ALL OVER AGAIN. AND LAST TIME IT TOOK THREE MONTHS TO RECEIVE MONEY BECAUSE SO MANY PEOPLE APPLIED.
WHAT WILL I DO ABOUT RENT? WHAT ABOUT FOOD?
I CAN'T ASK MUM FOR MONEY AGAIN. I FEEL SO BAD WHEN SHE DOESN'T HAVE MUCH EITHER.
...MY HEAD HURTS...
MORE BENEFIT CUTS? BUT I DON'T FEEL LIKE A SCROUNGER.
OPENING TIMES
DAILY MAIL
SCROUNGERS FINALLY PUNISHED
MAYBE £50 A WEEK IS WHAT MOST WORKING PEOPLE ARE GETTING?
MAYBE I'M REALLY NOT TRYING HARD ENOUGH.
AH!
GRWWWL

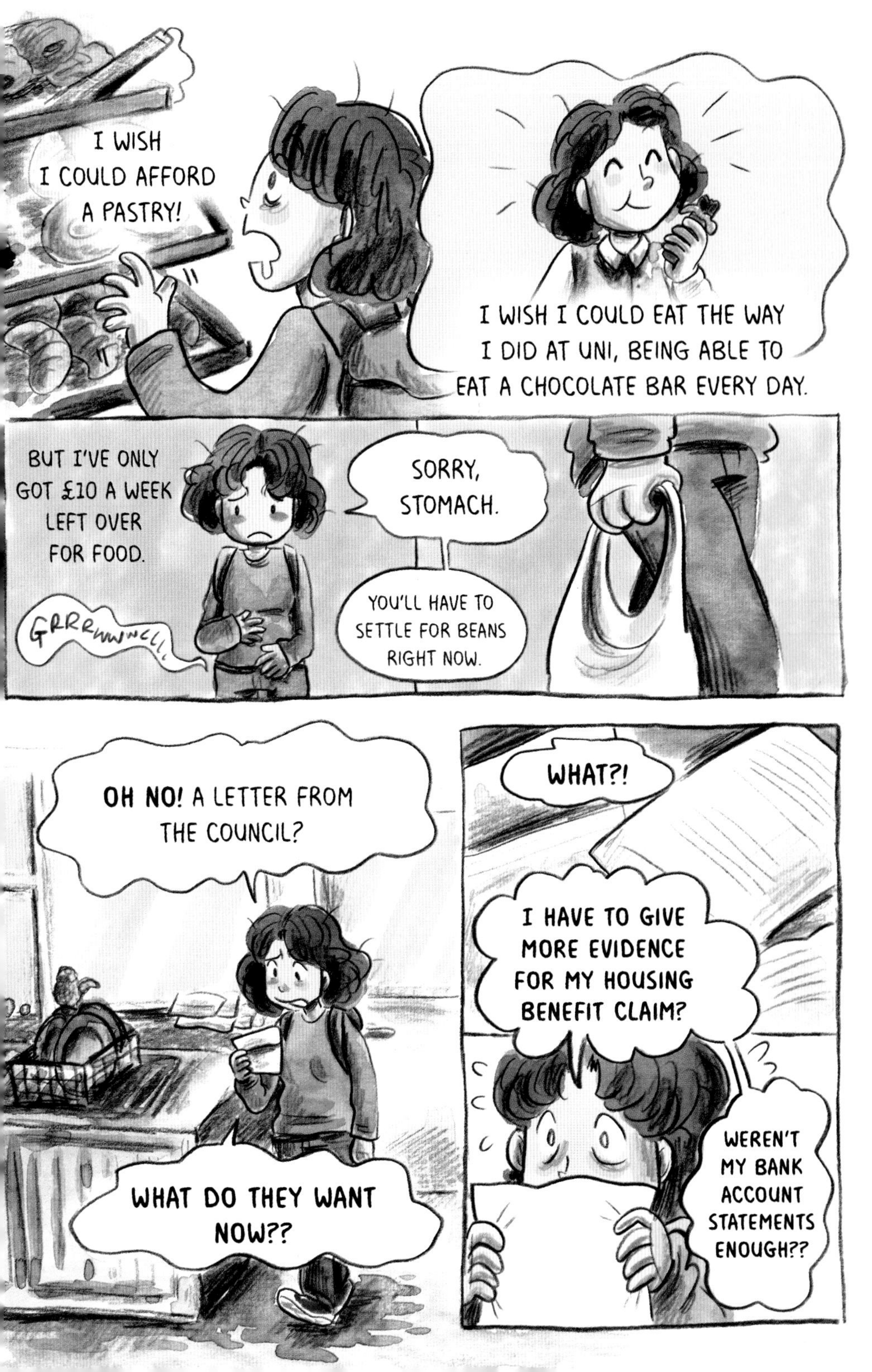
I WISH I COULD AFFORD A PASTRY!
I WISH I COULD EAT THE WAY I DID AT UNI, BEING ABLE TO EAT A CHOCOLATE BAR EVERY DAY.
BUT I'VE ONLY GOT £10 A WEEK LEFT OVER FOR FOOD.
GRRRWWWWLL
SORRY, STOMACH.
YOU'LL HAVE TO SETTLE FOR BEANS RIGHT NOW.
OH NO! A LETTER FROM THE COUNCIL?
WHAT DO THEY WANT NOW??
WHAT?!
I HAVE TO GIVE MORE EVIDENCE FOR MY HOUSING BENEFIT CLAIM?
WEREN'T MY BANK ACCOUNT STATEMENTS ENOUGH??

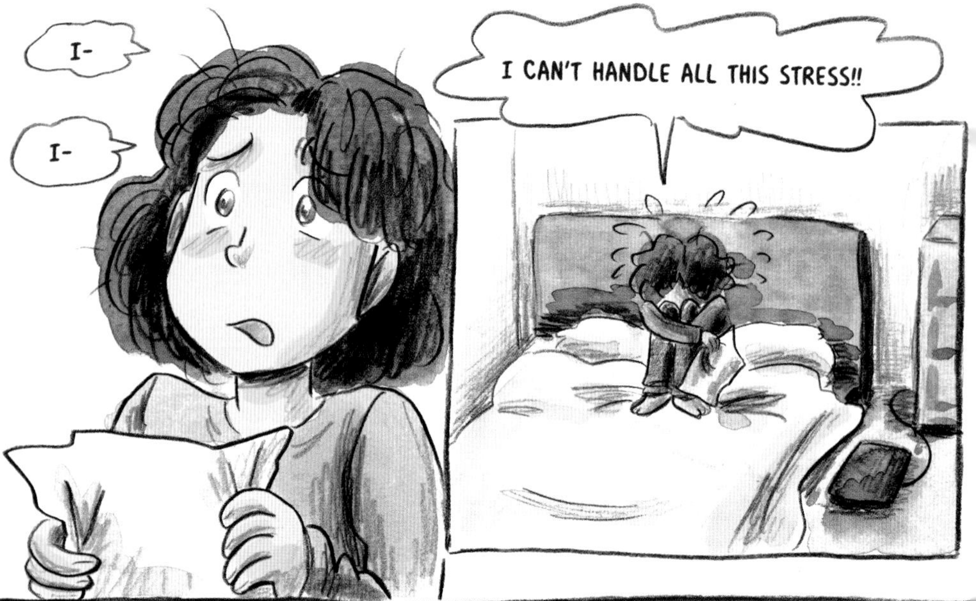
I-
I-
I CAN'T HANDLE ALL THIS STRESS!!

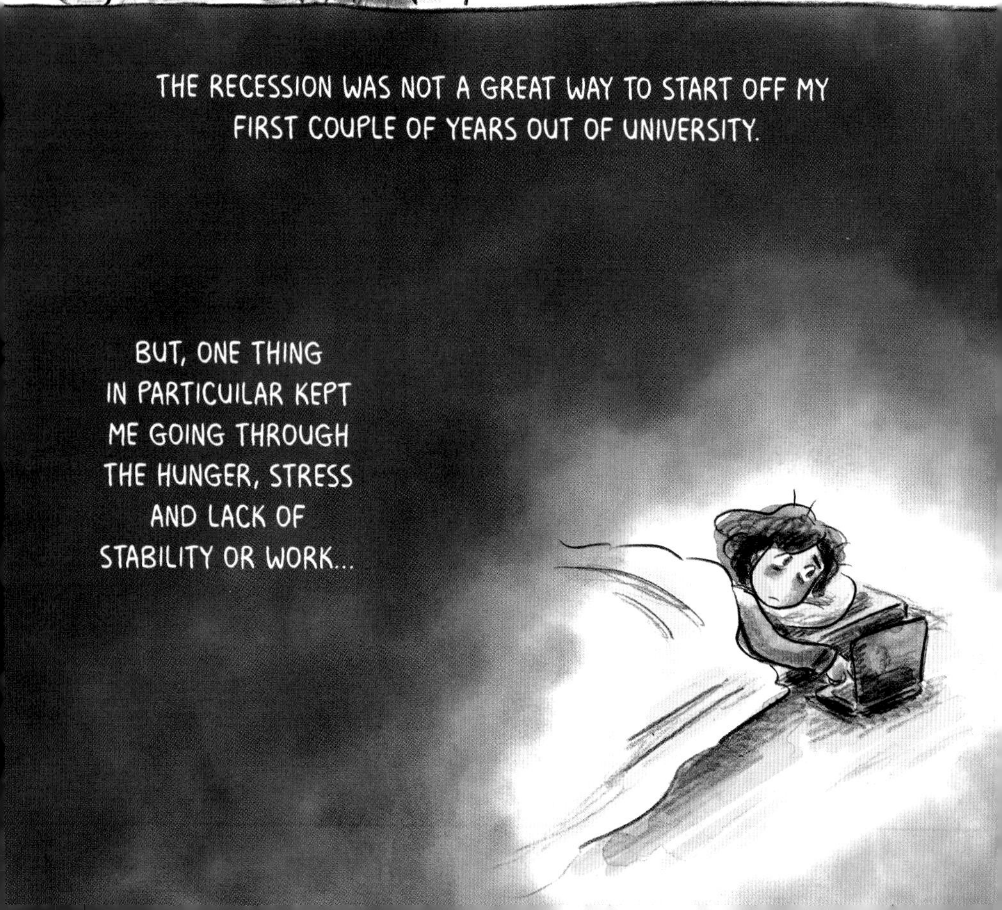
THE RECESSION WAS NOT A GREAT WAY TO START OFF MY FIRST COUPLE OF YEARS OUT OF UNIVERSITY.
BUT, ONE THING IN PARTICULAR KEPT ME GOING THROUGH THE HUNGER, STRESS AND LACK OF STABILITY OR WORK...

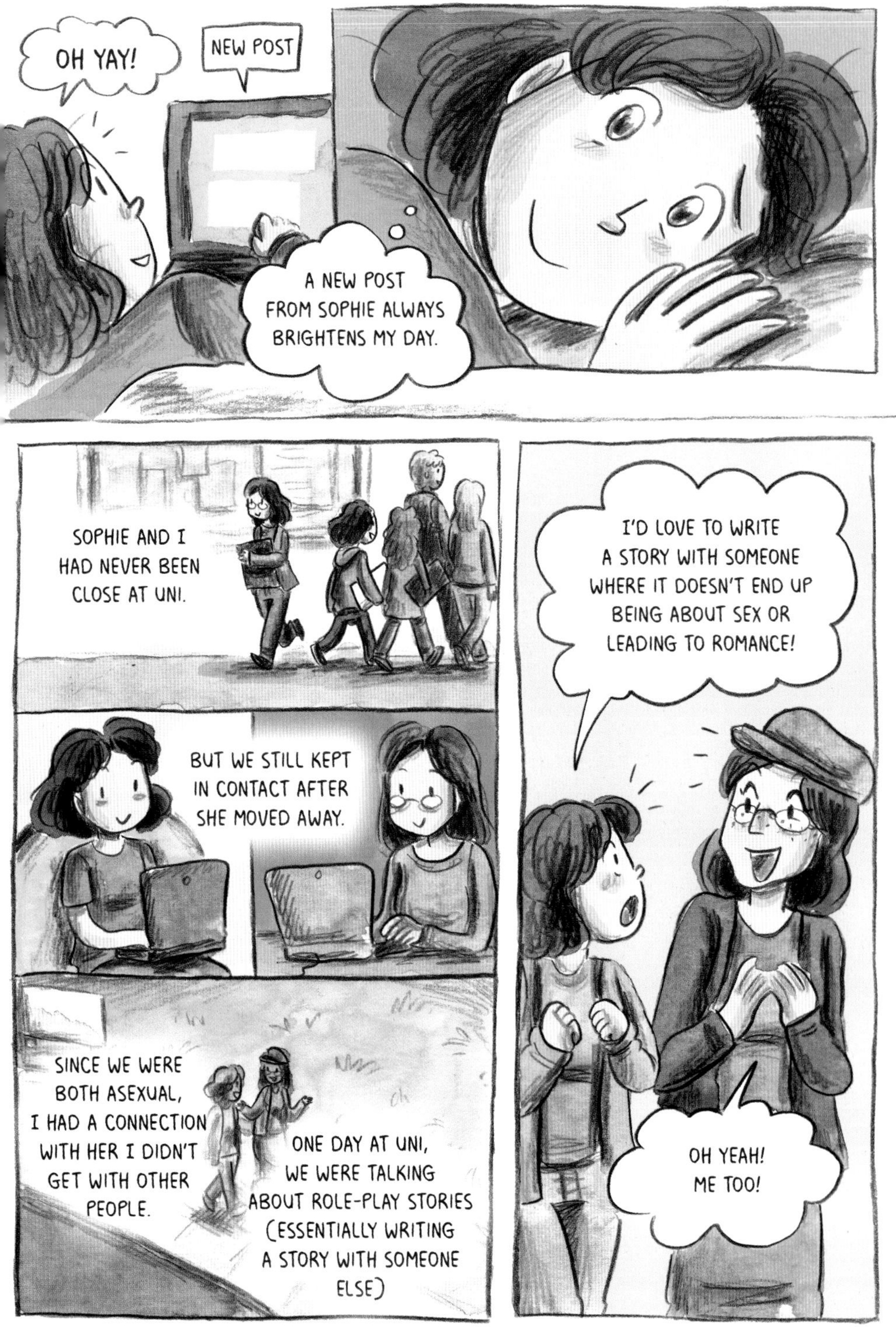
OH YAY!
NEW POST
A NEW POST FROM SOPHIE ALWAYS BRIGHTENS MY DAY.
SOPHIE AND I HAD NEVER BEEN CLOSE AT UNI.
BUT WE STILL KEPT IN CONTACT AFTER SHE MOVED AWAY.
SINCE WE WERE BOTH ASEXUAL, I HAD A CONNECTION WITH HER I DIDN'T GET WITH OTHER PEOPLE.
ONE DAY AT UNI, WE WERE TALKING ABOUT ROLE-PLAY STORIES (ESSENTIALLY WRITING A STORY WITH SOMEONE ELSE)
I'D LOVE TO WRITE A STORY WITH SOMEONE WHERE IT DOESN'T END UP BEING ABOUT SEX OR LEADING TO ROMANCE!
OH YEAH! ME TOO!

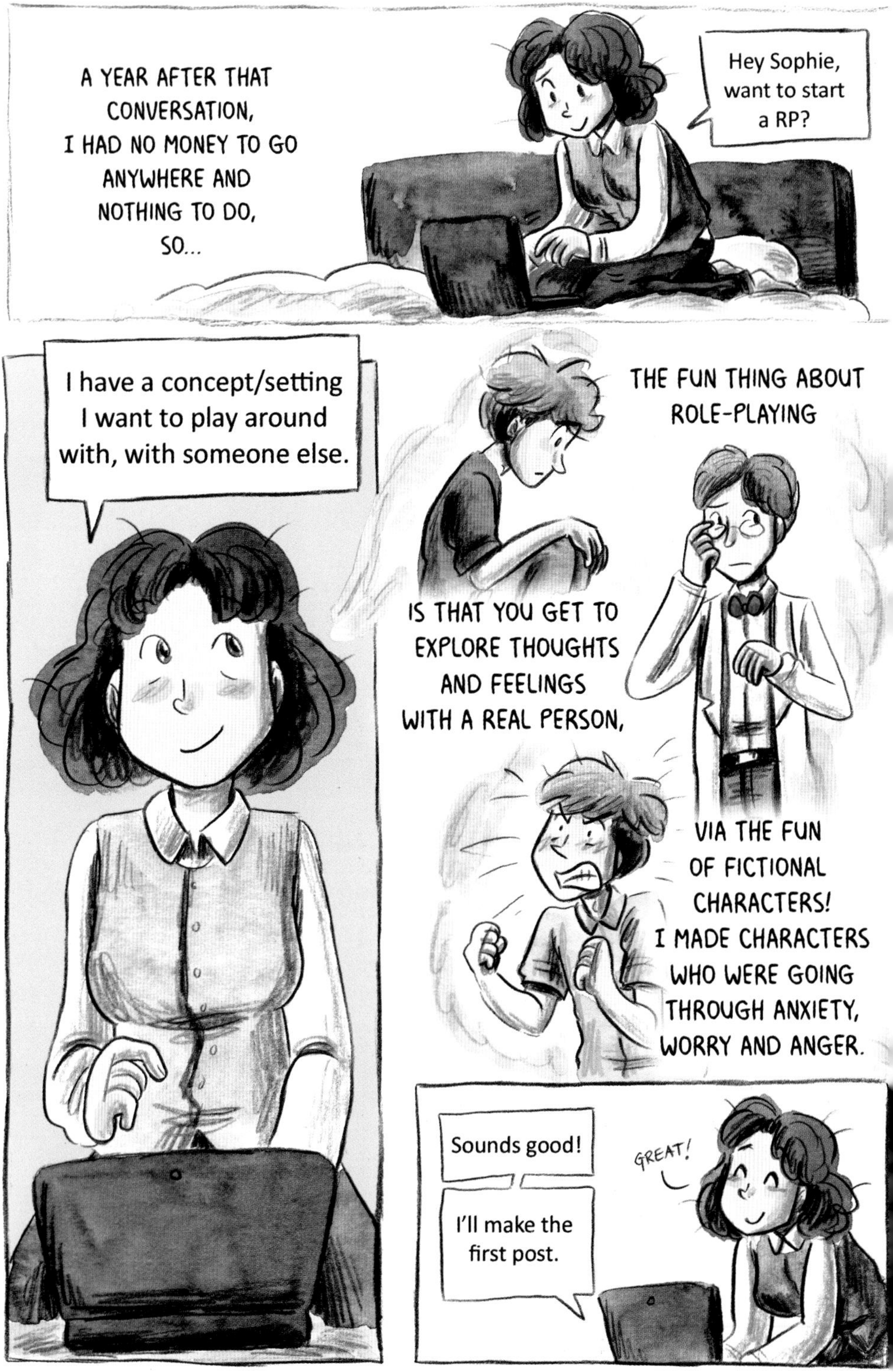
A YEAR AFTER THAT CONVERSATION, I HAD NO MONEY TO GO ANYWHERE AND NOTHING TO DO, SO...
Hey Sophie, want to start a RP?
I have a concept/setting I want to play around with, with someone else.
THE FUN THING ABOUT ROLE-PLAYING
IS THAT YOU GET TO EXPLORE THOUGHTS AND FEELINGS WITH A REAL PERSON,
VIA THE FUN OF FICTIONAL CHARACTERS! I MADE CHARACTERS WHO WERE GOING THROUGH ANXIETY, WORRY AND ANGER.
Sounds good!
I'll make the first post.
GREAT!

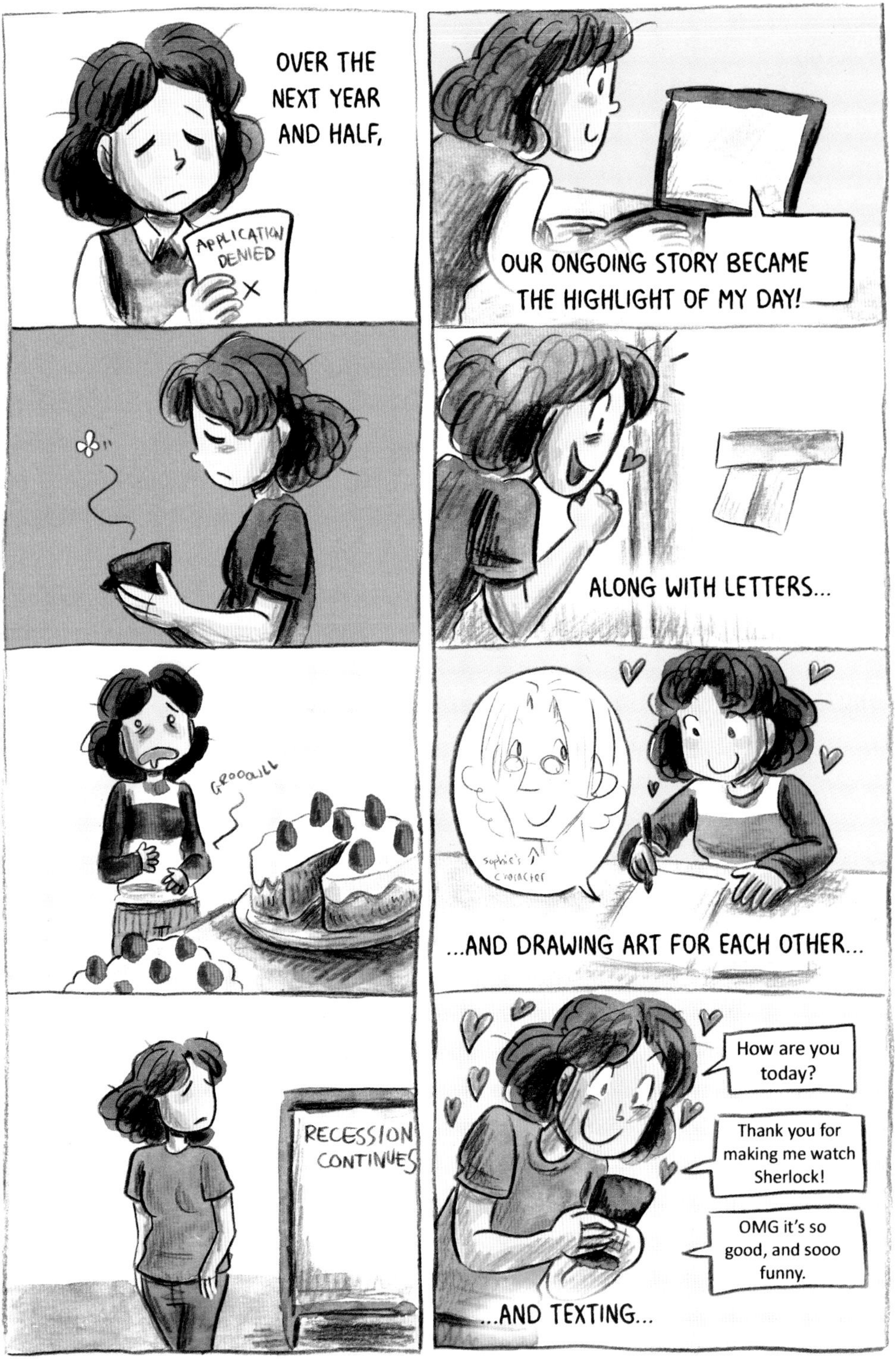
OVER THE NEXT YEAR AND HALF,
APPLICATION DENIED
OUR ONGOING STORY BECAME THE HIGHLIGHT OF MY DAY!
ALONG WITH LETTERS...
GROOOWLL
sophie's character
...AND DRAWING ART FOR EACH OTHER...
RECESSION CONTINUES
How are you today?
Thank you for making me watch Sherlock!
OMG it's so good, and sooo funny.
...AND TEXTING...

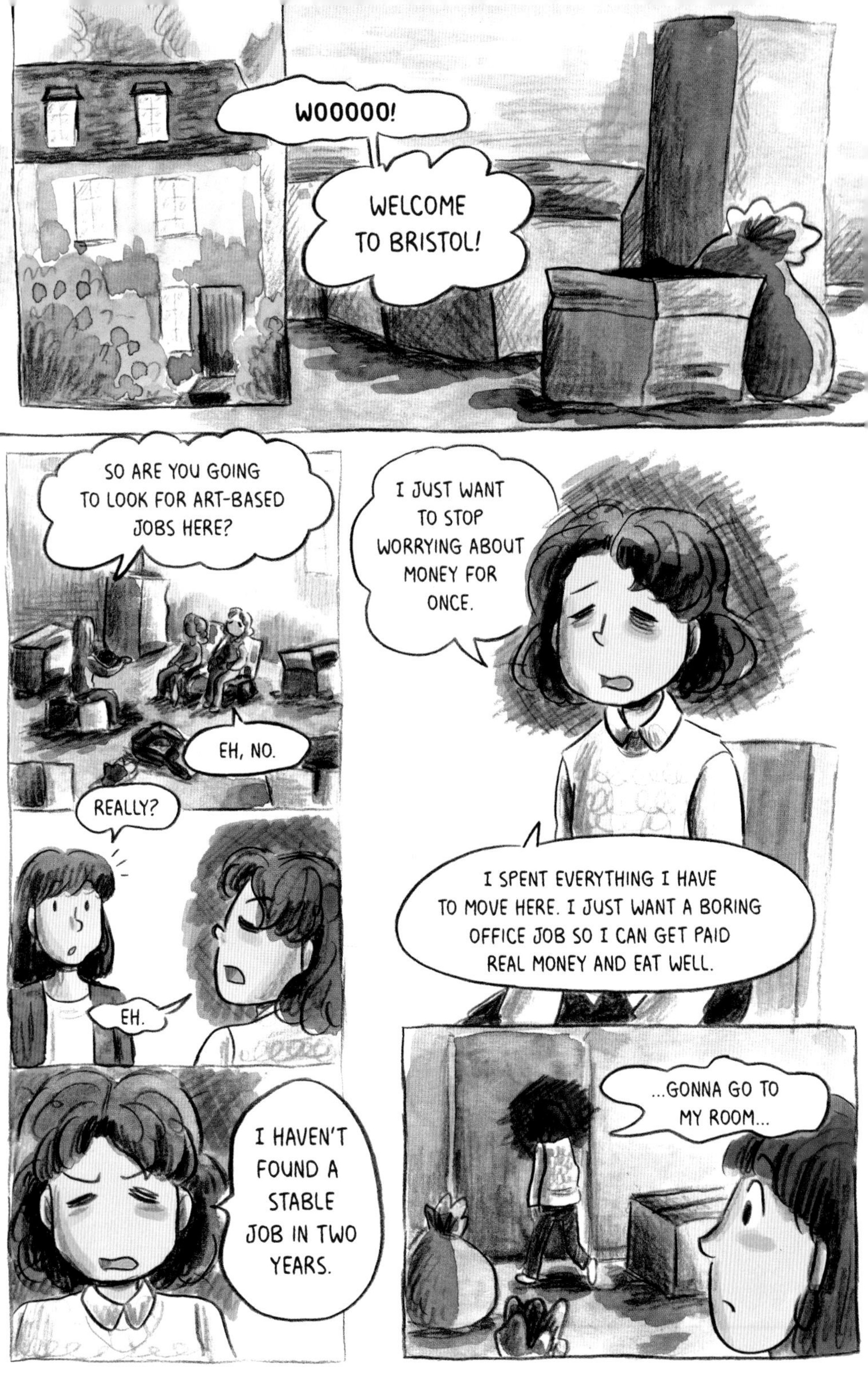
WOOOOO!
WELCOME TO BRISTOL!
SO ARE YOU GOING TO LOOK FOR ART-BASED JOBS HERE?
EH, NO.
I JUST WANT TO STOP WORRYING ABOUT MONEY FOR ONCE.
REALLY?
EH.
I SPENT EVERYTHING I HAVE TO MOVE HERE. I JUST WANT A BORING OFFICE JOB SO I CAN GET PAID REAL MONEY AND EAT WELL.
I HAVEN'T FOUND A STABLE JOB IN TWO YEARS.
...GONNA GO TO MY ROOM...

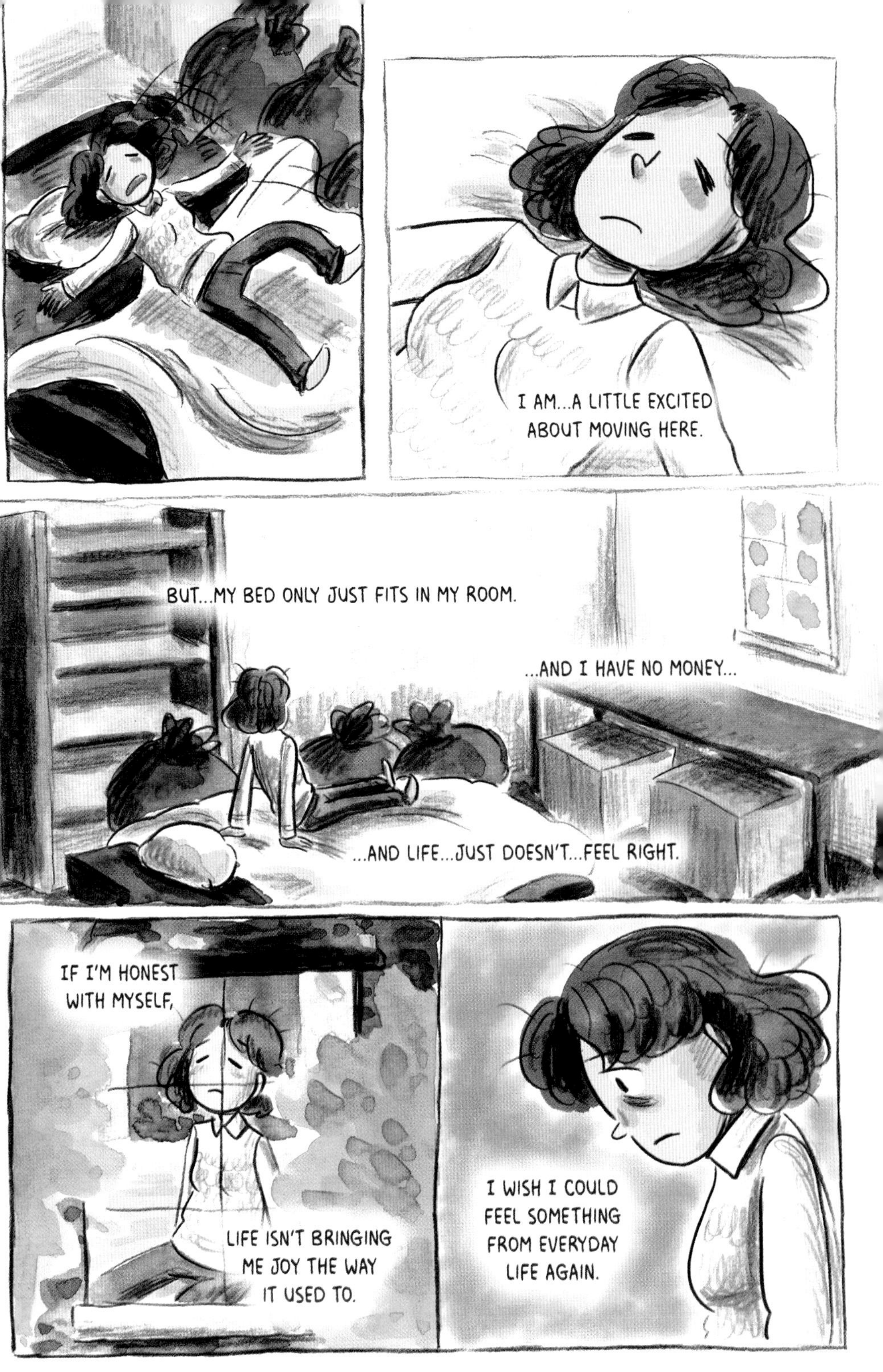
I AM...A LITTLE EXCITED ABOUT MOVING HERE.
BUT...MY BED ONLY JUST FITS IN MY ROOM.
...AND I HAVE NO MONEY...
...AND LIFE...JUST DOESN'T...FEEL RIGHT.
IF I'M HONEST WITH MYSELF,
LIFE ISN'T BRINGING ME JOY THE WAY IT USED TO.
I WISH I COULD FEEL SOMETHING FROM EVERYDAY LIFE AGAIN.

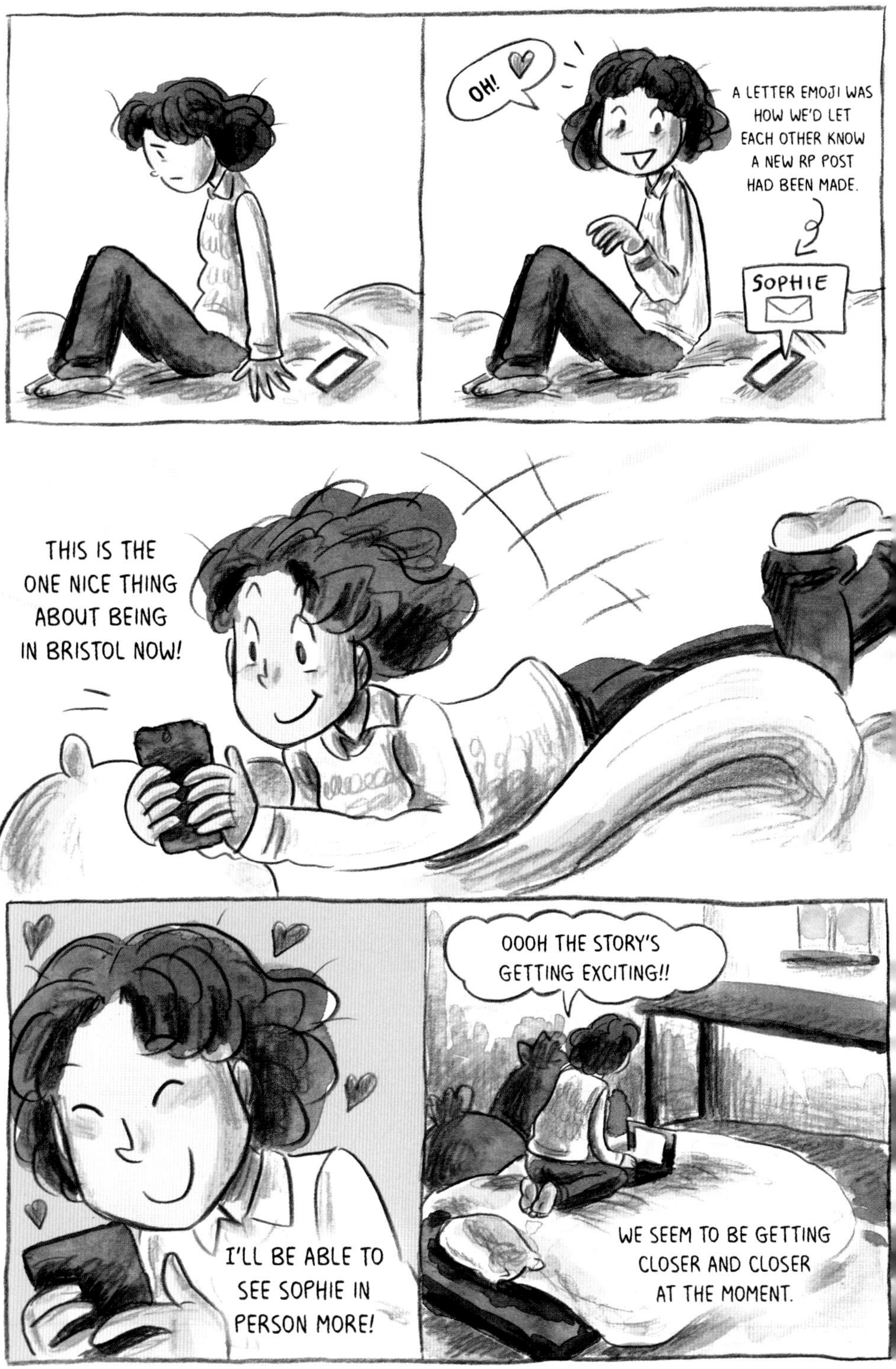
OH!
A LETTER EMOJI WAS HOW WE'D LET EACH OTHER KNOW A NEW RP POST HAD BEEN MADE.
SOPHIE
THIS IS THE ONE NICE THING ABOUT BEING IN BRISTOL NOW!
I'LL BE ABLE TO SEE SOPHIE IN PERSON MORE!
OOOH THE STORY'S GETTING EXCITING!!
WE SEEM TO BE GETTING CLOSER AND CLOSER AT THE MOMENT.

SOPHIE AND I WOULD CREATE OUR STORY BY GOING BACK AND FORTH IN POSTS. AT THE END OF EACH POST, BELOW THE MAIN STORY, WE WOULD OFTEN START HAVING MINI CONVERSATIONS LIKE THIS.

Archie's eyes widened and he started to panic. Faced with what was to him, something more terrifying than death, he didn't know what else to do except whimper helplessly with his hands over his ears.
**((Aaah I'm sorry Archie!))**

OCT 2nd 12:48am

FOR ME, MY CHARACTERS OFTEN BECAME WAYS TO EXPRESS MYSELF TO SOPHIE.

REAL LIFE WEAVED ITSELF INTO OUR CREATIVITY THROUGH OUR MINI CONVERSATIONS.

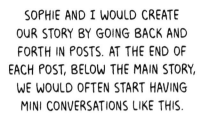

**((the way that Archie reacts here, that's how I react when I'm really scared too. We have the same phobias))**

. . .

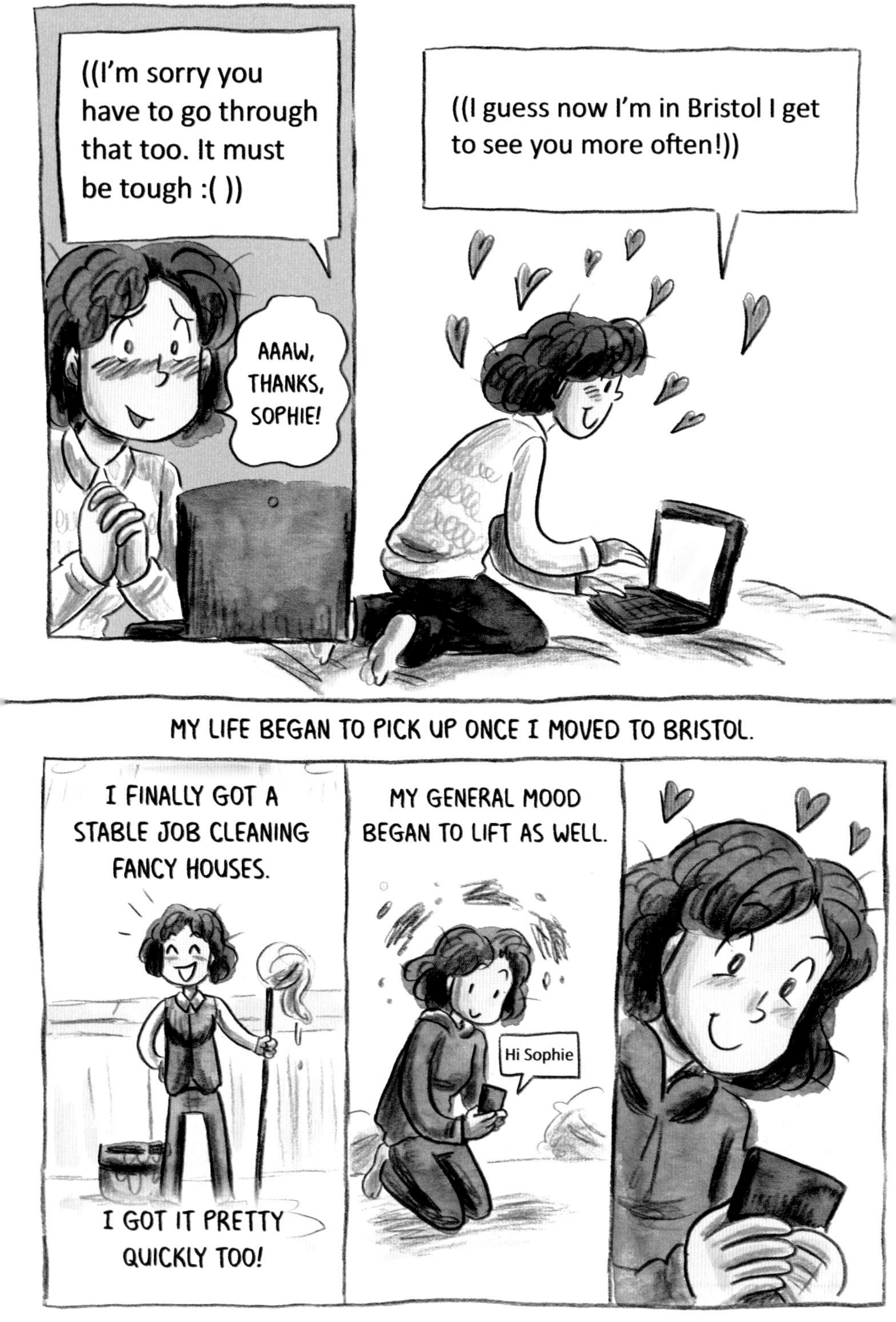

((I'm sorry you have to go through that too. It must be tough :( ))
AAAW, THANKS, SOPHIE!
((I guess now I'm in Bristol I get to see you more often!))
MY LIFE BEGAN TO PICK UP ONCE I MOVED TO BRISTOL.
I FINALLY GOT A STABLE JOB CLEANING FANCY HOUSES.
I GOT IT PRETTY QUICKLY TOO!
MY GENERAL MOOD BEGAN TO LIFT AS WELL.
Hi Sophie

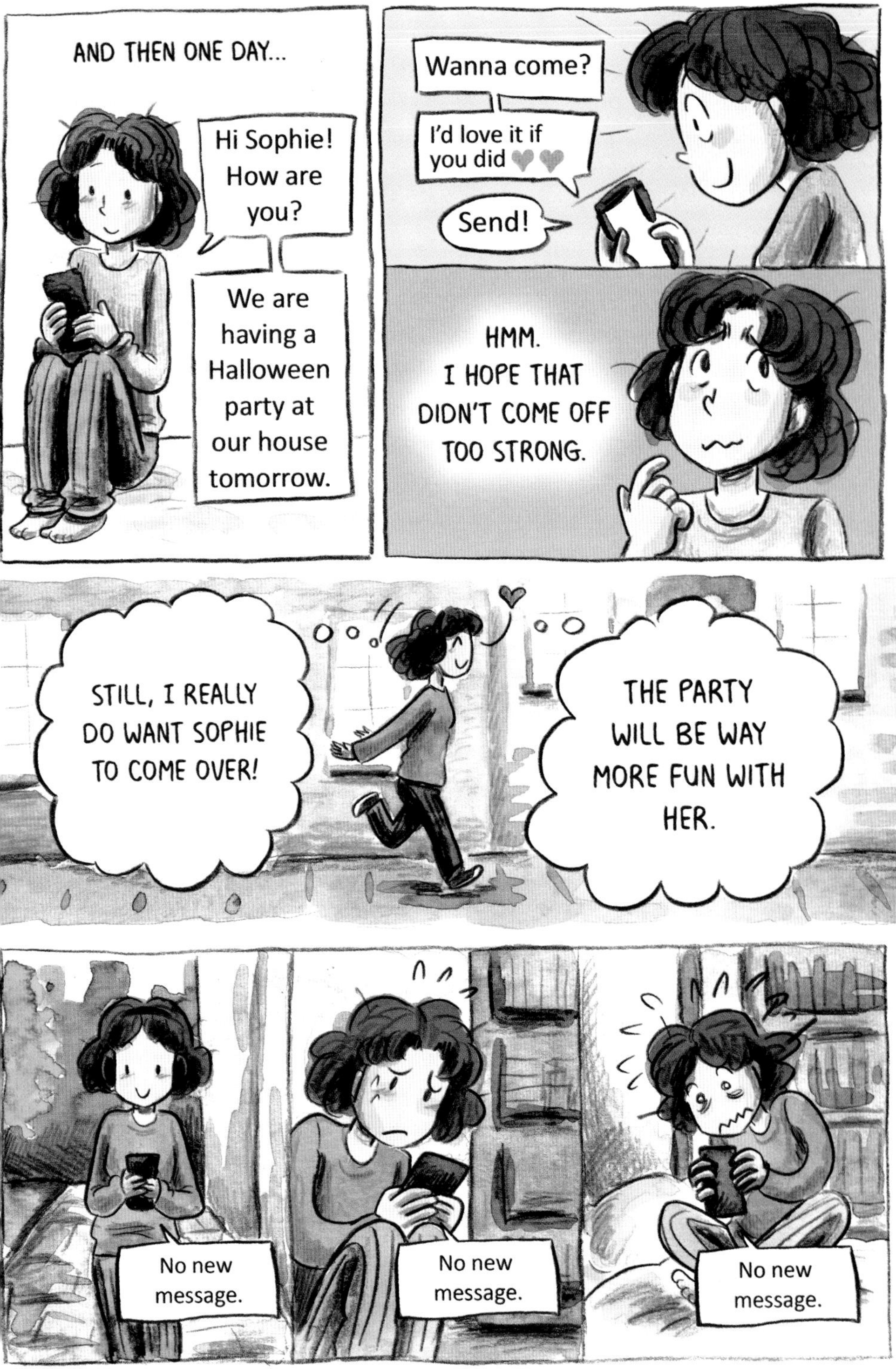

AND THEN ONE DAY...
Hi Sophie! How are you?
We are having a Halloween party at our house tomorrow.
Wanna come?
I'd love it if you did
Send!
HMM. I HOPE THAT DIDN'T COME OFF TOO STRONG.
STILL, I REALLY DO WANT SOPHIE TO COME OVER!
THE PARTY WILL BE WAY MORE FUN WITH HER.
No new message.
No new message.
No new message.

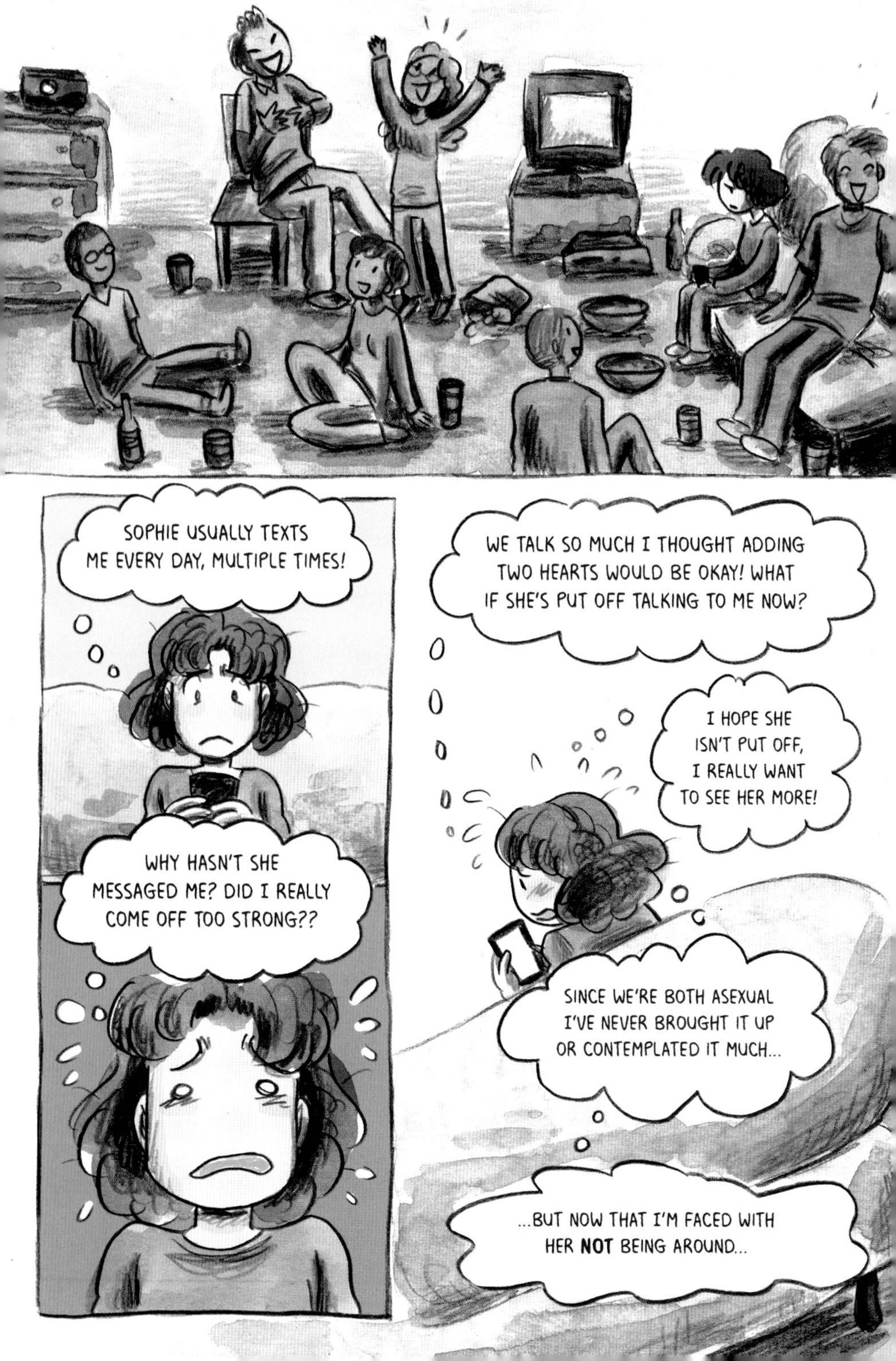
SOPHIE USUALLY TEXTS ME EVERY DAY, MULTIPLE TIMES!
WHY HASN'T SHE MESSAGED ME? DID I REALLY COME OFF TOO STRONG??
WE TALK SO MUCH I THOUGHT ADDING TWO HEARTS WOULD BE OKAY! WHAT IF SHE'S PUT OFF TALKING TO ME NOW?
I HOPE SHE ISN'T PUT OFF, I REALLY WANT TO SEE HER MORE!
SINCE WE'RE BOTH ASEXUAL I'VE NEVER BROUGHT IT UP OR CONTEMPLATED IT MUCH...
...BUT NOW THAT I'M FACED WITH HER **NOT** BEING AROUND...

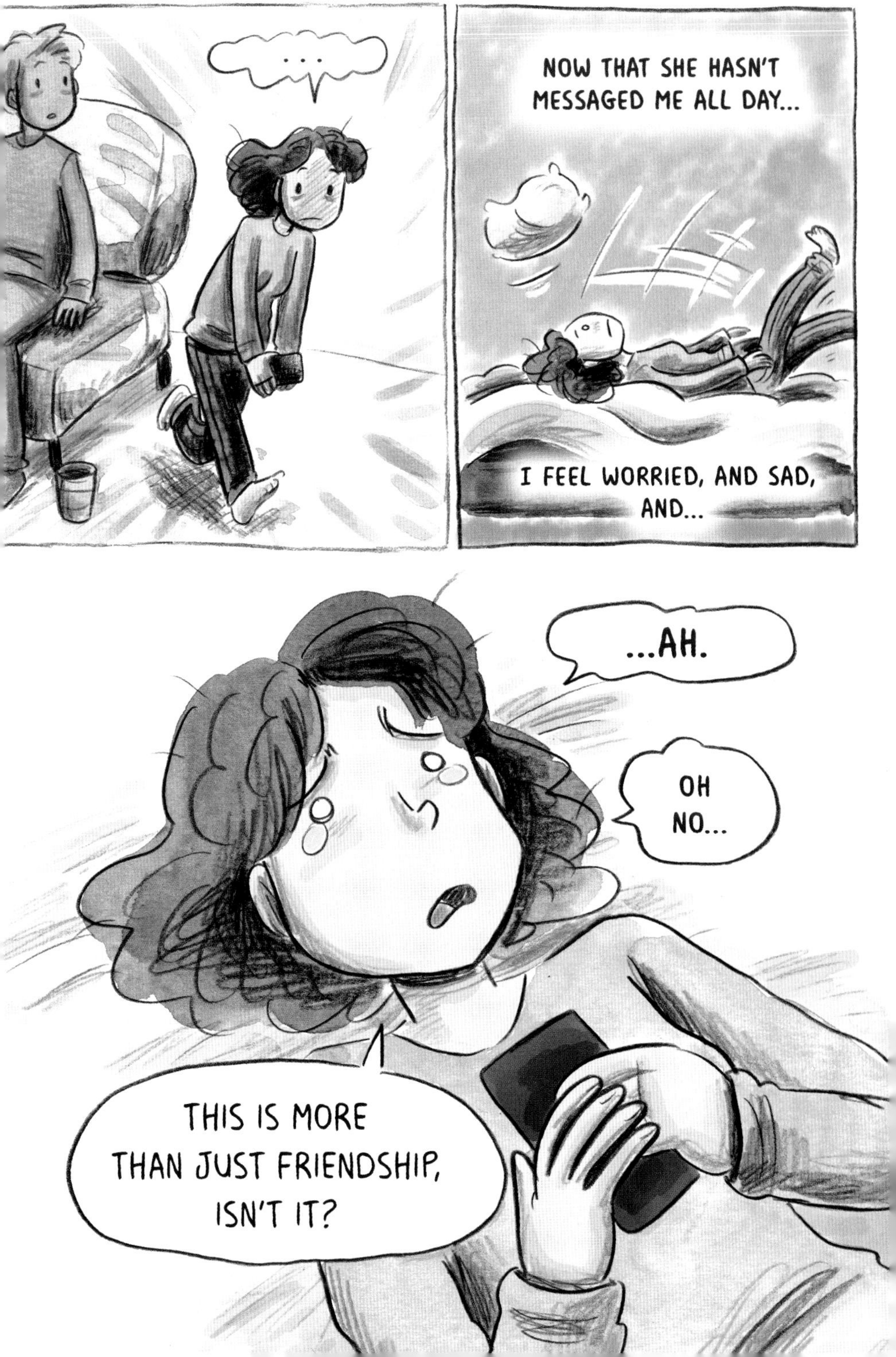
...
NOW THAT SHE HASN'T MESSAGED ME ALL DAY...
I FEEL WORRIED, AND SAD, AND...
...AH.
OH NO...
THIS IS MORE THAN JUST FRIENDSHIP, ISN'T IT?

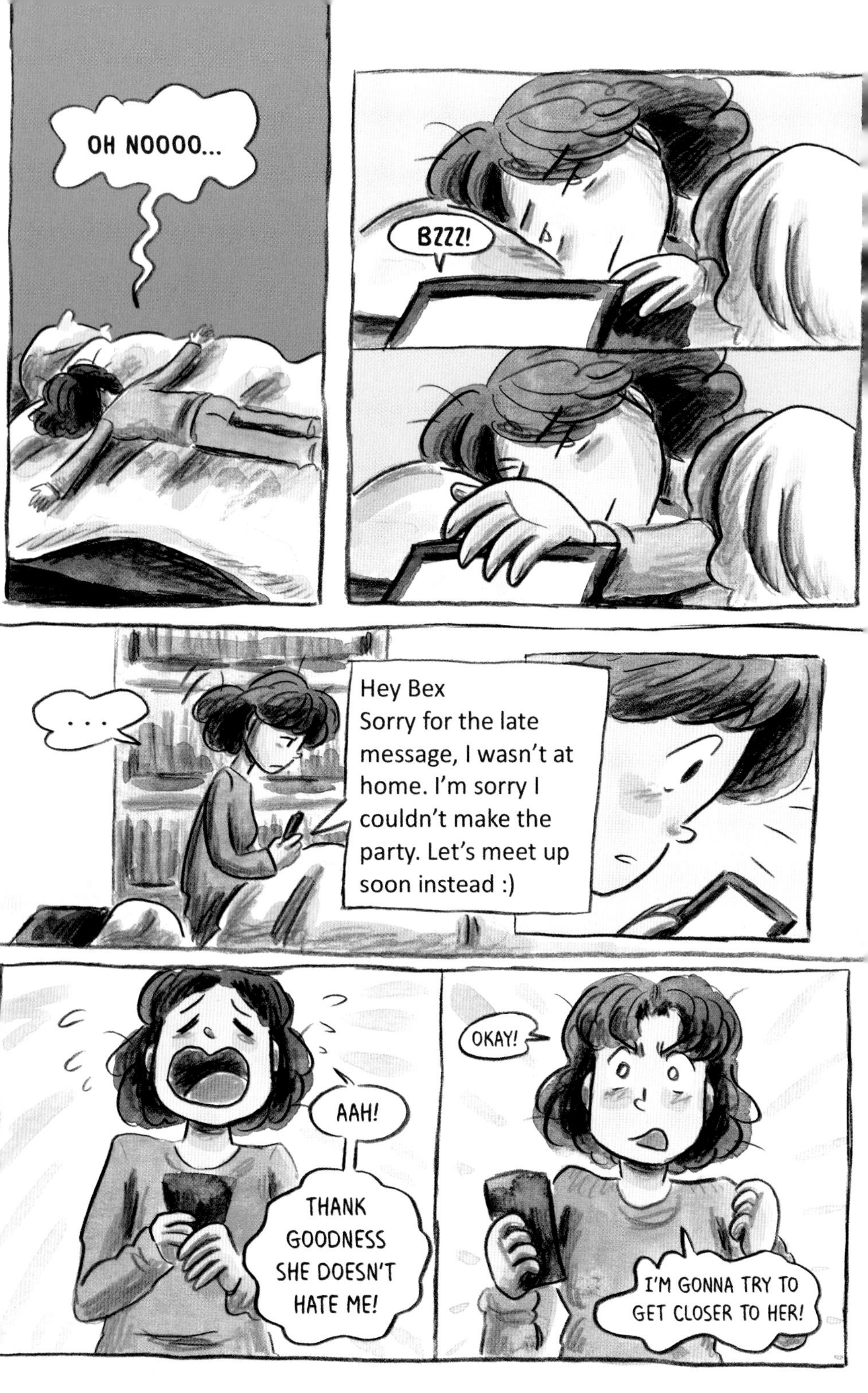
OH NOOOO...
BZZZ!
...
Hey Bex
Sorry for the late message, I wasn't at home. I'm sorry I couldn't make the party. Let's meet up soon instead :)
AAH!
THANK GOODNESS SHE DOESN'T HATE ME!
OKAY!
I'M GONNA TRY TO GET CLOSER TO HER!

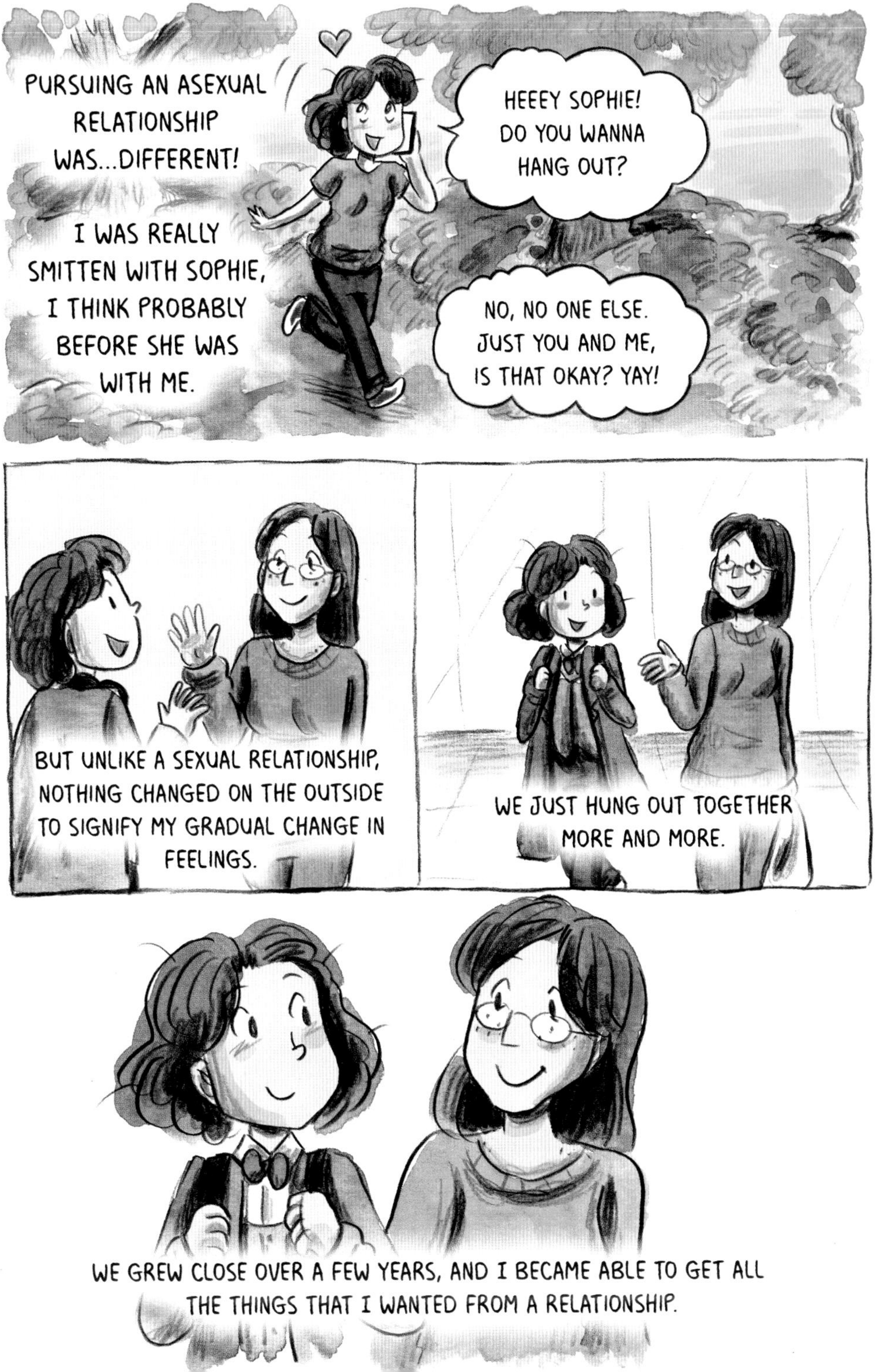
PURSUING AN ASEXUAL RELATIONSHIP WAS...DIFFERENT!
I WAS REALLY SMITTEN WITH SOPHIE, I THINK PROBABLY BEFORE SHE WAS WITH ME.
HEEEY SOPHIE! DO YOU WANNA HANG OUT?
NO, NO ONE ELSE. JUST YOU AND ME, IS THAT OKAY? YAY!
BUT UNLIKE A SEXUAL RELATIONSHIP, NOTHING CHANGED ON THE OUTSIDE TO SIGNIFY MY GRADUAL CHANGE IN FEELINGS.
WE JUST HUNG OUT TOGETHER MORE AND MORE.
WE GREW CLOSE OVER A FEW YEARS, AND I BECAME ABLE TO GET ALL THE THINGS THAT I WANTED FROM A RELATIONSHIP.

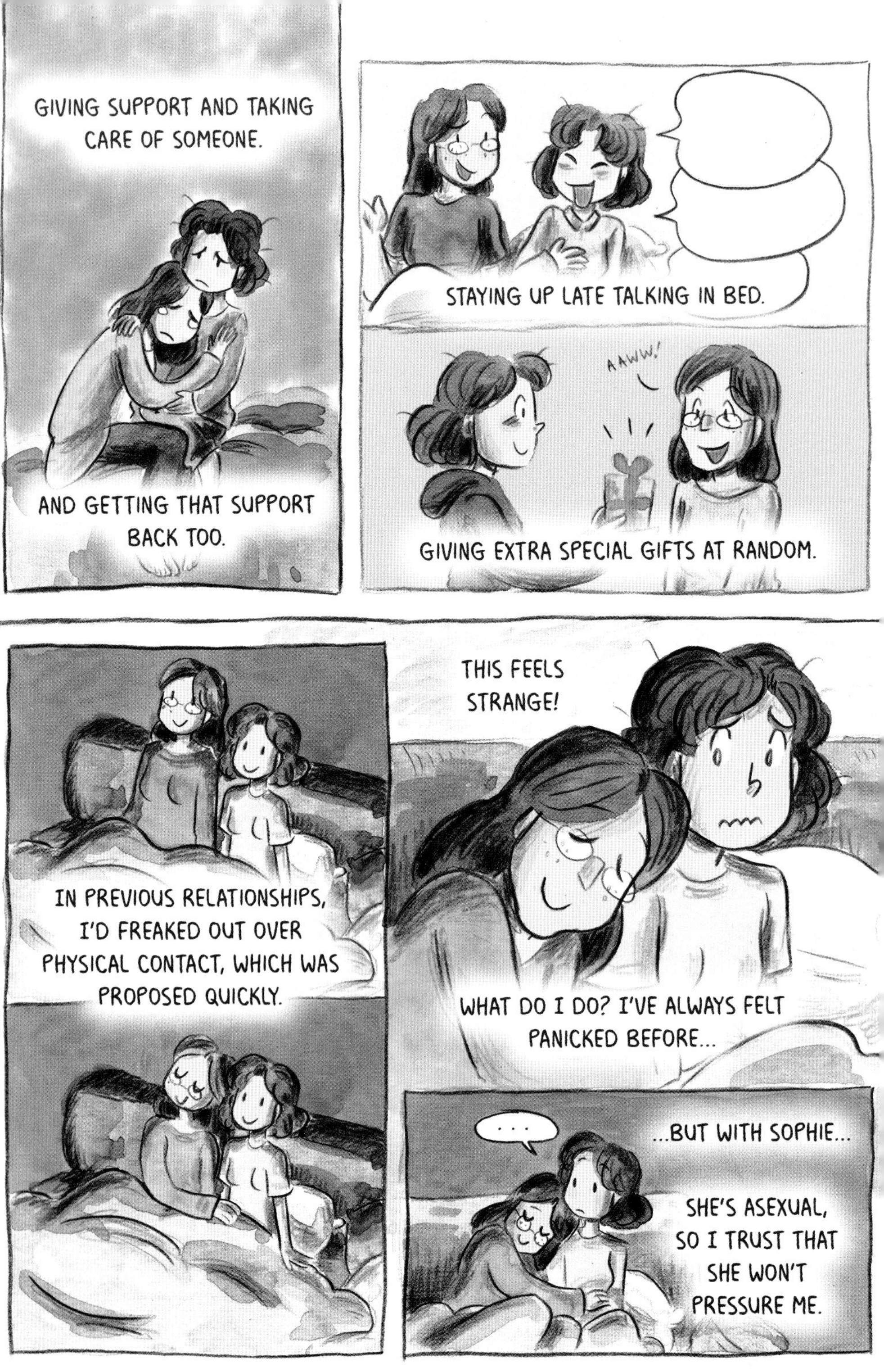
GIVING SUPPORT AND TAKING CARE OF SOMEONE.
AND GETTING THAT SUPPORT BACK TOO.
STAYING UP LATE TALKING IN BED.
AAWW!
GIVING EXTRA SPECIAL GIFTS AT RANDOM.
IN PREVIOUS RELATIONSHIPS, I'D FREAKED OUT OVER PHYSICAL CONTACT, WHICH WAS PROPOSED QUICKLY.
THIS FEELS STRANGE!
WHAT DO I DO? I'VE ALWAYS FELT PANICKED BEFORE...
...
...BUT WITH SOPHIE...
SHE'S ASEXUAL, SO I TRUST THAT SHE WON'T PRESSURE ME.

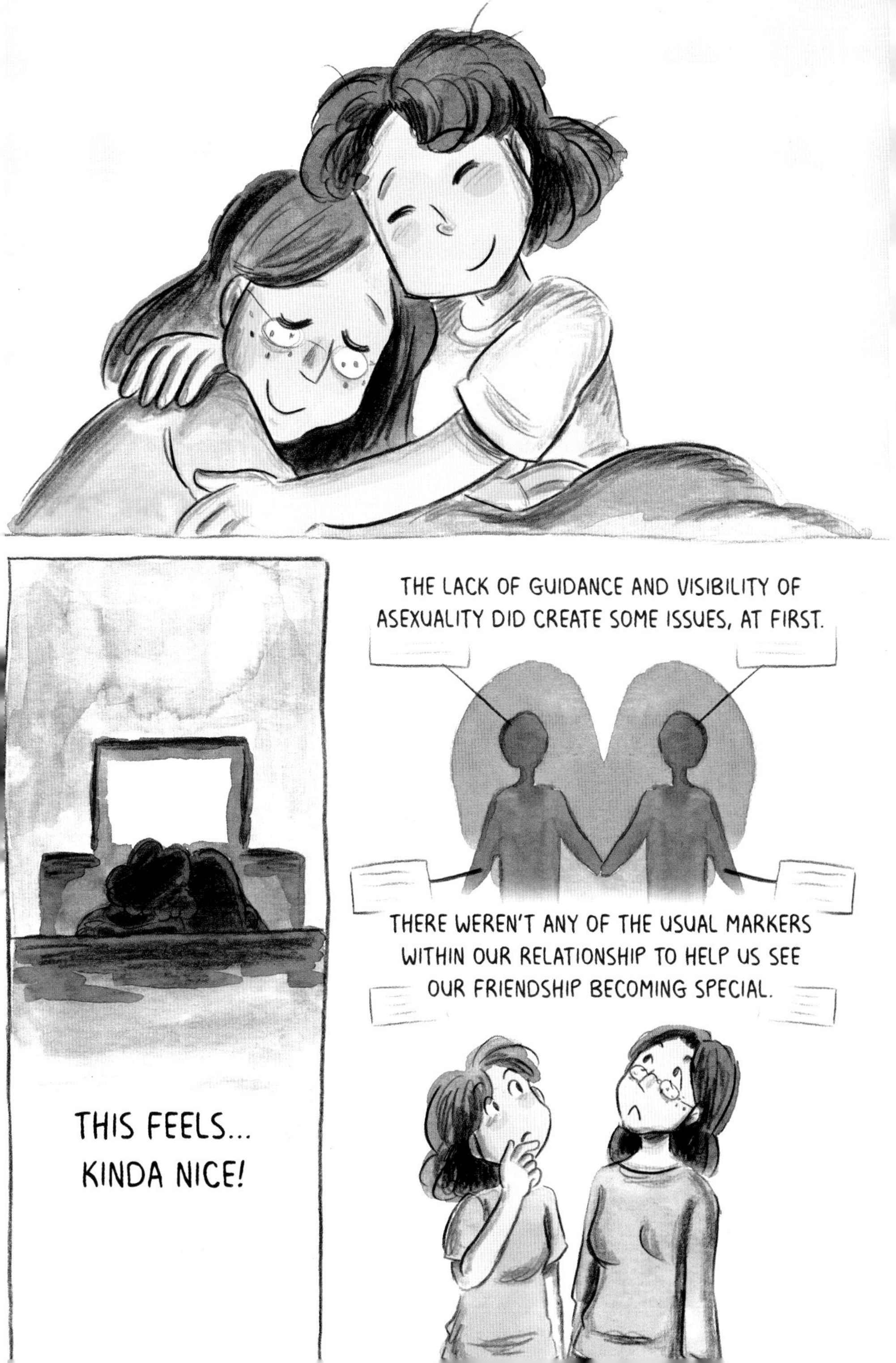
THIS FEELS... KINDA NICE!
THE LACK OF GUIDANCE AND VISIBILITY OF ASEXUALITY DID CREATE SOME ISSUES, AT FIRST.
THERE WEREN'T ANY OF THE USUAL MARKERS WITHIN OUR RELATIONSHIP TO HELP US SEE OUR FRIENDSHIP BECOMING SPECIAL.

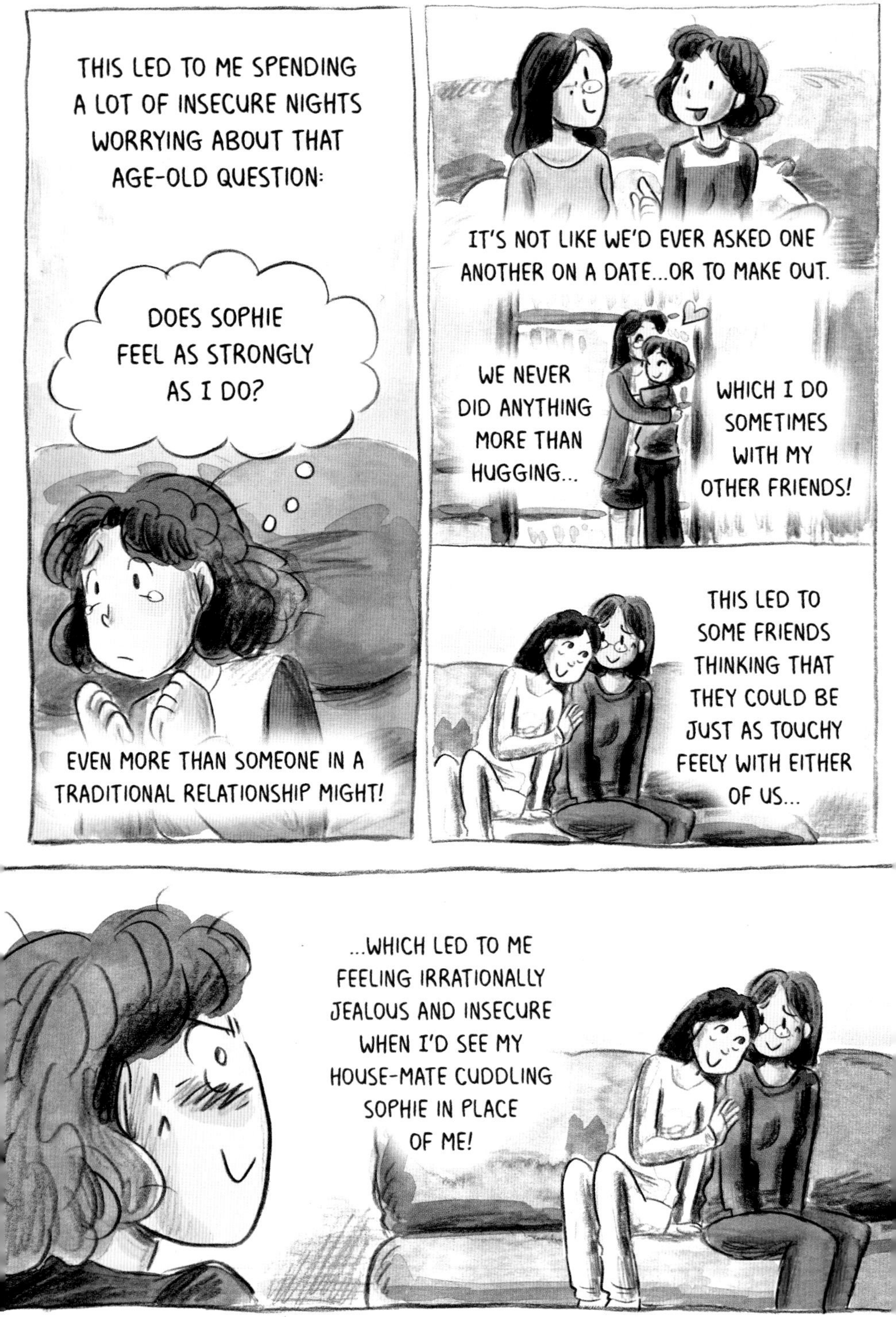
THIS LED TO ME SPENDING A LOT OF INSECURE NIGHTS WORRYING ABOUT THAT AGE-OLD QUESTION:
DOES SOPHIE FEEL AS STRONGLY AS I DO?
EVEN MORE THAN SOMEONE IN A TRADITIONAL RELATIONSHIP MIGHT!
IT'S NOT LIKE WE'D EVER ASKED ONE ANOTHER ON A DATE...OR TO MAKE OUT.
WE NEVER DID ANYTHING MORE THAN HUGGING...
WHICH I DO SOMETIMES WITH MY OTHER FRIENDS!
THIS LED TO SOME FRIENDS THINKING THAT THEY COULD BE JUST AS TOUCHY FEELY WITH EITHER OF US...
...WHICH LED TO ME FEELING IRRATIONALLY JEALOUS AND INSECURE WHEN I'D SEE MY HOUSE-MATE CUDDLING SOPHIE IN PLACE OF ME!

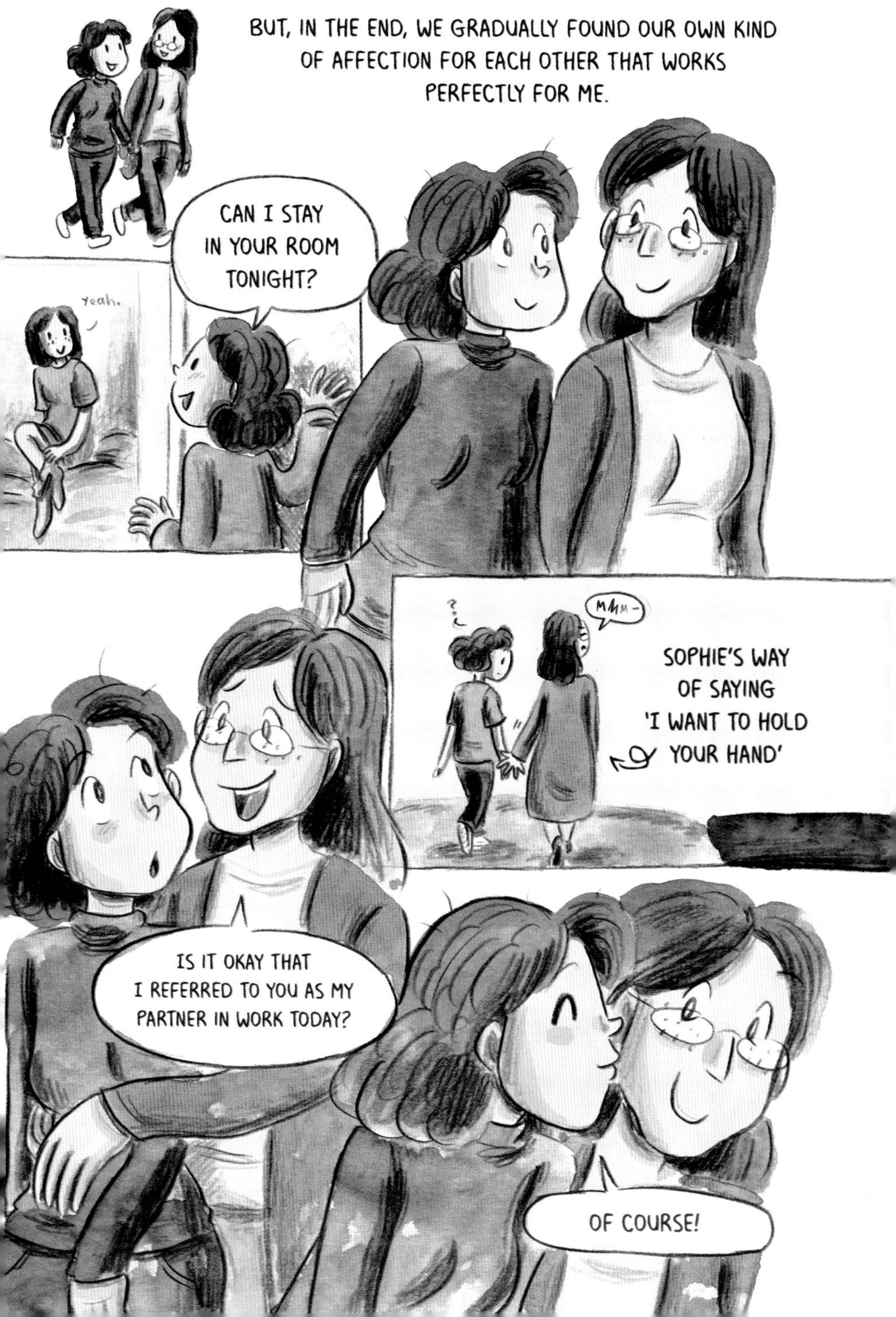
BUT, IN THE END, WE GRADUALLY FOUND OUR OWN KIND OF AFFECTION FOR EACH OTHER THAT WORKS PERFECTLY FOR ME.
Yeah.
CAN I STAY IN YOUR ROOM TONIGHT?
MMM-
SOPHIE'S WAY OF SAYING 'I WANT TO HOLD YOUR HAND'
IS IT OKAY THAT I REFERRED TO YOU AS MY PARTNER IN WORK TODAY?
OF COURSE!

# THINGS PEOPLE SAY TO ME IF I HAPPEN TO MENTION THAT I'M ASEXUAL DURING A CONVERSATION...

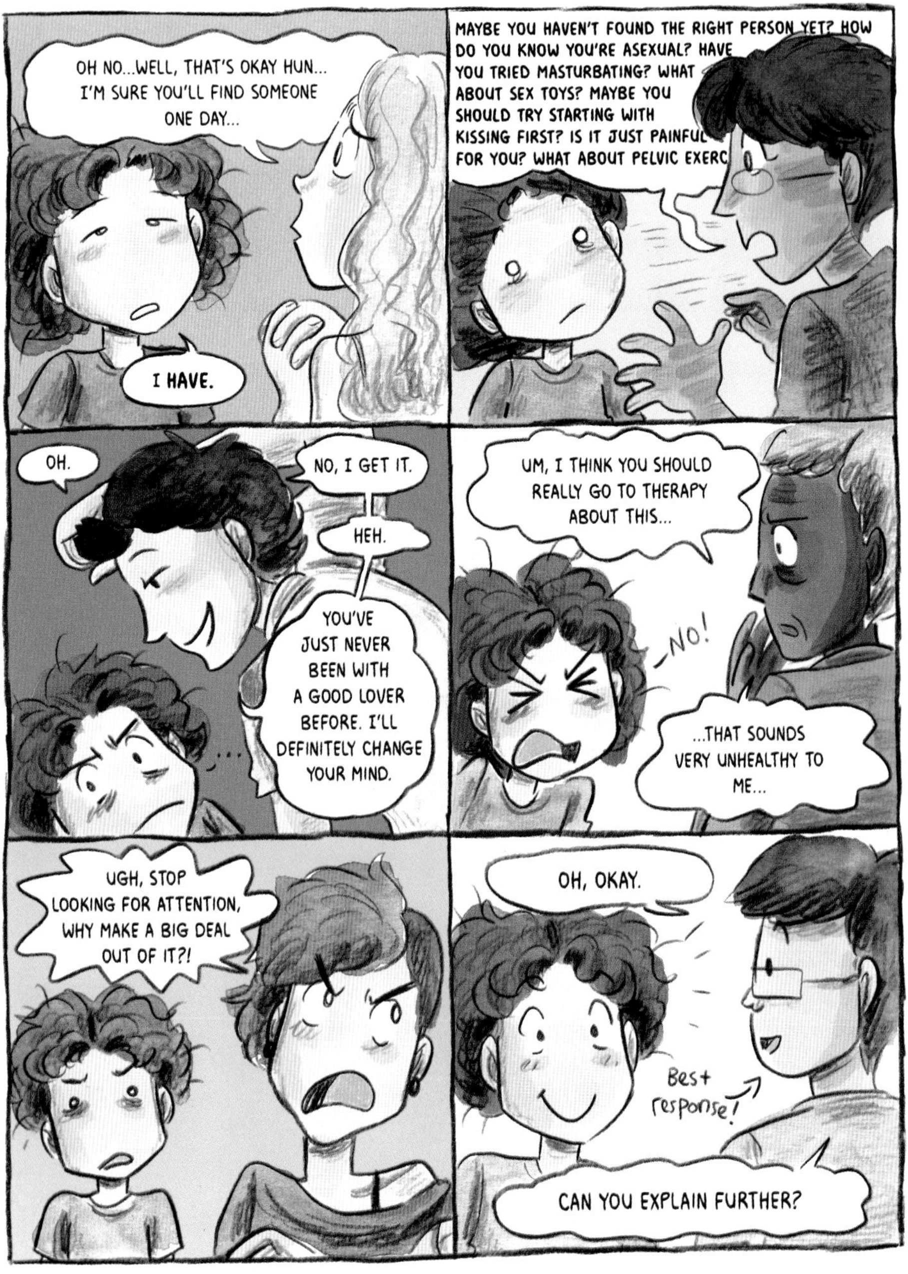
OH NO...WELL, THAT'S OKAY HUN... I'M SURE YOU'LL FIND SOMEONE ONE DAY...
I HAVE.
MAYBE YOU HAVEN'T FOUND THE RIGHT PERSON YET? HOW DO YOU KNOW YOU'RE ASEXUAL? HAVE YOU TRIED MASTURBATING? WHAT ABOUT SEX TOYS? MAYBE YOU SHOULD TRY STARTING WITH KISSING FIRST? IS IT JUST PAINFUL FOR YOU? WHAT ABOUT PELVIC EXERC
OH.
NO, I GET IT.
HEH.
YOU'VE JUST NEVER BEEN WITH A GOOD LOVER BEFORE. I'LL DEFINITELY CHANGE YOUR MIND.
...
UM, I THINK YOU SHOULD REALLY GO TO THERAPY ABOUT THIS...
NO!
...THAT SOUNDS VERY UNHEALTHY TO ME...
UGH, STOP LOOKING FOR ATTENTION, WHY MAKE A BIG DEAL OUT OF IT?!
OH, OKAY.
CAN YOU EXPLAIN FURTHER?
Best response!

# CHAPTER SIX

## HOW TO BE ACE

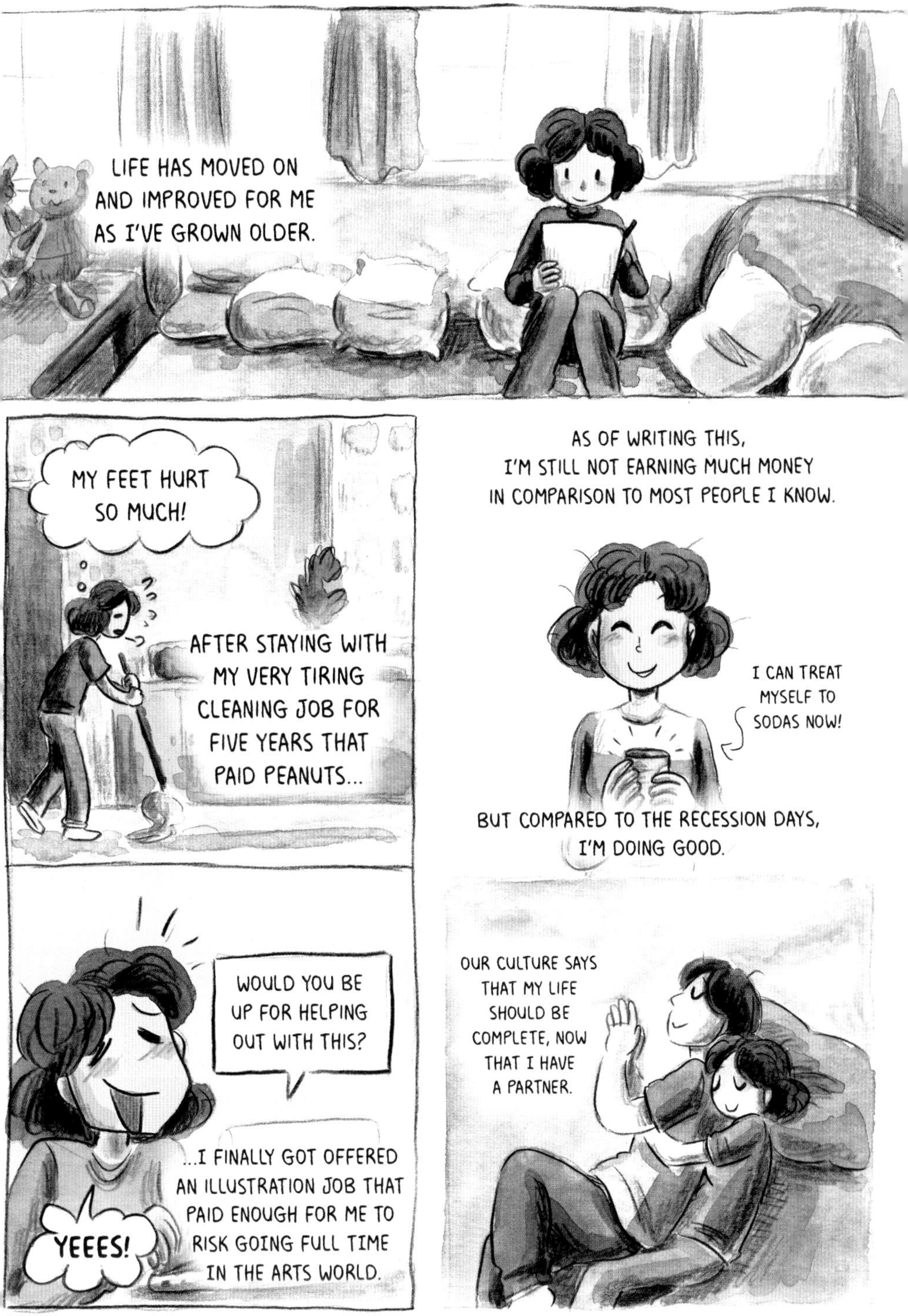
LIFE HAS MOVED ON AND IMPROVED FOR ME AS I'VE GROWN OLDER.
MY FEET HURT SO MUCH!
AFTER STAYING WITH MY VERY TIRING CLEANING JOB FOR FIVE YEARS THAT PAID PEANUTS...
WOULD YOU BE UP FOR HELPING OUT WITH THIS?
...I FINALLY GOT OFFERED AN ILLUSTRATION JOB THAT PAID ENOUGH FOR ME TO RISK GOING FULL TIME IN THE ARTS WORLD.
YEEES!
AS OF WRITING THIS, I'M STILL NOT EARNING MUCH MONEY IN COMPARISON TO MOST PEOPLE I KNOW.
I CAN TREAT MYSELF TO SODAS NOW!
BUT COMPARED TO THE RECESSION DAYS, I'M DOING GOOD.
OUR CULTURE SAYS THAT MY LIFE SHOULD BE COMPLETE, NOW THAT I HAVE A PARTNER.

BUT OF COURSE, LIFE IS **NOT** A BINARY PATH WHERE THE END GOAL IS A HAPPY PERFECT ENDING.

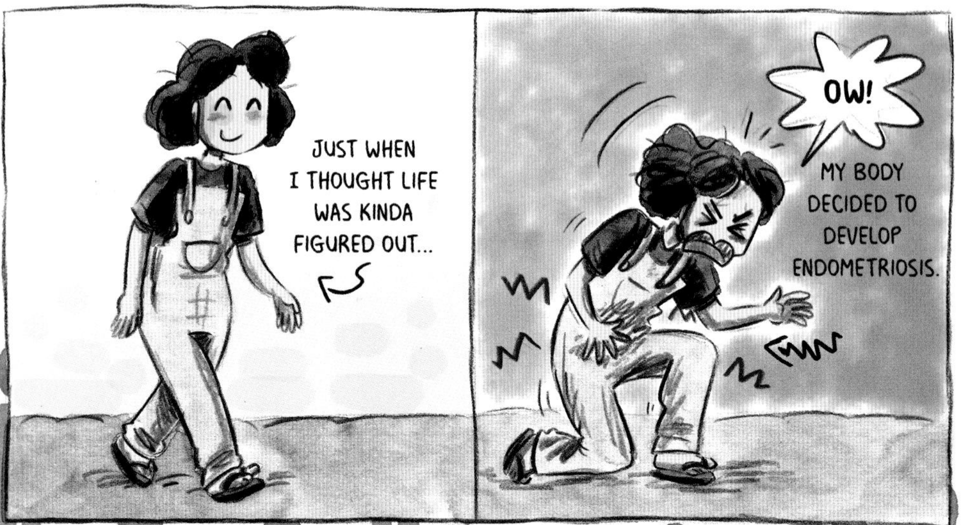
JUST WHEN I THOUGHT LIFE WAS KINDA FIGURED OUT...
OW!
MY BODY DECIDED TO DEVELOP ENDOMETRIOSIS.

AND I LEARNED BACK AT UNI TO NOT RELY ON RELATIONSHIPS BEING THE END GOAL OR WHAT WILL SOLVE ALL MY PROBLEMS.

SINCE MY OWN REALIZATION THROUGH TRYING TO PURSUE SEXUAL RELATIONSHIPS, IT'S MADE ME AWARE OF HOW MANY DIFFERENT KINDS OF PEOPLE THIS CULTURALLY ACCEPTED CONCEPT EXCLUDES.

IF BEING IN A RELATIONSHIP IS THE BIG THING NO ONE SHOULD BE WITHOUT, ARE WE SAYING THAT PEOPLE WHO ARE AROMANTIC HAVE LESS MEANINGFUL LIVES?

WHAT ABOUT PEOPLE WHO WOULD HAVE RELATIONSHIPS, BUT ARE NOT CURRENTLY ABLE TO BECAUSE OF PHYSICAL OR MENTAL HEALTH PROBLEMS?

WHAT ABOUT PEOPLE WHO DIVORCE LATER ON IN LIFE, LOSE THEIR PARTNER OR SIMPLY HAVEN'T FOUND THE RIGHT PERSON...WHY DO WE ACT AS IF THEIR LIVES ARE MEANINGLESS?

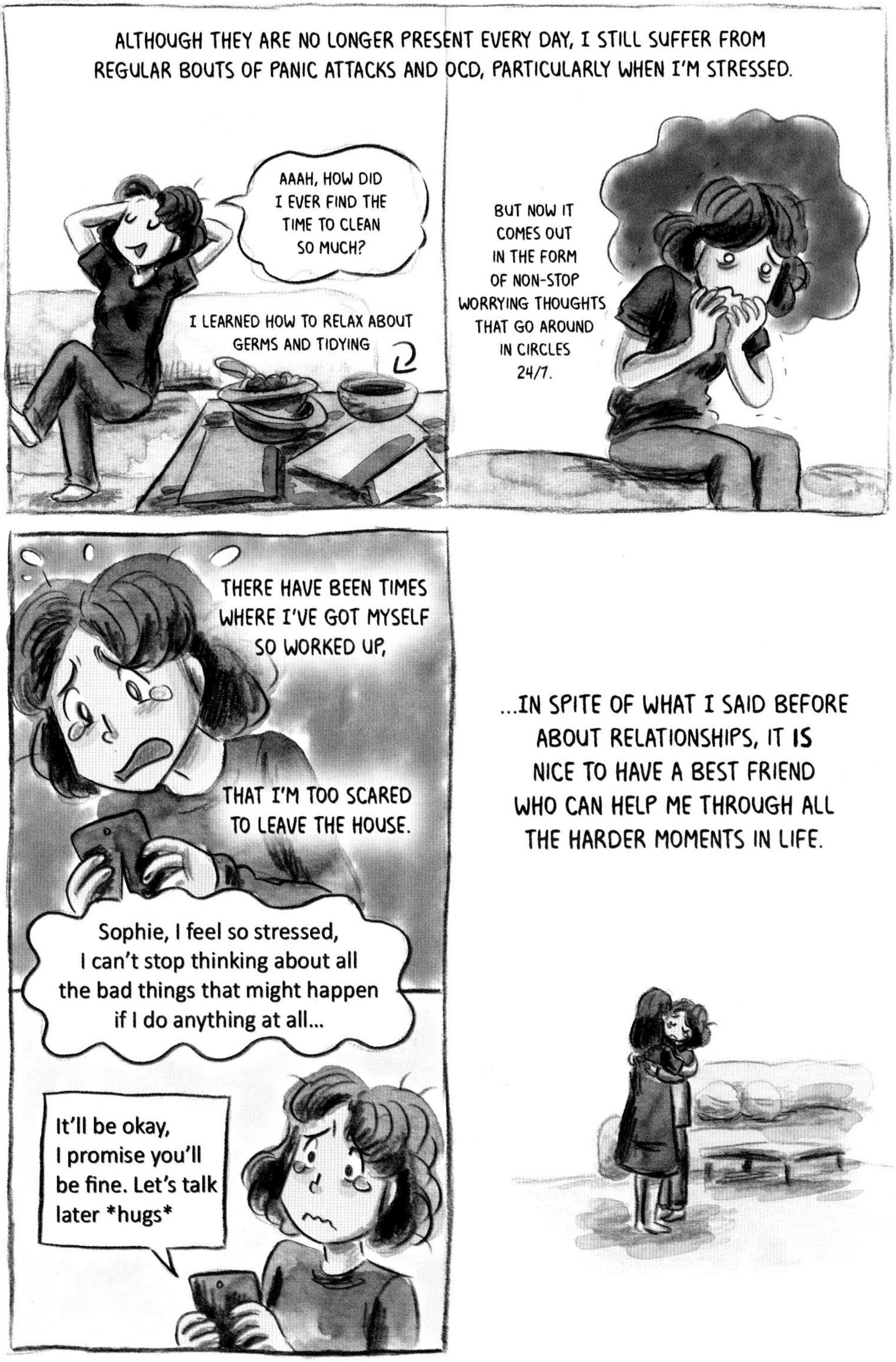
ALTHOUGH THEY ARE NO LONGER PRESENT EVERY DAY, I STILL SUFFER FROM REGULAR BOUTS OF PANIC ATTACKS AND OCD, PARTICULARLY WHEN I'M STRESSED.
AAAH, HOW DID I EVER FIND THE TIME TO CLEAN SO MUCH?
I LEARNED HOW TO RELAX ABOUT GERMS AND TIDYING
BUT NOW IT COMES OUT IN THE FORM OF NON-STOP WORRYING THOUGHTS THAT GO AROUND IN CIRCLES 24/7.
THERE HAVE BEEN TIMES WHERE I'VE GOT MYSELF SO WORKED UP,
THAT I'M TOO SCARED TO LEAVE THE HOUSE.
Sophie, I feel so stressed, I can't stop thinking about all the bad things that might happen if I do anything at all...
It'll be okay, I promise you'll be fine. Let's talk later *hugs*
...IN SPITE OF WHAT I SAID BEFORE ABOUT RELATIONSHIPS, IT IS NICE TO HAVE A BEST FRIEND WHO CAN HELP ME THROUGH ALL THE HARDER MOMENTS IN LIFE.

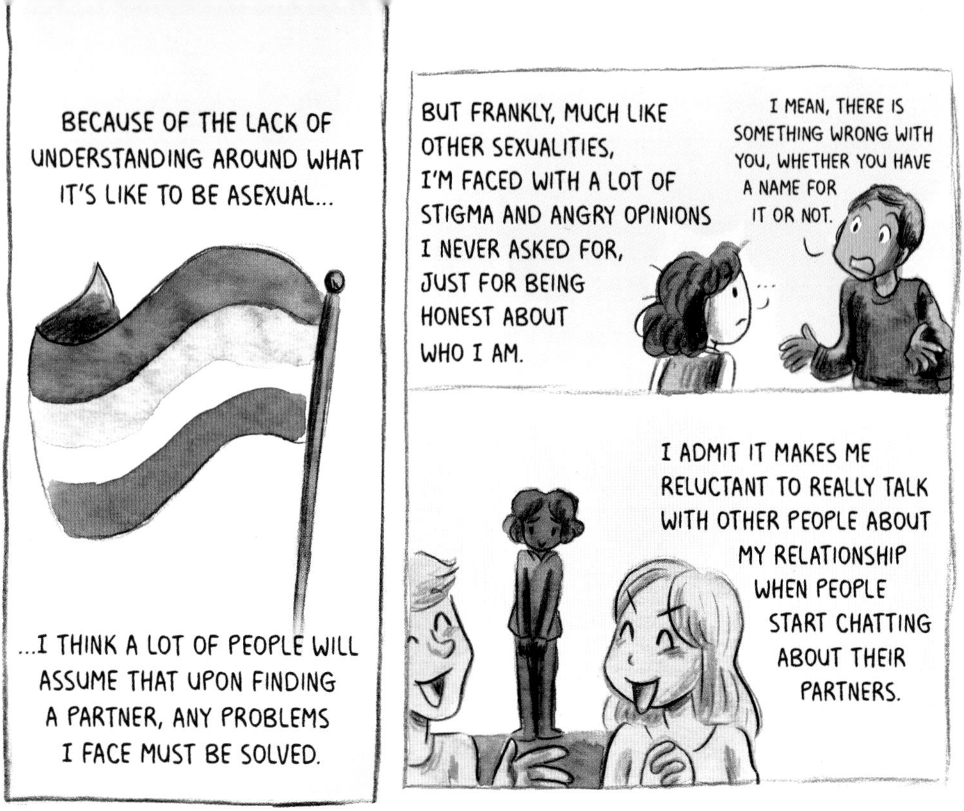
BECAUSE OF THE LACK OF UNDERSTANDING AROUND WHAT IT'S LIKE TO BE ASEXUAL...
...I THINK A LOT OF PEOPLE WILL ASSUME THAT UPON FINDING A PARTNER, ANY PROBLEMS I FACE MUST BE SOLVED.
BUT FRANKLY, MUCH LIKE OTHER SEXUALITIES, I'M FACED WITH A LOT OF STIGMA AND ANGRY OPINIONS I NEVER ASKED FOR, JUST FOR BEING HONEST ABOUT WHO I AM.
I MEAN, THERE IS SOMETHING WRONG WITH YOU, WHETHER YOU HAVE A NAME FOR IT OR NOT.
...
I ADMIT IT MAKES ME RELUCTANT TO REALLY TALK WITH OTHER PEOPLE ABOUT MY RELATIONSHIP WHEN PEOPLE START CHATTING ABOUT THEIR PARTNERS.

PEOPLE MAY BE SURPRISED TO FIND THAT ASEXUALS GET JUDGED ON A POLITICAL SCALE TOO:

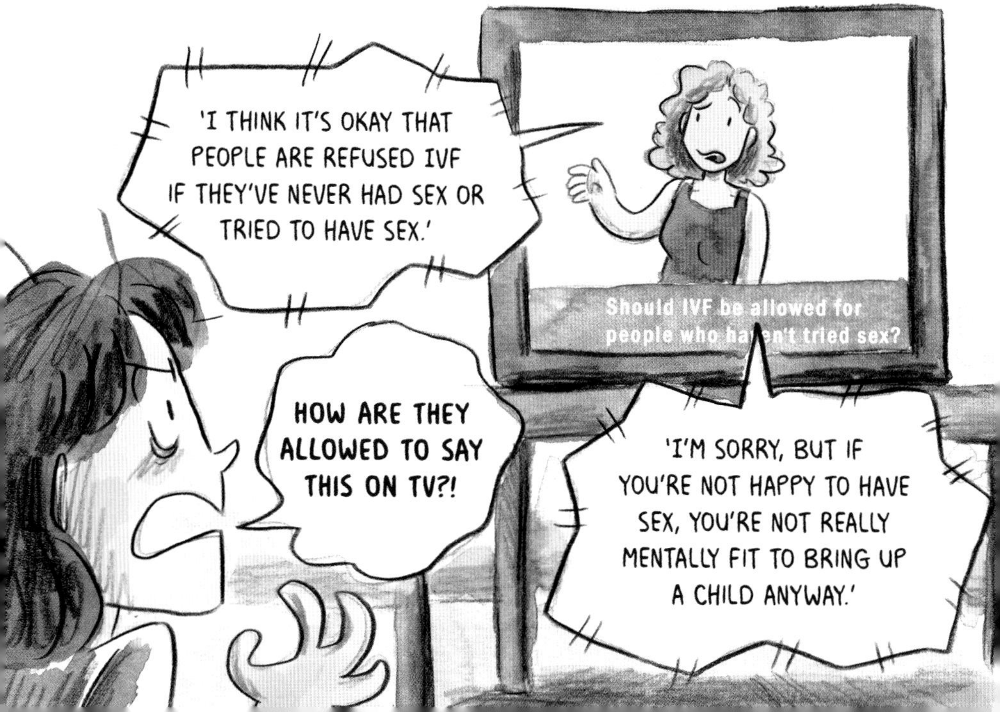
'I THINK IT'S OKAY THAT PEOPLE ARE REFUSED IVF IF THEY'VE NEVER HAD SEX OR TRIED TO HAVE SEX.'
Should IVF be allowed for people who ha en't tried sex?
HOW ARE THEY ALLOWED TO SAY THIS ON TV?!
'I'M SORRY, BUT IF YOU'RE NOT HAPPY TO HAVE SEX, YOU'RE NOT REALLY MENTALLY FIT TO BRING UP A CHILD ANYWAY.'

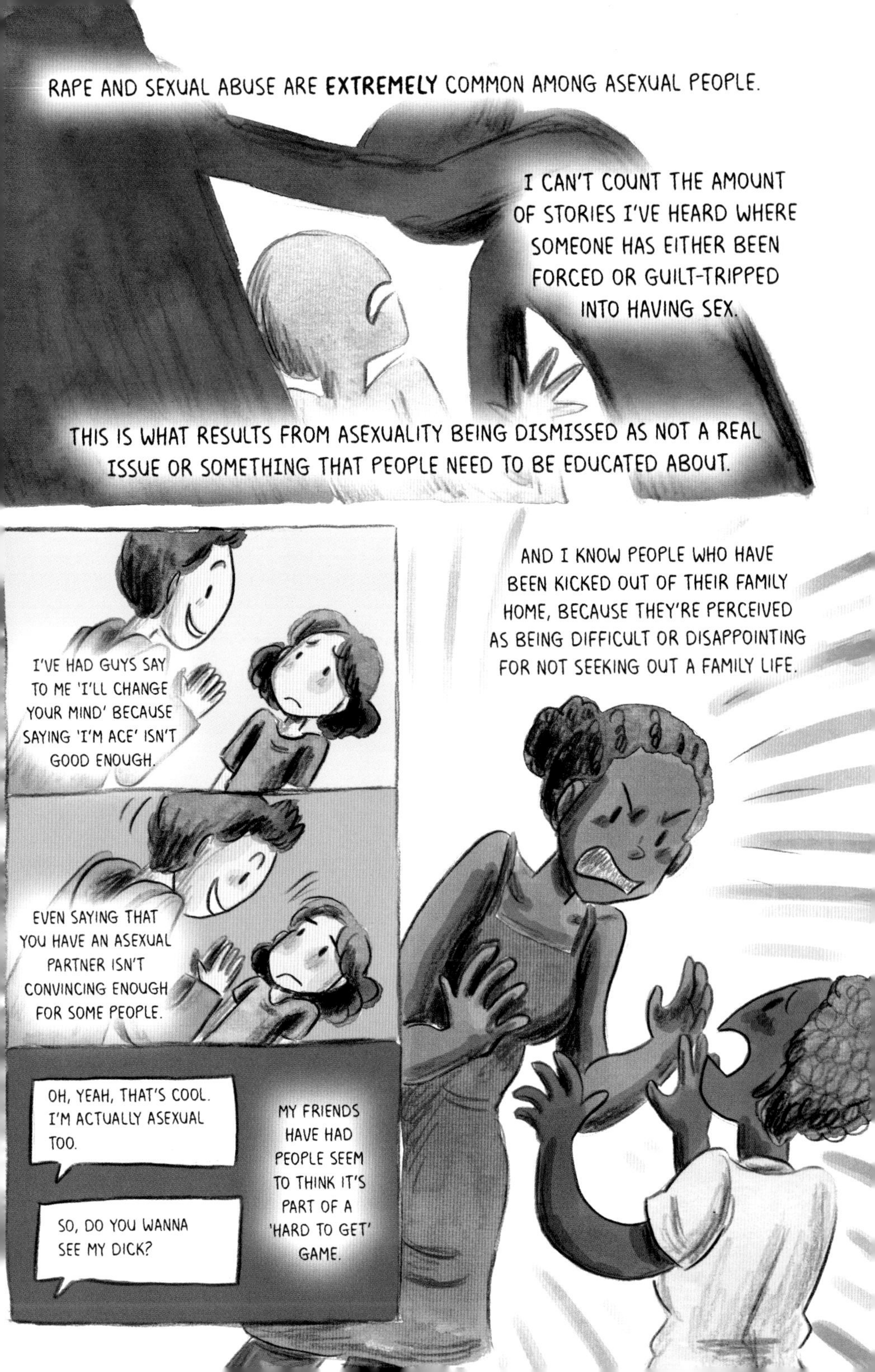
RAPE AND SEXUAL ABUSE ARE **EXTREMELY** COMMON AMONG ASEXUAL PEOPLE.
I CAN'T COUNT THE AMOUNT OF STORIES I'VE HEARD WHERE SOMEONE HAS EITHER BEEN FORCED OR GUILT-TRIPPED INTO HAVING SEX.
THIS IS WHAT RESULTS FROM ASEXUALITY BEING DISMISSED AS NOT A REAL ISSUE OR SOMETHING THAT PEOPLE NEED TO BE EDUCATED ABOUT.
I'VE HAD GUYS SAY TO ME 'I'LL CHANGE YOUR MIND' BECAUSE SAYING 'I'M ACE' ISN'T GOOD ENOUGH.
EVEN SAYING THAT YOU HAVE AN ASEXUAL PARTNER ISN'T CONVINCING ENOUGH FOR SOME PEOPLE.
OH, YEAH, THAT'S COOL. I'M ACTUALLY ASEXUAL TOO.
SO, DO YOU WANNA SEE MY DICK?
MY FRIENDS HAVE HAD PEOPLE SEEM TO THINK IT'S PART OF A 'HARD TO GET' GAME.
AND I KNOW PEOPLE WHO HAVE BEEN KICKED OUT OF THEIR FAMILY HOME, BECAUSE THEY'RE PERCEIVED AS BEING DIFFICULT OR DISAPPOINTING FOR NOT SEEKING OUT A FAMILY LIFE.

ALL OF THESE ISSUES ARE FELT HARDER WHEN THEY ARE SO OFTEN TRIVIALIZED BY CONSISTENTLY ANGRY COMMENTARY FROM PEOPLE ONLINE, EVEN WITHIN THE LGBT+ COMMUNITY.

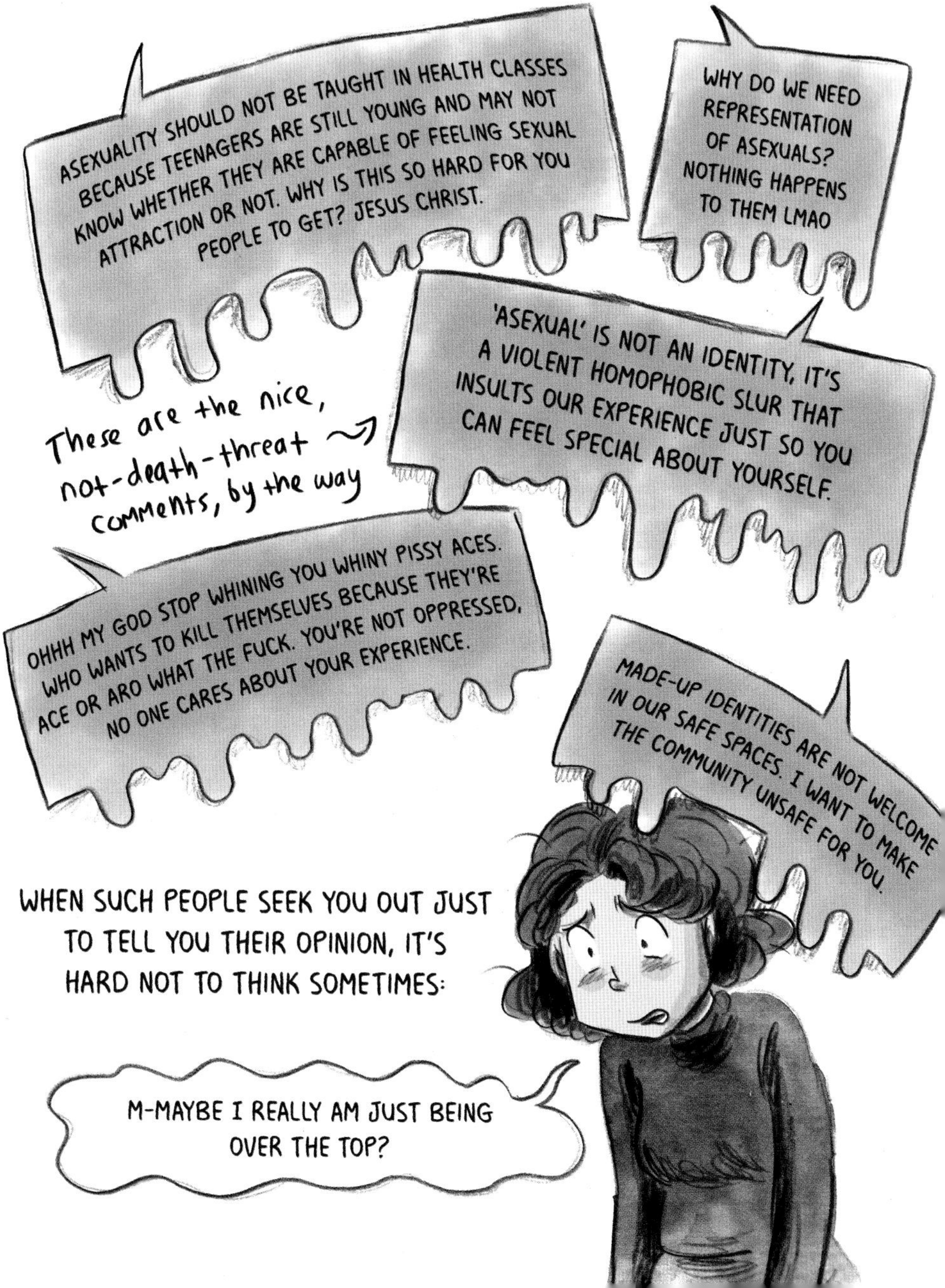
ASEXUALITY SHOULD NOT BE TAUGHT IN HEALTH CLASSES BECAUSE TEENAGERS ARE STILL YOUNG AND MAY NOT KNOW WHETHER THEY ARE CAPABLE OF FEELING SEXUAL ATTRACTION OR NOT. WHY IS THIS SO HARD FOR YOU PEOPLE TO GET? JESUS CHRIST.
WHY DO WE NEED REPRESENTATION OF ASEXUALS? NOTHING HAPPENS TO THEM LMAO
'ASEXUAL' IS NOT AN IDENTITY, IT'S A VIOLENT HOMOPHOBIC SLUR THAT INSULTS OUR EXPERIENCE JUST SO YOU CAN FEEL SPECIAL ABOUT YOURSELF.
These are the nice, not-death-threat comments, by the way
OHHH MY GOD STOP WHINING YOU WHINY PISSY ACES. WHO WANTS TO KILL THEMSELVES BECAUSE THEY'RE ACE OR ARO WHAT THE FUCK. YOU'RE NOT OPPRESSED, NO ONE CARES ABOUT YOUR EXPERIENCE.
MADE-UP IDENTITIES ARE NOT WELCOME IN OUR SAFE SPACES. I WANT TO MAKE THE COMMUNITY UNSAFE FOR YOU.
WHEN SUCH PEOPLE SEEK YOU OUT JUST TO TELL YOU THEIR OPINION, IT'S HARD NOT TO THINK SOMETIMES:
M-MAYBE I REALLY AM JUST BEING OVER THE TOP?

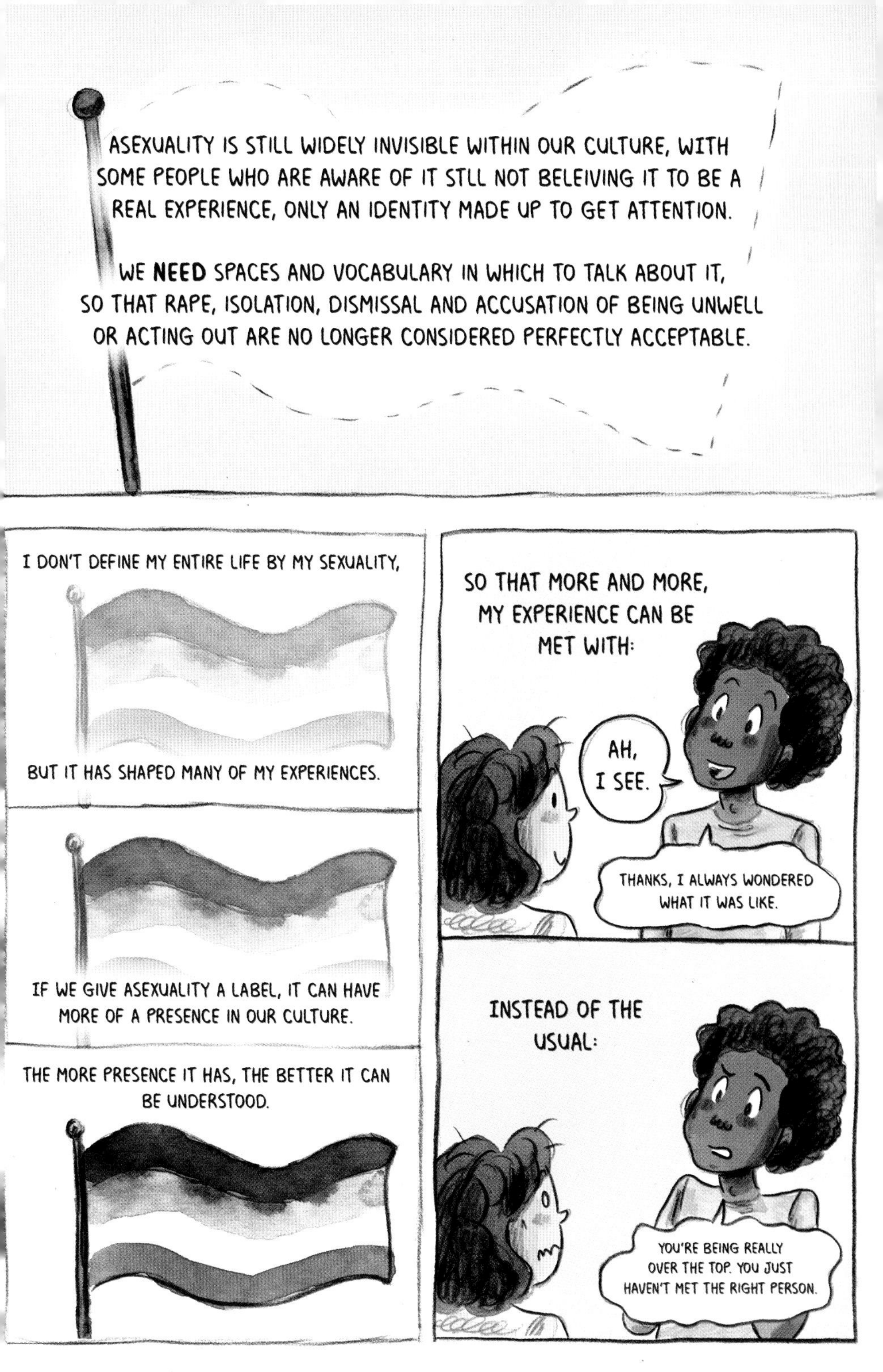
ASEXUALITY IS STILL WIDELY INVISIBLE WITHIN OUR CULTURE, WITH SOME PEOPLE WHO ARE AWARE OF IT STLL NOT BELEIVING IT TO BE A REAL EXPERIENCE, ONLY AN IDENTITY MADE UP TO GET ATTENTION.
WE **NEED** SPACES AND VOCABULARY IN WHICH TO TALK ABOUT IT, SO THAT RAPE, ISOLATION, DISMISSAL AND ACCUSATION OF BEING UNWELL OR ACTING OUT ARE NO LONGER CONSIDERED PERFECTLY ACCEPTABLE.
I DON'T DEFINE MY ENTIRE LIFE BY MY SEXUALITY,
BUT IT HAS SHAPED MANY OF MY EXPERIENCES.
IF WE GIVE ASEXUALITY A LABEL, IT CAN HAVE MORE OF A PRESENCE IN OUR CULTURE.
THE MORE PRESENCE IT HAS, THE BETTER IT CAN BE UNDERSTOOD.
SO THAT MORE AND MORE, MY EXPERIENCE CAN BE MET WITH:
AH, I SEE.
THANKS, I ALWAYS WONDERED WHAT IT WAS LIKE.
INSTEAD OF THE USUAL:
YOU'RE BEING REALLY OVER THE TOP. YOU JUST HAVEN'T MET THE RIGHT PERSON.

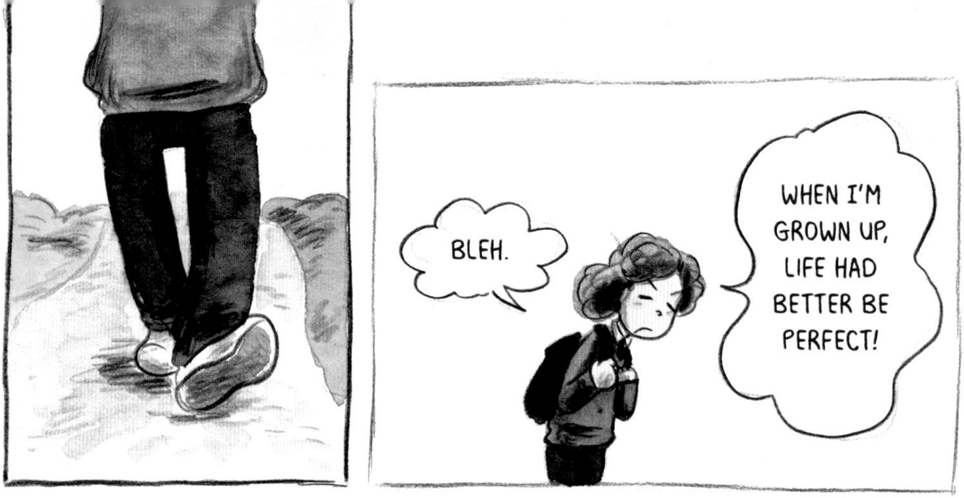
BLEH.
WHEN I'M GROWN UP, LIFE HAD BETTER BE PERFECT!

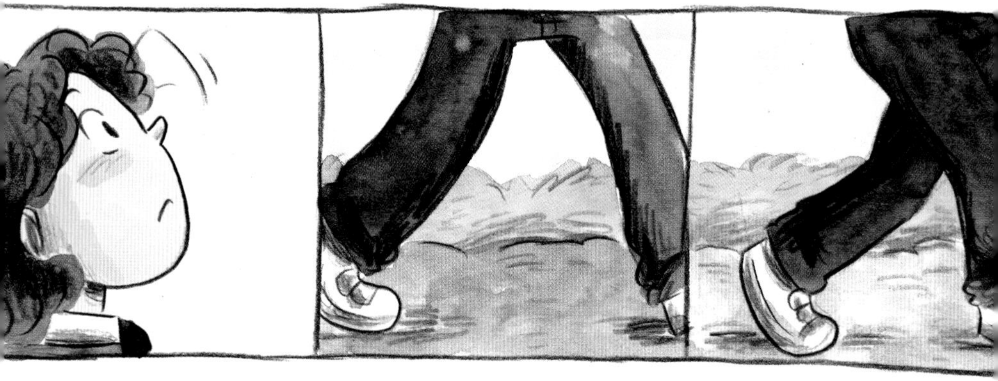

...LIFE IS NEVER WHAT YOU EXPECT IT TO BE.

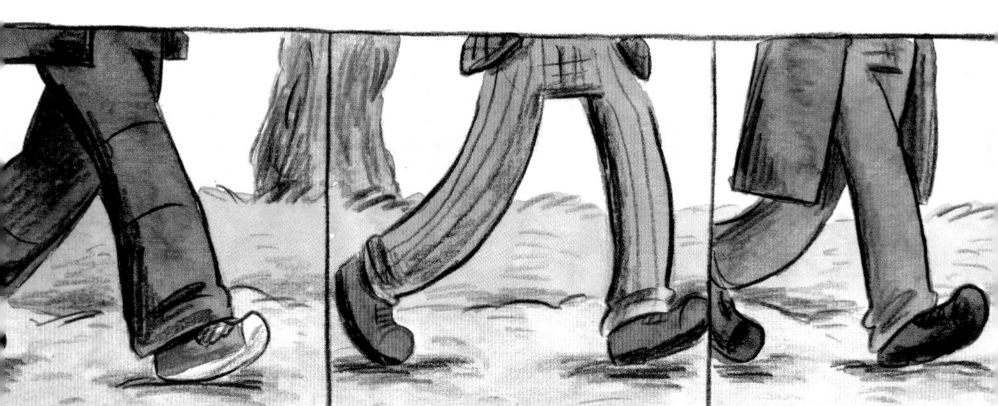

NO MATTER WHO YOU ARE, NO ONE EVER **REALLY** LIVES UP TO THE EXPECTATIONS THAT ARE GIVEN TO US.

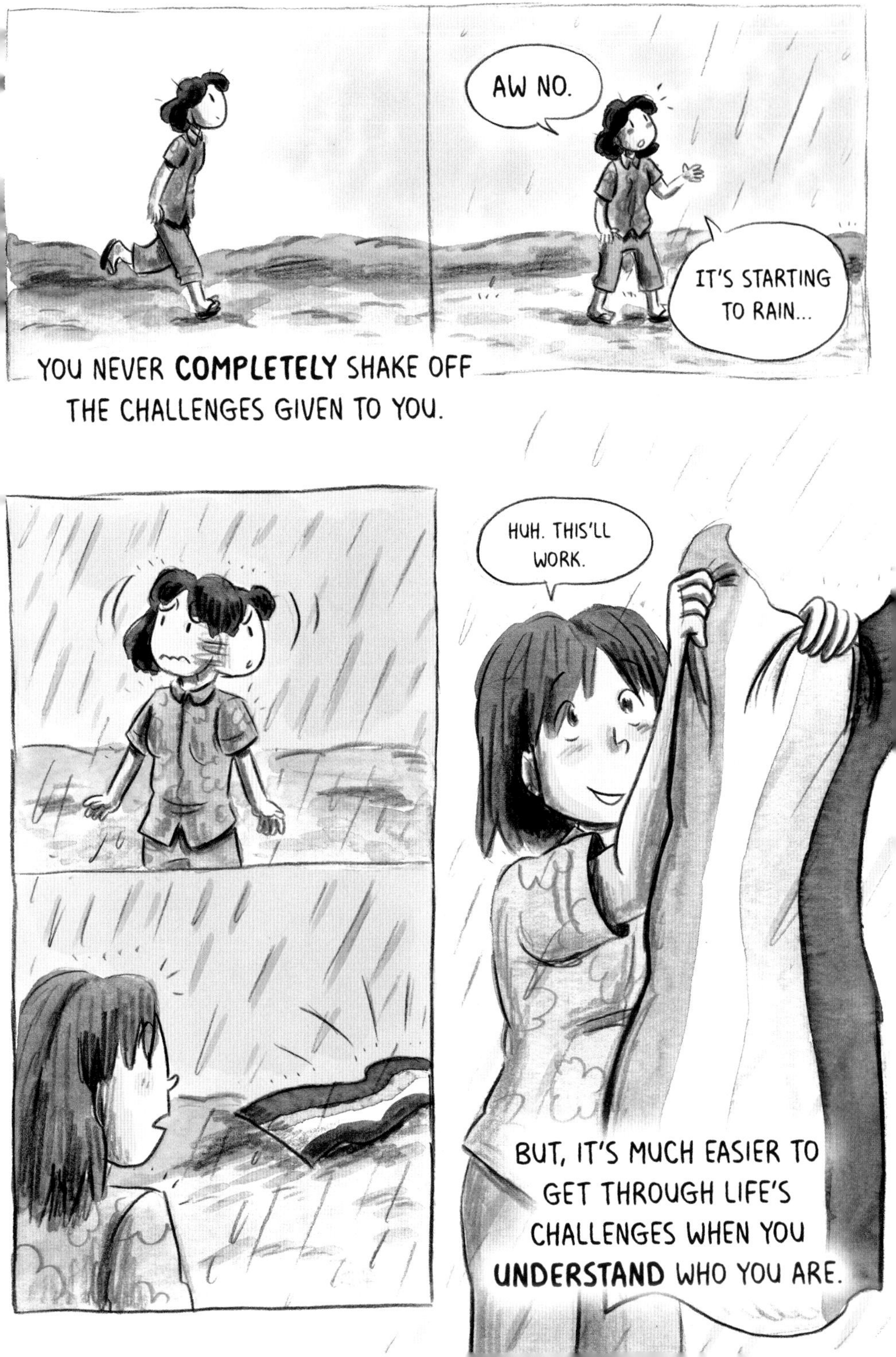
YOU NEVER **COMPLETELY** SHAKE OFF THE CHALLENGES GIVEN TO YOU.
AW NO.
IT'S STARTING TO RAIN...
HUH. THIS'LL WORK.
BUT, IT'S MUCH EASIER TO GET THROUGH LIFE'S CHALLENGES WHEN YOU **UNDERSTAND** WHO YOU ARE.

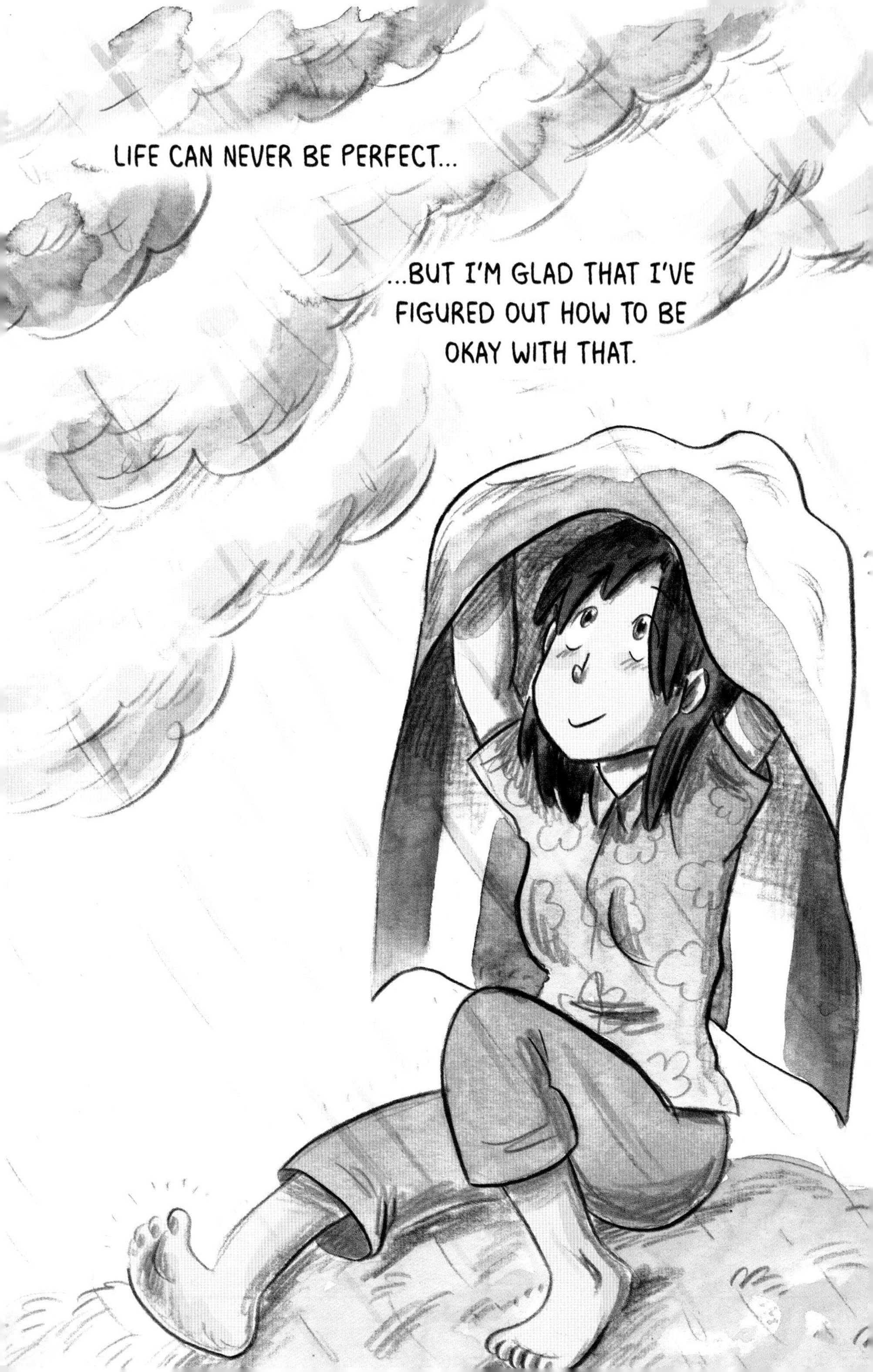
LIFE CAN NEVER BE PERFECT...
...BUT I'M GLAD THAT I'VE FIGURED OUT HOW TO BE OKAY WITH THAT.

# RESOURCES

### GENERAL INFORMATION AND RESOURCES/WRITING
WWW.ASEXUALITY.ORG
WWW.WHATISASEXUALITY.COM/INTRO
ASEXUALSURVIVORS.ORG
AZEJOURNAL.COM

### ASEXUAL AWARENESS WEEK
ACEWEEK.ORG

### COMMUNITY SPACES
WWW.THETREVORPROJECT.ORG/TRVR_SUPPORT_CENTER/ASEXUAL
ASEXUALGROUPS.WORDPRESS.COM

### OTHER COMICS EXPLORING ASEXUALITY
EVERYDAYFEMINISM.COM/2014/10/5-MYTHS-AND-MISCONCEPTIONS-ABOUT-ASEXUALITY
**HEARTLESS:** HEARTLESS-COMIC.COM
**ACES WILD:** WWW.DEVIANTART.COM/SALLYVINTER/GALLERY/63329389/ACES-WILD

### SEX EDUCATION WEBSITES/COMICS
WWW.SCARLETEEN.COM

### BOOKS (FICTION AND NONFICTION)
THE INVISIBLE ORIENTATION: AN INTRODUCTION TO ASEXUALITY BY JULIE SONDRA DECKER
LET'S TALK ABOUT LOVE BY CLAIRE KANN
TASH HEARTS TOLSTOY BY KATHRYN ORMSBEE

FIRST
YEAR
OUT
A TRANSITION STORY
SABRINA
SYMINGTON

## FIRST YEAR OUT

A TRANSITION STORY
SABRINA SYMINGTON

ISBN 978 1 78592 258 9
EISBN 978 0 85701 303 3

AN EMPOWERING AND INTIMATE GRAPHIC NOVEL DEPICTING A TRANS WOMAN'S EMOTIONAL, SOCIAL AND PHYSICAL TRANSITION.

TAKE IT AS A
COMPLIMENT
MARIA STOIAN

## TAKE IT AS A COMPLIMENT

MARIA STOIAN

ISBN 978 1 84905 697 7
EISBN 978 0 85701 242 5

A COLLECTIVE GRAPHIC MEMOIR TELLING REAL LIFE STORIES OF SEXUAL ABUSE, VIOLENCE AND HARASSMENT AND A CALL TO ACTION FOR CHANGE.

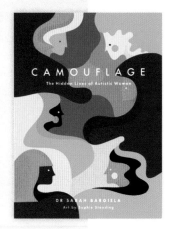

CAMOUFLAGE
The Hidden Lives of Autistic Women
DR SARAH BARGIELA
Art by Sophie Standing

## CAMOUFLAGE

THE HIDDEN LIVES OF AUTISTIC WOMEN
DR SARAH BARGIELA
ILLUSTRATED BY SOPHIE STANDING

ISBN 978 1 78592 566 5
EISBN 978 1 78592 667 9

AN ENGAGING AND BEAUTIFULLY ILLUSTRATED GRAPHIC BOOK SHEDDING LIGHT ON THE UNDER-EXPLORED CONDITION OF FEMALE AUTISM.